AVENUES
TO THE PAST

Sir Charles Brett C.B.E.

AVENUES TO THE PAST

Essays presented to Sir Charles Brett on his 75th Year

Edited by

TERENCE REEVES-SMYTH
AND RICHARD ORAM

Published by the

ULSTER ARCHITECTURAL
HERITAGE SOCIETY

Published by
Ulster Architectural Heritage Society
66 Donegall Pass, Belfast

6 5 4 3 2 1

Designed by April Sky Design, Newtownards
Printed by W&G Baird

ISBN 0 900457 60 0

Front cover:

Watercolour by David Evans of the Temple of the Winds in its surrounding parkland setting at Mount Stewart as viewed from Strangford Lough.

Frontispiece:

Sir Charles Brett C.B.E.

Title page:

Carved frame, 1741-1742, attributed to John Houghton, Trinity College, Dublin, see page 57, Figure 9 (Green Studios, Dublin).

CONTENTS

FOREWORD

Festschriften are usually filled with essays written by distinguished senior scholars who are contemporaries, or near contemporaries, of the person to whom the volume is addressed. Whilst this book is not lacking such contributors, it is perhaps a reflection of Sir Charles Brett's singular contribution as an architectural historian and conservationist, that this publication contains papers from widely differing generations. The scope of subjects covered could have been much broader were they to include Sir Charles's other interests, but we felt this volume would have greater value and import if it were focussed around a coherent theme. Accordingly, this *Festschrift*, which we have titled 'Avenues to the Past', contains essays on historic buildings and their conservation, architectural history, architects, garden history and the history of art.

In our capacity as editors to this volume and on behalf of the Ulster Architectural Heritage Society, we should like to thank those individuals and institutions who have so generously contributed towards the publication costs. None of this would have been possible without their support. Thanks are also due to Peter Marlow who has helped us raise the necessary funds. Finally, we should like to express our gratitude to the contributors, who have so enthusiastically given their time to writing these essays, which we are confident will serve as a long-lasting tribute to Sir Charles.

T.R-S.
R.O.

TABULA GRATULATORIA

The Ulster Architectural Heritage Society would like to thank the following institutions and individuals for generously contributing to the costs of this publication

INSTITUTIONS
Arts Council of Northern Ireland
Belfast Buildings Preservation Trust
Esme Mitchell
Hearth Housing Association
Irish Georgian Society
The Marc Fitch Fund
The National Trust
Ulster Architectural Heritage Society
Ulster Garden Villages

INDIVIDUALS
Mr and Mrs Kevin Baird
Mrs M.A. Bell
Mark Bence-Jones
Mr and Mrs Harvey Bicker
Marcus Binney
Mr and Mrs W.B. Boyd
Lady Mairi Bury
Sir Robert and Lady Carswell
Sheila Carden
Colonel and Mrs R. Charley
John Cornforth
Sheila Lewis Crosby
Mr and Mrs J.A.K. Dean
Martin Drury
Dorinda Lady Dunleath
Mr and Mrs Brian Ferran
Barbara Fitzgerald
Angela Fitzpatrick
Rita Harkin
Mr and Mrs Desmond Hodges
Erskine Holmes
Lyn Gallagher
John Gamble
John Green
Joan Kinch
Anne Lynch
Peter and Fiona Marlow
Andrew McClelland
Professor Kevin Nolan
Fionnuala Jay-O'Boyle
The Lord O'Neill
J.H. Torney
Mr and Mrs J.F. Rankin
Professor Gavin Stamp
W. Vaughan
Edward and Primrose Wilson
Anne Weatherup
D.R.M. Weatherup

PREFACE

Peter O Marlow
Chairman, Ulster Architectural Heritage Society

It is a great pleasure to write the Preface for this volume published in honour of Sir Charles Brett. It is also rather intimidating because CEB Brett, as he has always signed himself (except when he has assumed the pseudonym Albert Rechts), has written so much himself. The Brett bibliography which Karen Latimer publishes here more than amply demonstrates that he is both a prolific and a wide ranging author, and there is yet more to come.

No less than twenty one of her entries have been published by the Ulster Architectural Heritage Society of which he is now the President, having served for many years as Chairman. Beginning with the Lists in 1968 (his Buildings of Belfast appeared the previous year, published by Weidenfeld and Nicholson) and ranging from Lists to Monographs, the latest phase has culminated in a series of three major tomes on the Buildings of County Antrim, Buildings of County Armagh, and Buildings of North County Down. Beautifully illustrated, full of well researched, intelligent information, they also contain an iconoclastic sense of detached humour which makes reading each entry a pleasure.

Among his other publications is *Long Shadows Cast Before: Nine Lives in Ulster, 1625-1977*, essentially a family history and autobiography. It is a fascinating kaleidoscopic interweaving of generations of family history and contemporary insights in to the social and political situation of Belfast and Northern Ireland in the late 1970s in which he has played a significant part. His affiliation with the Northern Ireland Labour Party and canvassing for it may well have awakened his interest in the local architecture of Belfast. Certainly his Oxford education, exposure to poetry and a year in Paris as a journalist and broadcaster with Radiodiffusion francaise will have helped prepare him for a life-long commitment to the arts.

He served for two terms on the Arts Council of Northern Ireland, was its Vice Chairman and Chairman of its Lottery Arts Committee, and for longer than any other member, was on the Regional Committee of the National Trust; he also served on the Trust's Council for fourteen years. Although pre-eminently a buildings man, he helped formulate the policy for protection of the coastline in the north of Country Antrim. The resulting Ulster Coastline Appeal was the precursor of Enterprise Neptune, the Trust's most successful national fundraising campaign.

He frequently travelled to Trust properties throughout the UK when on holiday and sent back to the Director-General in London long and highly perceptive letters commenting on what he had seen. Some of these are classics, including an exchange with Jack Boles about a property which must remain nameless.

Dear Charlie,

...It is extremely helpful when shrewd and sympathetic observers take the trouble to give Head Office and the regions their impressions... XXXX is a management disaster, largely because the National Trust made a rotten bargain nearly 30 years ago and it does not own what it has to own in order to improve things. We have struggled and struggled at all levels regionally and nationally to get a better deal with XXXXX and I truly believe that we have no prospect of making any advances while XXXX still wishes to run it all his way. We have tried inducements and pressure, charm and skulduggery and you see we have been quite ineffective. By way of consolation, we are eternal and mortals are mortal.

It was his initial involvement with the National Trust that started him off on the road of architectural history. For many years he was the Trust's committee's publicity and membership sub-committee chairman, producing numerous guides, pamphlets, policy papers and other ephemera. His aesthetic eye, soundly based on architectural knowledge, was frequently brought to bear on such properties as Derrymore, both in discussions with Lord Antrim when first acquired and later with Trust staff when the house was reopened to the public in the 1990s, and also at Castle Coole in the mid-1980s when the debate raged about the relative values of Wyatt's clean crisp neo-Classical design for the interior spaces versus the elaborate, rich, and gilded decorations overlaid for the 2nd Earl of Belmore by Preston. Alas, the decision to paint the entrance hall and staircase "germolene pink" cannot be attributed to him!

Throughout his chairmanship of both Hearth and the Ulster Architectural Heritage Society he championed the cause of preserving Ulster's built heritage, not only by improving legislation and lobbying for more resources from government but also by showing through practical examples how buildings can be restored to productive use.

As Chairman of the Northern Ireland Housing Executive he brought that concern for well designed, socially responsible housing up to the present day.

Not long ago at a large formal luncheon in Dublin, he was asked, without prior warning, to offer his thoughts to the assembled dignitaries about a proposal to construct a government building along the Liffey. Architectural history shows, he said, that successful buildings in such locations are of human scale, are made of natural materials, and respect the horizontality of the river. And he sat down. Such an ability to come up with clear, simply stated maxims reflects a deep and wide knowledge not to mention the quick mind of someone trained in the legal profession.

In Long Shadows Cast Before he refers to himself, depending on his assessment of the person he is talking to, as either “inter-denominational anticlerical” or a “militant atheist”. His real faith is in words. As a long-serving solicitor, as a prolific author, as a debater, as an advocate for social causes and especially for the preservation of the built heritage, his accomplishments more than merit the publication of this *Festschrift*.

CHARLES BRETT: WIDER PERSPECTIVES

JENNIFER JENKINS

CHARLES BRETT DESCRIBES HIMSELF as a provincial Irish attorney, the sixth generation of his family in a line of solicitors. But when I visited Northern Ireland for the first time in 1986 soon after becoming chairman of the National Trust his name came up at every turn, not as a lawyer but as a conservationist and architectural historian – the author of the first book on Belfast's historic buildings, founder of the Ulster Architectural Heritage Society and a housing reformer in the tradition of Octavia Hill. He was a beacon of optimism and solid achievement rising above the fortified police stations, the menacing 'peace' lines and the defiant images of King Billy on the walls of bombed-out buildings.

At that time Brett represented the province on the National Trust's Council and had already served on its Northern Ireland Committee for almost thirty years. Here he made use of his place in the city's establishment to recruit the editor of The Belfast Telegraph and the BBC's publicity officer to help in raising the Trust's profile and boosting its membership. His formidable energy and legal skills were directed to creating a path along the North east coast of Ulster, not an easy task when the small farmers were reluctant to sell their land or to allow access for the public. The Ulster Coastline Appeal led the way for the Trust's wider Enterprise Neptune campaign and caused the spectacular cliffs of Antrim with their view across the sea to Argyll to be one of the best preserved stretches of the Irish coast. Brett was less successful in persuading the Trust to take on a wider selection of historic buildings. In the 1960s and 1970s the Trust's leaders did not share his interest in Victorian architecture or social history and were not willing to acquire either one of the linen manufacturer's mansions on the outskirts of Belfast or any group of small town houses. The former have now all been demolished but for the latter he turned to HEARTH, the charity set up for their repair and re-use (see Patton in this volume).

Brett knows Dublin well and has served on the Board of the Irish Architectural Archive, himself compiling lists of historic buildings for the towns of Monaghan and Cavan in these cross-border counties. His visits were not always welcome but on one occasion suspicious householders were reassured by an accompanying pop star. He was perhaps more at home in the intellectual company of writers and academics when we met at a dinner given by Jean Kennedy Smith, the American ambassador to Dublin, at her Phoenix Park house, which had been occupied by the Chief Secretary of Ireland before independence in 1921.

It was as the first chairman of the International Fund for Ireland that Brett was able to make his most important contribution to fostering links between North and South, appointed jointly by the Taoiseach, Garrett Fitzgerald and the Secretary of State for Northern Ireland, Tom King. The Fund was set up in 1986 'to encourage the economic and social development of those areas of both parts of Ireland which have suffered most severely from the consequences of the instability of recent years'. Under the leadership of this 'interdenominational anti-clerical' (his own words) the four Catholic and two Protestant members formed an effective team, never dividing along sectarian or north-south lines, their independence demonstrated by the decision not to meet on government property. Each member of the Board took the lead on the projects in which he was most interested. Brett himself was particularly concerned with the regeneration of the bomb-damaged towns of Ulster and with a scheme for sending unemployed young people to gain work experience abroad, using his contacts for some of them to help restore historic buildings in Paris. Summing up the Board's first year's experience, Brett concluded that 'It has provided, for the first time ever, a practical mechanism for cross-boarder cooperation without political or constitutional implications'.

The International Fund for Ireland took Brett across the Atlantic to Washington, New York and Ottawa, but he had already forged long-standing connections with the continent of Europe. After leaving Oxford in 1948 he became a stagiaire with *Radiodiffusion Francaise* (the English Service), taught in a school where girls little younger than himself ogled him from the front row and boys pelted him with chalk from the back. He graduated to the Continental Daily Mail gossip column, on which a colleague covered the Duke of Windsor and other high-life figures while he covered Montparnasse and its low-life, making friends in Anarchist and Trokskyite circles.

Since then he has visited most countries of Europe often in connection with Europa Nostra annual conferences or study tours. Asked to advise on the listing of historic buildings in the Channel islands, he spent several summer holidays, armed with notebook and pencil, surveying St. Peter Port in Guernsey, St. Helier in Jersey and the Isle of Alderney, thus depriving his children of his legendary skills in constructing sandcastles.

He and Joyce, whom he married in 1953 and whom I met some years later when she came to Glasgow to help my husband in the Hillhead bye-election, have also pursued their architectural explorations further afield, sometimes at meetings of the International Committee for Monuments and Sites and most recently in the Crimea. Here he was captivated by the Alupka (or Vorontsov) palace on the slopes of the Black Sea, which Churchill found distinctly less captivating when he stayed there during the Yalta conference. Brett was particularly intrigued by the part played in its design by the English architect, Edward Blore, and has published a study comparing drawings in the Victorian and Albert Museum with those in the palace and with the building itself. He concluded that the 'astonishing synthesis of English Jacobean, moghul and moorish styles' have 'made Alupka perhaps the most successful romantic palace in Europe'. Now retired from all his offices and committees, he has more time to devote to his ever widening studies of historic buildings.

GENDER AT SEA

MAURICE CRAIG

A YEAR OR TWO AGO I wrote to the Marine Correspondent of the *Irish Times* to protest at ships being referred to as 'it' instead of as 'she'. The lady in question, a capable journalist and a graceful writer, replied to tell me that there is, now, a house rule of the paper forbidding it. She, like me, regretted it, but there it was.

I was appalled. The usage was admittedly, not as common as it had been. Clearly, it was losing ground, though it is still not unusual to see, in other papers, both 'she' and 'it' used in the same article or report. But what was the reason for banning 'she'? When I was young, in the 20s and 30s, I never heard a ship spoken of as anything but 'she', except, very occasionally, by the kind of people to whom a ship is nothing more than a means of transport, people, who, if they mentioned a ship at all, referred to it as a 'boat'. I recalled an American film-star who, on first stepping abroad the *Queen Mary*, was heard to enquire 'When does this place get to London?'

It may seem trivial, but to me it appears symptomatic of a dissociation between ends and means, a loss of feeling and imagination. The real world of things, of work, of experience, obliterated in favour of a world of status, of convenience, of button-pressing and the twiddling of knobs. It results, no doubt, from the fact that our servants – our computers, our television sets, our washing-machines – are increasingly incomprehensible to most of us. We ask them questions and they give us answers; we give them orders and they either carry them out or tell us that it cannot be done. But they, in their inner being, are a mystery to all but a small minority of us, the users. It was not always so.

'The righteous man regardeth the life of his beast'. My father was fond of quoting this, from the Book of Proverbs, with reference not to his horse, for he never owned a horse, but to his motor-car, which he rightly regarded as entitled to every care and consideration which he could legitimately give it. He did not, of course, think of it as having a 'soul' or subscribe to any such sentimental concept. But it was, at the very best, entitled to respect. He was pained if he saw or heard such a mechanism being brutally or insensitively treated. So am I.

In that most prosaic of texts, the *Metropolitan Police Driving Manual* [1] we read: 'car sympathy is a quality to be admired in any driver'. Those policemen knew what they were talking about.

In the 20s and 30s my father had a chauffeur who, when polishing the car, would blow out between closed lips in the way that grooms do when dealing with horses. Because, of course, that is what he had been before economic necessity drove him to the care of machines. Some vestigial animism survived the change.

To return to the subject of ships. Throughout human history, down to about thirty years ago, every line in every part of every ship was a curve, except only certain vertical or near-vertical lines, which need not concern us. There were, and there still are, sound technical reasons for this. Insofar as these are dictated by hydrodynamics they remain, of course valid, so that the underwater shapes (which nobody ever sees except when the ship is in a dry dock) are as beautiful as ever, if not more so. The reason is that, good as the instincts of the older craftsmen and draughtsmen were, working by experience and with old saws in their heads such as 'cod's head and mackerel tail', the shapes prescribed by electronic analysis of flows and eddies are even more effective and aesthetically satisfying. But above the waterline things are very different.

In the first place, it was discovered that it is very much cheaper to cut everything at right angles than to shape each plate to an individual profile. Secondly, the advent of the roll-on roll-off system, and of the container, rectilinear and modular, dictated a flat deck, or decks, for almost the whole length of the vessel. So the ship becomes visibly a box, from which any feminine grace of line is entirely absent. There is little temptation to endow such an object with any gender but 'it'.

On top of all this, there are now no passenger-ships. Car-ferries are the most impersonal of all craft, in sharp contrast to their predecessors on the same routes, which had very marked personalities. Habitual travellers had strong attachments and antipathies. There are no passenger-liners. The cruise-ships which appear to be their successors are no such thing. Apart from their transcendent ugliness, they are devoted to assuring their clientele, subliminally at least, that they are not at sea at all. Here, indeed, 'this place' will in due course 'get to' London, then Southampton or Miami or wherever. They look, at best, like blocks of flats, or even, as a friend has suggested, like prison-hulks. The only way in which to make a sea-voyage, now, is to book a passage with one of the cargo-liner companies whose ships carry a few passengers, usually up to a dozen.

A land building, however noble or graceful it may be, is nevertheless static. But a ship is mobile, and may, and usually does, wander far and wide. *La donna e mobile.* The 'ship's husband', a functionary charged with seeing to the ship's business, remains at home. But the ship's master must accompany her everywhere, and if he takes action at variance with her essential character and capabilities, disaster may occur. Even at the quayside the ship is not completely motionless, the mooring-ropes creak and the fenders grunt. You know that at any moment she may take off and vanish beyond the horizon.

About a year ago, I looked out of the window and there, on the horizon, at anchor in Dublin Bay, was the unmistakable silhouette of the *France*, still at least in that range, as beautiful as ever. At the almost unprecedented age of thirty-seven, exceeded in my recollection only by the *Stavangerfjord* (1913-1959), now in Norwegian ownership and renamed as *Norway*, painted in different colours, altered in various ways and now employed only in cruising, she is still recognizably the one and only France, the last of the true succession of *Mauretania*, *Aquitania* and *Normandie*, as a top-link express Atlantic liner. I had seen her first from Las Canteras beach when she was on her maiden voyage in 1962, and two or three times afterwards in Le Havre and Southampton. The sight of her now, on this last occasion, affected me as the sight of Helen on the battlements of Troy had affected the old men in Book Three of the Iliad, who lowered their voices and said to one another 'Indeed she is the very image of an immortal goddess'.

Perhaps the most emotive passage I know in which such feelings are evoked is in Kipling's 'The Mary Gloster', which, as his son relates, Duff Cooper was fond of being asked to read aloud after dinner, and could never finish without the tears pouring down his cheeks. I am not surprised. The theme is the familiar one of a rugged self-made man who has become very rich and is now dying. As not uncommonly happens, he has a son who has received an expensive education and developed tastes and a way of life at variance with his father's. The mother has long since died, but not before he had named one of his ships after her: the *Mary Gloster*, and buried her at sea from that ship. He is now giving his son instructions that he is to be taken, in the same ship, to the same place. ('Hundred and eighteen East, remember, and South just three') where the ship is to be scuttled so that he and his ship go down together. In the concluding lines of the poem it is well nigh impossible to distinguish when the 'she' who is mentioned is the ship or his dead wife, since they both go by the same name. Mawkish it may be, but it has undeniable power.

So what, in the end, inspired the editor of the *Irish Times* or whoever it was who issued this, to me, so regrettable edict? I would like to think that it was a desire to distance himself from those saloon-bar types in their double-breasted brass-buttoned blazers who can be heard boasting about their cars or their yachts and referring to them as 'she'. I have some sympathy with this. You may be accustomed for years to using an expression, yet, imperceptibly perhaps, the feeling glows upon you that it sounds awkward or outlandish or affected. When you no longer feel like using it in public, it is time to stop. None of us except the least sensitive, can effectively resist something which is happening unnoticed, all around us, in, so to speak, the air we breathe.

But should we try? Don't we know that change is inevitable, and that the pace of it is increasing and that none of us has the faintest chance of stopping it or even slowing it down? Don't we know that over a period of three centuries the speakers of what was to become English were blissfully unpoliced, with no grammarians to tell them what to say and what not to say? If any of us doesn't know this already he has only to read Hugh Sykes Davies' *Grammar Without Tears* which tells, very readably, how 'unlettered men' so misused the Anglo-Saxon and so freely allowed importations to prove, or fail to prove, their survival value, that at the end of that period they had forged the language of Chaucer and of Shakespeare and of Swift and of Evelyn Waugh. You could make mistakes in those days and get away with it. Your social superiors spoke Norman French and took no notice of what you were up to.

Things are much the same today, though for quite different reasons. Nobody polices the electronic media which are wide open to the unlettered, who are busy changing the language as quickly if not more quickly that they did in the past. But this is surely no excuse for outlawing a graceful usage long practised by people better than ourselves and no yet dead?

NOTES

1. *Metropolitan Police Driving Manual.* 1955. London, HMSO, p.01.

SOME RECOLLECTIONS OF PATRICK O'BRIAN

DONNELL DEENY

ONE CHRISTMAS IN THE EARLY 1980s a close male relative enquired what I was reading. 'A novel by Patrick O'Brian. About the Navy of Nelson's time but with other aspects ...'. 'Oh, sub Hornblower' said my relative discouraging further elucidation, the curl on his lips being more eloquent than his comment.

I fear this exchange discouraged me for many years from proselytising on behalf of Patrick O'Brian. I was not, happily, discouraged from reading him but felt sufficiently inhibited to refrain from explaining to anyone I met that the novels made up a fascinating romain fleuve of which the Navy against Napoleon was only the principal stream. As well as Jack Aubrey, unworldly sailor on land, a cunning warrior at sea and, unlike the novels of C. S. Forester himself and his other successors, there was a second protagonist. Stephen Maturin was half Irish and half Catalan, doctor, naturalist and spy. The two characters from the beginning shared a love of the music of the eighteenth century movingly described in the books. At some point not specified they were elected Fellows of the Royal Society. The author had raided the stores of knowledge of the period from 1800 to 1815, assisted in that by possession of a substantial library including Encyclopaedia Britannica for 1810. He selected mouthfuls for the amusement and enlightenment of his readers e.g. casual references to 'old Bach' and 'London Bach', the latter's sheet music found neglected and bought for a few pennies at the back of a book shop. He had tremendous narrative drive.

As time went on and the paperback editions emerged one saw increasingly that one was not alone in being a fan. Many critics, writers and academics began praising him enthusiastically, including Iris Murdoch, her husband John Bayley, A. S. Byatt and Sir Alec Guinness.

Of equal moment was the chance discovery one by one that virtually all ones men friends who still read books (about half) were also fans of Patrick O'Brian. Notable among these in more than one sense was Charlie Brett. His interests – antiquarian, aesthetic, romantic, eclectic were naturally attuned to O'Brian. In

Fig 1.
Photograph of Patrick and Mary O'Brien (courtesy Donnell Deeny)

honour of that joint interest I jot down these few recollections. I am encouraged to do so by the fact that the recent and very good biography of O'Brian by Dean King is written with little or no personal knowledge of its subject. Indeed it does not even have a photograph of his wife of 50 years to whom so many of the books are dedicated.

We sought the O'Brians out in the South of France, obtaining their address from a mutual friend. I invited them for dinner in our hotel in Collirure. This village on the Mediterranean coast of France close to the Spanish border had become famous as a home of artists including Derain and Picasso. Patrick and Mary O'Brian had lived there for over 40 years. The house was called *Correch d'en Baus*, a Catalan name, not surprising in a part of France that had been and in some ways was still part of Catalonia. No doubt that partly explained the parentage of Stephen Maturin y Domanova.

On arriving at our hotel at about 7.00 p.m., having driven down from Andorra, I found an elegantly penned note declining the invitation to dinner but inviting us for drinks at 6.30 p.m. I hurriedly rang and the author himself answered. Time for the drink was extended. Directions were given. I must turn right outside my hotel and go down the hill into the village turning left into 'the odiously named *Rue De La Democracie*'. We found the house easily. It was not large. It was white. One went through a gate into a small courtyard with a single orange tree and then into a pleasant study the walls of which were lined from floor almost to ceiling with crowded bookshelves. (He did not write there but in a smaller building at the bottom of his vineyard).

Patrick was small, straight and spare. He had about him something of the Naval Officer as if an imaginary peaked cap still rested on his head. In fact it does not seem that he ever served as such. He was by then 77 years old. His wife Mary of similar age and height was small, stooped and charming. We were offered Taittinger and accepted. The conversation flowed. We must have passed some invisible litmus test because after half an hour Patrick said we must leave directly for dinner in Port Vendres. As his note has said they were far too decrepit to go out to dinner I looked a question at him. 'Your hotel, while I entirely understand why you chose to stay there, is really quite spoilt. We are taking you to the best fish restaurant in the region.' We piled into our hired car.

The restaurant was right on the quay side at Port Vendres and our hosts were greeted very much as honoured guests. Without much consultation lobster was ordered and we moved on to Roederer. The ladies talked with animation, and as is not infrequently the case, indiscretion Alison obtained rather more information from Mary than I did from Patrick. Indeed he came close to quoting Doctor Johnsons' remark that questioning was not a polite form of conversation among gentlemen. Incidentally this is quoted in the books without attribution to Doctor Johnson and quoted in turn by Mr. King in his biography without reference to the original source although, no doubt, O'Brian was aware of it. Given that asking questions was something of an occupational habit of barristers this might in other circumstances have stilted the conversation but it did not. He described how, out the very window we were looking, on the narrow z-shaped harbour of Port Vendres, Lord Cochrane had sailed in in his brig the Speedy and cut out an enemy merchant vessel, destroying others. This tacking in and out must have been phenomenal in the age before steam. Although Cochrane is the model for so many novels of this style in the period it is to O'Brian's credit that this incident is never used by him in his books.

A theme of Mary's conversation was the extreme poverty in which they lived in Collirure in the 1950's. Money was hard to take out of Britain because of strict exchange control regulations. In any event their income was small. Sometimes neighbours left food for them at the back door. This hardship eased somewhat when he began to translate French literature into English. He was proud that he was the translator of choice for Simone de Beauvoir. The next day, when we called with flowers and adieux, he gave Alison a newly published edition of de

Beauvoir's 'The Coming of Age' in his translation. They allowed themselves to be photographed in front of the orange tree in the courtyard, remarking that the oranges were only fit for marmalade. They stood with bowed heads as if awaiting some condign punishment. But afterwards their good humour resumed. I caught a delightful photograph of both.

His fame and standing continued to increase. In October 11th 1996 a dinner in his honour was held in the Painted Hall at Greenwich, a suitably grand naval venue for the celebration. He seemed delighted by it, quietly joyous at all that happened, particularly the expressive readings from his work by the actor Robert Hardy and the precise, indeed beautiful, drill of the Royal Marines. In conversation we compared it favourable to the more dramatic display of US Marines, seen on other occasions. This involved hurling carbines along the line to one another while eyes remained firmly fixed to the front. He told me that he had enjoyed the Bushmills single malt I had sent him, a new taste he had not previously encountered.

In 1998 he sustained two severe blows. His wife died in the spring of that year. They had no children although she had a son, Count Tolstoy-Miloslavsky by a previous marriage. He seemed to regard her grandchildren as his also. When next I saw him he acknowledged condolences for his loss but clearly did not wish to talk about it.

On October 24th 1998 the Daily Telegraph published a long piece entitled 'The Secret Life of Patrick O'Brian'. The paper 'revealed' that he was not in fact Irish at all but the eighth of nine children of an English doctor of German extraction. They also stated that he had not in fact worked as a secret agent in occupied Europe during the Second World War but had had a desk job in England. The article caused considerable distress to him, alleging dishonesty in one already sensitive on points of honour.

I can only say for my part that he never said anything to us to suggest either that he was in fact Irish or that he had been on active service in the war. As to the former he seemed one of those Englishmen who was proud of some connection with Ireland which in his case he did not elaborate on. He reminded me in that regard of Sir Patrick Mayhew who was proud of his connections with a distinguished literary family in the south of Ireland.

The suggestion that he was in some way being deceitful by changing his name from Russ to O'Brian seems to me a charge that is not made out. The use of pseudonyms by authors is, of course, commonplace. C. S. Forrester was merely a pseudonym although one he used even on private inscriptions. Indeed in Patrick's own case he had formally changed his name by deed poll to O'Brian as, oddly enough, had one of his brothers.

The journalist Kevin Myers, who knew him much better than I, said he was extremely touchy on any questions relating to his Irishness. No doubt this is so but to me he described coming to the north of Ireland and spending some time there. Indeed he said that his first love was from Belfast. She was called Mona Fitzpatrick. At the time of his death I mentioned this on BBC Radio Ulster but unfortunately it was edited out! It would be interesting to know whether there is an old lady now who was that girl.

I have to say that he also admitted to taking another girl up to MacArts Fort which she told him she was not meant to climb.

It is also right to say that the article revealed that he had been married before and that he had a surviving son. This, I confess, came as some surprise. He and his son were estranged. He had also had a daughter who died in childhood.

He had mentioned to me that his own mother had died when he was a child but he paid tribute to the kindness of his stepmother. All these matters might suggest to any reasonable person that he would tend to avoid discussion about a past life which was painful to him.

In this difficult time he was greatly cheered by the kindness of the then Provost of Trinity College, Dublin, Dr. Tom Mitchell. Not only did Trinity give him a LL.D, which he greatly valued, along with his C.B.E. but he extended an invitation to the elderly widower to come and stay in College. This O'Brian did. We found him in Bottany Bay, an aptly named square, evocative at it was of the penal colony, of which indeed, O'Brian had written.

On the table of his sitting room was the manuscript of what was to be 'Blue at the Mizzen'. Although there were a lot of reference books on the shelves none cluttered the table. One had a strong impression that he wrote almost entirely from his memory and imagination. Indeed he said that he never even re-read the novels. He once had summaries of them but they were inadvertently sold with his manuscripts by Heywood Hill to a university in the United States.

I gently suggested to him that that habit of not referring back to the earlier novels on his own part might explain why, for example, the names of his French characters all tended to begin with the same letter of the alphabet ie Dumesnil, Dubreuil, Duhamel, Dutourd, Duplessis. He was greatly amused at this and had not realized that that was the case. I have to say that I did not point out to him that his other Frenchmen all had double barrelled names although I think this is an unusual thing to find in France but perhaps less so in the early nineteenth century.

He took us to dinner in the club I knew as a former honorary member as the University Club but which he preferred to call the Kildare Street Club. He enjoyed being a host. It is true that his anecdotes did not tend to belittle him (who's do!), but that was consistent with them being chosen for the interest they might give his listener. For example, on asking him once what he actually thought of C.S. Forester he said that his descriptions of action scenes were very good. He had been recommended to Patrick by no less a person than Winston Churchill during the war. Certainly Forester had started the Hornblower novels before the war and had, of course, been an established novelist before that. Furthermore he wrote semi-propaganda for the Allied cause so this recommendation seems entirely credible although one is a littler surprised at Churchill having the time to read novels let alone recommend them at that time. O'Brian made the point that he had never read Forester after he started his own series of naval novels.

It seems indisputable that both his own divorce and that of his wife were painful to him. Perhaps for this reason he had a strong hostility to lawyers and judges who get a bad press in the novels. In trying to defend them, on this or another occasion, I quoted to him Flaubert's line in Madame Bovary: 'Not a lawyer but carries within him the debris of a poet.' He had not remembered this and liked it.

When later recounting this conversation to Sir Charles Brett I was forcibly corrected. It was not 'Not a lawyer' but 'Not a notary who carried within him the debris of a poet.' Typically he then sent me a photocopy of the page of the original vindicating his recollection. I will leave to others to consider the relative poeticism of notaries and lawyers and solicitors and barristers and I hope that these recollections may lead them to enjoy the works of Patrick O'Brian of which there will be no more as he died in Dublin on Sunday 2nd January 2000.

NOTES

1. King, D. 2000. *Patrick O'Brian: A Life Revealed. London,* Hodder & Stoughton.

SUBDUING THE LIGHT

COLIN HATRICK

THE GENERIC TERM OF stained glass is applied indiscriminately to coloured and leaded glass without giving a great deal of thought to the process of production involved. When it was discovered in the 14th century that the application of silver nitrate to the outside of glass produced rich gold colouring when viewed from within the necessity of cutting separate pieces for the depiction of haloes, crowns, weapons or armour was no longer necessary. Variety of intensity is achieved according to the number of coats applied. A further advantage is the ability to effect colour changes in particular a range of greens that may be achieved by adding stain to blue glass. This insight into the medium is unlikely to generate public interest in a subject that remains low in priority despite the efforts of a number of devotees.

For a short time attention to the resource was thrust upon communities by the programme of destruction that became a way of life in Northern Ireland. Glass is an element that is extremely vulnerable and in some locations damage was experienced at a considerable distance from the seat of an explosion.

It was inevitable that windows were lost but it is to the credit of many congregations, particularly the persons responsible for caretaking, that fragments were collected to enable repair to proceed. Occasionally opportunity was taken to restore inappropriate parts that had been added over the years. Some use of matching antique glass or salvaged material was required and judicious re-painting was carried out. Discussion about the methods to be used and the selection of aspects of repair such as plating, edge jointing and cleaning using de-ionised water resulted in acceptable restorations.

The city of Londonderry was targeted many times and the windows lighting the north side of St Columb's Cathedral were damaged badly. The protection afforded by the storm glazing enabled records to be made of the glass before removal to the workshop for piecing together of the fragments. Before re-installation a second explosion removed the temporary glazing that had been added to the openings. The final restoration may be viewed and admired. A scheme is in preparation to recondition the fenestration on the opposite side of the building.

Only a small number of publications and articles has drawn attention to the important resource of leaded glass in Northern Ireland[1] and investigation of the medium is best carried out on site. This may start conveniently by a visit to St Malachy's Church in Hillsborough, Co. Down, where a complete set of 18th century coloured glass, by Francis Eginton of Birmingham, may be viewed. His other authenticated window in the chapel of the Bishop's Palace at Armagh has been replaced.

One may then move to other locations to view the work of our earliest local practitioners Francis Coates and William Pearson both of whom started as house painters. From his base in Castle Street, Belfast, Coates produced a series of strongly coloured windows the most remarkable of which occupy the chancel lights of St John's Church of Ireland, Upper Kilwarlin, Co. Down. William Pearson, whose premises were in Talbot Street, Belfast, concentrated on patterned designs containing symbols and texts. An example of his work may be seen in the south wall of St Philip and St James Church of Ireland, Holywood, Co. Down.

In contrast to these relatively simple installations the work associated with Harry Clarke represents the full flowering of the art and technique of stained and decorative glass.[2] In Northern Ireland only the huge rose window at the west end of the Dominican College chapel on the Falls Road, Belfast, is by his hand and it is the output of his father Joshua's firm and of the Studios that is available for study. The chapel of St Malachy's College on the Antrim Road, Belfast, contains a complete set of windows by the firm of Harry Clarke Stained Glass Ltd. Depictions of St James and St Michael in the Roman Catholic Church in Hilltown, Co. Down, are signed J Clarke & Sons.

A few examples exist of the production of scenes without the use of paint relying instead on striations within the glass to give the impression of natural features. This medium did not achieve popularity and only a pair in the Presbyterian Church, Castledawson, Co. Londonderry, has been discovered so far together with a rendition of a Collin Glen landscape in the Non-Subscribing Church, Dunmurry, Co. Antrim. Campbell Brothers who produced the window at Dunmurry were in partnership for a short time with W H Clokey in premises at King Street, Belfast, from 1896. Conventional windows by Campbell & Co. may be seen in the chancel of Fisherwick Presbyterian Church, Belfast. (Fig 1).

Fig 1. Daniel: 12.3. James B. Campbell & Co, 1901. Fisherwick Presbyterian Church, Malone Road, Belfast.

Fig 2. Noah: Isaac. The Clokey Stained Glass Studio 1953. St James Church of Ireland Church, Lower Kilwarlin, Co. Down.

During some ninety years of existence the Clokey Studio was responsible for an enormous amount of decorative glass involving many artists and a variety of techniques to produce work that was most often of quality. Identification is not difficult as many of the windows bear a signature. The attention given to the production of war memorial panels may be appreciated at Downshire Road Presbyterian Church, Newry, and a bright jewelled style, popular for a time, may be examined at St James Church of Ireland, Lower Kilwarlin, Co. Down. (Fig 2)

As time progressed many of the artists who made up the Clokey Studio established successful businesses on their own account. Jack Calderwood's speciality was in the field of etching and engraving and his work may be seen at St Patrick's Roman Catholic Church, Ardboe, Co. Tyrone.

Fig 3. St. Peter: Daniel 1. Braniff, c.1965. Dominican College Chapel, Fortwilliam Park, Belfast.

After leaving Clokey, Daniel Braniff developed an unmistakable style that may be appreciated at the Dominican College chapel, Fortwilliam Park, Belfast. (Fig 3). A move in the opposite direction was made by Francis Ward when he joined Clokey about 1930 bringing with him a portfolio of designs. His firm of Ward and Partners, founded in 1895, was responsible for many well researched windows such as a Fall of Jericho at Knock Presbyterian Church, Belfast. Identification of the work of W J Douglas is relatively difficult as signatures are rare and considerable development of style is apparent. The Crucifixion in Duneane Presbyterian Church near Toomebridge, Co. Antrim, is typical of the work of the firm at that period. Rarer still is the discovery of a window by the workshop belonging to John Frackelton. Unusually a pair of lights installed in the Presbyterian Church, Bellaghy, Co. Londonderry, also bear the signature of Daniel Braniff. Brief mention may be made of other local workshops that have contributed to our resource of stained and decorative glass. Joseph McManus, first appearing in the Belfast Directory in 1907 and now operating as McNeill McManus had a brief essay into large-scale composition under the name of York House Studios Ltd. CWS Design of Hilden near Lisburn remains in full production and is engaged currently on the restoration of the windows at St Patrick's Cathedral, Armagh.

James Watson's style was considered to be of sufficient merit to use for the completion of a series of windows at St McNissi's College, Garron, Co. Antrim, that was started by Daniel Braniff before he took ill. R McClure and Sons Ltd., operate from Ballyclare and Art Glass N I Limited has a studio outside Londonderry City. The founding of the Tower of Glass Studio in Dublin in 1903 by Sara Purser brought a fresh approach to the subject.[3] Each artist was expected

Fig 4. John Leading Mary from Calvary. Mayer of Munich, Post 1890. St. Mathew's Church of Ireland, Richhill, Co. Armagh.

to be responsible for most of the processes involved. Examples of the output of the artists engaged may be seen throughout the country. Catherine O'Brien at Saul, Co. Down, Wilhelmina Geddes at St Cedma, Larne, Co. Antrim, A E Child at St Peter, Fintona, Co. Tyrone and Michael Healy at Holy Trinity, Magheralin, Co. Down. World War I memorials made up of armoured figures or angels produced by William McBride, of the Craftworkers Ltd., Dublin, may be found in a number of locations.

The style of painting used by Earley of Dublin is unmistakable and the work of the studio occupies the chancel of St John's Church, Carnlough, Co. Antrim. Firms from Great Britain or abroad have featured prominently throughout Northern Ireland. The lion's share has gone to Heaton Butler and Bayne but fine installations by Clayton and Bell, Ward and Hughes or William Wailes may be identified. Karl Parsons,[4] an exponent of the Arts and Crafts style, contributed only two windows and these may be viewed at Saintfield and at Helen's Bay, both in Co. Down.

Rare examples of the work of Morris and Company, using designs by Edward Burne-Jones, have been identified at Fisherwick Presbyterian Church, Belfast, and at the Presbyterian Church at Helen's Bay, Co. Down. At Drumalis, Larne, Co. Antrim, the collection of glass by George Walton of Glasgow is of international importance. Many churches used the services of Mayer of Munich, mostly of the Roman Catholic faith but occasionally at other locations such as St Matthew's Church of Ireland, Richhill, Co. Armagh. (Fig 4). The output of studios such as Gabriel Loire of Chartres, Lubin of Tours, Nicod et Jubin of Lyons or G Spreters of Brussels may be examined occasionally. Arid

Rosenkrantz, originally from Denmark, was responsible for an impressive Joseph window at St Patrick's Church of Ireland, Drumbeg, Co. Down. It is thought to be necessary to travel to Great Britain and beyond to view medieval glass but a visit to the chapel at Mount Stewart, Co. Down, and to St Mark's Church nearby in Newtownards will reveal this type of material that was brought in by the Londonderry family. Fragments have been dated variously from the 13th to the 17th centuries. At Kilcoo Parish Church, Bryansford, Co. Down, four little roundels of 16th century Flemish glass were the gift of Lord Roden.

The medium of stained and decorative glass, unlike other artistic expressions, depends on the transmission of light and the efforts that have been made to enhance or subdue it by means of little pieces of translucent material held in place by lead cames deserves more study and attention.

NOTES

1. See Hatrick, C. 1991. *Northern Ireland's Rich Heritage of Stained Glass*, Yearbook & Directory of the Royal Society of Ulster Architects; Hatrick, C. 1992. *Irish Stained Glass*, Ulster Architect.
2. Bowe, N.G. 1989. The Life and Work of Harry Clarke. Dublin, Irish Academic Press.
3. Larmour, P. 1992. The Arts and Crafts Movement in Ireland. Belfast, Friar's Bush Press, pp.163-171.
4. Cormack, P. 1987. 7 and 9 Chichester Street.

CRACKS AT THE ROYAL ACADEMY

NICHOLAS K ROBINSON

EVERY YEAR, BETWEEN 1780 AND 1836, artists put their reputations 'on the line' as the Royal Academy of Arts mounted its annual exhibition in the Great Room of Somerset House. Pictures chosen to rest on the famous 'line', a narrow moulding that ran around the room about eight feet from the floor, were best placed to be viewed by the crowds who thronged to the show.

Presiding over the Academy from its foundation in 1768 until his death in 1792 was Sir Joshua Reynolds. In the centre of Pietro Martini's engraving and etching after J.H.Ramberg [Figs 1 and 2] he is to be seen, ear trumpet in hand, as he guides a guest of honour around the exhibition of 1787: the Prince of Wales, resplendent in scarlet coat. The engraving shows how the canvases above the line have been canted forward to catch the eye and to alleviate light reflections from the great Diocletian windows beyond. Given that the 'skied' pictures were difficult to view, and those below the line obscured by the audience, the politics of the hanging procedure were, for the academicians, lively and absorbing.[1]

However, an incident occurred in the Academy in December 1790 that put a reputation on the line in the way the phrase is now generally used, and reflected internal politics of a more bitter kind. Caught up in the affair were Reynolds, Sir William Chambers, and Edmund Burke.

Chambers had designed the great Somerset House complex, whose Strand block was (in the words of John Harris) 'a polished academic jewel intended as an appropriate casket for the Academic bodies inside',[2] and he had been centrally involved in the establishment of the Royal Academy itself, obtaining the patronage of his former drawing pupil, George III. One writer notes the skill with which he thus outflanked rivals at the Society of Artists: this was not a committee man to trifle with.[3] William Robinson, clerk of the works at Somerset House and a very ordinary practitioner, was charged originally with designing the new complex: had Robinson not died providentially in October

Fig 1. Pietro Martini after Johann H. Ramberg, *The Exhibition of The Royal Academy, 1787*, published 1 July 1787 by A.C. DePoggi, No. 7 St George's Row, Hyde Park. A remarkable recreation *in situ* by the Courtauld Institute in 2001 showed how strikingly the RA summer shows were mounted, with pictures hanging cheek by jowl above and below the 'line' that runs around the room at doorcase height.

Fig 2. [Detail of Fig 1] In later years gout and corpulence would end the Prince of Wales's mounting of the steep staircase at Somerset House to attend the annual show. Here, in youthful finery, he appears content to be the prime exhibit as Sir Joshua Reynolds, ear trumpet in hand, points to other attractions.

Fig 3. [Thomas W. Rowlandson], *The Exhibition Stare Case*, c.1811. BM 11820. Rowlandson (not for the first time) uses an excitable animal – a dog on the fifth stair – to provoke a spiral of chaos and indecency up and down the staircase. Such disarray may be contrasted with the smooth passage of a reclining goddess along the frieze, while various bottoms mirror inadequately that of the Callipygian Venus in the niche.

1775 leaving the coast clear for Chambers to succeed him, further outflanking skills would surely have been displayed.[4] As treasurer of the Academy he wielded considerable power.

Edmund Burke's name has been suggested as a prime mover in the scheme to create at Somerset House a centre that would house both government departments and academic bodies,[5] and he certainly championed the project to the extent that Chambers at one stage wrote to him referring to Somerset House as 'a child of your own'.[6] In a guide to the new academy premises in 1781, Joseph Baretti credited 'Mr Burke, and various other Men of taste in Parliament' with 'having suggested the propriety of making so vast and expensive a Design at once an object of national splendour as well as convenience'.[7] Splendid it was, inspiring a future Irish president of the Academy, Sir Martin Archer Shee, to write in 1805:

In yonder pile by royal bounty plac'd
The Graphic Muse maintains the throne of Taste,
Surveys again reviv'd, her ancient powers,
And smiles as genius there unfolds her flowers.[8]

To gain the inner sanctum one climbed one of the most famously caricatured staircases in London [Fig 3] and passed through a door bearing the inscription (in Greek): 'Let no Stranger to the Muses enter'; to be on the safe side, an entrance charge of one shilling sufficed to discern those on at least nodding terms.

Baretti (for whom Burke and Reynolds once testified in his successful defence of a murder charge)[9] admired the stairs as having the merit of being contained in a very small space, without prejudice either to its commodiousness or magnificence; and, though all the light it has is brought from the top, yet so has it been managed, that there is a sufficiency even to the depth of seven stories, some of them very lofty ones. As the Exhibition-Rooms are necessarily, for the light, at the very top of this Stair, the Architect felt the necessity of supplying amusement to the Spectators while mounting towards the sky, and of furnishing them with stations of repose, where they might find entertainment, to compensate for the labour past, and be encouraged to proceed. In this he has certainly been successful, as every flight of stairs affords a new piece of scenery replete with amusing objects of various sorts.[10]

We do not know whether Thomas Rowlandson had Baretti's description in mind when he captured both Chambers's brilliant handling of the staircase and some of the more entertaining pieces of scenery to be viewed from the 'stations of repose'. But his illustration reminds us that the crowds came to see and be seen, to enjoy the mêlée every bit as much as the artists' endeavours, as the Morning Post had pointed out in 1785: 'some perambulate the rooms to view the *heads* – others remain at the bottom of the stairs to contemplate the *legs*'.[11]

On 10 December 1790 the great and the good mounted these stairs, as they had done for many years, to hear Reynolds give the fifteenth and last of his celebrated discourses and distribute the annual prizes of the Academy. His biographer, James Northcote, RA, takes up the story. It was, he says:

> *a very numerous and even crowded audience, composed of persons of the highest rank in the state, as well as all those who were the most eminent in art, and just at the moment when a respectful and solemn silence prevailed, on a sudden, a loud crash was heard, and a sensation felt, as if the floor of this great room, which is at the top of the house, was giving way and falling. The company immediately took the alarm, and rushed towards the door, or to the sides of the room, tumbling one over the other, in the utmost confusion and consternation, expecting, every moment, that the floor would fall away, and precipitate them down to the lower part of the building.*[12]

Northcote praises Sir Joshua for his courage and composure in remaining calmly in his seat (it surely helped that the elderly painter was deaf and partially blind), and when members of the audience had recovered their composure he 'continued his discourse, as coolly as if nothing extraordinary had occurred'.[13] At the end Burke stepped forward to acclaim his bravura performance in Milton's words:

> *The angel ended, and in Adam's ear*
> *So charming left his view, that he awhile*
> *Thought him still speaking, still stood fix'd to hear.*[14]

But neither Reynolds nor Burke was in a mood to play down the incident. When Dr Charles Burney came forward to offer his congratulations Reynolds told him 'we had pd. him the highest possible Compt. by staying perhaps at the risk of our lives', and Burney, writing to his daughter, admitted 'we are universally abused by our friends for our foolhardy complaisance to Sir Jos. in not making the best of our way out at the 1st. warning'.[15] There is surely an edge to Reynolds's complimentary remark of his audience, remembered by Northcote:

> *that if the floor had really fallen, most of the persons assembled must have been crushed to death in consequence; and if so, the arts in this country would have been thrown two hundred years back.*[16]

The incident was bound to cause a stir, despite the reassurance of Chambers's assistant John Yenn, present in the audience, that he knew from its construction that the floor was quite safe. A breathless paragraph or two might be anticipated in the morning papers, a few jibes from the Academy's critics. But Burke's response went much further. On 22 December he raised in the house of commons the issue of the safety of the whole building:

It had cost the public a great deal of money; and it was highly necessary that care should be taken to see that it answered the purpose for which it was designed... The king, the queen, the prince, with others of the royal family, the bishops, the judges and very many of their worthy constituents, Mr Burke said, went every year to honour the arts, and to honour themselves in countenancing the arts. From what he had remarked it was obvious that they were exposed to the danger of their lives in such visits and he entreated the right hon. gentleman [William Pitt, first lord of the treasury] *to set on foot an examination, and to appoint builders to survey and examine the whole of the works of that place and to control its completion... Mr Pitt said, that the information of the right hon. gentleman demanded the most serious attention, and that an inquiry should be instituted.*[17]

Why did Burke – admittedly excitable – take this course, one which so threatened the reputation of the leading architect of the day, and the Academy's treasurer? Had the experience made him truly fear for the safety of the Great Room, to such a degree that parliamentary scrutiny was called for, rather than simply questioning Chambers in a less public forum? Or was he (as one of Reynold's closest friends, an executor named in his will) getting back at the architect for a humiliation inflicted on the Academy's president earlier in the year? Internal politics had been developing into internecine warfare, the diarist Joseph Farrington noting that Chambers:

in many respects had too much considered himself and had assumed improperly great power... Sir Joshua had felt it, & had told him in the Council that though He (Sir Joshua) was President, Sir Wm. [the king's old drawing master] *was Viceroy over him.*[18]

Now, in February 1790, a cabal led by Chambers successfully challenged Reynolds's attempts to see his *protégé* Joseph Bonomi elected as an academician and as professor of perspective. The Bonomi affair, says Richard Wendorf, was Sir Joshua's French revolution and, moreover, 'but one episode in a series of disputes at the Academy that usually pitted Reynolds against the Academy's "Viceroy"'.[19] His colleagues' refusal to endorse Bonomi, in a heated meeting on 10 February (described by Reynolds in an unfinished, unpublished '*Apologia*') is summed up by Wendorf as 'in short, a world turned upside down for the aging President of the Academy: large numbers, ominous silence, feigned deafness, bad manners, collusion, and open rebellion'.[20] (Reynolds had asked Bonomi to send drawings to the meeting to demonstrate his qualification to become professor of perspective. When he requested the secretary, John Richards, to show them to those present, Richards walked past the two drawings and rang a bell for a servant to mount the long staircase and move the drawings from one side of the room to the other.) Reynolds, outraged, resigned both from the presidency and from the Academy itself. He was prevailed upon to return to the chair only after weeks of negotiation and a face-saving resolution of the Academy's general assembly. Whatever motivated Burke's intervention in the commons, Chambers had no doubt about his animus. Letters to George Rose, a secretary of the treasury, from his 'most Obedient and humble Servant' bristle with indignation.[21] On 24 December 1790 he writes that:

finding on my arrival in town yesterday, that much had been inserted in the papers, and much said in the house of Commons, about the ruinous state of a floor in the Royal Academy; I am under the necessity of troubling you with an explanation of the whole business… When the President gave his lecture about ten days ago, a very numerous Audience crouding to one end of the exhibition room, a crack was heard, or said to be heard, in the floor.

His assistant Yenn, he went on to say, had reassured the audience that:

the report could not proceed from any material failure in the floor of which he knew the Construction, and it had been sufficiently tryd by twelve Exhibitions, when more than a thousand persons had often been upon the floor at the same time.

The next morning, observing 'a couple of Cracks in the ceiling of a room underneath... and a rent in the Girder about nine inches long', Chambers had sent for Mr. Samuel Wyatt 'whose Skill and Great experience as a Carpenter are sufficiently acknowledged'. Wyatt, agreeing with him that no accident could happen, advised certain repairs:

[B]oth Mr Wyat [sic] *and myself thought the business too trifling, and the means of proceeding too obvious, to trouble other inspectors for more advice. but since the crack has been magnified into the report of a Cannon or a Clap of Thunder, and one nine inch wound into two dreadful gaps, I am humbly of Opinion other inspectors will be necessary: and have in Consequence, explained to the Messrs Adam what is doing, and obtained their promise of a meeting on the Spot next week; with Messrs White, and Samuel Wyat*

Their report, he felt sure, would 'quiet the Apprehensions of the Publick, which have been artfully wrought up to a Very unnecessary height'. In a further letter of 6 January 1791, Chambers reports that he has gone further:

judging, from the great, though very unnecessary clamour which has been excited upon the Occasion, that more Surveyors might be yet more Satisfactory to the Lords Commissioners of his Majesties Treasury; and still more effectual towards silencing the newspapers, and removing the doubts of the Publick; I invited twelve of the principal Architects, master builders and Carpenters in town...

He encloses the report, signed by nine of them – Robert Adam, Richard Jupp, James Wyatt, John Johnson, John Soane, Richard Norris, John Hobcraft, James White, and Samuel Wyatt – that one piece of timber, only one half of the girder in question, had split or opened:

about a foot in length, and about an eighth part of an Inch at the Opening of the Rent, diminishing to nothing at the extremity. but the timbers being perfectly sound, and having suffered in no other way, except for this small crack – We are decidedly of Opinion, that there was not any danger from the Weight that was upon it, at the time the noise was heard.

On 17 February James Wyatt, Soane and White attended upon the board to confirm this. Even so, they were requested to undertake with their colleagues – and to be further joined by 'Mr Dance Mr Holland Mr Milne & Mr Cockerell' – a survey of 'the whole of the Buildings at Somerset Place.'[22]

Meanwhile, the caricaturists were on to the story. An anonymous artist (possibly Samuel Collings) mocks Chambers as *A Great Architect Modelling* with a deck of cards [Fig 4], his self-importance reflected in the treatise at his side, *Art of Building and Rebuilding or Palladio improved by S.W.C* (a sly alteration to the title of his own famous treatise), his annoyance evident as the model collapses.[23] The picture frame supporting an elevation of the Strand front has also given way, the drawing's triple arcade echoed in the arrangement of the playing cards. Projecting from the architect's pocket, a document, *Art of Grant of Parlt* testifies to other skills and connections, and hints at the ever mounting costs of the project, as does a bundle of *Bills for repairing S.H.* on the floor (In the commons in 1788 one cynical MP, Daniel Pulteney, had complained that 'as Sir William Chambers had 5 per cent on all the money expended, it was his interest to find as many ways of adding to the expense as possible'.[24] (In fairness, the 'oeconomical' Burke had always stoutly defended the project against attacks of cost.) Also on the floor, an affidavit – *It was only*

Fig 4. Anon. (possibly Samuel Collings), *A Great Architect Modelling or Sr W – in his study*, published 13 January 1791 by S. W. Fores, No. 3 Piccadilly. BM 8016. Sir William Chambers watches, exasperated, as his playing cards (arranged to echo the triple arcade of the Strand front of Somerset House) come to grief.

a crack signed Adam, Wyat – contrasts mischievously with a painting of supposed devastation, *A View on the Thames*, which represents, no doubt, Burke's extravagant description.

More indecent and vulgar abuse was to follow in *A Report of the Surveyors* [Fig 5], as Rowlandson depicts three of the worthies called in by Sir William, baring their posteriors to defecate with alarming consequences at an unfortunate building that bears little resemblance, but has always been taken to be Somerset House[25] (It has all the signs of a Rowlandson 'pot-boiler', run off quickly and casually; even working at frenzied short notice, his contemporary, James Gillray, would have provided a façade as recognized as it was lampooned.) Scatological imagery was commonplace in the late eighteenth century. These not inexpensive prints reflected and pandered to a vulgar taste then prevailing. But such images did more; they allowed the artist to denigrate by excremental association the targets of his abuse. Rowlandson's customers are thus invited to mock in a particularly disedifying way the goings on of high art and architecture at Somerset House.

Only two days earlier, on 4 February 1791, Rowlandson had displayed poor taste of a different kind in *Chaos is Come Again*, treating readers to the horrific spectacle of an imagined collapse at Drury Lane Theatre [Fig 6];[26] the theatre, condemned as unsafe, was due to be pulled down and rebuilt. 'Music hath charms to soothe the savage breast' reads the sub-title, 'To soften bricks and bend the knotted oak'. A buxom diva on stage in front of the orchestra pit, arms aloft as her aria reaches its dramatic climax, appears to have triggered just such a response from bricks and beams alike, with terrifying consequences for players and audience.

Prints such as these reflect concern (or at least gossip) about the safety of public buildings: that, in Chambers's own words, 'the Apprehensions of the Publick' had been 'artfully wrought up'. Tragic incidents had, of course, been recorded over many years. In Ireland the gallery of a Dublin theatre, Smock Alley, had collapsed in 1701 killing several of the audience, and about two hundred people had been killed and wounded when the Roscommon courthouse fell down in 1718.[27] Tragedies real or apprehended were enough to

Fig 5. [Thomas W. Rowlandson], *A Report From the Surveyors*, published 6 February 1791 by S.W.Fores, No. 3 Piccadilly. BM 8017. Scatological prints, commonplace in the late eighteenth century, were used by caricaturists to abuse and degrade. Here Rowlandson's customers are invited to mock in a particularly disedifying way the goings on of high art and architecture at Somerset House.

oblige Pitt and the lords of the treasury to take every precaution, while Chambers gritted his teeth and lined up his professional colleagues.

Meanwhile, for the Academy's critics there was always something else to grumble about, a newspaper chiding it that:

> *this season… the EXHIBITION, with the usual penury, which has too often disgraced it, opens without any public annunciation of it. The PRESIDENT should take better care. The large sums received from the kindness of the public at the door, demand that the common respect should be paid them, of* advertising when *it opens. All that has been done at present is "Letting the people know, that in the opinion of different SURVEYORS, the building will not come about their ears".*[28]

The minute books of the meetings of the Board of Treasury (whose quorum of three invariably shows Pitt sitting with two of the other four members) serve as a reminder of the extraordinary detail in which the prime minister constantly immersed himself. When on 30 June 1791 the several architects

Fig 6. *Qui Capit invent Ille Habet fect* [Thomas W. Rowlandson], *Chaos is Come Again*, published 4 February 1791 by S.W. Fores [No. 3] Piccadilly. BM 8009. Another print of February 1791 excites anxiety about the dangerous state of public buildings. Despite the artist's dire warning, the old Drury Lane Theatre continued in use until 4 June. It was then pulled down and rebuilt.

attended upon Pitt and his board, they confirmed that all of the Somerset House components were, indeed, substantial and permanent buildings.[29]

And so they proved to be. The storm in the teacup abated, and their lordships proceeded to items about the Sandwich Islands, calico shipments, smuggled salt, depredations in Windsor Forest, petitions from dispossessed American loyalists, and, alas, problems in Ireland.[30]

ACKNOWLEDGEMENTS

For their help, generously given, the writer is grateful to Antony Griffiths and his colleagues in the Department of Prints and Drawings at the British Museum; to the staff of the Public Record Office, Kew; Mark Pomeroy, Archivist of the Royal Academy Archives; Edward McParland; and – especially – Rosemary Baker.

For kind permission to reproduce material, thanks are due to the Trustees of the British Museum, Andrew Edmunds, and Edward McParland.

NOTES

1. For an account of these exhibitions, and of the politics involved, see Solkin D.H. (ed.) 2001. *Art on the Line: The Royal Academy Exhibitions at Somerset House 1780-1836.* New Haven and London, Yale University Press. The Paul Mellon Centre for Studies in British Art and the Courtauld Institute Gallery.
2. Harris, J. 1967. 'Somerset House, London - 1'. *Country Life*, (16 Nov.1967), p.1252.
3. Wendorf, R. 1996. *Sir Joshua Reynolds: The Painter in Society.* Cambridge, Mass, Harvard University Press, paperback edition, 1998, p.183.
4. As soon as the project was decided upon, Chambers, not commissioned, took off to study new public buildings in Paris. Harris, *op.cit.*, p.1250.
5. E.g. Summerson, J. 1945. *Georgian London*, London, Penguin Books, p.123; Harris, *op.cit.*, p.1251; Sir Howard Colvin believed the credit could not be given to any one person on the evidence available: Colvin, H.M. 1976. 'Somerset House', *The History of the King's Works.* London, HMSO, v, p.363.
6. Undated, Sheffield Univ. Lib. Fitzwilliam mss., Bk 2/543.
7. Baretti, J. 1781. *A Guide Through the Royal Academy*, p.3.
8. Quoted in Cullen, F. 1997 *Visual Politics: The Representation of Ireland, 1750-1930*, Cork, Cork University Press, p.21.
9. In 1769; Robinson, N.K. 1996. *Edmund Burke: A Life in Caricature.* New Haven and London, Yale University Press, p.20.
10. Baretti, *op.cit.*, p.15.
11. Quoted in Kriz, K.D. 2001. '"Stare Cases": Engendering the Public's Two Bodies at the Royal Academy of Arts,' in Solkin D.H. 2001 (ed.).,*op cit.*
12. Northcote, J. 1813. *The Life of Sir Joshua Reynolds*, London, Colburn, ii, p.263

13. *Ibid.* Northcote's recollection is slightly inaccurate: Reynolds had concluded his address and was in the process of awarding the first gold medal. *Parliamentary History of England from the earliest Period to the Year 1803.* London, Printed by Hansard, 1816, vol. xxviii, p.1191.
14. Quoted in Leslie, C.R. and Taylor, T. 1865. *Life and Times of Sir Joshua Reynolds: With Notices of Some of His Contemporaries.* London, John Murray, ii, p.594
15. Quoted in Wendorf, *op cit.*, p.17-18
16. Northcote, *op cit.*, p.263
17. *Parliamentary History, op cit.*, p.1191-2
18. Cited in Wendorf, *op.cit.*, p.185
19. Wendorf, *op.cit.*, p.249, fn.106
20. *Ibid.*, 182. For his absorbing analysis of the affair, see pp.176-205.
21. They are to be found in the Public Record Office, TI/689
22. PRO, T29/63
23. Anon [possibly Samuel Collings], *A Great Architect Modelling or Sr W- in his study,* published 13 January 1791 by S.W.Fores, No. 3 Piccadilly. BM 8016
24. Cited in Colvin, *op.cit.*, p.379.
25. [Thomas W. Rowlandson], *A Report From the Surveyors,* published 6 February 1791 by S.W. Fores, No 3 Piccadilly. BM 8017. In her catalogue note M.D.George assumes the building to be Somerset House.
26. [Thomas W. Rowlandson], *Chaos is Come Again,* published 4 February 1791 by S.W. Fores, [No.3] Piccadilly. BM 8009
27. These and other examples are given in McParland, E.J. 2001. *Public Architecture in Ireland, 1680-1760.* New Haven and London, Yale University Press, p.32.
28. Newspaper cutting (dated 'May 1791' in a contemporary hand) in the Royal Academy Archives *Critiques*, I, p.137.
29. PRO, T 29/63. The architects and surveyors in attendance were George Dance, James Wyatt, S.P.Cockerell, Samuel Wyatt, Richard Jupp, John Johnson, James White, Richard Norris, John Hobcraft, Robert Brettingham, and John Soane.
30. Chambers, however, did not forget the attack on his reputation and when Reynolds died in February 1792 tried to prevent the founding president's body from lying in state at the Academy, arguing that no such provision had been made in the Academy's charter: Pressly, W.L. 1981. *The Life and Art of James Barry.* New Haven and London, Yale University Press, p.219 fn.45.

7 AND 9 CHICHESTER STREET

ROBERT MCKINSTRY

NUMBERS 7 AND 9 Chichester Street, Belfast, date from 1804. Originally these two houses along with Number 11, now a shop, formed part of a handsome terrace. Numbers 7 and 9 still survive intact, having served for some one hundred and fifty years as the offices of L'Estrange and Brett, Solicitors – Sir Charles Brett's family firm.

The building is of dark-coloured brickwork, six bays wide, four storeys high with a basement. All the windows still have their glazing bars and on the first floor the tall windows are particularly elegant. Further distinguishing features are the two entrance doors with their generous flights of steps, Doric columns and segmental fanlights.

While the grid pattern of the layout of Belfast's late Georgian streets still forms a backbone to the centre of the town, its appearance was utterly transformed by the Industrial Revolution of the nineteenth and early twentieth centuries: Belfast became a city and grand public buildings, churches, large offices and factories expressed this fact. However, L'Estrange and Brett's two houses in Chichester Street have stood to one side, a unique reminder of the plain elegant brick terraces built at the end of the eighteenth century in and around Donegall Square and Collage Square, each house a well balanced and integral part of the Classical whole.

7 and 9
Chichester Street.
Watercolour by
Jason McKinstry.

REFLECTIONS ON SOME EIGHTEENTH CENTURY DUBLIN CARVERS

ANNE CROOKSHANK AND THE KNIGHT OF GLIN

THERE WERE TWO IMPORTANT artists who were very influential on early eighteenth century Irish wood carvers. The first of these was the great French Huguenot carver, James Tabary who together with his two brothers almost certainly carved the stone and wood work on the exterior overdoors, trophies and armorials, of the Royal Hospital, Kilmainham where James's documented masterpiece is the superb wood carving of the chapel and its altar table dating from 1680-84.[1] The other influential craftsman of lesser quality was the English statuary, William Kidwell, 1662-1736, who had been apprenticed to the English sculptor, Edward Pierce, and came to Ireland in 1711. All of Kidwell's known works are in stone, mostly funerary monuments and many of them are of considerable quality. This was unlike the usual habit of carvers who worked in both stone and wood. Kidwell may have introduced into Ireland the habit of consulting engravings by other artists for details and for compositions.[2]

The profession of carver usually ran in families, for instance John Kelly, who worked in Trinity College in 1711, was probably the father of the younger John Kelly who is mentioned from the 1730s onwards. Again Henry Houghton who died in 1727 was the father[3] of John Houghton who was regarded as the finest carver in the mid century, dying in 1761. David Sheehan, died 1756, was the father of a dynasty, leaving a son Cornelius who was succeeded by his own son Mordecai. Sheehan's known work is mainly church monuments and therefore is outside the confines of this article. However he worked with Houghton on a number of occasions particularly in mantel pieces of which a splendid example is the Kentian work at Curraghmore, County Waterford, which we will mention later.

Edward Lovett Pearce, the architect of the Parliament House (now Bank of Ireland) employed a number of distinguished carvers in his public and private buildings though they are rarely documented. At Castletown, Co. Kildare for instance in the 1720s, in the upper storey of the main hall, the baskets of flowers (Fig 1) which form the capitals of the tapered pilasters are in fact not plaster but

Fig 1. Carved wood capital painted white on one of the pillasters in the front hall at Castletown, designed by Sir Edward Lovett Pearce, circa 1730. (Irish Architectural Archive)

Fig 2. Detail of one of the carved overdoors in the back drawing room of No.10 Henrietta Street, a house designed by Sir Edward Lovett Pearce circa 1730. (Irish Architectural Archive)

of carved wood.[4] They are robustly handled in deep relief and the detail of the flowers and cane work is finely executed. Very similar carved wood baskets filled with flowers and shells, occur in the spandrels of overdoors and in keystones of the door cases in the front and back drawing rooms on the ground floor in 10 Henrietta Street (late 1720s), one of the three houses designed by Pearce. In one of the rooms other keystones show a bust of a warrior's head with a martial trophy surmounted by a crest (Fig 2) which echoes in a small way Tabary's trophies, and another is a bust head of a woman. In Beaulieu, Co. Louth there are some large overdoors of trophies of arms and musical instruments and carved wood armorial sconces. These certainly show Tabary influence though they date from the early eighteenth century. Dublin carvers of this period must all have worked under their shadow. These baskets of flowers also appear on contemporary furniture such as the carved basket of flowers on the walnut stand for a Flemish nest of boxes at Castletown.

These rooms in No.10 Henrietta Street have other features in superb carved wood such as the chimney piece in the back drawing room with its acanthus decoration incorporating monkeys and with a centered crest. Under the main pedimented door case is a charming frieze incorporating mice and serpents entwined in the acanthus decoration. In the next door house, No.9, there are similar keystone heads on some of the door cases. Putto's heads and pairs of putti holding baskets also occur in No.10. Sadly we have no idea who executed these elaborate and imaginative decorations. It could well be the elder Houghton or the elder Kelly. We know no works by the latter but there are descriptions of his work in Trinity College.[5] In other parts of Dublin carved work with baskets,

Fig 3a. Carved basket and acanthus at Lisle House, Molesworth Street, circa 1725-1730. The staircase is now in No.13 Henrietta St. (Davison and Associates Ltd)

Fig 3b. Detail of the carving formerly on the staircase of No 8 Henrietta Street circa 1725-1730. (Irish Architectural Archive)

Fig 4. The organ case at St. Michan's Church, the carving of the case attributed to Henry Houghton, circa 1724. (Irish Architectural Archive)

acanthus and birds show much similarity, for instance the carved staircase frieze (Fig 3a) from Lisle House in Molesworth Street, now reassembled in 13 Henrietta Street, is very close in style to the frieze on the staircase which used to exist in No.8 Henrietta Street (Fig 3b), now known only through old photographs. Number 8 Henrietta Street was also designed by Pearce. One of the rooms in Lisle House had finely carved keystones of similar type to those in Henrietta Street. which suggest that the same major workshop was employed both sides of the Liffey.

We have only two references to Henry Houghton, when he was working in St. Michan's Church in 1725 and was paid 10 shillings and tenpence for repairing the altar rails and the fact that he was working there suggests that he may have been the carver of the magnificent organ case (Fig 4). The organ itself was made by John Baptiste Cuvillie and he had been contracted in 1724 not only to make the organ but to arrange for a 'good substantial case ... most beautiful and proper'. He obviously sub-contracted the carving of the case to a sculptor as he was not a carver and therefore the carver's name does not appear among the accounts or vestry books.[6] In style it strongly reflects the work of James Tabary with finely carved winged puttis heads, realistically carved festoons of fruit and flowers and as its *piece de resistance* has an exquisite trophy of musical instruments worthy of Grinling Gibbons. It is very similar to the trophy on the overdoor on Kilmainham Hospital's Banqueting Hall. Two other musical frieze-like trophies decorate the side of the case. It is all a tour de force of wood carving. Henry Houghton also worked at Trinity College where he was paid for work in February 1712-13.[7] It also reminds one, as will be seen, of the work of Henry's son, John Houghton, which we will now turn to.

Houghton is first recorded in 1729, as working as a carver in Pearce's Parliament House[8] and must have done a great deal of work as he was paid £333.8.3d, a huge sum at that date. It did include carving capitals and £50 for the royal arms on the south pediment. He may have carved the wooden caryatid herm figures on the chimney piece in the House of Lords after a design by Inigo Jones, though it was completed by Thomas Oldham in about 1750. A white marble chimney piece (circa 1754) on which he collaborated with David Sheehan, was for Lord Kenmare in Killarney and was again based on a design by Inigo Jones. Faulkner in his *Dublin Journal* for 19-22 January 1754 says that 'the stone cutting work was executed by the ingenious Mr Shehan, stonecutter, in Marlbrough-street and the carving by the great Mr Houghton'. The carving of the swags of flowers on the House of Lords herms reminds one of similar flowers in his father Henry's work in St Michans. There are a number of similar chimney pieces which may well be from Houghton's or Sheehan's workshops. Houghton carved in wood an overmantel in relief, now missing, once at Curraghmore, Co. Waterford, of *St Paul Preaching in Athens* after the Raphael cartoon. The Dublin Society had given him a prize of £20 (a very large sum) for this work in 1742. The overmantel frame by Houghton is a fine example with its Corinthian columns, broken pediment, central cartouche and a pair of putti reclining on either side. The fireplace surround is by Sheehan in the Inigo Jones manner.[9]

A very interesting notice in Faulkner's *Dublin Journal* of 28-31 July 1753 praises Sheehan and Houghton's work for the Earl of Barrymore's monument at Castle Lyons, Co. Cork, saying it shows 'to what perfection these Arts are now arrived in this Kingdom and demonstrate that performances of this nature need not now be purchased in other countries, which by ill judged prejudice against home productions, has too long been a discouragement to our own artifices.' The writer credits the Dublin Society schools, then in Shaw's Court, as responsible for these skills and these sentiments reflect the philosophy of self-sufficiency propagated by the patriotic propaganda of Samuel Madden, Thomas Prior, Dean Swift and Bishop Berkeley.

Other similar overmantel reliefs exist in Bishop Clayton's house, now Iveagh House, in Stephen's Green. The quality of the bas reliefs is varied. An upright pair of them were described by Strickland as being done in the Houghton manner by Richard Barrington Boyle 1811-1891[10], for Sir Benjamin Lee

Fig 5. Bacchic bass relief scene of carved wood with overmantle by John Houghton in Bishop Clayton's House now part of Iveagh House, St Stephens Green circa 1730. (Courtesy of Commissioners of Public Work)

Fig 6. Carved bass relief of Marcus Aurelius, by John Houghton, with its overmantle part of the decoration of the old Presence Chamber in Dublin Castle circa 1750. (Courtesy of Commissioners of Public Work)

Guinness when he was altering and enlarging the house. However the most important of them is a bacchanalian scene in the hall, which with its surround is borrowed from one at Houghton Hall, Norfolk. It has a broken pediment centered by a superbly carved shell motif (Fig 5). The fireplace below is probably by Barrington Boyle. Mrs Delany[11] noticed these reliefs when she saw them in 1731, in the oak panelled rooms in Bishop Clayton's first house in Stephen's Green. She called them 'panels, doors and chimneys finished with very fine high carving'. Some of these were moved to Claytons's second house in 1736 by Richard Castle when it was built on the South side of Stephen's Green. Mrs Delany must have been referring to the overmantel mentioned above.

An engraving of the dining room (the presence chamber in the eighteenth century) in Dublin Castle in *The Graphic* for 14 April, 1888, shows another of Houghton's reliefs of classical subjects, this time, a scene from the life of Marcus Aurelius[12] (Fig 6) above its original chimney piece. It dates from 1750-51. The design is directly taken from the marble example by Rysbrack published in Isaac Ware's *The Plans. Elevations and Sections, Chimney Pieces and Ceilings of Houghton in Norfolk*, 1735. Its elaborate pedimented frame similar to that in Bishop Clayton's second house which we have just described, is also taken from one by William Kent published in Ware who had Irish connections with the Earl of Kildare and his brother in law, Thomas Conolly. The treatment of the carving of the relief is very different between the work in Iveagh House and that in the Castle. The subjects are far apart, one being dignified and sober while the earlier is a bacchic sacrifice. They may also show the difference in style between an early

Fig 7. Detail of carved staircase frieze from Bishop Clayton's house now part of Iveagh House, St. Stephens Green. (Courtesy of Commissioners of Public Work)

Fig 8. Detail of the carved oak frame, by John Houghton, of Francis Bindon's portrait of Jonathan Swift in St. Patrick's Deanery, circa 1735-1740.

and a late work. The frieze (Fig 7) in Iveagh House set into the grandiloquent nineteenth century staircase is almost certainly eighteenth century and from Houghton's workshop. The Roman profile bust is the centre of the design which incorporates putti, acanthus and birds.

Houghton may have carved a bas relief for Bishop Synge for his house in Kevin Street, as in his letter to his daughter in June 1747 he includes a comment that John Houghton was responsible for putting up carvings in one of the main reception rooms. They were in place by September of that year and the bishop was recommending that they should be varnished with nut oil.[13]

Houghton's most important documented work is the frame he made for Bindon's portrait of Dean Swift for the Deanery of St Patrick's where it still hangs (Fig 8). It has an oak frame, is elaborately carved with harps, books, quills, tasseled ropes, a lyre, and various other symbols with two cartouches at the top and bottom containing the arms of the dioceses of Dublin and Swift's own achievement. The picture was paid for by Lord Howth who commissioned three others at the same time, one for himself. He paid £18.13.0 for the frame. The pictures were painted between 1735-40 and this frame was made between these dates. The composition of the frame is very unusual and we think it shows much influence from his father's attributed musical trophies in St Michan's. The only frame in England with any similarity is one of Sir John Chardin in Oxford which shows mathematical instruments.[14] However in Dublin there is another frame (Fig 9) also for a Bindon portrait which was carved in mahogany of *Bishop Boulter preaching to the inhabitants of the poor house* 1741/2, now in Trinity College. Its symbolism is of charity and the picture originally hung in the Dublin

Fig 9. Carved frame attributed to John Houghton for Swift's portrait of Bishop Boulter of 1741-1742. Trinity College Dublin. (Green Studio Limited)

Fig 10. Carved mirror frame attributed to John Houghton circa 1750. (Christies Images)

Workhouse. Unlike the Swift frame it is lighter as the elements are not placed against a solid background.

Two delicate mirror frames, the details of which connect with the picture frames, exist in private collections. They are much influenced by French craftsmen and echo the designs of Daniel Marot with their lambrequins, foliage, birds and shells not to mention helmets. They are carved in mahogany, one with a parcel gilt border round the frame and they both have that criss cross diaper pattern background which is so typical of Irish furniture decoration. One is illustrated here (Fig 10). We attribute these to John Houghton and they date from the 1740s to 50s.

Fig 11. Parcel gilt frame attributed John Houghton, which originally hung in the Weaver's Hall and dated 1738. (Metropolitan Museum of Art, New York)

Another elaborate parcel gilt frame (Fig 11) is that of the tapestry portrait of George II (Metropolitan Museum, New York) originally from the Weaver's Hall dated 1738 which includes helmets (also in one of the mirrors), tasselled ropes and weaver's spools. It is parcel gilt and it is certainly attributable to Houghton. The Weaver's Hall, which no longer survives, we know from old photographs[15] had a magnificent interior with much carved wood including a pair of elaborate baroque chimney pieces, pedimented doors etc.

The magnificent frames of the full length portraits by Bindon of Provost Baldwin and by Benjamin Wilson of Archbishop Price in the Dining Hall in Trinity College may also be by Houghton though they are different in style. They date respectively from c.1746 and 1749 and both show rococo features

Fig 12. Carved and gilt frame of the portrait of Archbishop Price, in the Dining Hall of Trinity College, Dublin, attributed John Houghton circa 1746-1749. (Brendan P. Dempsey)

Fig 13. Carved and gilt pier glass, one of a pair from Russborough House, Co. Wicklow attributed to John Houghton circa 1752. (National Gallery of Ireland)

particularly the frame with its asymetrical shells on either side and the imaginative cornucopias (Fig 12). There are unfortunately no accounts for these frames. However as Houghton was supplying frames for Bindon it is certainly a likely possibility. They are both gilded and are composed of decorative motifs and overblown roses and other flowers.

By far the most important collection of frames hung in Russborough, Co. Wicklow and are now in the National Gallery of Ireland. They were for pictures and mirrors and are noticeably much more rococo than the frames already mentioned. A pair of full length pier glasses (Fig 13) show the influence of the engravings of rocaille carved work from Lock and Copeland's *A New Book of Ornaments* which was published in 1752. This was the time Russborough would have been furnished. The putti's heads which appear on these and other overmantel picture frames from Russborough lead us back to Henry Houghton in St Michans. The grandeur of the frames with their outspread eagles, their bacchic masks, their chinese and female heads make an astonishing surviving interior collection. The carving must have been worked in tandem with the stuccodores, the La Francini and others. This magnificence was in keeping with the newly built Russborough and its owners the first and second Earls of Milltown. The architect, Richard Castle, died in 1751 and the building was completed by Bindon which makes a definite link with Houghton. However there is no certainty in the attribution. It should also be noted that the carving of the overdoor rococo brackets in the hall and the doorcase in the saloon and staircase woodwork are of incredible opulence and are of superb quality and must come from one of the best Dublin workshops.

A very exciting piece of information has recently come to light.[16] The autobiography has been discovered of the English carver and designer, Thomas Johnson, so well known for his pattern books[17] of high rococo ornament published 1755-62. He was working in Liverpool in 1746 and came to Dublin where he found employment aged 22 with a carver, one Smith of William Street. He then moved to 'Mr. Houghton [who] was the most eminent carver in Dublin'. He described Houghton as a 'wood Statuary' and also called him 'the best wood carver, for basso relievo figures I ever saw before or since'. He only stayed about eight months in Dublin but came back in 1753-55 when he worked for a mirror maker from the Partridge family. He said he learnt a lot from Houghton and in turn taught Houghton's apprentices a great deal. His visits may well have influenced Irish rococo carving, even though on his first visit he was young.

The mention of Houghton's death in 1761 in Faulkner's *Dublin Journal* for 9-13 June includes interesting details of his possessions. They called him a carver and said that the auction would include large pier glasses, frames, chimney glass frames in the Chinese manner and other goods and pattern books. This reminds us of the Russborough frames.

It has been suggested that Houghton was the teacher of John Kelly the younger and certainly he collaborated with him. They are first mentioned in a no longer surviving bill in the Carton accounts for £60, for the Kildare armorial achievement in the pediment at Carton in 1739. They seem to have collaborated on and off until Houghton's death. One would like to think that the pair both worked on the lovely Chinese state bedroom at Carton with its elaborate rococo mantelpiece and overmantel with its brackets for Chinese porcelain.

Fig 14. Carved cabriole foot, from Dr Mosses bed from the Rotunda Hospital. Made for Dr Moss in 1759 by John Kelly.

Kelly is best documented for the bed he made for Dr Bartholomew Mosse. The bill is, according to Strickland, dated 15 September 1759, months after Dr Mosse had died. The bill is extraordinarily detailed and mentions all the carving though strangely the Corinthian order with which Kelly described the bed on the bill heading is in fact changed to Ionic on the bed. The bed board with Mosse's crest is the most expensive item costing £3.8.8 and the whole bill is for £19.8.6. The legs and feet with their carved shell decoration, diaper pattern, tassels and realistic lion paw feet with prominent claws, sum up at its best all the quality of Irish furniture (Fig 14). A second four poster in Castlecoole Co. Fermanagh has very similar clawed removable feet and acanthus on the leg which as in Mosse's bed comes off to show the bolts. In this bed the posts are decorated with beautifully carved climbing vines both leaves and fruit and the decoration is probably from the Houghton workshop as he is recorded as working with David Sheehan at old Castle Coole in 1748.[18] The third four poster bed attributed to Kelly is now in Florencecourt, Co. Fermanagh.[19] It has many of the features of the Mosse bed and the legs with their masks are surmounted by removable shells hiding the bolts. The drapery on the top of the bed head is akin to the drapery which conceals loaves of bread under the Boulter frame in Trinity College which we have discussed. Mosse in his will proved on 2 Apri1 1759, calls his own bed Ionic and leaves it to his daughter Jane. Mosse was a furniture maker himself as his will makes plain, and in an auction of his effects on 19 May, 1761 'a complete set of tools fit for a gentleman mechanic for working in wood' is mentioned.[20]

Figs15a. Carved overdoor from Dr Mosses house, 15 Cavendish Row. Carved by John Kelly circa 1759.

Fig 15b. Carved overdoor from Dr Mosses house, 15 Cavendish Row. Carved by John Kelly circa 1759.

Kelly did a great deal of work for Mosse in his house in No.9 Cavendish Row including overdoors (Figs 15a & b), window surrounds and carved staircase brackets. The overdoors are among the most exquisite, delicate carvings done in Dublin[21] and are very similar in quality of carving to the overdoors made for No. 20 Lower Dominick Street where he was working for Robert West. The floral festoons hang from rings, are centered with a bird and are composed of mixed flowers executed with superb crispness. One example from No.20 (Fig 16), now in a private collection has been stripped of its paint and gives a true picture of the carver's skill. The charm of Kelly lies in his lightness of touch and despite his lack of asymmetry he is a rococo master.

Like Houghton, Kelly made basso relievos, six of which he exhibited at the Society of Artists in Ireland in 1765, 68, 69 and 73. None of these are now known and some of them may have been centre plaques for chimney pieces, but one exhibited in 1765 is described fully. The catalogue says 'An allegorical basso relievo, in wood, representing Hibernia presenting the heart of the people

Fig 16. Carved overdoor from No. 20 Dominic Street carved by John Kelly for Robert West, circa 1759-1760.

to the King, attended by Industry etc', which sounds more like an overmantel. In Doneraile House in Kildare Street Kelly carved a staircase in 1749 for Col. Hayes St Leger. The bill survives[22] and is countersigned, as was that of the Mosse bill by the architect John Ensor who was another of Richard Castle's pupils. Strickland assumes Kelly dies in 1773 as there is no further mention of him. It is strange that the papers do not as far as we know mention his death.

The best period of the art of wood carving in Dublin continued for at least another generation with the work of Richard Cranfield and also his sometime collaborator William Robinson, whose work can be seen in Trinity College and Newbridge. In this article we have been adventurous in our attributions to Houghton in particular, but we considered it worthwhile to try a positive approach to identifying the unknown oeuvre of Dublin's greatest master carvers. We agree with Thomas Johnson's opinion of Houghton as being 'the most eminent carver in Dublin' in the mid eighteenth century.

NOTES

1. McParland, Edward. 2001. *Public Architecture in Ireland 1660-1760*, London and New Haven, Yale University Press, pp.68-69.

2. Potterton, Homan. 1975. *Irish Church Monuments.* Belfast, Ulster Architectural Heritage Society, pp.9-10.
3. Glin, Knight of, 2000. Introduction to Catalogue of Johnston Antiques *An Exhibition of Irish Georgian Furniture.* Dublin, p.12 for extracts from Houghton Wills in the *Welply Irish Wills and Proceedings.* 11 & 13 (1740-49), Society of Genealogists, London IR/G 101/8.
4. Information from David Griffin, (Irish Architectural Archive).
5. Crookshank, Anne, 1986. 'The Long Room' in Peter Fox (ed.) *Treasures of the Library: Trinity College Dublin.* Dublin, Royal Irish Academy, pp.16-28; T.C.D. Mun, P2/20/39.
6. Crookshank, Anne, 1975. 'Eighteenth-century alterations, improvements, and furnishings in St. Michan's Church, Dublin', *Studies* Vol. I xiv, pp.391-2.
7. T.C.D. Mun. p2/24/15
8. See Curran, Constantine P. 1949 'The Architecture of the Bank of Ireland', in F. G. Hall (ed.) *The Bank of Ireland,* Dublin, Hodges Figgis, pp.438-39, p.454.
9. See Girouard, Mark, 1963. 'Curraghmore, Co. Waterford'. *Country Life,* Vol. CXXXIII, Nos.3440-2 (7th, 14th & 21st February), pp.256-60, 308-11, 368-71.
10. Strickland, Walter G, 1913. *A Dictionary of Irish Artists.* Dublin, Maunsel, Vol.1. pp.74-5.
11. Llanover, Lady (ed.), 1861. *The Autobiography and Correspondence of Mary Granville. Mrs Delany.* (first series) London, Richard Bentley, Vol. 1 pp.288-9 and p.305. The Bacchanalian scene still exists in No.120 Stephen's Green and must be by Houghton.
12. This is fully described in Róisín Kennedy, *Dublin Castle Art,* Dublin, Office of Public Works, 1999, pp.86-87.
13. Legg, Marie-Louise (ed.), 1995. *The Synge Letters: Letters of Bishop Edward Synge to His Daughter Alicia, Roscommon-Dublin, 1746-52,* Dublin, Lilliput Press, pp.38, 44, 75.
14. Information kindly given by Jacob Simon of the National Portrait Gallery. For illus see Mrs. Reginald Lane Poole *Catalogue of Portraits...* Oxford, 1912, Vol. 1, p.186, No. 453.
15. Photographs taken by OPW during demolition in 1954, now in the Irish Architectural Archive.
16. We are indebted to Jacob Simon of the National Portrait Gallery, London for this information, which he intends to publish in the *Furniture History Society Journal.*
17. Hayward, Helena, 1964. *Thomas Johnson and the English Rococo,* London, Alec Tiranti.
18. Curran, *op. cit.,* p.439
19. Glin, Knight of, 1997. 'Furniture at Florence Court', *Apollo,* April, pp.16-20.
20. Kirkpatrick, T. Percy, edited by Henry Jellett, 1913. *The Book of the Rotunda Hospital - An Illustrated History of the Dublin Lying-in Hospital from its Foundation in 1745 to the Present Time.* London, Adlard; for his will pp.209-214 and the sale, Appendix 4.
21. Curran, Constantine P, 1945. *The Rotunda Hospital, its Architects and Craftsmen.* Dublin, O Lochlainn, pp.23-24, publishes Kelly's accounts for work in No.9 Cavendish Row, all of which still survives.
22. Griffin, David, 1996-7. 'The building and furnishing of a Dublin townhouse in the 18th century', *Bulletin of the Irish Georgian Society.* Vol. 38, pp.24-31 and the inventory of the house, pp.32-39. David Sheehan supplied marble tables, fireplaces and Thomas Oldham a pier glass with a white carved frame.

THE STORY OF A SMALL BUT HIGHLY ARCHITECTURAL OBJECT

EDWARD MCPARLAND

THIS IS A STORY FOR Sir Charles. It is set in a college presided over as provost, from 1904 to 1914, by his great-grandfather. It starts in Paris where he once lived (and where, according to his family tradition, his great-great-great grandfather Charles Brett was present at the fall of the Bastille). To check its claims fully would involve a trip – which he might enjoy – starting in Bordeaux and moving through Margaux to Pauillac and beyond St Estèphe to the northern tip of the Médoc. It will tease him, by rehearsing the good works of a cleric. Its hero is a Belfast architect whom he has studied for fifty years. And its subject is a building in Dublin, a city which he loves, and which admires him. There is even a coda involving a distinguished lawyer of independent mind.

* * * * *

A sensible architectural historian, on looking at the church of La Trinité in Paris (Figs 1, 2), might jump to an obvious conclusion. There, in Théodore Ballu's tower, is surely the source for Charles Lanyon's Campanile in Trinity College Dublin (Fig 3)? True, the four standing evangelists of Paris have yielded their perch to the more academic seated personifications of Dublin. And the dome of one boasts dormer aedicules missing in the other. But from large scale to small, the similarities are so telling that – even disregarding the twin invocations of the Trinity – it is difficult to resist the idea that Ballu made Lanyon's work a lot easier.

Pedantry, I'm glad to say, intervenes to make the simple complex. For work was started on La Trinité in 1861, but on the Campanile about ten years earlier.

Since we need not entertain the idea that the Chaussée d'Antin had its eye on College Green, academics may come into their own. Perhaps plans for the Paris church were prepared earlier, and Lanyon had sight of them? (Such ingenuity of reasoning is not unknown among the architectural historians of Ireland). But the

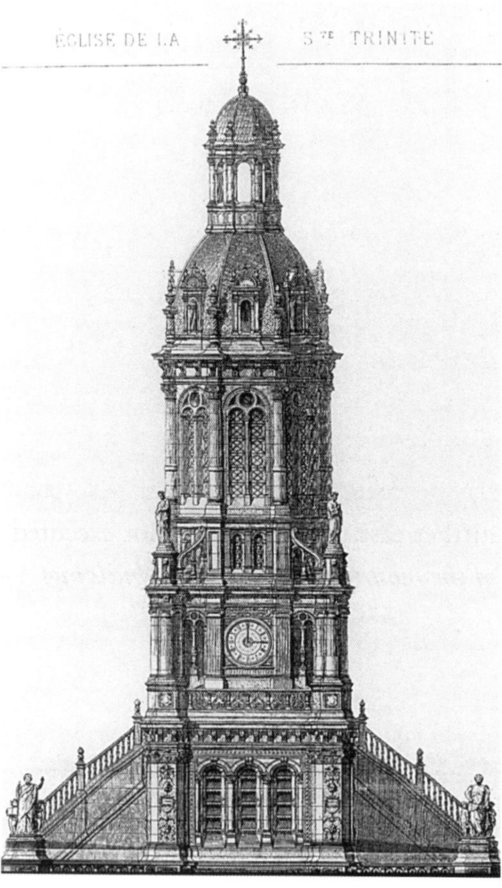

Fig 1. The church of La Sainte Trinité, Paris, from M.Th. Ballu, *Monographie de l'eglise de la Sainte Trinité…*, Paris, 1868.

Fig 2. Detail of fig. 1.

Fig 3. Campanile, Trinity College, Dublin (Lawrence Collection, National Library of Ireland). The building to the left of the campanile was replaced by Thomas Drew's Graduates' Memorial Building of 1902

difficulty of disproving this proposition need not recommend it. The prosaic explanation is likely to be the right one: Ballu and Lanyon probably had the same pattern-books on their shelves.

* * * * *

Lanyon's was not the first bell tower in the college. Richard Castle had built one in the 1740's to succeed a still earlier tower which may have been a survivor from the monastic period of the site. Within Castle's tower was the great bell which Abel Rudhall of Gloucester agreed to cast in 1744. Castle's bell tower was demolished in 1791: it stood half-way between the Examination Hall and Chapel porticoes, and was effectively condemned when William Chambers decided in the 1770's to erect these porticoes. Chambers proposed his own bell tower further east: his design was not executed but is recorded in Pool and Cash's *Views of the most remarkable public buildings ... in the city of Dublin* of 1780.

A design incorporating a bell tower by Thomas Rickman survives in the RIBA. In 1837 the west side of Library Square was cleared of buildings, opening up the possibility of erecting there a new range, and Frederick Darley's proposals for this included a campanile crowning lecture-rooms and museum. As is well known it was Decimus Burton who, in 1849, suggested that, in order to preserve the view from the West Front to Rubrics, the line between Library and Parliament (or Front) Squares be left open, except for 'a small but highly architectural object with a central arched opening from East to West ... connected either by an open colonnade or handsome piers and railing to the buildings North and South of the Library Square ... The building ... should be surmounted by a low Campanile to receive the celebrated bell now so unworthily located' (Fig 4).

Like any good external consultant Burton had been sensitive to local sentiment, connected in this case with Rudhall's bell, sentiment which Provost MacDonnell adverted to on the occasion of the laying of the foundation stone of the Campanile. 'In spite of the advanced years of many among us' he said (Archbishop Beresford who was paying for the Campanile was 79) 'we are not ashamed of the boyish gladness with which we exult in the restoration of our bell'. Said, by obscure tradition, to ring of its own initiative if the unchaste pass beneath its bell, the Campanile happens to lie, alas (with its transverse axis blocked by lawns) on a little used line of movement in Front Square. MacDonnell was exaggerating when he continued: 'for many a year & at many a meeting, the event of this day will be the cheerful topic of Collegiate intercourse'. Outside the rarefied medium of *festschriften* for the learned, the sentimental

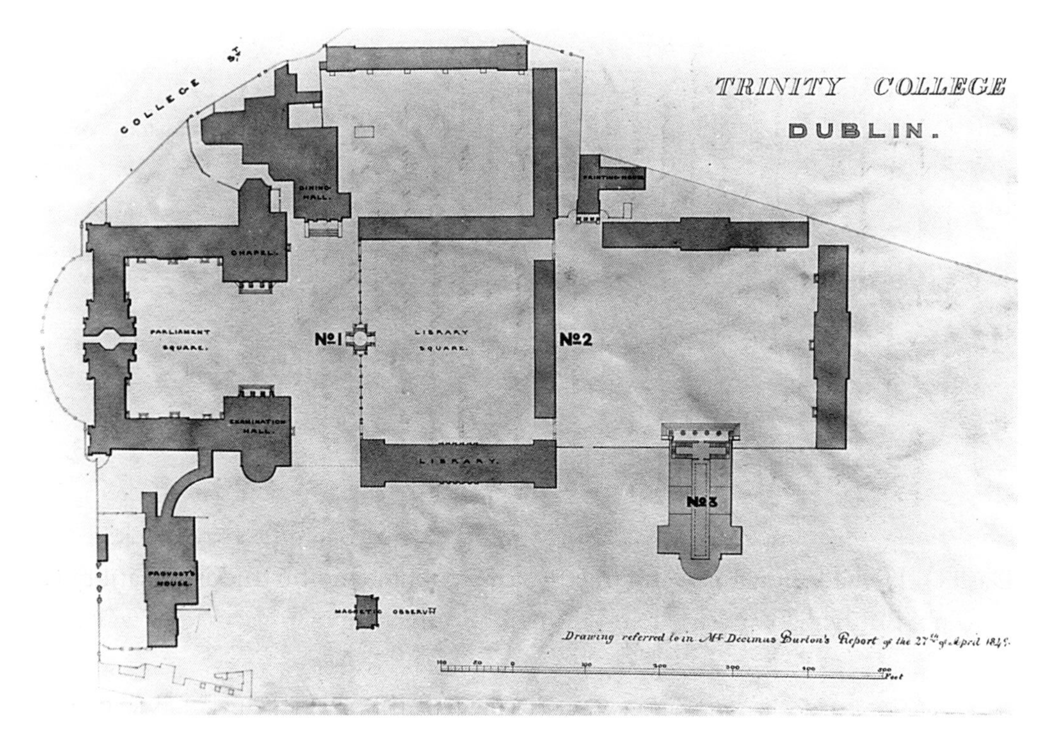

Fig 4. Decimus Burton, plan of Trinity College, 1849, proposing a campanile (No 1) and screen between Library and Parliament (or Front) Squares, and a large neo-classical building (No 3) on the south side of New Square where Deane and Woodward's Museum Building was erected (Trinity College Dublin, MUN/V/5/9, p.107).

associations of Rudhall's bell are sombre rather than cheerful: it summons undergraduates to examinations and, muffled, it announces the deaths of fellows.

* * * * *

Lord John George le Poer Beresford, younger son of the first Marquess of Waterford, was born in 1773. Appointed bishop of Cork by 1805, he moved through the sees of Raphoe, Clogher and Dublin to become Archbishop of Armagh in 1822. Pleased to mark his succeeding the king of Hanover as chancellor of the university in 1851, and amenable to a proposal of Provost MacDonnell, he viewed 'the humble shed' then housing the bell of the college, and decided to build for it the present Campanile. He forwarded designs for it to the college for approval (the choice of Lanyon as architect must have been his: he approved the estimate – £3241.19.0 – of the contractor Henry Kingsmill whom, the records suggest, he paid directly). And on 1 December 1852 he laid the foundation stone. A cantata to celebrate the completion of the work, composed by Messrs Waller and Stewart, was presented to the board in March 1855.

McDowell and Webb's intrepid biographical ventures have left a vivid picture of Beresford vis-à-vis Richard Whately, Archbishop of Dublin while Beresford was in Armagh: 'Beresford was a solid aristocrat who had been a bishop for as long as anyone could remember, and who looked down on Whately as the eighteenth upon the nineteenth century, as Christ Church upon Oriel, as a slow-moving Tory on a radical logic-chopper, and above all as an Anglo-Irish nobleman, and a Beresford to boot, on ... the son of a prebendary of Bristol'. Beresford was a builder. In the 1840's he had faced criticism for the radical re-edification of the Cathedral in Armagh, towards which he contributed £24,000 privately. In 1825 he had added an upper storey to his palace in Armagh. In choosing Charles Lanyon, he chose for Trinity the most distinguished architect then at work in Ulster.

When an architect has books on his shelves dealing with styles of architecture other than those of the gothic and of classical antiquity, he is called eclectic. Lanyon was eclectic. By the time the Trinity commission came his way, he had already broken free from the archaeological *impasse* in which many early 19th-century figures found themselves. (Such was the college architect Frederick Darley). He had shown his Attic mettle at Kircubbin, and his Tudor versatility at Queen's. But he had also by then ventured into the choppier waters of a wider classicism, mannerist and baroque, which we call Victorian. In the same years, Deane and Woodward in their Museum Building were escaping the archaeological *impasse* by going Ruskinian. For his Campanile, Lanyon brightened up the Augustan solemnities of Front Square by looking to a 16th-century lighthouse in the Atlantic.

Or something very similar, since the lighthouse at Cordouan at the mouth of the Garonne (Fig 5) is only one of a type of domed, lanterned, towered

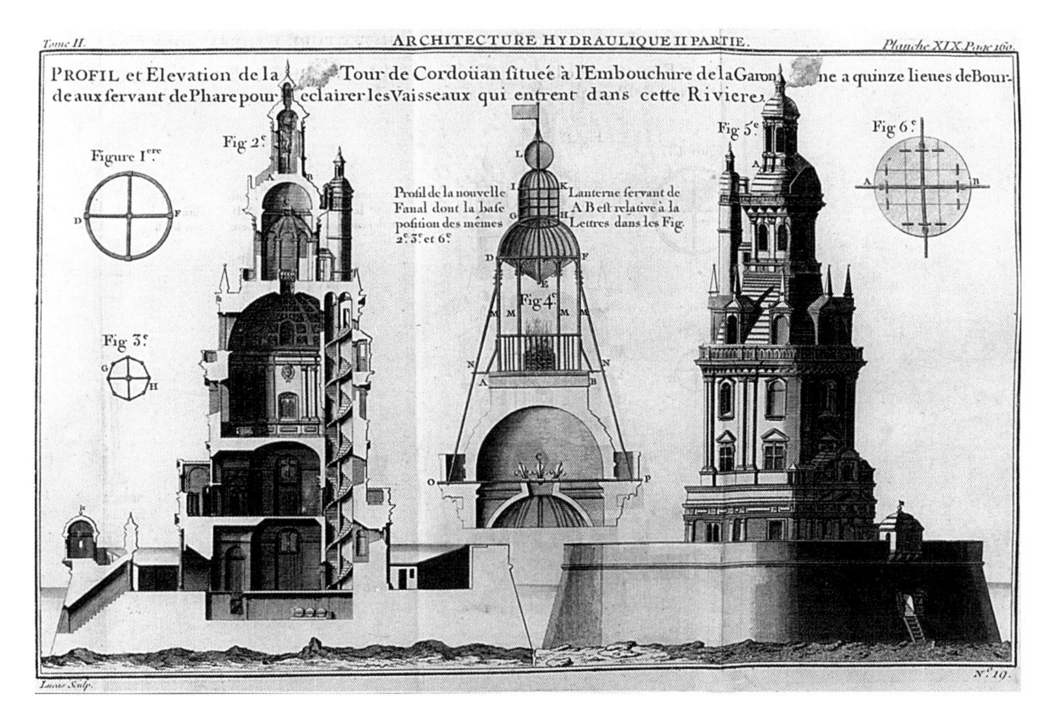

Fig 5. Lighthouse at Cordouan, France (Bernard de Belidor, *Architecture hydraulique, seconde partie*, II, Paris, 1653, plate 19)

structures from around 1600 in France. Cordouan was known in Ireland, not just by mariners, but from a plate in Belidor's *Architecture hydraulique.* Lanyon and Ballu are closer to each other than either is to Cordouan: very likely another similar tower was the shared model for the architects' independent bell towers.

Lanyon's Campanile is really two structures, a Frenchified Portland stone belfry above a Doric arcade in granite. The redundant transverse arcade (avoided by Burton in his notional 'small but highly architectural object' of Fig 4) probably survives from plans to link the Campanile by an arcade, colonnade or even loggia to the buildings north and south. Burton, we know, wanted such a screen. So did Lanyon, at least as his design developed. His first proposal was to site the Campanile a little to the east of its present position, perhaps to mark the east end of the former college chapel, long demolished. The board of the college, however, decided to align it approximately with the west pavilion of the Library, but to reject any plan 'particularly that of a corridor, for connecting the Library with the Campanile'. If the corridor (or 'cloister' as Lanyon called it) went, maybe there could be a screen: Lanyon thought 'The campanile will not look complete without it'.

Fig 6. Model of Campanile inscribed R. Day. Modeller. London (Provost's House, Trinity College, Dublin)

An early model of the Campanile by 'R. Day. Modeller. London' survives in the Provost's House in the college (Fig 6). It differs from the executed building only in details, but these probably record original intentions, altered in execution. All four of its coats of arms are archiepiscopal; in execution two Beresford arms yielded to those of the college and

Fig 7. Model of Campanile executed in butter, present whereabouts unknown

the royal arms. And perhaps the model shows how Lanyon originally intended to rusticate the lower storey: it is close to the Doric treatment of the governor's house at his Antrim County Gaol on the Crumlin Road, Belfast, of 1843-5. A more recent model, displaying interesting variants is, unfortunately, less instructive (Fig 7). Constructed in butter for a feast in the college some years ago, its present whereabouts is unknown.

* * *

It must have been during the few hours of darkness one night in late May 1872 that some undergraduates headed for the Campanile with paint and brushes, intent on paying tribute to William Keogh. Keogh was a judge who had just heard a petition lodged by William le Poer Trench against Captain J.P. Nolan. Trench and Nolan had fought a bye-election the previous February. Trench was a tory. Nolan was a home ruler supported by the Roman Catholic clergy (and, according to a later account, 'carloads of cudgel-bearing supporters'). Nolan was returned.

Trench's petition before Judge Keogh was based on a claim of undue clerical influence on the electorate. Keogh was a catholic. His judgement, in favour of Trench, included an 'unrestrained denunciation of the manners and influence of the catholic priesthood'. And in the ensuing sectarian unrest, those undergraduates with their paints and brushes decided to do their bit. Recent cleaning has not managed to efface wholly their work on the north-east pier (so much for restoration treating building as palimpsest). In the right light, and with the right kind of confidence in your guide, and with enough in your glass to remind you of the Médoc (and its lighthouses) where the origins of this story lie, you can convince yourself that you can see traces of a J and a U, of a K, an E and an O, which is all that survives of that nocturnal epigraphical expedition of l872: 'Bravo! Judge Keogh'.

ACKNOWLEDGEMENTS

I am grateful to the board of Trinity College Dublin for permission to quote from their records, and to Brendan Dempsey, David Griffin, Eugene McGovern and Peggy Morgan

NOTES

This essay is based largely on the correspondence of Archbishop Lord John George Beresford (mss 2770-4), and the college muniments (MUN/P/2 series of building accounts and MUN/V/5/9,10 records of meetings of the board) in the Manuscripts Department, Old Library, Trinity College Dublin. The vignette of Beresford *vis-à-vis* Whately is from R.B. McDowell and D.A. Webb, *Trinity College Dublin 1592-1952, an Academic History*, Cambridge, 1982. For Judge Keogh see R.V. Comerford, 'Isaac Butt and the home rule party, 1870-77', in W.E. Vaughan (ed), *A New History of Ireland, VI, Ireland under the Union, II, 1870-1921*, Oxford, 1996

CONSERVATION AT THE COAL-FACE A SHORT HISTORY OF HEARTH

MARCUS PATTON

WHEN THE FIRM OF L'Estrange & Brett moved from their ancestral offices at the end of the 20th century, Sir Charles Brett delivered several large cardboard boxes to me. It may have been merely good housekeeping, since he no longer had the basement or the secretarial staff to assist him in maintaining them, but no doubt he also had in mind that some poor archivist was some day going to spend days going through them, and perhaps felt some relief that it would not be him. With the invitation to contribute this essay, I realised that it was to be my job, since those boxes contained much of the early history of Hearth, an organisation which owes its genesis largely to Charlie.

It was he who on 16 July 1970 chaired the inaugural meeting of a steering committee set up by the Northern Ireland Committee of the National Trust to establish a Public Utility Society under the Housing (Ireland) Act 1919. By the time of its next meeting in November the group had acquired the name HEARTH (standing for Historic Environmental and Architectural Renovation Trust for Housing) and a more detailed prospectus had been drawn up, including the proposal that the organisation should be steered by the Trust in association with the recently formed Ulster Architectural Heritage Society. It duly reported to the main committee of the Trust that this was:

> *an eleventh-hour attempt to rescue at least some remaining examples of Ulster's architectural character which are disappearing fast as a result of redevelopment and neglect. If this effort fails, and does not inspire imitators, most of the buildings which give character to the towns and villages of Northern Ireland will vanish.*

It went on to say that it could not afford to delay 'because the Government is planning wholesale redevelopment, having promised to introduce statutory listing and to bring improvement grants into line with the rest of the United Kingdom'. A number of possible schemes were identified right away, of which the village of Seaforde and two lockhouses on the Lagan Navigation were eventually to come to fruition.

The new Trust was inspired by the Little Houses scheme of the National Trust for Scotland and a scheme in Amsterdam known as Bond Heemschut, as well as the early building preservation trusts being promoted in England by the Civic Trust. However due to the prevailing circumstances in Northern Ireland – then at the height of the Troubles – it was decided to work closely with the newly formed Housing Executive and to provide houses for letting as well as for sale.

The rules under which Hearth was registered in December 1972 as an Industrial and Provident Society stated that its primary object was:

> *to secure by such means as are available for the public benefit, and in accordance with the purposes and policies of the National Trust and the Ulster Architectural Heritage Society, the preservation, protection and improvement of buildings of particular beauty or of historic, environmental architectural or constructional merit or interest in Northern Ireland, and to stimulate and educate public interest therein.*

It was set up with powers to achieve those objects through restoration, improvement or new building, and to provide or manage houses, flats, shops or commercial premises.

The people involved in the steering committee of Hearth are worth naming individually, since each played – and in some cases continues to play – a large part in the quality of our built environment. The chairman was Lord Clanwilliam, then chairman of the Northern Ireland Committee of the National Trust. His vice-chairman was C E B Brett, chairman of the UAHS and a member of the NI Committee of the National Trust as well as of the Board of the NI Housing Executive. The other members were Brian Boyd, an architect managing the National House-Builders Registration Council in Northern Ireland; Lady Dunleath, an active member of the UAHS Committee; Bill Montgomery, described as a property developer; Brian Rankin, another member of the local National Trust committee and a former chairman of the NI Housing Trust; and John Williams-Ellis, another member of the National Trust committee and a nephew of the architect Clough Williams-Ellis. The Secretary to the steering group was John Lewis-Crosby, who ran the regional office of the National Trust and also served on the UAHS Committee. He was assisted by David Good and Nigel Hughes of the National Trust's staff.

When the new Trust was set up and held its first official meeting in March 1973, negotiations were already well advanced to buy, for a fairly nominal valuation, two groups of houses in Seaforde, Co Down, from the local land owner, Patrick Forde – another member of the National Trust committee. Plans were commissioned from a Mr Gordon, who was retiring as Chief Inspector with the Housing Division of the Ministry of Development, and he was to be employed at a sum of £1500 per annum for a three day week.

At first it was thought that the Housing Executive would be likely to offer 100% capital loan for forty years together with an annual grant to cover the loss resulting from letting properties at a suitable social rent rather than the commercial level, although the Executive had not then defined its policy towards housing associations. It was also thought then that the Executive might appoint its own conservation team to look after historic buildings, something which sadly did not happen. The Executive's loan never materialised either, but the National Trust and the Pilgrim Trust offered loans of £10,000 each, and Arthur Guinness Ltd provided a grant of £100. On the strength of this, it was proposed in October 1974 to restore two houses in Seaforde and offer them for sale.

Work seems to have gone slowly, being expected to finish in mid-1975 and then by late October 1976. There was concern about the enforceability of covenants and the National Trust agreed to covenant the properties itself, but then with housing association funding becoming a possibility with the Housing Order of 1976, the decision was taken to let out the houses rather than sell them. However it soon became clear that with its primary objective of looking after historic buildings rather than 'providing housing', Hearth was not going to be eligible for funding unless it set up a subsidiary organisation. In January 1977 it was resolved to set up Hearth Housing Association, and that October HEARTH changed its name to the full monty of 'Historic Environmental and Architectural Renovation [or Rehabilitation – there is some confusion about this] Trust for Housing' to allow the new housing association to be called Hearth.

Fig 1. Seaforde almshouses Hearth's first scheme was the restoration of the 1830 Almshouses in the estate village of Seaforde, Co Down.

At a meeting on 23 January 1978 the details of the new association were finalised. It would acquire the two cottages at Seaforde which had already been restored by the holding trust; the DoE and the NI Frederation of Housing Associations would assist in drawing up conditions for permanent staff; and the DoE would make seeding finance available. Lord Clanwilliam stood down as Chairman to allow Charlie Brett to take over, and it was reported that planning permission had been received for the completion of the restoration of the Seaforde Almshouses. In early February an advertisement was drawn up to attract a Director to manage the association, suggesting that it would grow rapidly and have rents coming in from 194 properties by year 6. (Hearth is still far from that target after nearly 25 years!) I was lucky enough to be appointed to the new job.

By this time two more essential committee members were in place, Karen Latimer and David Evans, and our first secretary, Anne Tredgett, had been appointed. The Antrim Arms hotel in Glenarm and houses at Camden Street in Belfast had been identified, and we managed to hold a committee meeting in one of the snugs of the Crown Bar, where Charlie hoped we could hold all our meetings if we managed to get promised offices in the upper part of the building.

On the staffing front, Carol Mills became secretary the following summer (and later housing manager), and she was joined shortly afterwards by Tony Merrick as architectural technician, both of whom are still with Hearth. For a few years Jon Sampson worked with us as a planner with the brief of developing work in the Killough HAA, and Elaine McCreight joined us in 1987. Our permanent staff

Fig 2. Glenarm Schoolhouse
Many of Hearth's projects start with derelict buildings. The Old Schoolhouse in Glenarm was in only poor condition, but with windows altered (see above), and had lain empty for about ten years. The conversion into two houses involved the insertion of a new floor in each of the school rooms.

has been constant ever since. For a period around 1990 Dawson Stelfox, who now runs Consarc Conservation, worked with us on a freelance basis when not preparing to climb Mount Everest.

When Charlie Brett took over the chairmanship of the Housing Executive he stood down as Chairman of Hearth, and John Lewis-Crosby took his place. His chairmanship was almost casual, but he was highly supportive of Hearth and was a passionate believer in the importance of little houses. When Charlie Brett returned to the chairmanship after his enforced absence he brought back his much more hands-on style. He expected virtually a continuous correspondence by first class post, which was time-consuming but meant that he was very much involved in all the decisions and that excellent records were kept. When Charlie eventually stood down in 2000, Karen Latimer succeeded him and Primrose Wilson became Vice Chairman.

The Housing Association

In August 1980 Hearth Housing Association acquired its first two tenants when it officially took over the Seaforde Almshouses, and soon it was on site with its own schemes in Seaforde, Glenarm and Belfast.

Although Hearth remains a small association, with around a hundred houses and flats in management, they have been developed over nearly twenty contracts, and a further dozen projects (over thirty houses) have been carried out by Hearth Revolving Fund, mostly for sale, along with a further fifteen or so projects where Hearth has performed an architectural consultancy for outside clients restoring historic buildings. In addition to those, Hearth surveyed many other buildings it wasn't able to take forward to contract, often helping to delay demolition until more appropriate users arrived to restore the buildings.

Sadly, many others were lost. Not to depress readers unduly, during its first year of operation Hearth looked at buildings in Brook Terrace Enniskillen, Orchard Street and Church Wall Londonderry, Maryville Street Belfast, Riverside Antrim, McNeill's Hotel Larne, Shore Street Donaghadee, the old forge in Hillsborough, 50-58 Irish Street Downpatrick, and Waterford Place Coleraine, all of which were demolished shortly after. Other buildings were restored subsequently by other owners, and a small number remain standing but in much worse condition.

Falling between the two stools of housing and conservation, Hearth often found it hard to raise the necessary funding to restore buildings in poor condition to acceptable standards. Under the legislation at that time, housing associations were eligible for 100% capital funding – up to a point. Beyond that point they could not get historic buildings or conservation area grant, but support for housing expenditure above the yardstick would be sought from Historic Monuments and Buildings Branch (HMBB) of the DoE.

The groundlessness of the optimism that had predicted such a rapid growth for Hearth soon became apparent, and indeed few of our schemes have taken less than five years from initial contact to completion. In the first year we also looked at a terrace in Hamilton Street which was 'in the ownership of NIHE, which appears to be taking no steps to rehabilitate them at present' – it was to be ten more years before the application was made for their demolition which led to our restoring them; and the village of Glenoe was still unspoilt with its old corn mill standing - good material for a revolving fund scheme, but difficult for a housing association.

As early as 1979 it was obvious that there was still a role for the old revolving fund to play. A sub-committee in 1979 reported that:

> *The Rehabilitation Trust provides a necessary function because Hearth is unable to carry out acquisition and restoration where NIHE can provide no evidence of housing demand; where the District Valuer's assessment is not sufficiently competitive...; or where the property concerned has a purely commercial use. [It] could also acquire property where urgent action was required, and sell it at a later date to Hearth.*

Nearly three years of a moratorium in the early 1980s meant that no sooner was the housing association getting under way than it found all its proposals being quietly knocked on the head and dropped. When we were unable to get HAG (Housing Association Grant) for the restoration of the little 18th century lockhouse at Drumbeg which was decaying and becoming vulnerable to vandalism, we decided the time had come to revive the revolving fund. It duly acquired and restored Drumbeg with the help of loans, but when the house had been sold and the loans repaid there was no money in the kitty to develop further, and more funds would be needed. However, as John Lewis-Crosby put it, "the idea of launching an appeal for the Historic, Environmental and Architectural Rehabilitation Trust for Housing makes me shudder!". It was not until 1991 that we rationalised the two organisations as Hearth Housing Association and Hearth Revolving Fund.

It would be tedious to list all the buildings involved, nor can we pretend that many have involved cutting-edge conservation techniques. Hearth's role has not been to carry out sophisticated restorations of grade A buildings, but to ensure the survival, in spite of dereliction, social problems and for many years against the backdrop of the Troubles, of some of the most threatened historic buildings in Northern Ireland. Some were not even listed when we took them on, many were derelict for twenty years or more, quite a few were roofless or riddled with rot, and many were in areas where no sensible developer would put his money. Our job was to keep the buildings standing and try to bring them back into use with a minimal loss of fabric. The stitch in time to save these buildings would, it was hoped, encourage others to restore better buildings nearby, and set an example which the planners could point to when faced with applications to demolish buildings that were more important or in better condition. And at the same time we would provide social housing.

The anecdotes that follow are not for the most part about architecture, but about life at the coal-face of conservation: a mixture of architectural ideals, compromises with tight costs and bungalow builders, life in rural Fermanagh and urban Belfast with people in fear of their lives or aggressively defending their corners of the lacerated city. All Hearth's schemes have involved compromise, and they continue to do so as we look after the needs of the people who live in them as well as the maintenance of the buildings. Architectural purists should stop here.

Surveys

Restoration starts with a survey of the building, scrambling over it with rod and tape and sketching the plans that will be drawn up back in the office. For some reason you usually find yourself doing surveys on cold wet days in the winter instead of those sunny days in the spring when you would love to be away from the telephone. It is usually a fairly routine process, but every building has unusual facets that you uncover at this stage. Sometimes the survey is made memorable by the weather or the history of the building. In Castle Street Armagh we were glad to have the mountaineering skills of Dawson Stelfox who was able to make light of the lack of stairs and floors and clamber fleetly up the crumbling walls to take measurements.

Since it can be difficult to assess the conversion costs and how buildings might best be adapted without carrying out quite detailed surveys, we have often visited and measured up buildings that didn't eventually come off. One such was

Jackson's Almshouses in Aughnacloy which we surveyed on a freezing cold day in 1981, when snow was falling thick and even on its lawns, enormous icicles dangled from its overhanging eaves, and its forest of heavily corbelled chimneys reared themselves dark and gaunt above the snow-covered roof – shades of Christmas Day in the Workhouse! Inside the mostly derelict shell lived the sole denizen, a cheery old man who had arrived when all sixteen units were full. He had a corner room and the rest of the building was empty and freezing cold. A fine well-panelled board room decorated with a portrait of Dr Jackson and a copy of the Rules enjoyed a breathtaking view from over snow-covered fields behind and below, but the cold was absolute.

Another memorable visit was to Barry's Amusements in Bangor in 1982, when it was lying derelict and threatened with demolition from which we had hoped to save it. It was pouring rain inside and out, and was a sad sight – derelict dodgems, wrecks of amusement machines, corpses of penny in the slots under suspended repair and covered in dust downstairs, while spilling out of upstairs rooms were cardboard boxes of chocolate for vending machines. Paint peeled off the walls and rain dripped into the ballroom where the panelling and hammerbeams were green and rotting.

Not everything was so dramatic: a house on the Shore Road in Belfast was outwardly derelict and there was no sign of life when you knocked on the door. Its occupant was a man in his seventies, very deaf since naval service during the war. The house was damp and cold, in very bad repair with smashed windows and flaking ceilings – but had super fireplaces throughout, and good plasterwork – and dust everywhere. No housework had been done for a long time, but he said it had been a palace in his aunt's day; as disrepair had set in he "just lost heart" and couldn't be bothered.

Rural cottages, of which we surveyed quite a number in the mid 1990s, were little better. Many had yards several inches deep in slurry and liquid mud, with sheep or cows browsing round the front door (and sometimes beyond), but occasionally you would find one still furnished as it had been left by an old lady who had died a few years before.

Builders

It would be nice if all our projects were restored by craftsmen with a deep knowledge and love of their work. There have been some, but quite a number of men started off deeply sceptical of the merits of repairing the ruins they were being asked to restore, only to develop an interest as the work progressed and go on to work on other old buildings afterwards. "is the challenge I tell ye,' said one builder on opening up his Pandora's Box - "Anneka Rice couldn't do nothing with this one.' Needless to say at the end of the job he was very proud of it.

Builders had often learnt from painful experience that good work was not appreciated. One told me that he had worked on some houses off the Ormeau Road for the Housing Executive – pepperpotting in a little terrace of polychrome houses. When it came to re-roofing, he said to the architect, Look these tiles are going to look wrong, let's put up natural slate: so the architect said okay, and he did. Then it came to replacing windows: Look said the builder, all the other houses here have sash windows, let's match them, so the architect said okay. Then it came to replacing cracked chamfered stone lintels over windows: It seems a shame to put in standard lintels, said our builder, and took one home and made up a mould and produced a concrete replica, and the architect said, That's nice. So it was a good job. But when the Executive did the next phase, a different contractor got it and put in night vent windows, and rendered the whole terrace. Was it any wonder that builders had learnt to offer their clients the cheapest and quickest option, assuming that that was what they wanted?

When we restored Drumbeg Lockhouse our builder was a Brazilian gentleman. We were told that his motto, 'I Do All', extended beyond routine subcontracting work like plumbing and electricity into the higher realms of masonry as well. This was because his brother, who spoke very little English and seemed never completely certain whether his visa was in need of renewal, was a mason. He had not learned to speak much English during his sojourn and when a sub-contractor called at the site one day when Jeremias was on his own, he was greatly puzzled to find what he took to be a Frenchman who didn't speak any English working on a crazy project to restore a burnt-out ruin!

One bricklayer who worked on several of our projects had some favourite terms for styles of brickwork, such as Ham and Eggs for Flemish bond. When he came across two nearly adjacent courses of brickwork with uneven numbers of courses which had to be matched up, he described it as "a Pig", and cleverly managed to fudge it. As for a bit of more modern walling that had been badly built, he looked at it then snorted and laughed, and said "The wall ties in that wall is only there on Thursdays," meaning they were pretty uncommon.

For some years now there has been very stringent legislation in place governing safety at work, which has gone some way to making building sites safer places to work, although there is a school of thought that the safer you make a site the more risks the men on it will take.

Back in 1982 the builder was entirely responsible for the conditions his men worked under, and I could only watch two labourers gutting out some houses that had been full of plaster, rotten clothes and dry rot, absolutely filthy work. I suggested to their boss that they should be wearing masks, and he said, Well sometimes they do and sometimes they don't. 'It's dreadful work really, but they seem to Relish it.'

Ironically, the first site where we had a serious accident was also the first where I had known a contractor to employ a safety consultant. Two demolition men fell to the ground while dismantling an old fire escape, apparently having performed the old trick of sawing off the branch you are sitting on.

Difficult Buildings

We decided early on that Hearth should try to restore not just attractive buildings but also ones that were seen as problems. If we could restore those buildings, it should be easy for everyone else to look after the rest. Difficulty could be a factor of location, or of structural problems, or of sheer dereliction and hence of costs – or more often a combination of those.

Structurally speaking, our project at Camden Street in Belfast was probably one of the most challenging, certainly for the time we did it in the early 1980s. A pair of two-storey returns were demolished and replaced with larger returns incorporating fire escapes for the flats being created in the houses – not in itself a difficult operation, but greatly complicated by the extent of dry rot in the five storey building, spread through timber battens built into the walls. These had rotted and been crushed by the weight of brickwork above, leading to vertical cracking where the party walls had lost lateral support. Many floors were virtually suspended on thin air due to the absence of sound timber built into the walls. Our builder maintained that he never lost any sleep over the structure, but he must have been the only one – even our structural engineer, John McCaughey of Kirk McClure & Morton, who was usually quite unflappable, always said when looking at subsequent problems that 'after Camden Street, anything looks good'.

Sometimes the difficulties were bureaucratic: the terrace of low whitewashed houses in High Street Comber were granted a curious planning permission which

Fig 3. Comber
This vernacular terrace of whitewashed houses with their irregular fenestration probably started life as housing for the local distillery, but were later occupied by workers at the nearby Andrews' Spinning Mill.

required us not only to make 'no external changes to the front elevation' but also to provide 'floor and front door levels as agreed with the Roads Service'. It turned out that the Roads Service had assumed the houses were to be demolished and were proposing to raise the road and footpath levels by as much as 9 inches. The two conditions were incompatible since many of the doors and windows were already very low, and it would have been impossible for us to comply with the Roads Service levels without rebuilding several houses, adding to our costs and reducing the historic interest of the terrace. At one meeting with the Roads engineers, they suggested that if the houses really had to be kept perhaps they could be used as a museum and just entered from the back, to allow the pavement to be built up at the front!

An example of a difficult location in which to restore housing for sale was the terrace of Georgian houses in Hamilton Street in the Markets area of Belfast. One of only three Georgian terraces surviving from some twenty such in the area before it was redeveloped by the Housing Executive, it was surrounded by social housing in an area where no Protestant (and not a lot of Catholics) would have considered living, with bombs still going off in the nearby city centre. When the terrace had been emptied of residents it was seen at once as a target by local vandals, and they had clambered in with saws to remove the (perfectly sound) joists and floorboards, leaving the walls unrestrained. Stair balustrades, shutters and architraves had gone, and even the roof purlins. Unsurprisingly, the Executive declared it was a dangerous building and went for LBC to demolish it. The UAHS objected to the loss of this bookend to the very important Joy Street terrace which the Executive had restored. And when the Executive said, if you want it kept, you restore it – it was Hearth that had to find the means to do it. Since it was too urgent to put through the housing association system, we had to

Fig 4. Hamilton Street
Almost the last of the three-storey Georgian style houses that once typified the Markets area of Belfast, the restoration project was adapted to include the corner shop that was being demolished nearby.

find ways of funding it with our Revolving Fund. It did seem ironic that the Executive, with its annual budget of some £500m, couldn't afford to restore it, and Hearth was expected to do it with a total capital of less than £100,000.

No sooner had we agreed to take the buildings on and become responsible for them than there was a violent storm, and I fully expected to find chimneys collapsed into the street the next morning. As it happened, the only casualty was a car which had been parked nearby and become the victim of a falling slate. It belonged to a structural engineer working for the DoE, who stormed furiously into the site to demand compensation from the foreman. When the man said he was an engineer and that the buildings were highly dangerous and should be demolished, Albert slyly asked him why then he had parked in front of them, under a notice saying 'Dangerous building – keep out', on a day when hurricane force winds were forecast?

Around the same time we took on another building which had already partly collapsed. Nos.201-205 Donegall Street were the rump of a much larger terrace of buildings thought to date from about 1800, which Roads Service had demolished for a road widening scheme. While we were negotiating to buy the three houses which had been blighted for twenty years but were no longer required by Roads, the back wall of one collapsed. Roads Service repeated their view that the houses were dangerous, and HMBB agreed and more or less said they would not stand in the way of demolition. However DoE were being faced with the alternatives of demolishing the (soon to be) oldest dateable buildings in

Belfast due to their own neglect over the years, or transferring them to us at a realistic valuation, and when we went back to Lands Service, they were glad by now to dispose of the buildings for a nominal sum. Moving in before full purchase could be completed, we put up a temporary skin to support the remaining structure, and in due course were able to carry out full restoration.

Over the years, we have examined many buildings labelled dangerous, and in nearly every case found ways of bringing them back into daily use. In moments of doubt I would consult the structural engineer John McCaughey for his comforting rules of thumb, such as 'What has stood for a hundred and fifty years can probably go on standing for another fifty' (which he qualified however with the warning that 'A wall is either standing or not standing, and there is no in-between').

Costs and Bureaucracy

A prominent businessman once told me that he was on the board of the Housing Executive when they decided to introduce 'Parker-Knoll standards'. A vision of social housing filled with leather sofas and coffee tables was amusing, but actually not so far from the mark. In the early days of housing associations, plans had to be prepared showing exactly where all the furniture in a house was going to go.

In addition, Hearth always found it difficult meeting the sometimes contradictory requirements of Housing Associations Branch and Historic Monuments & Buildings Branch, and it led to some interesting, if protracted meetings. To be fair, we found a fair level of support for our work within the system too, because even if our schemes were complex or expensive, they were always quite small and the total expenditure on Hearth's projects remains a minor (and publicly much appreciated) part of the overall housing budget. Indeed, even if some of Hearth's schemes seemed expensive at the time, few of them look so now.

We early took the view that it was better to do things to a high standard than to mass produce housing units, but it did mean we ran into problems early on when our schemes went over the cost yardstick. Charlie Brett was a firm supporter of quality and principles, and opposed to cutting corners or risking the quality of our projects. When things got really difficult he would say in mock piousness, 'The Lord will provide!'

In 1985 we had a useful meeting with senior housing officials in which we discussed the way in which our schemes kept getting rejected by the system like bad coins in a slot machine, because they didn't conform to room areas (too large or too small), ceiling heights (too high or too low), house types (too large or too small) or costs (too high!). Initially HAB did not realise that interiors were listed as well as front elevations, but eventually it was agreed that a better system was necessary, and over the years additional allowances have been made to take account of the cost of the unusual features of listed buildings. But even with good will on all sides it was not easy to stretch a rigid system to embrace our projects. At one meeting, a DoE official remarked 'I get the distinct impression that [the Department's QS] is bending over backwards to meet you two-thirds of the way'!

One of our most successful early Revolving Fund schemes was at Moira, where originally we had tried to carry out a housing assocation scheme. When it was turned down and we had to raise money to do it with our revolving fund, we thought we might get funding from a building society, and talked to several at length without making much progress – as with other financiers, it seemed they could have helped us much more easily if we hadn't needed their help. Giving up on that I talked to our bank, who offered a loan without any difficulty; and later on when it came to our second loan application the bank manager glanced at the photographs of our recently acquired ruins which I was rather timidly showing him, and said he was quite happy to lend to us; the appearance didn't bother him, as he knew what Moira had been like!

When we came to restore Hamilton Street, one obvious source of grant was Urban Development Grant, designed to encourage developers in central Belfast. When they saw from my calculations that I was going to make a loss (even with their help), the UDG officers declared the scheme non-viable and said they couldn't help after all. I was puzzled that they were prepared to give money to developers who were already covering their costs, but not to charities who were putting their own resources at risk for the public benefit. The Housing Executive applied similar principles here and in Armagh, refusing to grant-aid some properties which they considered were too expensive, and hence non-viable. In the end, seeing that we were going to go ahead without them, the UDG officers did offer a modest grant.

If the system made problems for us, we certainly also made problems for it. When Carol Mills was at a housing conference a couple of years after she started, she got chatting to a QS in the Housing Advisory Unit of DoE, who asked

Fig 5. Main Street, Moira
The restoration of this group of buildings sparked off the renovation of a much longer terrace of unlisted buildings and has contributed to the revitalisation of Moira.

which association she was with. 'You work for Hearth?' he said in some alarm. 'You mean you work with Marcus Patton? I have nightmares about Marcus Patton!'

Partnerships

Hearth aims to have some influence beyond its own schemes, in educating students and in influencing or talking to others involved with historic buildings.

At its simplest, this might mean surveying and demonstrating that a building was viable so that others could carry out the restoration. On other occasions we were asked to proffer advice to architects who were proposing radical and damaging work to buildings that could survive well without such intervention.

Campaigning to rescue buildings as they are about to be demolished is never satisfactory, and it is much better to be able to restore buildings and set an example. From that point of view perhaps our greatest success was in Moira where we had only been able to acquire and restore three houses out of a terrace of about twenty that were mostly derelict. However our houses were snapped up when they came on the market, and our agent said he had suddenly done £500,000 of business in Moira, and had never had such interest in any property as in one of ours.

Less successful was an attempted partnership with a commercial developer and his architect over buildings at College Square North. They were slightly puzzled by our philosophy of starting from what was suitable for the building rather than what might maximise profits (just as I was puzzled by their obsession with figures rather than designs), so it was an educational exercise for all concerned, and one which did not get very far. Everntually we managed to acquire the buildings ourselves and restore them with a complex package of HAG, Heritage Lottery Funding, historic buildings grant and conservation area grant.

Sometimes it did seem as if we were fighting an uphill battle persuading people of the merits of old buildings, but conservationists are an enthusiastic bunch and rarely deterred. Attending a meeting in offices in Donegall Square South I enthused to our host about the art nouveau tiles on the staircase of his building. Oh, he said, we think they're just like lavatory tiles. Then Ian McQuiston of HMBB arrived and remarked on the splendid view of the Scottish Provident Building across the square from us which had recently been very thoroughly cleaned and restored, even keeping the tiles on the staircase. I said I'd just been remarking on the ones in the present building. Did the people there like the tiles, asked our host. No, said Ian, they thought they were like lavatory tiles...

There was much public relations work in our scheme at Hamilton Street, where the Markets Tenants Committee had made it clear that they wanted new houses. Dan Craig, the Executive's architect, had kindly prepared the ground however by saying that there was no question of Hamilton Street being knocked down, so it was just a choice between derelict property or private housing! After a little discussion at a meeting one evening they warmed to the idea, and admitted that quite a few Markets people did want the old houses kept. When the houses were put up for sale in due course there was considerable interest, and our agent rang to know where else a development like it could be done. I had to say nowhere, as they were about the last group of Georgian houses in the city, and many such blocks had been demolished in the last ten to fifteen years. His disappointment was audible!

The Troubles

All housing associations have problem tenants, and all building preservation trusts deal with problem buildings. Hearth has had its share of both, and in addition like all housing bodies in Northern Ireland over the last thirty years it has had to carry out its work against the backdrop of the Troubles. Sometimes the effect was of a general economic kind, with depressed property values and sometimes inflated tender prices; but often there were more specific problems.

I have already mentioned our project to restore six houses in Hamilton Street. Because we had very little finance at the time we took the buildings on, we played for time by using the direct labour squad of Heritage Repairs to carry out holding repairs while raising money for the more serious restoration as a second phase. However it coincided with one of the periodic outbreaks of lunatic violence in the history of the Troubles, and it is perhaps worth recording the kind of effect these times had on day to day life. In March 1988 we lost several days work during a week of Troubles-related funerals following the Gibralter incident, when the site had to be closed although there was no direct trouble in the area. Many of the men lived in West Belfast and would have had difficulty getting back after midday. One of our joiners was at school with both a fellow who was killed in a random shooting that week and with another man that had died during the week having been shot the previous summer, and both those funerals were from nearby St Malachy's. Later in the week two soldiers were set upon in Andersonstown and brutally murdered. Every day there seemed to be a funeral, and another murder. That St Patrick's Day I recorded:

> *Almost all the men had turned up, including G. who lives only half a dozen doors up from where today's funeral victim (an IRA sniper shot by police on Monday or Tuesday night) lived. K. said he had to walk about four miles to get a taxi to get in as the Falls was deserted. A. pointed out a fellow sitting in a car at the cul de sac up the road, who he said was watching movement in the area and waiting to see what they'd do. The site next door was shut and had closed early yesterday. A. is jittery because he served time in jail in the early part of the troubles for some paramilitary offence, and as a Protestant is aware of being something of a marked man in the area.*

You could get paranoid walking around Belfast in those days, and if you had any imagination it could run away with you. David Evans told me about visiting Newry in the late eighties to make a print of the Cathedral. While he was taking photos for it he noticed he was being watched by a villainous looking gentleman, probably a vigilante, who was looking very suspiciously at him. Eventually the man sidled up to him and said 'You'll never get a good view from there, you'll have to come on up to the flats' – and guided him up to the better location!

Although we have restored some buildings after bomb damage, only one of our buildings has been bombed while tenanted. This was the terrace of houses in Castlederg which we took over with some tenants in situ. One morning in 1990 we heard there had been a bomb at the police station in the town. It contained between five hundred and a thousand pounds of explosives, and was less than a hundred yards from our houses. When I got up there I found the front roofs and windows of our houses all blown in, doors flattened and rear windows and slates mostly damaged too. Fortunately our two houses closest to the bomb were empty. The bomb had been left in a van at the entrance to the station, and had been spotted in time for the police to be evacuating the area, but the bomb went off as a couple of children from one of our houses were in the hall about to leave, and they were injured by the door coming in. Strangely enough, despite the devastation, there was hardly a crack in the lime-built stone walls of our houses, although every window and door had been blasted in.

When we eventually completed the restoration of the houses, and the Dalys had moved back into their old house, Charlie remarked how in this still quite

Fig 6. Castleefin Road, Castlederg Some towns in Ulster have lost so much through demolition and alteration that quite a modest terrace like this can be of great local significance. This was originally a factory, and later converted into housing which had become unfit before Hearth restored it.

severely divided town 'Everybody was civilised, pleasant, and polite, across all divides. I am confirmed in my view that bodies such as ours have as much to contribute to better relations in Ireland as either the politicians or the churches.' Historic buildings are a common factor to everyone in an area, and all can take a pride in them.

Difficult Areas

The Troubles may have been unique to Northern Ireland, but every city in the world has its problem areas and issues of crime, and Belfast has these 'ordinary decent criminals' too.

When we took over the old Home for the Blind in the Cliftonville Road, which had had difficulty keeping staff there and decided to move to the safer pastures of south Belfast, we put in a caretaker to keep vandalism at bay until such time as building work could start, and found a family in nearby Hillman Street who were willing to move into the large empty building. Speaking to Mr McNeice when the caretaker phase came to an end, he talked enthusiastically of the peace and tranquillity of the lower Cliftonville Road (compared to his old home), saying he had only had about three windows broken and one attempted break-in during his tenancy!

The problems of retaining a building within a redevelopment area are considerable, since the whole area is seen as condemned, and vandals will smash or steal from every house in the vicinity. When we took on Rose Cottage in the Donegall Pass RDA many local people supported its retention, but we were concerned that as soon as the tenant moved out the vandals would move in. We were not entirely reassured by the words of one of the locals: 'I'll tell you what it is, all the boys have been told, if any of them touches the house they'll get the kneecaps blew off them.' Somehow that threat didn't seem to have got through to the vandals, as the house was broken into at once and shortly after the slates were stolen, and it was an uphill struggle protecting the house until restoration could start.

One of the earliest houses on the Antrim Road is Woodbine Cottage, a small cottage ornée which had been surrounded by larger buildings over the years. When its owner had moved out of the house it began to be vandalised, and then the newel post was stolen and a fire was lit in it, leaving it badly smoke-damaged, locally scorched and extremely vulnerable. We were able to arrange for work to restore it while the legal transaction to buy it took place (and while the building was listed), and put a caretaker in as soon as it was habitable. She could not be there all the time of course, and one night when work was nearly finished thieves broke in and stole the (reproduction) Victorian fireplaces we had put in. Again, the incident was only one of many problems in the area.

Caretakers are an invaluable way of stabilising buildings awaiting restoration. It is the thought that a building is going to be pulled down, and might as well be done by locals as by professionals, which tempts vandals. If they think the house belongs to someone who cares for it, they may not leave it alone altogether, but they will certainly be less vicious. However there are caretakers and caretakers. When we finally got inside the vandalised shells of the houses in College Square North, I wandered up to the attic of one house and encountered a wino who bestirred himself and rose to meet me saying 'Scyoosh me, I'm the Shecurity'!

When we were finishing off the fourteen houses in Castle Street, Armagh, in 1992 there was concern about the possibility of squatting, which had been common in Belfast in the 1970s, so I sought local advice, and was told:

> *There's never been a squatting problem in Armagh. Not since the early days of the troubles. Actually, my brother squatted in a house in Irish Street. But he had to, because he was forced out of his own house by the troubles. That was the only reason there was ever any squatting in Armagh. So the squatters were recognised in due course by the Executive, and a cousin of mine was working for the Electricity Board and sent along to connect the supply. 'I'm from the electric board,' he said to the wife when she answered the door, 'I've just come to connect the supply for you' – whereupon a cloud of steam issued forth from the kitchen much to the wife's consternation. The cousin said he could see she was busy and he'd call back in twenty minutes, by which time the wires had been disconnected! But there's no squatting in Armagh any more!*

In the nineties we bought a burnt-out gate lodge at the entrance to Alexandra Park in north Belfast, and met with the Parks Department of the city council to discuss aspects of its restoration. They told us that it was their worst park for vandalism, and indeed *after the ceasefires* a peaceline was erected along the centre of the park to separate Catholic youths at the upper end from Protestant ones at the lower end; there were also problems of alcoholics and ordinary vandalism. When our builder started work he encountered some of the most sustained vandalism we have ever experienced – most nights half his work of the day would be knocked down, and every weekend the security fencing he had put up would be ripped apart as if Godzilla had been passing through. After a fire one weekend damaged most of the timber that had been put in so far, and spalled stonework, I asked the police (who had a station overlooking the top end of the park) what we should do about the house. 'Pull it down', I was advised. Seemingly, that station's area of operations stopped at the park gates, another station on the other side of the peaceline being responsible for the park itself. We didn't pull the house down of course, but managed to find a local family that wanted to live in it and were prepared to be caretakers from the shell stage on. Overnight the vandalism ceased, as Brian talked to the youngsters who were doing most of the damage, explained how important the house was, and won them over from being vandals to becoming defenders. The Council has now reinstated missing gate pillars nearby, and the Park looks much more attractive and well kept than it did ten years ago.

Difficult Owners

It is often said that there are no problem buildings, only problem owners: and there is a good deal of truth it that, because when you see a building lying derelict the chances are that it is owned by someone who has an inflated idea of its value or has no interest in it at all. It is fairly easy to cast your eye over a town and pick out the two or three buildings whose restoration would really turn it round, but much more difficult to trace their owners and persuade them to sell. In Hearth's experience it can often take a number of years (in one case about twenty!) before the owner, if he can be identified, can be persuaded to part with his little treasure.

Usually the owner has the means to restore but no interest; but we encountered the opposite in the lady who owned a small terrace house in central Belfast which was full of pigeons but had, she thought, the potential to become a law library.

When we were trying to acquire the terrace of early 19c houses in Donegall Street, which had been blighted and vacant for twenty years while Roads Service decided they were surplus to the requirement of a road-widening scheme, I received a letter saying that 'whilst the walls of the property are in a sound condition, Roads Service is of the opinion that these properties should be demolished as soon as possible'. As Charlie remarked on hearing this, 'A cynic might be tempted to wonder whether there exists any building of architectural merit or historical interest which the Roads Service considers should not be demolished as soon as possible!'

Developers always assume that there is a vast urban development grant available on the property they are selling, and you wonder why they haven't proceeded with their own plans on the strength of it. Not surprisingly, like the crock of gold it seems to evaporate as you get closer to it, but it can raise the 'hope value' of a property to ludicrous heights and greatly delay purchase.

Listing

During the housing moratorium of the early eighties we took on some listing work for HMBB, looking at wards in parts of Belfast and particularly in border areas in south Fermanagh and Tyrone. Often we had beautiful weather for it, and there would be a bizarre mismatch between the peace and beauty of the countryside and the very different mindset imposed on it by the modern world. Listing in England must be a pleasant activity, but exploring every country lane in a border area of Ireland is slightly nerve-wracking. Many roads were dead ends, coming to bridges that had been mined; others were marked not for cross border use, with a painted rectangle on the road. Sometimes it was hard to tell whether you had crossed the border or not, and the fact that you had gone off the end of your large scale OS map onto white paper might be the only indicator that you had crossed the border.

Parts of rural Ulster contained some very run-down and isolated houses, and often a stranger with a notebook and camera was a slightly frightening event for the inspected, as much as it was to the inspector who had no idea what he was walking into. Sometimes you found an architectural treasure, more often you encountered depressingly poor housing and social conditions. On one occasion near Killyman I came up to a fairly modest but odd farmhouse run by two old ladies, neat and sprucely kept but with disconcerting features like the valley gutter discharging into a downpipe and thence to a milk churn for a water butt. The old ladies were in the yard behind so I didn't see them till I went round the back, and obviously visitors were rare events at the farm. 'Enid there's a man out there!' Flutterings and flurryings and a large alsatian brought into play; but soon they were chatting away nineteen to the dozen, one plump and freshfaced with white curly hair and a polkadot apron, the other thin and stooped with a shawl over lanker locks.

Around Newtownbutler the country is mostly lough and field and derelict cottages. The people were always very friendly and trusting, yet they had to be on their guard as well. They lived on a disputed border and there had been many deaths there. One old man, living on his own in a cottage two hundred yards from the end of a mined road, was well sozzled before the morning was out. Another, living at the end of a long road, was slightly crazed and talked at great length of his mother's death from gangrene after spiking her foot with a fork; I asked about other cottages on an island marked on the map. All empty he said, so and so left ten years ago, and so and so died fifteen years ago, and so on.

One day I saw a beautiful group of thatched cottages across a lough, but the convolution of water, border, white paper on the map and twisting road was such that it was not clear how to get to it. I stopped and talked to an old farmer at another cottage to get directions. He was a bachelor farmer who had lost the sight of one eye in a farming accident fifteen years before and saw poorly with the other. In Fermanagh it is not easy to get directions without discussing a few other matters first, and conversation turned to his unionist politics, and the murder of various friends over the years. You couldn't trust anybody, he said, not even your neighbour. Eventually I managed to get directions for the thatched cottage. 'They'll give you a good welcome right enough', he said. 'But they're Catholics. Just so's you know who you're talking to. Black Catholics.' Since we had not discussed my politics or religion, he had no idea who he had been talking to, and for all he knew I might have been a rabid republican myself, but since I was a stranger he could trust me.

I went down the lane almost a mile, till I came to one of the most idyllic cottages I have seen. Small, neat, immaculately thatched and limewashed, with lavender and daisies growing in profusion in the flower patches around; even the outhouses were beautifully thatched, and a row of kitchen utensils hung outside the front door in a neat row. I went in and found an old lady sitting beside the turf fire on the open hearth. Her daughter, aged perhaps 40, came in, then an old neighbour who helped with the garden, and we talked for half an hour about the house, about the crane for cooking utensils, and the 'oven' (the black pot they hang over the fire). A beam running across the room carried about fifteen neatly wrapped parcels and constituted the attic of the little open roofed house. The only concession to modernity that I spotted was a white telephone – they didn't have electricity – though the old lady said the dresser was new. They were even drying clothes on thorn hedges at the back. As a stranger I had been made most welcome in both houses, but they obviously couldn't trust their nearest neighbour and hardly talked to one another. The contrast between the glorious beauty of the country and the wretched concerns of its inhabitants never seemed more harsh.

Occupants

One of the great satisfactions of Hearth is that you are providing houses for people; one of the great problems is that sometimes you get tenants who can be a thorough nuisance. The problem tenants are the exception however, for the most part we get to know our tenants and they are partners in looking after the buildings, often taking a great pride in them.

When we started we sometimes rehoused people from very poor conditions. Within a few years that became rare, and for the most part now the waiting list is made up of people who want to move to a different area, or whose family has split up so that a new home is needed.

The first houses Hearth bought were the almshouses in Seaforde, and when I went to meet the last old lady still living in the unimproved houses I was struck by the primitiveness of her accommodation:

> *A living room about ten feet square, a bedroom big enough to hold a bed and another room a bit smaller, plus an outside loo. It was very dark inside but out of courtesy she turned on the naked light bulb. Her dog, a plump 17 year old fox terrier she said was nearly blind, greeted me then flopped into a corner chair. Miss Kelly got her legs up under her on her armchair after getting me the other chair, a plain bentwood one, from the table. Sweetish confined musty smell. A "New Caledonia" cast iron range pumping out heat on a rather humid afternoon. There were a few ornaments: a dog whelk teapot (which she thinks is a tortoise), a sailorman corkscrew, and a plaque with the sentiment that the reader's life be as long as the beard of Paddy McGinty's goat.*

When we restored the larger houses in Seaforde, hardly any of the families were living in bad circumstances as the Housing Executive had provided so many family houses in the area, and many were simply transfers from Executive houses elsewhere. We also had our first experience of awkward tenants. One couple would reminisce through rose-coloured lenses about the comforts of the semi-derelict and damp house they had left in the Main Street, and complain bitterly about the draughts in their new centrally-heated house. Whether because of this disatisfaction or not, their rent was generally rather late.

An intriguing home which I visited some years before we had the chance to buy it was the Curfew Tower in Cushendall, which David Evans took me to see as a building in need of repair. The tower is five stories high with one room on each level and a very steep narrow staircase along one side, built in red sandstone with narrow oriel windows. The occupant, Bob Hume, was in his 70s and had retired to the tower as a caretaker for old Major Turnly, then bought it, and had done some very homely but quite painstaking alterations:

> *Second-hand windows slotted into some openings; corrugated perspex heated and flattened out to form fake old glass (surprisingly effective); a sliding door added to close the open stairs off from the living room, counterbalanced into a slot in the wall and pulled to by a sequence of cords and pulleys; the top of a Tuborg beer keg let into his corner living room fireplace, and his small living room (at second floor) crammed with mementoes, pipes, his own paintings, a model aeroplane in glass case, gas lighting, odds and ends. The basement was the cellar for locking up vagabonds and idlers ("seems a bit tough on idlers", said David), the living room had a gun rack and a device for ringing the curfew bell (which hangs up outside at the crenellations) from inside.*

Fig 7. Curfew Tower, Cushendall
The tower is the very much the symbol of the Co Antrim village it sits at the centre of, but because of its quirky design with four rooms stacked on top of a dungeon it was at risk when Hearth acquired it for restoration.

Bob had been there about ten years, and before that there was a family called Stewart who flew the Union Jack from the flagpole and rang the curfew bell at 1 pm, 3 pm and 6 pm (so I have been mostly told, although some say the last bell was at 7 pm). Mr Stewart had been in the navy in the first war, and had a wooden leg which did not prevent him from being a very active tree surgeon willing to climb any tree in the vicinity. He brought up a large family (some said ten children) in the tower, and ruled them with a rod of iron.

Some time after we had sold the tower to one William Drummond, who had described himself as a bookseller, Cushendall was agog at reports in the Irish Times that the tower was being used as a base from which to publish pornography through 'the notorious K Foundation'. In fact, this was hardly a Playboy kind of organisation. Having made approximately a substantial profit from their activities as a pop group which sent up the inanities of the pop world but managed to get a number one hit, Bill Drummond and his colleague had decided some years before to burn a million pounds in fifty pound notes, recording the destruction on a video which (having failed to interest the London art galleries in the ashes as a work of art)

they released in 1995 with the title 'Watch The K Foundation Burn A Million Quid'. (They were also behind the 'alternative Turner prize' a couple of years ago when the worst artist of the year was given £40,000, creating a nice moral dilemma for its recipient). While enjoying their anarchic sense of humour I was worried in case they decided to burn the Tower as a symbolic gesture! However it has since become a residency for artists to stay and produce work, and the tower continues to be opened for the Heritage Open Days each year.

Although the majority of our tenants are excellent, social housing by its nature throws up a number that give problems. Most commonly these are alcoholics. With one couple the husband would remain fairly quiet when drunk, but the wife would become violent and abuse the neighbours, ringing their doorbells continuously late at night, and could be extremely vindictive. Eventually she stabbed one of her neighbours in the hand with a bread knife one night, and they had to be evicted.

That couple went quietly enough when we threatened eviction, but another tenant was more difficult to shift. It had become apparent that she was sub-letting her flat and living elsewhere, and collecting very much higher rents from her tenants than she was paying to us. To cover her tracks, she asked if she could take in a lodger, but as she had two children and it was a two-bedroom flat the Committee refused this on the grounds that it would cause overcrowding. She argued that the children were only with her during school holidays while the lodger would be a student who would only be there during term time, and that she had a right to take in a lodger under the Tenants' Charter. She then announced that as she was now working in Dublin during the week, there would be no overcrowding as the lodger would not be there at weekends. This Box and Cox arrangement seemed unlikely, and we pointed out that a lodger would require services like breakfast which she could not provide if she was away. When her housing benefit was stopped we could not be told the grounds for the action but it confirmed our impression that something illegal was going on. Gradually we pieced together enough information to establish that she had several addresses in Belfast and some further afield, at which she was registered as a landlord and charging tenants rents; she might have owned some of them, but was certainly only a tenant of our flat, and a fraudulent benefits claim eventually gave us the evidence of sub-letting we needed and the case came to court. She didn't turn up and her poor barrister had to make excuses for her (very hard-working student, often out working, the phone was cut off) and said he would try to get her in to the court for the afternoon session. Spontaneous laughter broke out from our tenants who were there as witnesses (and knew fine well she was in Dublin), and was frowned on by the judge. The case went ahead in the afternoon, and there was a Lewis Carroll like episode when the defending barrister (still in the absence of his elusive client) maintained that she was living in the flat but that the reason her neighbours had not seen her for two years was that every time she went out the front door they had been looking out the back, and vice versa. When the evidence of fraud came up there was no doubt however that he had lost his case.

When we finished our scheme at Cliftonville Road in 1986, it coincided with a period of unrest in north Belfast, and our initial tenants were nearly all emergency rehousing cases from the Manor Street area. The cost of furnishing and heating the large flats was daunting enough for families in low-paid work, and we thought some would move on as soon as other accommodation became available, but its neutral location in a very polarised part of Belfast was ideal for tenants with mixed marriages. A few years later, one of the original tenants told me she was embarrassed when she was at the bakery with a cousin who said to the girl behind the counter that she lived in a 'mansion', with 'fancy cornishes and all'. She said you got used to such things but when visitors called they always noticed them!

Although we sometimes meet people who will talk of being brought up in a family of six or ten siblings, it is very rare to find it in these days. However when we took over the terrace in Castlederg we acquired three families, including one of husband, wife and ten children aged from six to 25, living in a two-bedroomed house. ('We kind of operate two dormitories really', said the father.) Charlie Brett said he thought 'that the fairest thing would be to redistribute the 10 children amongst the three families!' In the end we did distribute them between two houses, linking their house to the one next door, but by then some of the children had left home and the pressure was less. Incidentally, that overcrowded family, in a house with only cold water and a tin bath, was as clean, cheerful and pleasant as any of our tenants.

You do tend to hear a lot about medical conditions when visiting tenants, and Carol sometimes feels more like a social worker than a housing officer, but in a way that is what we are, and for tenants who may be confined to the house and don't get a lot of visitors the crack is important. One man told me that he was having to cut down on his intake of liquids: *'I don't drink pints of beer any more, just vodka'*, adding cheerfully, 'Oh, it's surprising what medical advice can do.'

It is very satisfying when a tenant takes pleasure in their new house. One Glenarm lady said to someone getting one of our houses *'You're lucky enough to be the next pope'*. One of the Joy Street tenants said he got on very well with his neighbours, saying by way of explanation that *'We work together here, the three of us, we're just a little click.'*

Housing association tenants sometimes come from hostels where they have been unused to running a household and can find the responsibility of housekeeping quite intimidating. One girl came from a Barnardo's hostel and having moved her rucksack of possessions into the main room she panicked and moved back to the hostel. Other tenants have had mental breakdowns and come to us after long periods of hospital care, but go on to settle in well. Occasionally such a tenant may forget to take essential medicines and develop strange behaviour. One tenant, who has always been forgetful and eccentric (losing her door key, accusing plumbers of changing the station tuning on her radio, etc), got quite manic after dropping her routine mental treatment for a period, and was seen sitting on a chair in the street diverting the traffic; she was accusing NIE of electrifying the water supply, and blaming the worn patch on the tapestry of her chair on nuclear fallout. In retrospect, with the mania under treatment again, it is amusing, but it was distressing at the time.

We don't really want to know the religion of our tenants, but in Northern Ireland there are few places that don't have a religious connotation and putting a Protestant into a Catholic area and vice versa rarely works, so in fact we always had to have some awareness of religion. With modern legislation we are actually obliged to ascertain religion in order to provide government statistics, however distasteful the process. Despite the folk myths about the other side having eyes too close together or digging with the wrong foot, you certainly can't rely on appearances to gauge religion, as Carol and Elaine found when visiting a tenant who was chatting away about her early life as a nun, and asked Are you Catholic too? No, said Elaine. Oh, said the tenant, you've got a real Catholic wee face on you!

With some common areas like staircases to flats, front gardens to almshouses and so on we have some routine cleaning to carry out, and from time to time have difficulty in getting suitable cleaners and landscape gardeners. One cleaner wrote us a touching letter offering her services, concluding with a plea to 'Please in the future think of me when you see a spot of dust.' I still do.

Fig 8. Glenoe
The picturesque hamlet of Glenoe above Larne should have been protected with conservation area status twenty years ago. Since then it has seen many inappropriate developments and demolitions, and the terrace Hearth restored is almost all that is left with historic character.

Conclusion

Hearth may not have grown at the rate envisaged by its original Committee, and it is one of the province's smaller housing associations, but it is quite large as a building preservation trust. Its permanent staff of four are stretched in carrying out their development or management work, but a small organisation has its advantages. We know, and are known by, our tenants, and we see projects through all the stages from survey to management. While not getting involved in campaigns like the UAHS does, Hearth enjoys a practical role in rescuing buildings that might not have survived otherwise.

A few years ago I received a post card out of the blue from Estonia, a place I've never been to. It says:

I keep the book 'Hearth' in my bag all the time and take it out on average once a week to support my arguments on modern heritage protection, I do not want to give you the impression that I've become some kind of missionary who is bashing his opponents with a black book, but I must say that it has helped me to convince some developers and architects that it is not only in Estonia that there are shabby old houses, and that it is possible to repair them.

Hearth is a small organisation, but size isn't everything!

PICTORIAL IMAGES OF THE FIRST DUKE OF WELLINGTON

PETER JUPP

WHEN WELLINGTON DIED IN 1852, aristocratic power in Britain was not significantly less than it had been in 1769, the year of his birth. Given the scale of economic and social change that took place during those years, this was no doubt a matter of both surprise and comfort to the Duke in his final years; and the causes for it have certainly exercised the minds of historians since then. Of the various explanations which have been put forward, most emphasise political and economic factors: the shaping of legislation to preserve aristocratic power – the most notable example of which was some of the provisions of the 1832 Reform acts; the wealth that flowed from investment in industry and from urban development on aristocratically owned property; and the lack of any sustained challenge from other sections of society. In recent years, however, the spotlight has shifted to cultural factors. It has therefore been argued that the elite reacted to threats to its position generated by the French Revolution by diminishing the sleaze associated with parliamentary politics and by establishing that political office should be a matter of public trust rather than private profit.[1] Linda Colley has drawn attention to the bonding effect of the mass mobilization that accompanied the French wars and suggested that victory accompanied (somewhat tardily) by reform helped make aristocratic leadership of a more powerful Britain acceptable.[2] These propositions have led, in turn, to much greater attention being paid to the transformation in the means by which information about the politics of the elite was transmitted to the public – most notably by the newspaper press – and to the messages conveyed and their impact.

It is in this context that pictorial images of the elite assumes particular importance for the political historian. A great deal of essential research on this topic is already in print: most notably, the catalogues of engraved portraits and caricatures in the British Museum, the National Portrait Gallery volumes on Georgian and Victorian portraiture,[3] and recent monographs on such subjects as satirical prints in George III's reign, the marketing of images of George III, graphic journalism during the 1830s and 1840s, and monuments constructed to commemorate victors of the Napoleonic wars.[4] However, there is room for a great deal more research on this theme and what follows is a case study of the pictorial images of the first Duke of Wellington – a subject of daunting scope but one in which much of the ground has been cleared by the catalogue of single works to be found in Lord Gerald Wellesley's and John Steegman's *The Iconography of the First Duke of Wellington*, published in 1935; and the digest of their work, together with subsequent additions, in Dr Walker's *Regency Portraits.*[5]

* * * * *

As is well known, there was a very considerable increase in the volume of portraiture and caricature during the course of Wellington's life. In the cases of oil, water-colour and pen portraits, their increasing number was due to a combination of factors: the increased artistic interest in the portrait as a result of the productions of the great portrait painters of the time – a point underlined by the fact that about one-third of all Royal Academicians were in the categories of portrait or history and portrait painters[6]; to the greater interest in art generally through the foundation of such institutions as the Royal Academy - one indication of which is the massive turnout for Lawrence's funeral in London in 1830[7]; and to the increasing demand by individuals to be painted.

Although it is impossible to provide even an approximate estimate of the number of portraits of these kinds produced in these years, it is possible to indicate the scale of the increase and the proportion devoted to Wellington. In the former case, the records of the National Portrait Gallery on the numbers of works, artists, and subjects, suggest that there was a four-fold increase in the volume of portraiture from about 1770 to 1830 and then a period of stasis.[8] As for the popularity of Wellington as a subject, some evidence of its scale is provided by the fact that nearly 300 different oils, water-colours and drawings are known to have been devoted to him in his lifetime.[9]

In the case of *engraved* portraits we are on firmer ground statistically. In common with engraving as a whole, there was an undoubted increase in this field in terms of the number of individual subjects engraved, the number of different engravings of individual subjects, the number of engravers and, as a consequence, the number of engraved portraits produced. These, at least, are the conclusions to be drawn from an analysis of the catalogue of engraved portraits published by 'Henry Bromley' (the pseudonym of Anthony Wilson) in 1793, the British Museum's index, and of the classified list of engravers to be found in Hind's *History of Engraving and Etching.*[10]

Several reasons for this development can be suggested. It seems likely, for example, that the flowering of portrait painting had the dual effects of enhancing interest in engraved portraiture on the part of artists and of stimulating a demand amongst collectors for engraved and therefore cheaper versions. It is certainly the case that there was a similar flowering of talent in the field of mezzotint portraiture in the late eighteenth and early nineteenth centuries, suggesting that there was an attempt to emulate the masters on canvass; and that throughout the period there was a very substantial increase in the number of stipple and line engravers of usually lesser quality working in the field of portraiture, suggesting that there was a growing market to be satisfied.[11]

Another reason may be that technical developments in engraving enabled artists and publishers not only to meet existing demand but also to increase it by producing more, and probably cheaper, impressions from individual plates. The key here was the use of steel. Thus it seems that the number of mezzotints or line engravings that could be taken from a single copper plate was limited to as little as 1-300 in the case of the former and from between 1-3,000 in the latter, thereby restricting the potential market that could be satisfied. In the late eighteenth and the early nineteenth centuries, however, it became increasingly common to harden the face of a copper plate with the much more durable steel or to engrave on steel plates, thereby increasing the number of impressions that could be produced to as many as 40,000. This development was accompanied by a revolution in the means of producing cheaper and larger quantities of paper suitable, or at least adequate, for printing. Overall it is likely that increasing demand and improved technology were developments that reinforced each other.[12]

A further important factor was the enormous increase in book production and the consequent increase in the demand for engraved portraits for the purposes of illustration. In this regard there were three related developments. The first was the proliferation of books which were devoted to presenting engraved images of, and often with written commentaries on, the good and the great in the artistic, military and political fields. An early pioneer was the Rev. Granger's *Biographical History of England from Egbert the Great to the Revolution* first published in 1769 and consisting of a catalogue of 'Engraved British Heads'. Granger's work was not illustrated but it was said in an advertisement for the fifth edition of 1824 that it had created such an interest amongst collectors to match his catalogue entries with the appropriate engravings, that prices of books that contained relevant examples had risen five times their original value by 1790; and that the prices for individual prints had risen from an average of 5s to as much as £70 to £80 over the same period of time.[13] Needless to say Granger's unillustrated catalogue was soon followed by a spate of specialised illustrated works, some of the most influential being Bell's *British Poets* (1776-1783), Bromley's and Mark Noble's revised editions of Granger, and later, Edmond Lodge's *Portraits of Illustrious Personages of Great Britain.*[14] The last featured many military and political figures (Wellington being the last entry) and, having been initiated in 1814 went through at least ten editions between the publication of the first part in 1821 and 1860.

A further development was an increase in the number of periodicals that regularly contained engravings, most notably the *Universal Magazine* (1747-1814), the *Lady's Magazine* (1770-1818), the *European Magazine* (1787-1826) and subsequently the less weighty *Forget Me Not, Friendship's Offering, The Keepsake* and *The Anniversary.*[15] In addition, there was an equally dramatic increase in the number of books published, most particularly historical works in the forms of biography, memoirs and monographs, most of which included engraved portraits as a matter of course. It was probably in these last two fields that line engraving on steel plates made its greatest impact, the *Times* pointing out on 5 Nov. 1828 that as many as 10,000 impressions could be taken from a single plate, thereby making them ideal for book runs.

It was through the medium of the engraved portrait that pictorial images of Wellington were most widely disseminated. To measure how widely is impossible at this juncture as a result of the lack of statistics on sales of individual prints and books, but it is possible to provide an indication of his popularity as a subject relative to his contemporaries. The source materials for this exercise are the British Museum indexes of engraved portraits and the files of items accumulated since their publication by both the Museum and the National Portrait Gallery. From these it is possible to establish the subjects of whom engravings were most frequently published, my minimum standard for any subject being 15 separate publications in order to reduce the number of candidates to manageable proportions. Admittedly this cannot be a fully accurate guide as it takes no account of the sales of individual publications which may have been greater in the case of a subject engraved and published once than of another engraved and published more frequently. In addition, it ignores the vital factor of the length of a subject's life. On the other hand a blunt methodological instrument is better than none at all.

Broadly speaking, the subjects that qualified for inclusion fall into five categories. The first and by far the largest consists of actors and singers. Of these the most frequently published in engraved form was Garrick with more than 180 publications. Next in this category came Mrs Siddons with more than 80 and following in her wake, Kemble, Francis Abington and MacCready. The rest commanded between 15 and 30 apiece. Then as now, it seems, the stars of the world of entertainment commanded greater public interest than any other category of individuals.

The second category in terms of the gross number of publications, if not, for obvious reasons, the number of individual subjects, consists of members of the Royal family. Well ahead of any other single figure of the eighteenth or nineteenth centuries came Queen Victoria with a staggering total of more than 370 different engraved portraits. This was more than twice that of her nearest competitors in this field – George III and George IV – who nevertheless achieved respectable levels of exposure with over 160 publications in the former's case and nearly 150 in the latter's. In fact the high figures for individual members of the Hanoverians strengthen the view that historians have seriously underestimated the popularity of the monarchy prior to Victoria's accession. In this respect it is interesting that the titular head of the anti-Catholic and 'ultra' tories, the Duke of Cumberland, merited at least 47 published engravings.

The next three categories are of roughly equal size in terms of numbers of both subjects and publications. One, which is most conveniently considered at this stage, consists of painters, poets, composers and writers. By far the most frequently engraved of all these subjects was Sir Walter Scott with more than 80 prints to his name. Of the rest, the next in line in their different categories were Reynolds, Byron, Johnson and Handel with Carlyle, Dickens, Burns and Lawrence not far behind. Overall the list of qualifiers in this category is not very surprising although it is perhaps odd that other 'Romantic' writers did not figure more prominently.

It is against this background that Wellington's popularity as a subject can be assessed. Thus, although he fits into both of the last two categories of military heroes and politicians, a fact which obviously inflated his marketability, he was far ahead of all other contenders with at least 180 published engravings. The nearest to him on the military side, inevitably, was Nelson with about 80; and on the political, with equal predictability, the younger Pitt and Fox with about 70 and 60 respectively. It is somewhat surprising, however, that these figures were considerably greater than anyone else in these two fields: the next in the military line being Kepple; and the next in the political being Gladstone, Brougham, Burke, Peel and another 'ultra' Tory, Lord Eldon.

Thus, it appears that Wellington was far less published in engraved form than Queen Victoria but in the company of Garrick, and to a lesser extent, George III and George IV, much more so than any other contemporary. As has been suggested, this is to some extent due to his dual role as soldier and politician and also to his longevity. On the other hand, the fact that soldiers and statesmen were not so frequently published as might have been expected, and appear to have been less popular subjects generally than stage personalities and royalty, makes his achievement more, rather than less, notable.

The final pictorial medium to be considered is political caricature. As is well known there was a remarkable flowering of technical artistry and textual subtlety in this field during Wellington's lifetime – as remarkable as in the various forms of portraiture. Moreover, it was also a medium that was subject to considerable technical innovation. Thus, the copper plate etchings of the great masters such as Gillray, George Cruikshank and William Heath, which yielded in the region of between 1-3,000 impressions each, gradually gave way to other forms: to the more cheaply and numerously produced lithographs which were the trademark of John Doyle ('HB'), the dominant caricaturist of the 1830s and 1840s; and to the even cheaper and more productive woodcuts first developed for popular consumption by Cruikshank prior to 1820 and, following further improvements in reproduction, by Leech and Keene amongst others, for *Punch* in the 1840s.[16]

Fortunately, as a result of the formidable scholarship of Mrs George for the period to 1832 and the dominance of caricature thereafter by the publisher McLean, and by Doyle and Punch, it is possible to provide a fairly precise estimate of Wellington's popularity as a subject. Thus of the 5,000 or so political caricatures produced in the years between his first appearance in 1808 and his death and of which the British Museum has copies, my estimate is that he appeared in about 1,000.[17] Admittedly this figure conceals considerable variations between phases of his career. He made very few appearances between 1808 and 1813; a great deal more, as might be expected, in 1814-15; and many fewer again between 1816 and 1826, when royalty and many other politicians were more popular subjects. The great increase took place between 1827 and 1834 when, as a result of his prominence at Westminster, he appeared in some 40% of all political caricatures. Thereafter his appearances were proportionately less but still compared favourably with the years when he was at the height of his political fame. Nevertheless, despite these variations, it seems probable that Wellington's popularity as a subject for caricature exceeded that of any other single figure during that period.

To sum up on this aspect of the subject. There seems to be sufficient statistical evidence to suggest that in a period of very rapid growth in pictorial depiction, Wellington was the most portrayed Briton in his own lifetime, to adapt a phrase of Wellesley and Steegman.[18] In each of the categories surveyed, he may have had rivals in frequency of depiction but no other person commanded such attention in all three where the number of single works and different published images can be estimated with a fair degree of reliability to have exceeded 1480.

*　　*　　*　　*　　*

The question of how widely these images were disseminated amongst the public is much more difficult to answer although two general propositions may be ventured. The first is that it seems likely that there was an increase in the opportunities for viewing individual images and a gradual broadening of the social ranks that took advantage of them. Initially, that is to about 1820, it is probable that viewers of oils and water-colours, for example, would have been restricted for the most part to owners and their friends, to visitors to the Royal Academy exhibitions and to those of other bodies such as the British Institution, most of whom were likely to have been drawn from the landed elite. After 1820, however, there appears to have been an increase in the number and size of London exhibitions, particularly of portraits, and an upsurge of interest in the English provinces. In the case of London, for example, it has been claimed that the first exhibition of a collection of 'national' portraits took place at The British Institution in 1820 when 183 works were put on show. Later, in 1823, 1830 and 1833, the Institution mounted exhibitions devoted to the works of Reynolds, Lawrence and West. In addition, there appears to have been a proliferation of other exhibiting bodies such as those based at Somerset House and the Egyptian Hall in Piccadilly. Moreover, all these developments took place in addition to the annual Royal Academy exhibitions which, to judge by the works devoted to Wellington, featured an increasing number of portraits in the 1830s and 1840s.[19]

A similar trend can be detected in the English provinces. In 1821 the Birmingham Society of Arts was founded and in 1827 it departed from the tradition of exhibiting locally made ornaments and brasses in order to display a selection of modern paintings. In 1828 Newcastle was host for the first time to an exhibition mounted by the Northern Academy of Arts; and the Artists' Gallery in Norwich was proud to advertise an exhibition of works belonging to seven local 'gentlemen' collectors. In the following year Manchester was the temporary home of a large exhibition of paintings and other works of art. Moreover, to judge by a study of some 50 provincial newspapers of the 1820s, there was a notable increase in their coverage of the arts in general and exhibitions of paintings in particular.[20]

Of course an increase in the number and the geographical spread of art exhibitions does not of itself attest to a more broadly based viewing public. On the other hand such figures as we possess of the numbers visiting some of the special exhibitions of the 1820s suggests a broadening of their social rank beyond the elite.

Thus, *The Times* reported in 1829 that 20,000 had paid 1/- each to view an exhibition of battle scenes at the Egyptian Hall 'including nearly all the whole of the nobility'; and in 1830 the *Birmingham Journal* claimed that over 22,000 had visited the Birmingham and Manchester exhibitions of the previous year of whom c.18,000 had paid 1/- and were therefore from 'the general public'.[21] It seems plausible to argue that this trend was continued in the 1830s and 1840s.

Much the same conclusion may be drawn in the case of probably the majority of engraved portraits and caricatures. Until the 1820s nearly all these were produced in London from copper plates and because of the use of that medium were sold for quite sizeable sums. It would appear that £1.10.0s was an average price then for a late impression of a portrait engraved on copper and that several shillings was a minimum price for an uncoloured caricature.[22] Such sums would probably have been within the reach of a significant proportion of the population of London and its perennial visitors but it nevertheless seems more likely that purchasers would have been of broadly the same social rank as the viewers of oils at that time. It was those who peered through print shop windows who would have been from lower down the social scale.

From about 1820 onwards, however, it seems there were a number of developments that gradually broadened the social rank of those who would have been familiar with these particular images of Wellington. In the case of engraved portraits, for example, it seems likely that the increasing use of steel plates to produce greater numbers of impressions led to a lowering of prices that brought them into the price-range of the middle classes and those below. Prices of engravings fell to as little as 1/- or less in the 1820s, some even being distributed free to purchasers of particular periodicals.[23] In addition, their increasing use as illustrations in books and the vast increase in book production after 1815 would have combined to make them available to broadly the same social classes, either as purchasers or as users of libraries. Finally, in the case of caricatures, the probability is that woodcuts, especially those that accompanied political tracts, reached a much wider audience than the copper plate or even the lithograph variety. Hone's tracts of the post 1815 period, such as *The Political House that Jack Built*, which was illustrated with woodcuts by George Cruikshank, achieved very high sales and were seen by artisans and other classes of workers, not least in the growing numbers of Mechanics Institutes, reading rooms, coffee houses and pubs. Moreover, woodcuts were the chosen medium of the *Punch* caricaturists of the 1840s and the 1850s when it has been estimated that sales reached about 10,000 per issue and were much more widely distributed than previous periodicals as a result of the use of the railway network.[24]

The overall conclusion therefore appears to be as follows: that until about 1820 the majority of these particular pictorial images were known only to the landed elite and the London art world; that thereafter there was a gradual broadening of the ranks of viewers in social, and perhaps geographical, terms through exhibitions, less expensive steel engravings, book illustration, periodicals and cheap tracts. This suggests, in turn, that in terms of reaching the widest public, these particular images began to rival those conveyed traditionally by other means: by the pub sign and by decorations on tableware and other household objects as far as pictorial images were concerned; and by three dimensional objects placed in public places or available for general purchase, namely the bust, statue or statuette.

* * * * *

A further aspect of this subject which merits examination is the types of pictorial images that were particularly influential in the course of Wellington's career. For this purpose it has proved useful to consider his career as passing through four distinct phases: the first encompassing the period to May 1814, during which he established his military reputation but was seldom in England; the second, from then until the beginning of 1827, when he achieved heroic stature as the victor at Waterloo and then gradually established himself in the centre of the political stage; the third, from 1827 to 1834, when his political influence was at its height; and the last, continuing until his death, when his role was more that of the country's most distinguished elder statesman.

In the first phase of his career, that is in the period to May 1814 when he returned to England in triumph from the Peninsular campaign, at least 50 or so different images of him in the forms of oil and water-colour portraits, miniatures, medals, wax profiles, busts and statues were produced.[25] These included some very well known works: most notably the oils by Home and Hoppner; the busts by Gahagen, Nollekens and Turnerelli; the wax profiles by Amatucci; and the oils executed in the Peninsular by Pellegrini and, of course, Goya. However, the important point in the context of this essay is that very few of these would have been known in England at the time to more than owners and their friends. Thus, of the works produced before he left for the Peninsular for the final time in May 1809, Home's were executed in India and of the rest, only the pencil and wash drawing by Edridge and Hoppner's oil are known to have been exhibited at the Royal Academy, the latter in 1806. As for the later works, those by Amatucci, Pellegrini and Goya would not, of course, have been known; and of the rest, only a small number of busts and medallions appear to have been put on public display. Moreover, it is interesting that none of last seem to have been based on sittings.

It follows therefore that the medium through which his image was most widely popularised was engraving. In this regard Wellesley and Steegman have suggested that the most influential works on which engravings were based were Pellegrini's portrait of 1809 and Amatucci's wax profiles of about 1812.[26] However, there are good grounds for questioning this verdict, at least for the period to May 1814. Thus, of the 20 or so engraved portraits published in that period, the majority are based on portraits by Home and Hoppner and the busts of Gahagen and Nollekens, the last of which drew heavily on the former's production.[27] Some 10 were based on their images whereas Pellegrini's portrait, although undoubtedly popular, inspired 3 engraved versions between 1811 and 1813. Moreover, of the engravings in the 7 periodicals which published portraits of him in these years and which probably reached the largest number of people, only one can be clearly identified as being based on Pellegrini although as it appeared in the *Lady's Companion* in 1813, its influence may have been disproportionately significant.[28] The conclusion seems to be that the most widely publicised images were those of British artists or those working in England, all of which happened to be based on sittings. Of these, the most popular appears to be Home's, which was published 5 times in England [Fig 1];[29] and Hoppner's production of 1806, Palser publishing Cook's engraving at least three times between 1808 and 1812 [Fig 2].

Fig 1. Portrait by Robert Home, 1804, National Portrait Gallery

Fig 2. Portrait by John Hoppner, 1806, Government House, Madras; exhibited Royal Academy, 1806.

Fig 3. Caricature by Charles Williams, 'The Last Harvest or British-Threshers Making French Crops', published Sept. 1808, BM Catalogue no. 11024.

It is probably a measure of Home's and Hoppner's influence on the popular impression of Wellington in this period that the first caricature of him, etched by Charles Williams and published in September 1808, bears some resemblance to their images [Fig 3]. The print is interesting, not least because it appears to make a strong allusion to Wellington's Irish connections. Thus, in a satire in which the main theme is the defeat of Junot at Vimeiro on 21 August, Wellington, with sword raised, is referred to as the leader of the 'British Threshers', the latter being the name given to Irish rural insurgents. The reference was topical as Wellington had spent some time during the Spring of that year considering means to control their activities in the west of Ireland in his capacity as Chief Secretary.

In the course of the next six years Wellington appeared in a further 30 satires, all of which were concerned chiefly with the merits of the Peninsular campaign. By and large they follow the ebb and flow of the war, being initially critical of what appeared to be yet another hopeless and expensive venture and then becoming more sympathetic and eventually, laudatory. However, the problem for the caricaturist as far as the ever more prominent Wellington was concerned, was how to make him instantly recognisable.

The answer, of course, was reference to the prominent 'bridge' on Wellington's nose depicted in Home's oil. The first caricaturist to display this prominently and to develop it in subsequent productions was George Cruikshank although there remains some doubt as to whether it was based on Home's image, on personal observation, or has some other explanation. It is worth noting, for example, that Cruikshank, like George Dance before him, had a particular fondness for noses and tended to exaggerate those of his subjects, particularly those of foreign royalty and soldiers. Whatever the reason, he clearly makes reference to the 'bridge' in his first drawing of Wellington (3rd from the left) presenting the Convention of Cintra to Junot in August 1808 (the print was published on 29 September) although it is noticeable that two other figures are similarly adorned [Fig 4]. In due course Cruikshank's somewhat restrained reference was made much more explicit. One of the reasons for this may have been Wellington's reappearance in London for the much publicised enquiry into the Cintra Convention in the early part of 1809 – an event which would have led to his being seen by caricaturists. Another may have been sight of a drawing by a Lieutenant Downman made at Badajos between 1809-10 that displays the 'bridge' side on and therefore much more clearly;[30] and which was certainly available in engraved form after Wellington was elevated to a dukedom in 1814 [Fig 5]. Whatever the precise reason might be, Cruikshank soon established a much more distinctive 'bridge' as the major clue to Wellington's presence in his

Fig 4. Caricature by George [?and I] Cruikshank, 'Whitlock the Second or Another Tarnish of British Valour', published 29 Sept. 1808, BM Catalogue no. 11035.

Fig 5. Engraving after a drawing by Lieutenant Downman, reproduced in Wellesley and Steegman, *Iconography*, Plate 8.

Fig 6. Caricature by George Cruikshank, 'More Trophies for White-hall' published 10 July 1813.

productions – as can be seen in 'More Trophies for White-hall' (10 July 1813), in which Wellington (on the left) tells his generals that the booty from the battle of Vitoria would pay for three nights of celebrations while his troops (led by an Irish Catholic) do the necessary on the right. [Fig 6].

In the subsequent phase of his career – from his return from the Peninsular campaign to the beginning of the political upheavals following the end of Lord Liverpool's prime ministership in 1827 – Wellington's fame and his availability as a subject for sightings and sittings led to a rapid increase in the number of single images produced: at least 100 or so. Moreover, a substantial proportion consisted of oils and water-colours, including some distinguished examples by Beechey, Couré, Dawe, Hayter, Isabey, Jackson, Lonsdale, Phillips, and, of course, Lawrence, who produced six portraits of him in these years. However, as in the previous period, few of the portraits would have been known to the general public in their original form, the only ones to be exhibited in the Royal Academy being three of the Lawrence portraits and that by Hayter, exhibited in 1826. Public knowledge of single rather than engraved images, of which Lady Jersey said that Jackson's oil of 1824 presented the best likeness, would therefore have been restricted, with the exception of those by Lawrence and Hayter, to miniatures, reliefs, those on household objects, and to busts and statues, particularly the busts produced by Chantry and exhibited at the Royal Academy in 1824.[31]

It was also the case, as in the previous period, that the engraved images that would have reached a wider public represented only a proportion of the single works. Thus, to judge by the frequency of publication, the most popular engraved portraits of these years were those based on a canvas by Beechey which was produced in 1814 but which Sir Herbert Maxwell consigned incorrectly to 1806 in the first page of his two volume *Life*. In all there were at least four publications of engravings after Beechey in this period (1814, 1816, 1817 and 1823), and probably another. These were followed, in order of frequency of publication and possibly of popularity, by engravings from paintings or reliefs by Isabey, Burney, Amatucci and Bauzil, Isabey's being reproduced at least three times. Of the Lawrence canvasses, only one, the 'Sword of State', was produced in engraved form [Fig 7], thereby depriving the public then of the now much better known canvass of 1814; and of the Jackson, there was no engraving at all until 1828. The most popular engraved images of this period therefore presented Wellington in a very particular light: as a warrior of course, but in the case of the Isabey and 'The Sword of State', as a triumphant, almost arrogant, one.

Fig 7. Engraving of a portrait by Sir Thomas Lawrence, 1814.

The images presented by the caricaturists in the 1814-27 period varied in frequency and meaning. In 1814 and 1815 he not only appeared in a substantial number of satires (in about 50 or some 20%), but was invariably presented in a flattering light: as a heroic symbol of a Britain that was less rapacious than her allies in the territorial settlement of 1814-1815; and the least ruffled by Napoleon's escape from Elba. However, the tide turned against him on 5 October 1815 when Cruikshank, in 'Louis XVIII climbing the Mat de Cocagne' mounted a comprehensive attack on the allies for their restoration of Louis XVIII and their alleged plans for future conquest and plunder, identifying Wellington (on the left) as a willing and self-interested accomplice [Fig 8].

It was this message, elaborated to suggest that the war had resulted in the elevation of a small band of soldiers and politicians – most notably Wellington, Castlereagh and Sidmouth – into a position from which they could enhance the power of the State to feather their own nests and crush the liberties of free-born Englishmen, that gradually prevailed over all others. Admittedly the dissemination of this message in the form of full-sized caricatures was restricted between 1816 and 1818 because the number produced and the proportion in which Wellington appeared, fell drastically. On the other hand the theme was underlined by Wellington's appearance in this guise on the front page of Hone's and Cruikshank's radical *The Political House that Jack Built*, which sold in large numbers following its publication in 1819; and was reinforced by identical images to be found in the flood of caricatures that poured onto the market from 1819 to 1821, most of them being comments on the Queen Caroline affair. About 900 caricatures were produced in those years – over 50% of the total number produced between 1814 and 1826.

Fig 8. Caricature by George Cruikshank, 'Louis XVIII climbing the Mat de Cocagne', published 5 Oct. 1815.

It was therefore during this period that the predominant image presented in the engraved portrait – particularly that in Lawrence's 'Sword of State' – was echoed and embellished by the caricaturists, the drawn sword with which Wellington was invariably depicted, being a convenient symbol of an oppressive state crushing the liberties of the subject. Moreover although interest in Wellington as a subject declined after 1821, along with the production of caricature, the image of a brutal, rapacious figure persisted, as can be seen in J. Lewis Marks' production of c.1822 [Fig 9].

In the politically most prominent phase of Wellington's career, between 1827 and 1834, about 40 individual works of all kinds were produced, of which about half were paintings. None of these was of major artistic merit although Jackson's two oils of 1826-7 and possibly 1830-31, Lawrence's finished production for Lord Londonderry and his three unfinished canvasses, as well as Wilkie's

Fig 9. Caricature by John Lewis Marks, 'Duke Achilles Defeated or the Opera Girl of Paris' published ?1822, BM catalogue no. 14409.

commission for the Merchant Taylors' Company of 1832-3, deserve notice. As far as the images they presented are concerned, there was, if all are taken into account, some softening of his traditional portrayal as a heroic, imperious warrior. This was to some extent due to a faithful representation of the passage of time on his facial appearance; and also to a tendency to present him in a cloak or frock coat which has the effect of diluting the impression of an exclusively military figure. In fact the canvasses as a whole convey the image of a somewhat olympian soldier-politician – an image which lay at the heart of the contemporary debate about his suitability for a major political role.

It is interesting in this respect that the engraved image which had the widest circulation in these years reinforced the civilian dimension of his career. In all only 7 different engraved portraits were published in this period but this may be due to the fact that the market was dominated by Lawrence's portrait of him painted for Charles Arbuthnot in 1821 but bought by the 5th Earl of Rosebery in 1878 and sometimes known as the 'Rosebery' Lawrence.[32] This was published in engraved form for the first time in 1827 and led to more than 50 further publications, at least 5 of which, and probably a great deal more, were produced in these years. Thus, although Jackson's and Hayter's canvasses of 1824 and 1825 were also produced in engraved form at this time, the image that was most widely disseminated, particularly as a result of its appearance in Edmond Lodge's *Portraits*, was Lawrence's [Fig 10]. As can be seen this presents him with a faint smile and in a largely civilian guise, his shoulders being enveloped in a cape with a soft velvet collar. It is therefore possible that in spite of the ambivalence of the canvasses, the highly popular engravings after this particular Lawrence helped to establish a civilian – politician, as an alternative to a soldier – politician, image of Wellington in the eyes of the public.

The question of a military or civilian image is also highly relevant in the case

Fig 10. Engraving of a portrait by Sir Thomas Lawrence, 1821.

of caricature. The years 1827-34 saw a very considerable increase in the number of political satires published: at least 1600, or about the same number that were produced in the much longer earlier period from 1814 to 1826. Moreover, there was an equally striking, although hardly surprising, rise in the proportion in which Wellington made an appearance: in some 40% – a proportion that far exceeded that recorded for any other individual. It was therefore in this period that the caricature competed most successfully with the engraved portrait in impressing an image of Wellington on the public mind.

In the period between the break up of the Tory forces on the formation of Canning's ministry in April 1827 and the passage of the Catholic Relief Bill in April 1829, the caricaturists, and most notably William Heath, were uniformly hostile to Wellington. The occasions for the expression of hostility are obvious enough. The break up of Lord Liverpool's coalition, the resulting political instability and the battles over the first stages of 'the constitutional revolution' in the shapes of the repeal of the Test and Corporation acts and the Catholic Relief Bill, were events that generated a political temperature higher than any seen since the days of the Peterloo and the Queen Caroline affairs. The reasons for it are more problematic. Caricaturists, by tradition as well as by profession, had to be critical of someone or something; and Wellington was a natural target. However, the virtually unanimous hostility suggests that more deep-seated reasons played a part. One possibility is that the tradition popularised earlier by Cruikshank was hard to dislodge and easier to follow. Another is that the caricaturists and publishers were themselves hostile to the weakening of the Protestant constitution that Wellington presided over in the first stage of his premiership, although this seems unlikely as they proved remarkably flexible on political issues over time. A third, and perhaps the most likely, reason is that they judged that hostility to Wellington's policies and tactics would sell the most caricatures – a conclusion which, if correct, would strengthen the argument that popular support for the *ancien regime* was a good deal stronger than has traditionally been thought. In this respect it is interesting that in their treatment of the Catholic question, the caricaturists concentrated on the threat to the Constitution from the means by which concession was achieved rather than on the religious dimensions.

Whatever the precise reasons might be, there is no doubting the consistency of the attack. Thus, the dominant image was of a military tyrant who, in his obsession with power, was prepared to subvert the constitution and fly in the face of majority opinion. He was consequently displayed for the most part in military costume with sword at the ready in order to crush all opposition. Of all the many caricatures conveying this message, one of the best is Thomas Jones' *'Porro unum est necessarium'* published just at the time (March-April 1829) when Wellington was forcing George IV and a largely hostile British public to swallow Catholic Relief – a concession, the artist prophesises, that would fail to appease Catholic Ireland [Fig 11].

Yet although the caricaturists were united on the message to a surprising degree, they were clearly eager to establish alternative devices to press it home: partly, I suspect, because of Wellington's reluctant surrender of his military role as

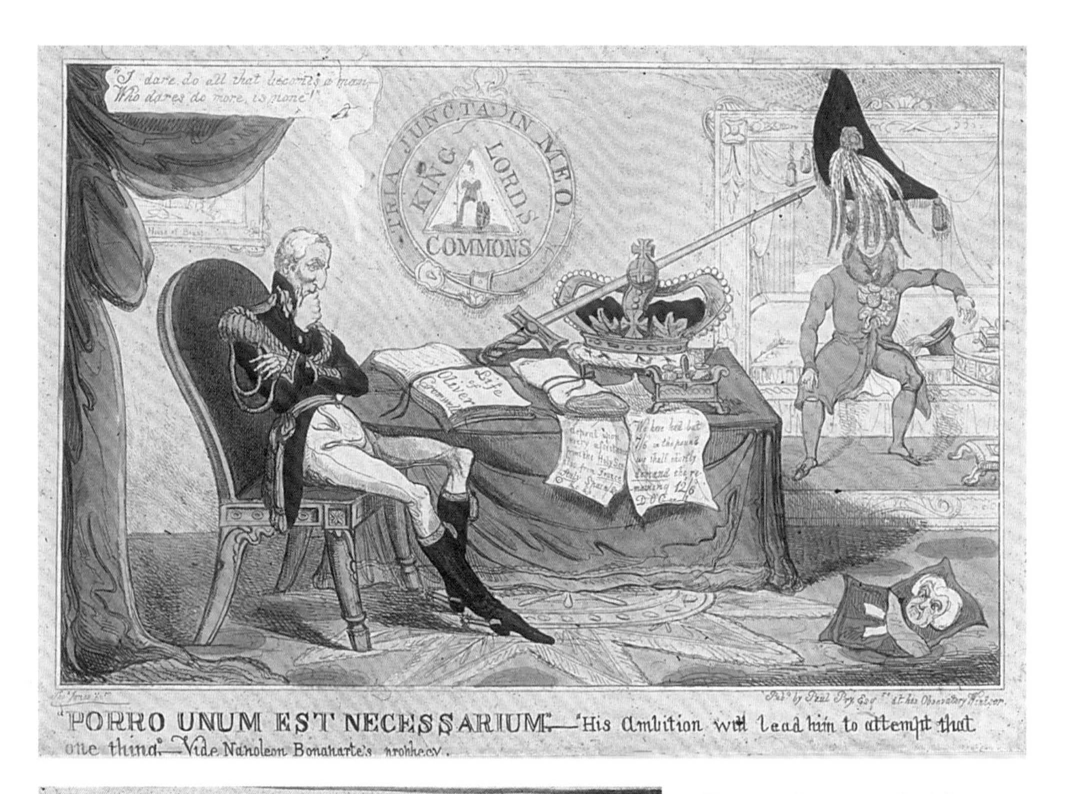

Fig 11. Caricature by Thomas Jones, 'Porro Unum Est Necessarium', published c. Apr. 1829, BM catalogue no. 15728.

Fig 12. Caricature by ?William Heath, 'Portrait of a Noble Duke', published [?Mar.] 1829, BM catalogue no. 15691.

Commander-in-Chief in January 1828; and partly because there appears to have been vigorous competition between them to succeed to Cruikshank's mantle – a competition which put a premium on individual 'trade marks'. Thus, variants on the military theme appeared in the famous 'A Wellington Boot', in 'The Prime Lobster', the lobster – being a term of abuse for a soldier – and most famously, 'Portrait of a Noble Duke' [Fig 12], all of which were published by Thomas McLean from his shop in Haymarket and were probably drawn by Heath. In addition, new images were established with Wellington portrayed as a mute, and therefore deaf to public opinion; as a cabinet maker or grave digger who dominated his colleagues and was preparing for the funeral of the Constitution; and most famously, as a coach driver who was prepared to drive his team through the obstacles presented by George IV's conscience and prerogatives in order to reach his destination of Catholic relief.

Following the passage of the Catholic Relief Bill, however, a distinct change occurs in the ways Wellington was portrayed. To a large extent this was the result of a transformation in the general features of caricature that had begun earlier in the 1820s. Thus, instead of the gross distortion of physical characteristics which had been typical hitherto, there was a growing tendency to present subjects in free-standing form with an emphasis on physical likenesses. Similarly, instead of the message and the messengers seeming to be ridicule of the elite by radical critics outside it, there was an increasing preference for more subtle, more wide-ranging, and in some cases, more informed, comment from the interiors of high politics. The reasons for this are still a matter of conjecture. Some historians argue that it was the result of changing elite and radical strategies. Philip Harling, for example, suggests that in the course of the late 18th and early 19th centuries the elite became aware of the threat of radical attacks on 'Old Corruption' or sleeze, and had taken substantial steps by the late 1820 to clean up its act.[33] Diana Donald argues that following Peterloo, radicals calculated that the written word was a more powerful tool for their purposes than caricature and that they left that medium to others.[34] But there may be other reasons. In the case of the artistic developments, for example, it seems plausible to suggest that they were due, in part at least, to the growing use of the lithograph in which the subject matter is drawn directly on the stone from which it is printed, thereby facilitating the making of likenesses. Another possibility is that it reflected the growing dominance of the market by McLean and his favourite artist, John Doyle, who, as a trained portrait painter, favoured a representational style. As for the more subtle and informed content of caricature, it may have been the result of politicians beginning to cultivate opinion and feeding information to the artists.

Whatever the precise reasons might be, the fact is that the caricatures of the 1830s, and particularly Doyle's, convey a very different impression from those of earlier years. Thus, whereas the caricatures of Cruikshank's hey day undoubtedly appear to have been composed from a standpoint outside the world of the political elite, those of the 1830s appear to have been composed from within it.

These developments bore heavily on the way Wellington was portrayed in the period from the middle of 1829 to the end of 1834. Thus, the thin, wiry, tense and almost manic figure was replaced with one that was more rounded, more sedate. In addition, the predominant use of military costume gave way to civilian dress, thereby reflecting faithfully the course of his career and the dominant image of the oil and engraved portraits of him. Parallel with these changes was the gradual fading of the image of the despot and the rise of that of the sometimes rascally, sometimes bemused, elder statesman: anxious to serve; eager to maintain the status quo but not to the point of provoking an irreversible radical backlash. It was in this new guise that he was presented as the titular leader of the new Conservative Party, Peel usually being displayed as a sycophantic second-in-command who was nevertheless biding his time until the patrician old guard faded away. The two most notable popularisers of this image were Robert Seymour and Doyle, the latter, as a Catholic Irishman, being particularly sensitive to Wellington's Irish ancestry and his labours on behalf of Catholic relief. Doyle's ' The Rival Artistes', 17 July 1832, is typical of the new image with Wellington depicted as superior to Lord Grey in the pirouette for having turned from opponent to proponent of Catholic relief, and in May 1832, for being ready to come to William IV's rescue and form a government to deal with the issue of parliamentary reform, the necessity for which he had hitherto denied. [Fig 13].

It was during the last phase of Wellington's life – from 1835 to his death in 1852 – that images of him were most widely disseminated amongst the public and when there was the greatest degree of uniformity between the images conveyed by the various different media. In the case of single works, for example, about the same number were produced in these years as in the whole of his previous life. Moreover, a substantial number of all kinds were made available to a much larger public than before. Thus, a significant number of busts and statuettes were exhibited at the Royal Academy and found homes in clubs, other private institutions, and town halls. It is also likely that more of these were sold than hitherto. In addition, a number of statues were erected in public places, most notably on Constitution Hill, and in Glasgow and Edinburgh. The same pattern can be observed in paintings. Hardly a year went by without at least one

Fig 13. Caricature by John Doyle ['HB'], 'The Rival Artistes', published 17 July 1832, BM catalogue no.17192.

portrait being exhibited at the Royal Academy and a fair proportion of the total number of canvasses produced was commissioned for display by private or public bodies such as the various service clubs, several of the London Companies and, following his election as Chancellor of Oxford in 1834, the Oxford and Cambridge, and the Examination Schools.[35]

In the case of oil and watercolour portraits, a significant indication of his tremendous appeal as a subject is the fact that he was painted by at least 30 different artists – a degree of popularity which certainly justified his well known irritation with the demands made of him for sittings. By far the most frequent was Benjamin Haydon who produced at least 27 variants but Briggs and Lucas contributed over 30 between them and Morton, Salter, Weigall, Simpson and D'Orsay, another 20. In fact it would appear that few portrait painters of note did not try their hand at a representation.

The pictorial images that ensued from this activity naturally varied but in accordance with the drift of his career and in response, possibly, to the growing reserve about dress that reflected the fading society of ranks, orders and degrees,

the dominant one was of a distinguished statesman with a military past but a largely civilian role, his dress and often the setting, being in sombre colours. One of the best known is D'Orsay's canvass of 1845 presenting him in socially neutral evening dress but adorned with the Golden Fleece and the ribbon of the Garter [Fig 14]. Briggs's canvass of 1837 and Haydon's and Hayter's of 1839, convey a similar overall impression. Of course the whole issue of pictorial representation was stirred by Claudet's famous daguerreotypes of Wellington, made on his 75th birthday on 1 May 1844. These were put first into the hands of Abraham Solomon who produced an enlarged portrait and this and the daguerreotype were then given to the engraver, H. T. Ryall [Fig 15].[36] However, as this image did not jar with the already dominant forms, it may be said to have reinforced them, especially as it has been said that it was copied extensively by painters and engravers.[37]

Fig 14. Portrait by Count D'Orsay, 1845 in the National Portrait Gallery and reproduced in Wellesley and Steegman, *Iconography*, Plate 39.

Somewhat surprisingly the huge production of single works of all kinds was not matched by a similar surge in the variety of engraved images. Thus whereas a half of all examples of the former were produced in these years only about 40, or a quarter to a fifth, of engraved portraits were published then. The reasons for this discrepancy are once again a matter of conjecture. It may reflect a falling off in demand for medium to large-sized impressions as a result of the generally lower quality of portrait painting by comparison with the later 18th and early 19th centuries. On the other hand, it may reflect the continuing popularity of the 'Rosebery Lawrence'. Thus, it was this earlier work which was engraved in by far the greatest number of forms in this period and which was the image used to illustrate the Duke in Lodge's immensely successful *Portraits*, the first edition of which was completed in 1834 and which ran through a number of subsequent complete editions. Once again it may have been a case of Lawrence driving contemporary painters into the category of being unprofitable as far as print

Fig 15. Engraving by H. T. Ryall based on Claudet's daguerreotypes, 1845, and reproduced in Wellesley and Steegman, *Iconography*, Plate 38.

publishers were concerned.

However, in spite of this particular discrepancy, it is the case that the general impression of the Duke as conveyed in oils and watercolours was faithfully reflected in those that were put into engraved form. This was to some extent ensured by the continuing popularity of the 'Rosebery' Lawrence which emphasised a human, civilian, image. But it was also due to the fact that the most popular artists for engraving were those that continued in that vein. Thus the most popular of all were the canvasses of Briggs and Haydon and Claudet's daguerreotype.

The probable dominance of Lawrence in the field of engraved portraits was matched by the dominance of Doyle and after 1841,of the various artists who produced the 'big cuts' for *Punch*. In general, the images produced by these artists matched those of most of the single works and the engraved versions. Thus, he was usually portrayed in civilian dress and as an elder statesman of a genial, gentle disposition: alarmed occasionally by novel ideas but essentially secure in the knowledge that the Reform acts had not resulted in the toppling of the landed elite and its conservative values. However, although this is the general impression conveyed by an examination of all the Doyle and Punch caricatures, there were differences of emphasis. In the 1830s Doyle took the view that Wellington was something more than an ineffective figurehead and often portrayed him as the guardian of Peel and after l837, the Queen – the implication being that under his stewardship both the Conservative Party and the Constitution would be immune to dangerous notions [Fig 16]. In the 1840s, on the other hand, both Doyle, the *Punch* cartoonists and others such as Henry Heath, presented him on occasion as an old woman, an antique ornament, a Chelsea Pensioner, or a Militia colonel, thereby suggesting that at long last he was out of touch with the real centres of power [Fig 17].

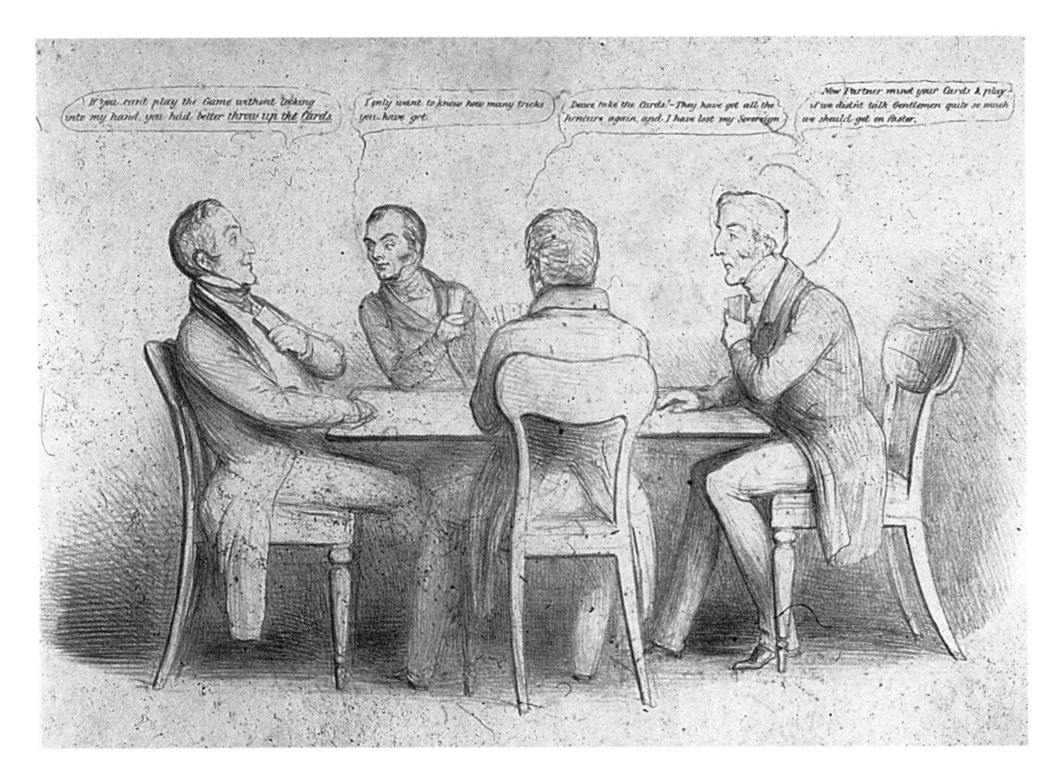

Fig 16. Caricature by John Doyle ['HB'], 'A Cautious Game', published 23 Oct. 1841, no.713.

Fig 17. Caricature by Henry Heath ['HH'], 'Ministerial Free Trade Militia Corps !', published ? 1846, no. 3 in *Political Sketches by HH – (New Sieries* (sic).

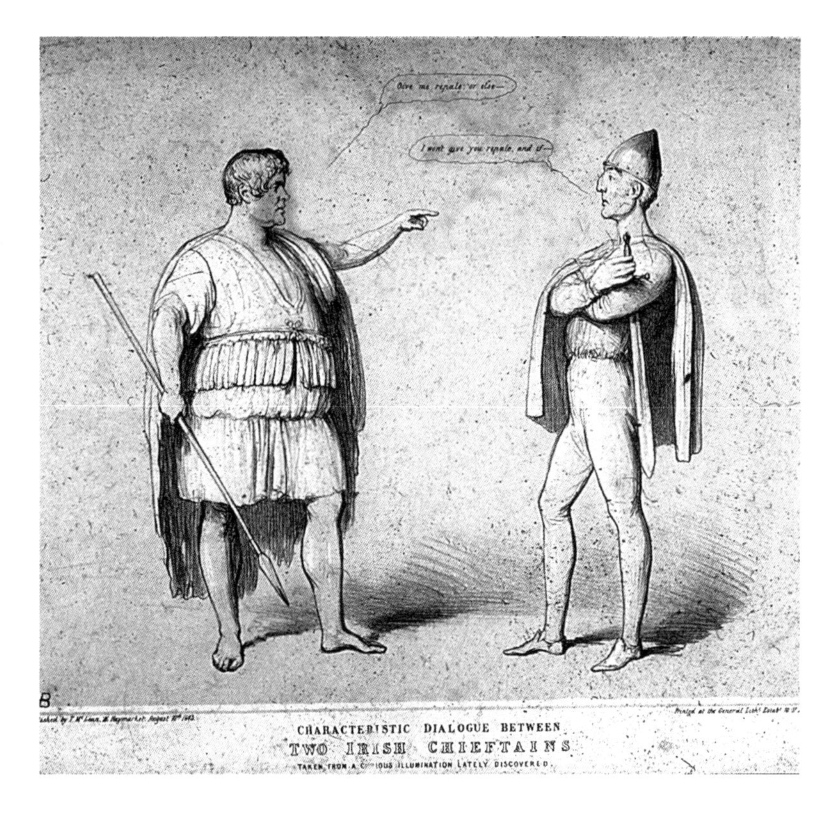

Fig 18. Caricature by John Doyle ['HB'], 'Two Irish Chieftains', published 10 Aug. 1842, no.772

By now of course Wellington was secure in the position of being the great national hero, a station underlined by the enormous scale of his funeral and by the spate of canvasses, busts, statues and engravings that were produced shortly after his death and in the course of the next few years. Portraiture in all its various forms, and caricature after 1829, had undoubtedly helped to give him this stature and in this respect it is interesting that very few productions made any allusion to the fact that he had been born into the Anglo-Irish landed elite, as opposed to the English. To the English it probably did not seem significant as it was assumed that the landed elite was multi-national. To the Irish, on the other hand, it probably was significant and it is perhaps fitting to conclude this commentary on the images with Doyle's direct reference to the subject in his 1842 caricature, 'Two Irish Chieftains' [Fig 18].

* * * * *

What light, then, has this study cast on the reasons why the power of the elite remained largely in tact during Wellington's lifetime – a period of unprecedented economic, social and political change? We have noted that this period was also characterised by a rapid increase in the pictorial representation of the elite, and after 1820, by the diffusion of those representations, particularly through exhibitions and engravings, amongst a larger and more socially diverse public.

This supports the view of other historians that there were cultural reasons for the survival of elite hegemony.

However, the role of pictorial images in this process turns on the question of the messages that they conveyed. In the single case of Wellington, stress has been placed on the need to consider all types of images: to identify not only the most widely known but also the similarities and differences between them. This suggests that engravings of oils and watercolours had the greatest currency and that virtually all of these presented Wellington, naturally enough, in a flattering light. Further, if the focus is restricted to caricatures – the medium disposed to be least flattering – it is remarkable that a transformation in the predominant images of him takes place precisely at the point when the elite was under its greatest strain – between 1828 and 1832. For the previous decade or so the predominant images in terms of their general currency were of a flourishing, arrogant, military figure who was bent on imposing his will on the political world. During and after 'the constitutional revolution' of 1828-32, however, the predominant images become that of an avuncular, kindly, more civilian figure, presiding benignly over changes he had hitherto opposed. Why this happened remains a matter of conjecture. Some would set it in the context of a general transformation in the style and content of caricature after 1820, the reasons for which were changes in both elite behaviour and radical strategy. Others, like myself, would place greater emphasis upon technical developments and the stylistic preferences of artists and publishers. What is not in doubt, however, is that Wellington is the perfect example of the transformation taking place.

NOTES

1. Harling, P. 1996. *The Waning of 'Old Corruption'. The Politics of Economical Reform in Britain, 1779-1846,* London and Oxford, Oxford University Press. For subsequent references to this and other works, I cite the surname followed by a short title. All books were published in London unless otherwise stated.
2. Colley, L. 1992. *Britons,* London and New Haven, Yale University Press.
3. Hake, H and O'Donoghue F. 6 vols.,1908-25. *The British Museum Catalogue of Engraved British Portraits*; George, M.D. 11 vols., 1935-54. *Catalogue of Political and Personal Satires Preserved In The Department of Prints and Drawings In The British Museum*; Kerslake, J. 2 vols., 1977. *Early Georgian Portraits*; Walker, R. 2 vols., 1985. *Regency Portraits*; Ormond, R. 2 vols., 1973. *Early Victorian Portraits.*
4. Donald, D. 1996. *The Age of Caricature. Satirical Prints in the Reign of George III*; Colley, L. 'The Apotheosis of George III', *Past and Present,* no.102, pp.94-129; Fox, Celina. 1987. *Graphic Journalism In England During the 1830s and 1840s*; Yarrington, A. 1987. *The*

Commemoration Of The Hero 1800-1864; Monuments to the British Victors of the Napoleonic Wars.

5. Wellesley, Lord G. and Steegman, J. 1935. *The Iconography of the First Duke of Wellington* (1935); Walker, *Regency*, vol. i, pp.533-542.Other works consulted which deal with the visual representation of the Duke are: Physick, J. 1965. *The Duke of Wellington in Caricature* (1965) and Percival, V. 1969. *The Duke of Wellington : a pictorial survey of his life.*
6. Garlick, K. and Macintyre, A. (Eds.) 1978-. *The Diary of Joseph Farington*, vol. i, pp.132-133.
7. The funeral was reported extensively in the *Times*, 18, 19, 22, 23, 25 and 26 Jan.1830.
8. Drawing on Kerslake, *Early Georgian*, Walker, *Regency* and Ormond, *Early Victorian*. I estimate the numbers in the NPG collection as c.1700 for the period 1714-60; c. 7,000 for 1790-1830; and c.5,000 for 1830-60.
9. Estimating the number of works in different categories is difficult, not least because of the question of whether to include variants and copies. My figures for single works are based on Wellesley and Steegman, *Iconography* and Walker, *Regency*, including the latter's abbreviated list and additions. They include variants and copies.
10. 'Henry Bromley' (Wilson, Anthony). 1793. *A Catalogue of Engraved British Portraits From Egbert The Great to the Present Time*; O'Donoghue and Hake, *Catalogue of Engraved Portraits*; Hind, A.H. 1923. *A History of Engraving and Etching*, pp. 378-388.
11. Hind, *History*, pp. 379-80, 385-86.
12. *Ibid.*, pp. 15-17, 284; Steinberg, S.H. 1961. *Five Hundred Years of Printing*, pp. 276-279. Estimates of the number of impressions from different kinds of plates vary considerably and these figures are approximate. On this point see Garlick and Macintyre, *Farington Diary*, vol. i, p. 26l, sub. 21 Nov.1794; *Times*, 5 Nov. 1828, p.2, col.(f), where the figure of 10,000 impressions is given. On 9 Oct.1830, *The Leeds Mercury* suggested that a double set of steel plates could yield 40,000 first rate impressions.
13. Granger, J. 2 vols., 1824 edition. *Biographical History of England from Egbert the Great to the Revolution*, vol. i, pp. ii-iii.
14. Bromley, *Biographical History*; Noble, M. 1806. *Biographical History of England from Egbert the Great to the death of George I*; Pinkerton, J. 1797. *Iconographia Scotica, or portraits of illustrious persons of Scotland*; Boydell, J. 1789, with further editions 1790-95. *A Catalogue of the Pictures in the Shakespeare Gallery, Pall-Mall.* Boydell also published a volume of 'illustrious' heads in 1811.An imitator of Lodge was the prolific cleric, the Rev. Henry Stebbing, who published a similar 'portrait gallery' in 1829.
15. In 1827 a Brighton bookshop, Taylor & Son of 134 North St., was selling *Forget Me Not* and *Friendship's Offering*, each of which contained 13 plates, for 12/- each, *Brighton Gazette*, 27 Dec.1827.
16. Price, R.G.G. 1957. *A History of Punch*, pp. 43-45, 356-57.
17. This estimate is based on George, *Catalogue*, vol. xi and an analysis of the caricatures of John Doyle ('HB'), and those appearing in *The Comic Almanac* and *Punch*.
18. Wellesley and Steegman, *Iconography*, p. ix.
19. Wheatley, H.B. 1897. *Historical Portraits*, p.114.
20. *Aris's Birmingham Gazette*, 3 Mar.1828; *The Tyne Mercury*, 24 June 1828; *The Norfolk Chronicle* and *Norwich Gazette*, 7 Nov.1829; *Birmingham Journal*, 2 Jan.1830.
21. *Times*, 13 Apr. 1829; *Birmingham Journal*, 2 Jan. 1830.

22. *Times*, l0 Feb 1829, p.1, clm. (a). The prices for proof impressions before and after lettering were 5 and 3 guineas respectively. McLean's monthly sheets of caricatures sold for 3/- uncoloured and 6/- coloured.
23. For typical lists of prints and prices in the late 1820s see *The Manchester Times*, 21 Nov.1828, 2 Jan.1829. Prices ranged from 1/- to £6.6.0. A steel engraving of George IV was distributed free to early subscribers to the *Country Times*, in 1830, see *Leeds Mercury*, l3 Nov.1830.
24. Price, *Punch*, pp.25-26.
25. Based on Wellesley and Steegman, *Iconography* and Walker, *Regency* including the latter's abbreviated list and additions.
26. Wellesley and Steegman, *Iconography*, p. xi.
27. Walker, *Regency*, vol. i, pp. 533-34.
28. *European Magazine*, 1808; *British Neptune*, 1809; *Royal Chronicle*, 1810; *Military Panorama*,1812; *Military Chronicle*,1812 and 1813.
29. In 1809, 1811, 1812, and twice in 1813.
30. According to Wellesley and Steegman, *Iconography*, p.56, the whereabouts of the original are unknown.
31. *Ibid.*, p. 24.
32. *Ibid.*, p. 28.
33. Harling, *Old Corruption*, passim.
34. Donald, *Caricature*, see in particular, pp.184-85.
35. Walker, *Regency*, vol. i, pp.538-42.
36. *Ibid.*, vol. i, p.540.
37. Press notice by Jean Liddiard for the exhibition of Claudet daguerreotypes at the NPG, March-April, 1985.

RICHARD CASTLE'S DESIGNS FOR CASTLE COOLE, CO FERMANAGH

DAVID J GRIFFIN

THE RECORDED ARCHITECTURAL HISTORY of Castle Coole during the eighteenth century is generally accepted as follows: The present Castle Coole, James Wyatt's masterpiece, was built between 1790 and 1798 on a different site to replace the house erected circa. 1709 by James Corry (c1683-1718) to the designs of John Curle, whose signed and dated drawings are recorded.[1] (Figs 1-5) This house, known as Old Castle Coole, was destroyed by fire in 1797, one year after the completion of the present house. However the discovery of five designs by Richard Castle (c1690/3-1751) in the collection of the Earl of Belmore[2] show that Castle produced designs for a proposed rebuilding of the house during the long tenure of Col. Margetson Armar (1726-1773), guardian and cousin of Leslie Corry, who was under-age when he inherited the house from his father John in 1726.

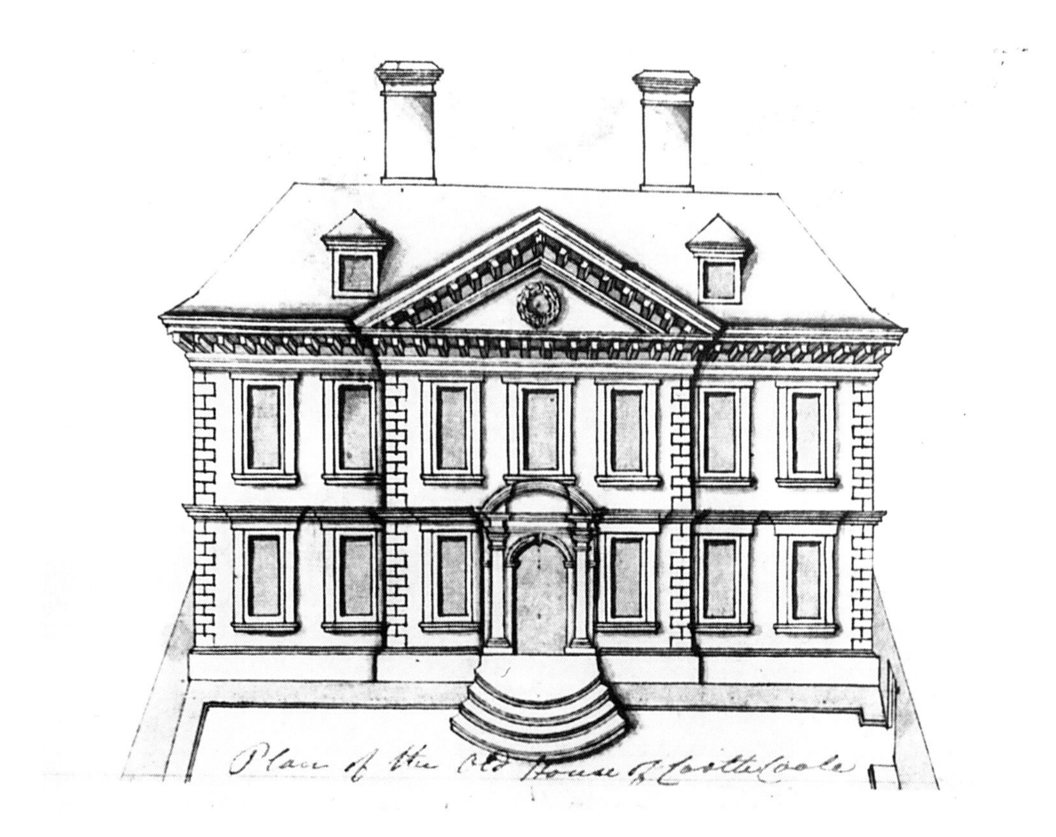

Fig 1. John Curle: Front elevation of old house at Castle Coole 1709

Fig 2. John Curle: Side elevation of old house at Castle Coole 1709

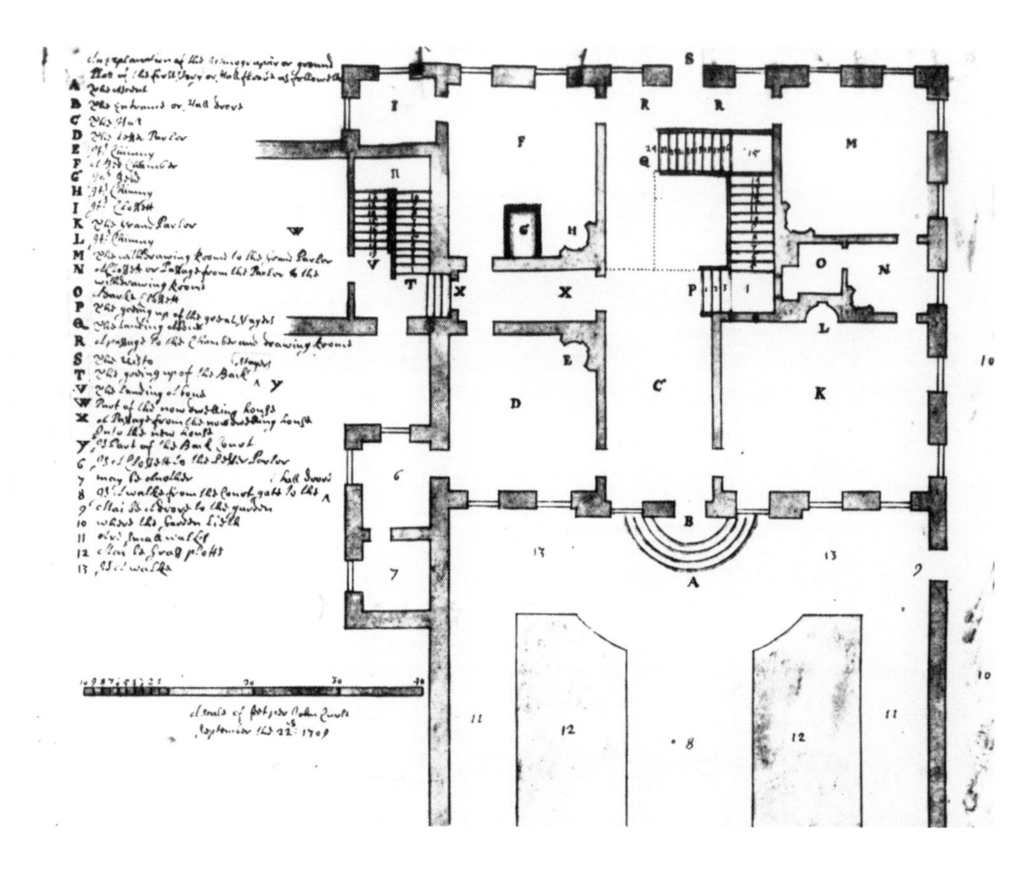

Fig 3. John Curle: Ground floor plan of old house at Castle Coole 1709

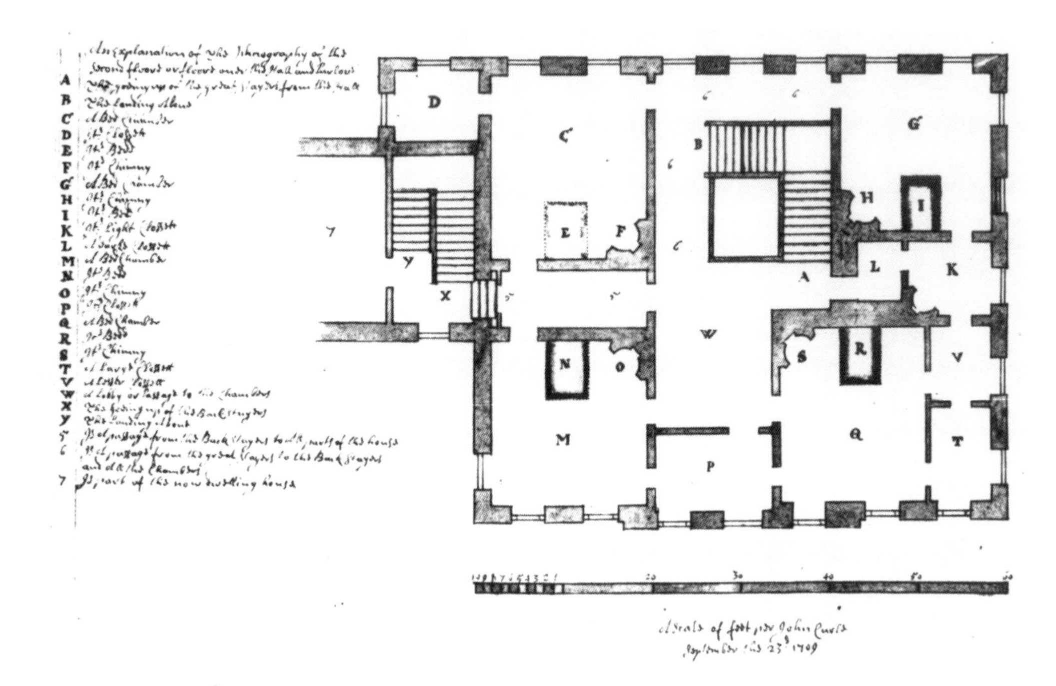

Fig 4. John Curle: First floor plan of old house at Castle Coole 1709

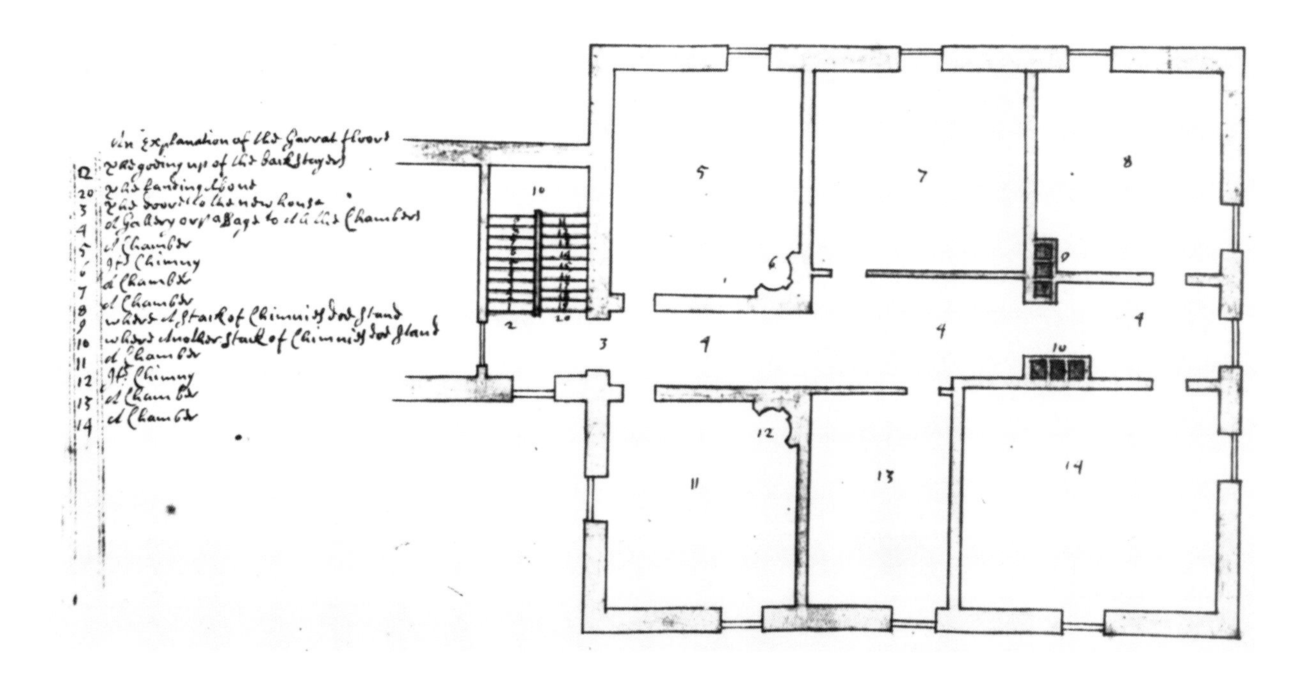

Fig 5. John Curle: Garret or attic floor plan of old house at Castle Coole 1709

Armar was in control of the estate from 1718 until 1741 when he eventually inherited the property. It is most probable that it was at this time that he first turned his attention to rebuilding the earlier house.

Richard Castle was of continental protestant stock (see Dixon this volume) and was brought to Ireland by Sir Gustavius Hume M.P. in 1728 to build a house at Castle Hume, also in County Fermanagh. In March of the same year the Surveyor General of Ireland, Sir Edward Lovett, while busy at work on the new Parliament House in Dublin, wrote recommending Castle to those contemplating new country houses:

His name is Castle, he is a present employed in building a House for Sir Gustavius Hume near Enniskillen but I hope will find more and constant employment, I thought I could not do a better service than mentioning this to gentlemen who may have occasion for such a person[3]

Castle Hume was destroyed by fire in 1729, rebuilt presumably by Castle and demolished in the early nineteenth century. Now little more than his stable block remains.

Four of the five surviving drawings, namely the front elevation and three floor plans by Castle (Figs 6-9) form a set or part of a set for a compact three bay, two storey villa with raised basement, measuring 59 feet 4 inches x 50 feet 6 inches as against Curle's house, which measured 60 feet x 50 feet, approximately the same size.

Fig 6. Richard Castle: Proposed elevation first scheme for new house at Castle Coole

Fig 7. Richard Castle: Proposed cellar or basement floor plan first scheme for new house at Castle Coole

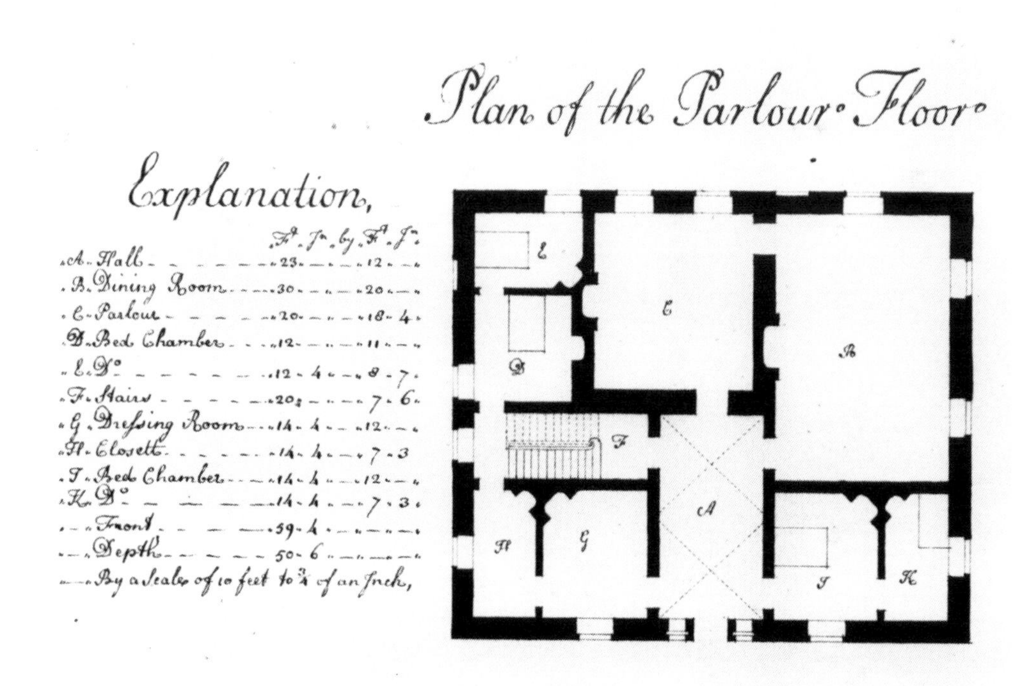

Fig 8. Richard Castle: Proposed parlour or ground floor plan first scheme for new house at Castle Coole

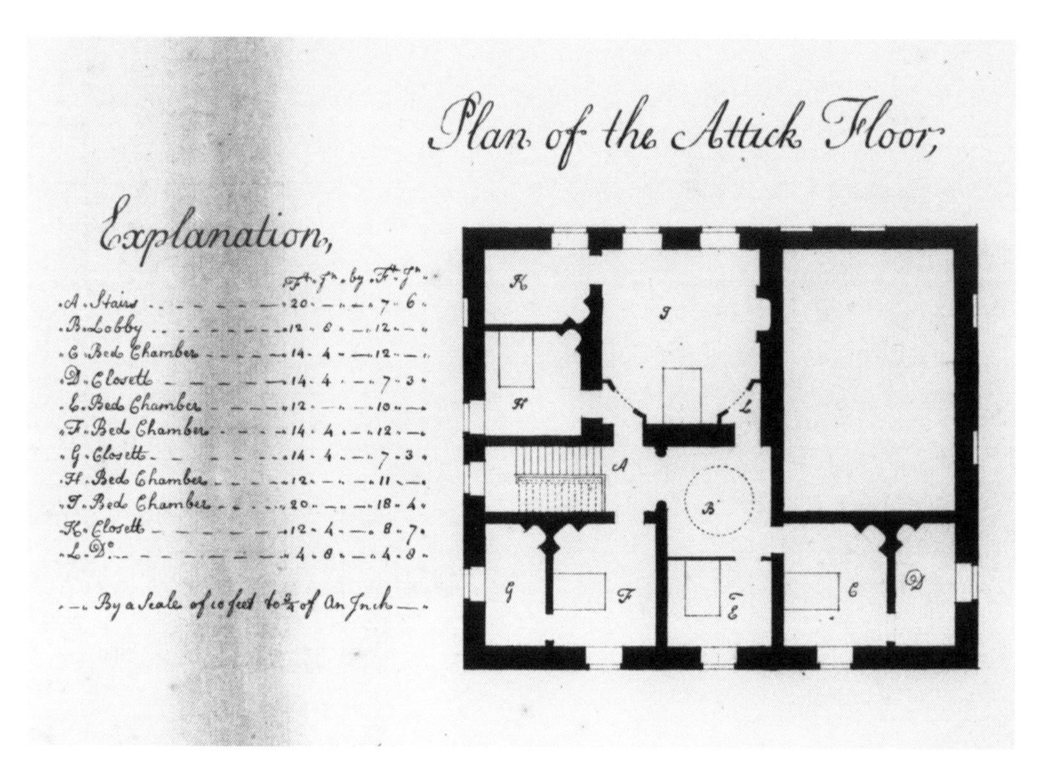

Fig 9. Richard Castle: Proposed attic or first floor plan first scheme for new house at Castle Coole

The vaulted basement (Fig 7) was to contain the usual offices, kitchen, scullery, larders, butler's pantry, wine and ale vaults and a servants lodging room and hall. A staircase was to give access to the ground and first floors. The parlour or ground floor (Fig 8), entered by a tripartite doorcase, was to have a groin vaulted entrance hall, a parlour and a large dining room taller in height, taking up the space above, unusual for taking up part of the attic or first floor, four bedrooms and a dressing room. The attic or first floor (Fig 9) was to have a central top lit lobby as at Castle's (later?) Bellinter, Co. Meath and Russborough, Co. Wicklow, where it was reached from the staircase via an opening flanked by engaged columns. Five bedrooms and closets are shown. The main bedroom in the centre of the garden front has an apsial end, a feature later used by Castle at Russborough, Co. Wicklow.

However, when we come to study Castle's fifth drawing 'General plan of House and Offices' (Fig 10) we can have no doubts regarding its proposed location, for Castle's drawing shows the layout of adjoining avenues confirmed by an estate map of circa. 1783, still at Castle Coole.[4]

This beautifully tinted drawing includes a ground plan for a house measuring 63 feet 8 inches x 42 feet 9 inches in depth. The seven bay house is shown as having a ground floor above a raised basement reached by a broad flight of steps. Unfortunately the plan of the house, unlike the attached wings

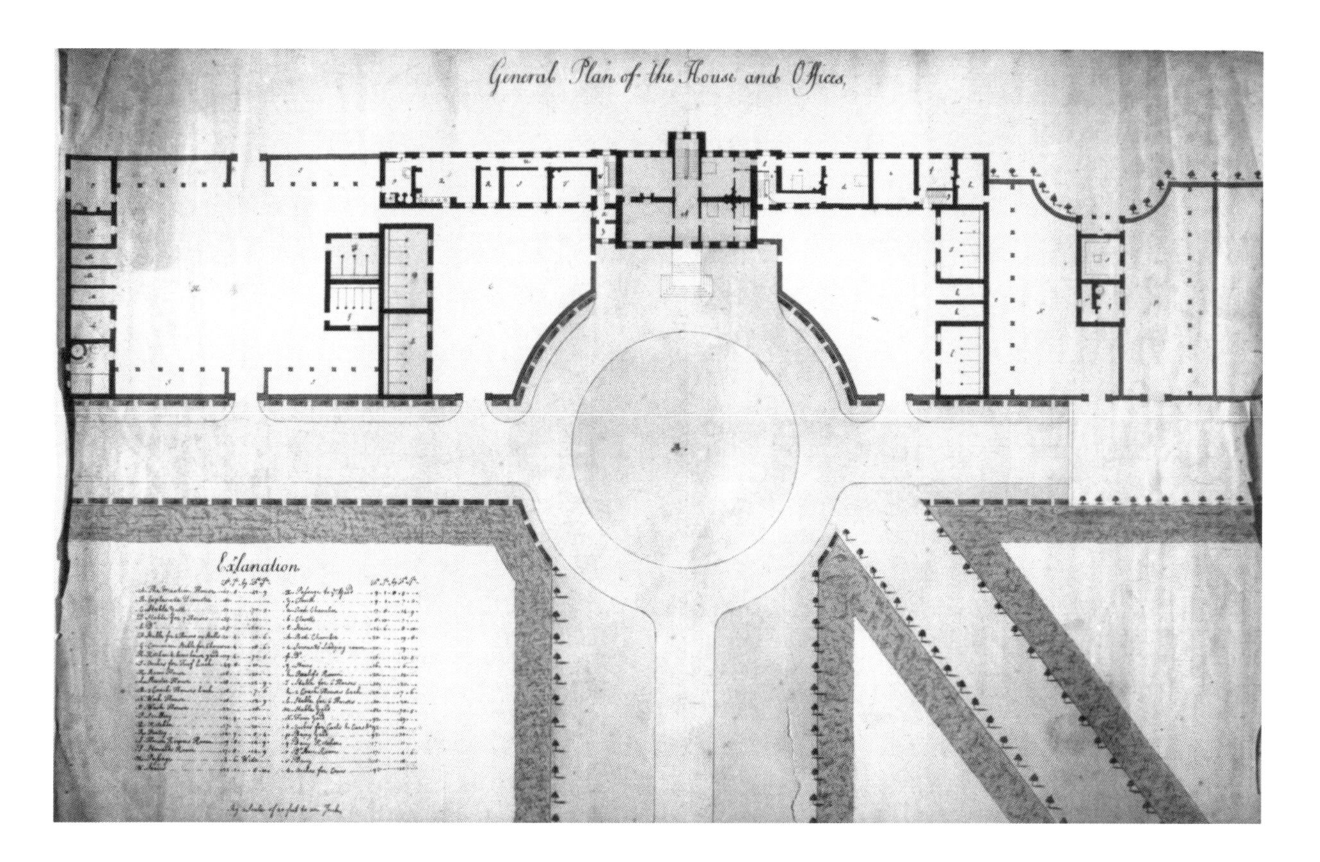

Fig 10. Richard Castle: General plan of the house and offices Plan of house as executed?

and adjacent building, is unlettered and therefore has no key identifying room uses, perhaps there was a separate set of drawings for it. The central hall is flanked to the right by suites of bedrooms, dressing rooms and closets, and to the left by two large reception rooms. A two bay staircase is partly contained in a central two bay projection to the rear. The map of circa.1783 shows a house with a similar central rear projection and a block plan of buildings to the left, not dissimilar to Castle's stable block, suggesting that his scheme may have been carried out at least in part. It is interesting and perhaps worth noting that in this drawing Castle depicts the surrounding trees in perspective, a device used by him on a drawing for proposed alterations at Carton, Co. Kildare circa. 1739.[5]

Whether either of Castle's schemes were ever built, his involvement at Castle Coole is documented in the Ordnance Survey Memoirs for Enniskillen Parish, written by Lieutenant John Clayton in 1834. Here there is a detailed history and description of Castle Coole, noting that the architect of the previous house was 'Castles, the man who built Castle Hume of Devenish Parish'.[6]

ACKNOWLEDGEMENTS:

The Earl of Belmore for permission to photograph architectural drawings in his possession. Edward McParland for first drawing my attention to the presence of drawings by Castle at Castle Coole. David Davison, photographer. All photographs are from the collection of the Irish Architectural Archive, Dublin.

NOTES

1. Original mislaid, photographs are in collection the Irish Architectural Archive, Dublin
2. The Earl of Belmore, Castle Coole, Co. Fermanagh.
3. Collection the National Library of Ireland Ms. D20 209
4. McErlean,T. 1984. *The Historical Development of the Park at Castle Coole*, National Trust Northern Ireland Region, pp.46-7.
5. Collection the Irish Architectural Archive, R.I.A.I. Murray Collection, No138.
6. See Day, A. and McWilliams, P. (eds.) 1980. *Ordnance Survey Memoirs of Ireland, Volume four, Parishes of County Fermanagh 1834-5. Enniskillen & Upper Lough Erne.* Belfast and Dublin, The Institute of Irish Studies and the Royal Irish Academy, p.68.

SIR CHARLES TAMERLANE PC A PERSONAL MEMOIR

ANNE DAVEY ORR

HIS LIST OF ACCOMPLISHMENTS is staggering: Chairman International Fund for Ireland, Chairman Northern Ireland Housing Executive, Northern Ireland's representative on the National Trust for over twenty years, the longest serving member of any National Trust committee in the UK, founder and President of the Ulster Architectural Heritage Society, founder of Hearth which has restored over 100 buildings of architectural merit. He has been involved with Europa Nostra and ICOMOS for many years.

In a grand celebration of the contribution which Sir Charles Brett C.B.E. has made to life in Northern Ireland – and Ireland, the National Trust and the Ulster Architectural Heritage Society hosted a special gala dinner at Malone House in Belfast on 30 October 1998. It marked the knight's seventieth year. Tributes were paid to Sir Charles by the Lord O'Neill, Dr. Edward McParland, and Hugh Dixon, among many others.

Sir Charles opened his response to the glowing tributes by quoting Samuel Taylor Coleridge: 'Swans sing before they die 'twould be no bad thing if some should die before they sing.' Sir Charles continues to 'sing' in his beautifully produced Buildings of North County Down published in June 2002 by the UAHS with photographs by Anthony C.W. Merrick.

For those of his many friends privileged to be at the grand gala dinner, Sir Charles was in particularly good voice on that special night. It was Lord Antrim, he said, who invited him onto the National Trust. When Charles asked him what books he should read, the good lord answered, "There aren't any." Charles determined that he would write them himself. That reply brought into existence Northern Ireland's leading architectural historian. He is pre-eminent in this field having, with *Buildings of North County Down*, completed a triumvirate of splendid publications which includes *Buildings of Antrim* and *Buildings of Armagh* – all attracting glowing reviews in *Country Life*, the *Times Literary Supplement* and *The Irish Times.*

Just as the man attracted glowing tributes from his friends and admirers back in 1998, Dubliner Dr. Edward McParland said that he had been asked by the National Trust's Peter Marlow to be 'southern' in his tribute to Sir Charles. The great abiding links between the Dublin civic group and the UAHS over the past thirty years, he said, had been presided over by Sir Charles and Kevin Nolan. Blowing the genteel civility of the world of conservation to smithereens he compared southerners to the followers of Genghiz Khan and northerners to the followers of Tamerlane and the followers of the Golden Horn, he described the many Charlies he knows. Among them Elegant Charlie – referring to the essay he wrote for Maurice Craig which had 41 foot notes. Stoic Charlie – who got through the Ulster Workers' Strike with candles and claret. Charlie of the Clocks – a stay at Charlie's house is full of quarter hourly chimes. Charlie the Belfastman following in the footsteps of his father and grandfather and last but not least the Charlie that everyone recognises – Charlie the Awkward Bugger. Enter Tamerlane.

"We all admire that certain element in Charlie – the forethought that leads to an even handedness." Some, he said, might like to raise a glass to Charlie the interdenominational, anti-cleric or to the Charlie who like his great grandfather, then aged sixty-one in 1906, hoped that his name would be remembered. In the case of the great grandson of that there is no doubt.

But where I asked myself was the Charlie I knew – Charlie PC? In his response to the tributes of his friends Sir Charles said that he was delighted to see so many young people involved in conservation at his dinner. There were several good reasons for taking up architectural history, he said, the first and most common is snobbery because it gets you into all the great houses; the second is social climbing and the third is the hope that eventually when you knock on all those doors a nice young lady will come out naked. This, he said, had happened to him twice – but he did not elaborate on those experiences except to say that one young woman had told him what he could do with himself.

As many other people had on that evening, Sir Charles paid tribute to his wife Joyce who, he said, had devoted forty-five years to conservation – mainly conserving him. His interest in architectural history he traced back to the Ruskin Lectures given during his time at Oxford by Sir Kenneth Clark. That inspiration led to the creation of a strong lobbying group without whose activities many of Northern Ireland's most noteworthy buildings would have been lost. It led to the black and white surveys which are now invaluable records, and the first flowering of a distinguished history of publication. What a debt historians and

Fig 1. The launch of the Ulster Architectural Heritage Society's book on Clandeboye. From left to right Dr. Bill Maguire, The Marquess of Dufferin and Ava, Robert McKinstry, the Marchioness of Dufferin and Ava, Charles Brett and Peter Rankin.

architectural corespondents owe to him.

On that night in October, fellow writer, Hugh Dixon, reminded everyone of the other force in Charlie's early life – Socialism. Had things been different in Northern Ireland, there is no telling what Charlie's membership of the Labour Party would have led to. Politics' loss is conservation's gain.

What people tend to forget about Sir Charles Brett C.B.E. is that while he was engaging in this unstoppable activity and forging an unassailable reputation as an architectural historian of wit and erudition, he was a full time solicitor – and a businessman. He also sketched and doodled, taught himself to work in gesso, tended his roses and maintained an active and critical interest in the visual arts.

I can't remember precisely when I first met Sir Charles but it was certainly during my days as a designer with the BBC and was most likely to have been in the BBC Club in Linenhall Street. Charlie had soon persuaded me, in all my 1960s psychedelia, to join one of the National Trust committees. In those days I had no idea that in later years, when I became editor of the *Ulster Architect* magazine, Charlie would become one of my most prized contributors. Nor did I suspect that after a stint with the BBC in London and a brief spell in Kilkenny, I would sit on the Regional Committee of the National Trust alongside him for nine years. During those years there were many hot issues such as the style to adopt for the restoration of Castle Coole which led to the 'germolene pink' row. When eventually I stayed in a Palladian villa bare of anything but intrinsic decoration, and the detritus of family history, I realised that he had been right in advocating a classical treatment for the interior. The memories which are most vivid of those years are of National Trust Charlie swathed in smoke from his untipped cigarette at Rowallane when everyone broke for tea. What I have come to recognise in Charlie over the years is a man whose abilities are hard to match – the very universality of them creating for him, perhaps, a kind of isolation which is sometimes compounded by Awkward Bugger Charlie.

Unexpectedly I received a book in the post recently by an author whose work I did not know. It had been sent to me by Charlie. Robertson Davies was a novelist, who, like Charlie was educated at Oxford. But he wasn't just a novelist, he was a playwright, a literary critic and essayist. When he died in 1995, Malcolm Bradbury said of him in *The Times*: 'Davies encompassed all the great elements of life.....His novels combined deep seriousness and psychological enquiry with fantasy and exuberant mirth.' That epitaph could in some respects so easily apply to Sir Charles Brett C.B.E. – except that it leaves out entirely Sir Charles PC.

It is Sir Charles PC who likes to gossip and can be irascible. When he was writing regularly for the *Ulster Architect* magazine he was prone to point out the many typographical errors which enabled the magazine to challenge *The Guardian* in that field: one he delighted in was copula for cupola. We photographed him in front of Rose Cottage when it had been restored by Hearth and while I am sure the quality of its architecture was uppermost in his mind, the comment I remember was: "Wouldn't it make a perfect place for a mistress!"

It was that Charlie who wrote a nostalgic article for *Ulster Architect* magazine about the offices of L'Estrange and Brett in Chichester Street, Belfast, on the occasion of the practice moving to new premises. Although semi-retired at the time, the move from the building with which his family had been associated for so many years, was obviously a wrench.

The person who really tuned into Charlie PC was my daughter. He was to give her a really stiff interview in preparation for her university entrance to study law. "You will grill her Charlie, won't you? Don't be easy on her."

My daughter, whom I expected to find in tears, met me beaming with the words, "Oh mum, he's a real pussy cat." So Sir Charles PC he has been to us ever since.

I meet Charlie irregularly for lunch. We chat and gossip and talk of old acquaintances. After a few glasses of good wine he isn't exactly feline but there might be the odd hint of a purr. I feel privileged and enjoy immensely being part of his 'territory'. The book he sent me by Robertson Davies was called *What's Bred in the Bone.* What an extraordinary person was bred in the bones of Sir Charles Tamerlane PC.

SOME COUNTRY CHURCHES BY JOSEPH WELLAND

ALISTAIR ROWAN

THE NAME OF JOSEPH WELLAND is well known to Irish architectural historians. Born in Midleton, Co. Cork on 8 May 1798, he was the son of William Welland, head agent to George Brodrick, 4th Viscount Midleton, who had responsibility for the new buildings on Lord Midleton's estates, including at least part of Cobh harbour. For almost twenty years, between 1802 and 1821, William Welland supervised repairs and alterations to Cashel Palace for Lord Midleton's brother, Charles Brodrick, DD, Archbishop of Cashel, and it was through the influence of the Archbishop that Joseph Welland became a pupil and subsequently an assistant to John Bowden, architect to the Board of First Fruits in Dublin.[1] Bowden also had a large secular practice and Welland, according to his Obituary in *The Dublin Builder*, 'enjoyed an extensive share of business' with responsibility for 'numerous works' including Monaghan Gaol and Court House.[2] In the late 1820s he is noted as the architect to the Commissioners of Education in Ireland building rural schools in Carlow and Cork.[3]

On Bowden's death in 1821 it would seem that Welland inherited at least some of his secular projects and clients. At the same time William Welland asked Brodrick to recommend his son as Bowden's successor for the Board of First Fruits post, and, after it had been decided that the position should be divided between four architects each of whom was to be responsible for an ecclesiastical province, Joseph was given charge of the province of Tuam. He retained this position when the Board was reconstructed as the Ecclesiastical Commissioners in 1833, took on a more general role in 1837[4] and was given sole responsibility for the whole country when the architect's department was further reorganised and centralised in 1843. It may have been at this point that the Commissioners introduced the requirement that their architect should undertake no outside work, a limitation which meant that Joseph was to become, the most significant architect of the Church of Ireland in the early and mid-Victorian age. According to his obituary, he designed over 100 new churches as well as carrying out alterations and enlargements to existing structures throughout the whole country.

Sir Charles Brett's *Buildings of Country Antrim* gives an account of one modest, yet characteristic, new work by Welland, Christ Church, Ballynure, built between 1856 and 1858. The same author's *Buildings of County Armagh* includes Welland's St. Saviour's Battlehill, Portadown, of 1856 to 1858. Both of these buildings represents an aspect of the Commissioners' architect's work, quite characteristic of the range of his activities, for what Joseph Welland did was to establish a clearly identifiable template for Irish church building in the nineteenth century and then to impose it. Indeed it was his destiny to stamp a new image on churches of the Anglican communion in Ireland, as enduring and instantly recognisable as its immediate predecessor, the late Georgian tower-and-hall churches promoted with grant-aid from the Board of First Fruits and put up on many an Irish hilltop, primarily to reassure ascendancy families that though they might have ceded power to Westminster, their way of life was not to be threatened by the passing of the Act of Union. Welland, while working with Bowden, began in this tradition, but in the late 1830s had moved to a more contemporary Gothic style which immediately became his own.

It is the ubiquitous and prolific nature of Welland's activity as the architect of the Ecclesiastical Commissioners which has perhaps obscured his remarkable ability. There is no county in Ireland where his work, or the work of his office and clerks, is not to be seen. As tastes in the pattern of worship changed, Welland added porches, robing rooms, chancels, planned new side aisles, replaced windows, made space for organs or, at the very least, re-ordered the interiors of older churches by providing new seating of pitch-pine pews with terracotta tiles on the aisleways between them, pine reading desks and Perpendicular panelled pulpits. It thus came about that a standard type of furnishing and finish was to be encountered throughout the Church of Ireland which, like the arrangements which characterised the buildings of a particular Order in the Middle Ages – Augustinian, Benedictine, Cistercian or Franciscan – or the rooms and planning of luxury hotel chains today, spoke of the norms and standard expectations of their time.

When Welland died, his son William and a district inspector from within the organisation, William Gillespie, were appointed joint architects to the Ecclesiastical Commissioners in his place. Although this outcome was not unexpected, professional outrage at the choice of two in-house candidates spilt over into the columns of *The Irish Times*. A correspondent, signing himself 'A Churchman' observed that candidates of calibre would have been deterred from applying for the post by the 'absurd condition' that they would be required to work exclusively for the Commissioners, 'absurd, because of the miserable equivalent offered in the way of a salary; to wit £600'.[5]

Of course Joseph Welland did not design all the buildings for the established church between 1843 and 1860. He worked through local assistants and clerks[6] and stepped aside when a large and influential congregation or prosperous local landowner wished to employ a particular architect. The Ecclesiastical Commission was however a government agency, and, where public money was involved, Welland, as its architect, had an obligation to review each proposal and to ensure that funds were properly spent. It is this role that must explain the confusing and conflicting accounts of the authorship of different parish churches that are sometimes found. It is none the less clear that Welland himself was the driving force that established the architectural style of the Church of Ireland in the early Victorian age. Inevitably, given the scale of the operations he had to direct, a certain way of doing things, an office style, set standard norms. Experienced assistants, clerks of works and even well-tried builders, such as Walter Doolin of Dublin, could be trusted to take design decisions within an established template: the shape and number of buttresses, the choice of a plain or cusped lancet, the use of a flat or shoulder arch on a doorway, the choice between plate tracery for an east window or a group of graded lancets, or the subtle difference between a trefoil as opposed to a quatrefoil at the apex of a gable. All these elements could be changed and substituted at will according to local circumstances and requirements. A Welland church did not cease to be the work of its chief designer simply because some elements were added or taken away in the process of its construction. It was the broad idea, the massing, the innate feeling for the shape and effectiveness of a buttress, the essential impact of the form that he determined and bequeathed to every county in the country. Though he had 'to contend against the difficulty imposed by limited funds', in the opinion of one contemporary, 'his designs [were] marked by a truthfulness and suitability of character, an effectiveness of detail and imposing proportions'.[7]

Welland's life deserves a full biography, for there are many questions which cannot be answered here. In the first place it seems remarkable that, from the relative isolation of Ireland, he should prove to be among the very first architects to understand the real significance of Pugin's ideas and to adopt completely the aesthetic principles put forward by Pugin's books and architecture.[8] Did Welland make study trips to England or was it the printed word and limited example of Pugin's early Irish buildings which caused his architectural transformation? Comparison of some of his designs for rural churches may illustrate both the distance he travelled and the essential economies that operated within a minority

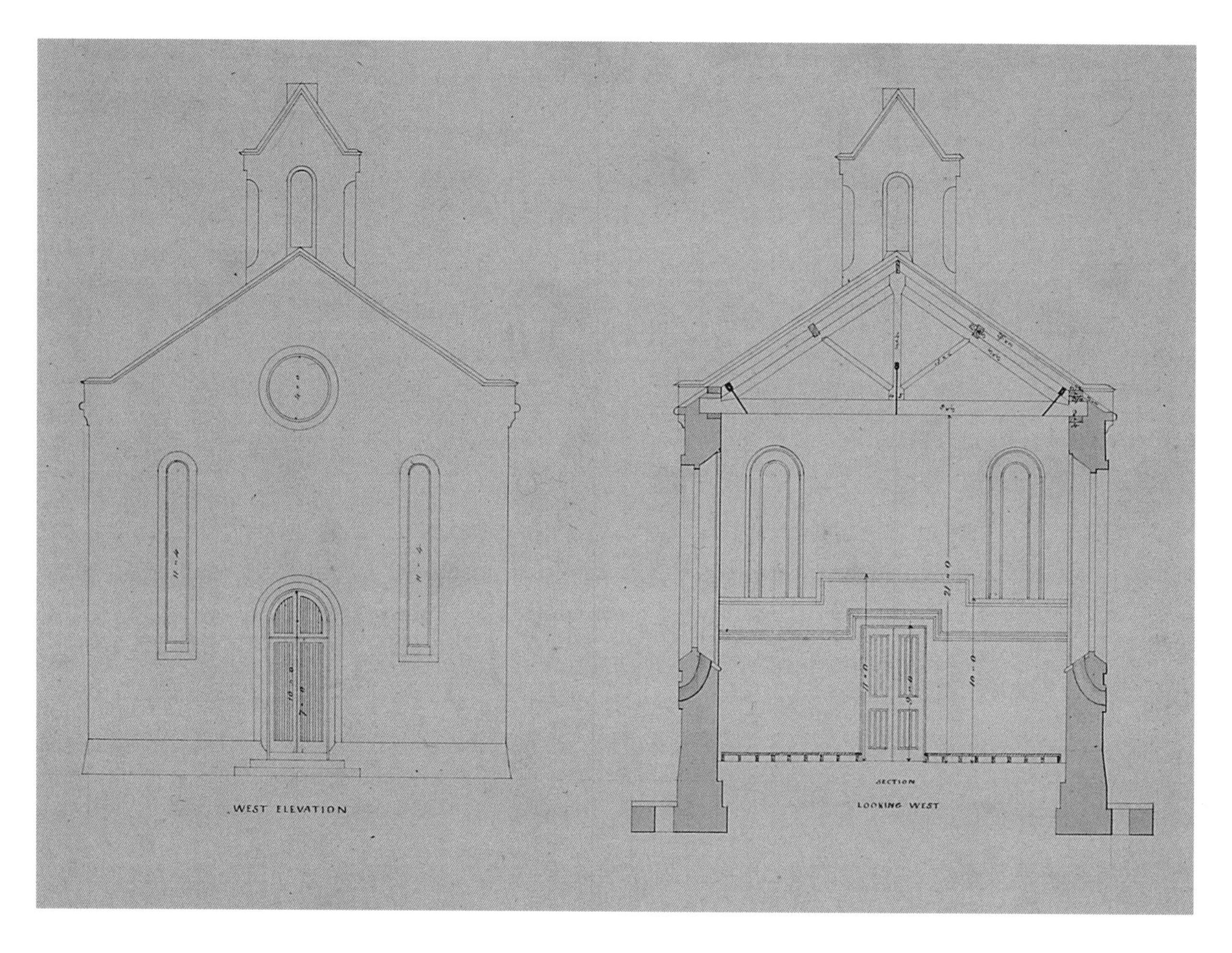

Fig 1. Joseph Welland, Design drawings for Church at Kilkenny West, Co. Meath: entrance front and cross section through the church c. 1838

denomination, even though it was always a privileged one. It may also provide some insight into the ways of Irish rural life in the mid-Victorian age.

The change which took place in Welland's architectural style is quite remarkable. Two rural churches built to his designs in the later 1830s, Kilkenny West in Co. Meath (Fig 1) and Eglish in Co. Offaly, are creditable works of a routine, even humdrum character. John Bowden, Welland's master, knew how to design more attractive and better articulated churches than these, yet for the Diocese of Meath Welland, then almost 40, was content to propose two plain rectangular stone buildings, roughcast, with low-pitched gables like any farm building and minimal dressed stone detail. Both churches have narrow round-headed lancet windows lighting each side, a bellcote at the apex of the entrance gable, and an orderly rectangular interior. Nothing is ground-breaking here.[9]

Move forward some ten years, however, and Welland's manner has changed completely. It is not a matter of the plan, since the needs of the Church of Ireland in the 1840s were essentially the same as they had been in the 1830s.

What was still required was a long, well-lit hall with a rational juxtaposition of lectern, pulpit and altar. Welland served the interests of the clergy equally well in both periods. What is different in the later work is the way he has envisaged the appearance of a rural church and how it is detailed. Three more churches in the Diocese of Meath may make this point: they are the churches at Balrath Boyne, Kildalkey and Laracor.[10] Like a great deal of Welland's work, the buildings are essentially similar, so that it is a matter of the choice of motif and placement of individual elements that distinguishes one from the other – or indeed from the example in Co. Antrim that Brett writes about, Christ Church at Ballynure.

Fig 2. Joseph Welland. Design drawings for Church at Balrath Boyne, Co. Meath: plan, east, west and south elevations. Ink and watercolour on cartridge paper. 1857

All these churches are long, stone-built halls, marked as a place of worship by the positioning of a bellcote on the ridge of the west gable, and by the judicious use of a limited vocabulary of Gothic elements. (Figs 2, 3 and 4) Two porches, differently detailed, project from different positions, on the north and south sides; one is for the congregation to enter the church, the other, nearer to the

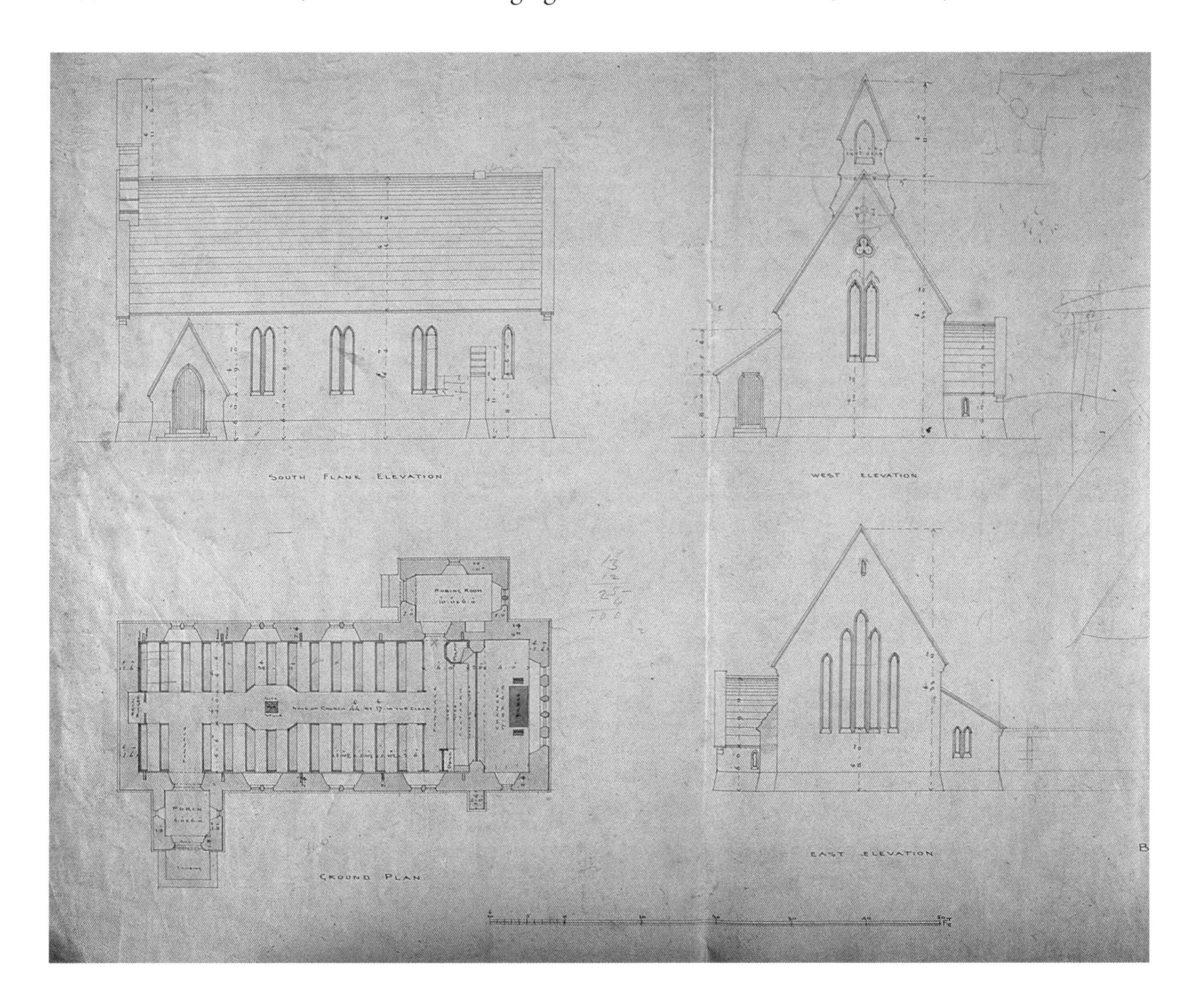

Fig 3. Joseph Welland. Design drawings for Church at Kildalkey, Co. Meath: plan, east, west and south elevations, with detail of trefoil window. Ink on tracing paper. 1855

chancel, is for the clergy and doubles as a robing room. The robing room doorway is the less important, so that, whereas a Georgian architect might have welcomed the opportunity to build two porches in a symmetrical way, Welland gives the different functions a distinctly architectural expression by making the porch for the congregation a broad gabled extension, which breaks forward from the side of the church roof and has an arched doorway, while the entrance for the clergy is played down, either as a modest addition with a lean-to roof or else as a smaller gabled porch, whose roof ridge comes below the line of the eaves of the church wall. Unlike his designs of the 1830s, in all these churches Welland is at pains to express the different functions of the different parts of his building. For the main body of the church he uses the high, 60 degree pitch of a medieval roof which contrasts with the separate roofs of the porches and which is (with one

Fig 4. Joseph Welland. Design drawings for Church at Laracor, Co. Meath: plan, east west and south elevations, with selected details. Ink on tracing paper. Not dated

exception) visually distinct from the chancel. The chancel roof is stepped down slightly so that the buildings, when seen from the east end, appear as a tightly knit conjunction of independent units with one steep gable rising above the other.

The elements which Welland assembled are changed from one design to another, partly for the sake of variety itself. Much depended on the money a congregation had to spend. Some churches, like Laracor, could be stripped down to a minimum so that Welland's most expressive motif – one that he took from Pugin – the diagonal stepped buttress, is entirely omitted and replaced, in its role of giving a sense of solidity to the structure, by no more than a pronounced batter to the lower courses of the walls. At Balrath Boyne a single buttress is introduced towards the east end of the south wall, marking the position of the chancel arch in the interior and, unusually, a stone stud is set on the ridge of the roof for the same purpose. At Kildalkey there must have been much more money to spend. Here every external angle was marked by a buttress, double-stepped for the body of the church and single-stepped on the two porches. The nugget-like quality of Welland's architecture was further enhanced here by the addition, under the west gable, of a projecting stone box to provide a space, accessed from within the church, for a person to ring the bell. The same projecting box occurs at Ballynure – where it is given a slate instead of a stone roof – but at Laracor and Balrath Boyne the parishioners had to make do with a simple recess on the inside wall at the end of the nave, with a timber screen to separate it from the church. The ceiling of all these churches make a positive use of exposed carpentry with scissors trusses supporting purlins and rafters. At Kildalkey, where the chancel was built on a polygonal plan, the exposed rafters seemed to form a corona around the altar.

For about a decade, from the mid 1850s to the early 1860s, Welland's office made copies on tracing paper – a new material for architectural draughtsmen which enjoyed some vogue at that time – of the drawings which were sent out to contractors. The set of designs which survive for Laracor and Kildalkey are in this medium and show a surprising juxtaposition of plans, elevations and selected details, traced, no doubt, from the larger number of paper sheets which will have been prepared for the builders' use. They are bound together as long flat books in dark brown covers with the name of the church painted on the cover in bold sans serif lettering.[11] Tracing paper becomes notoriously fragile and it would seem that, in later years, the office reverted to the more traditional cartridge paper even for the copies that were kept in Dublin.

Occasionally the cost of these smaller rural churches by Welland is recorded but the process whereby his ideas were transferred into a three-dimensional reality is not, like most country houses and larger public buildings, recorded in any known set of building accounts.[12] Faced with this lack of information we would have little means of understanding how the building work progressed were it not for the fortunate circumstance that one landowner in Co. Wexford was an amateur photographer who recorded the construction of one of Welland's country churches while the papers of another Wexford family document the finishing of the interior of yet another new church by Welland with stained glass that was supplied from London.

Between the summer of 1857 and the end of the following year, the parish church at Horetown, New Ross, was rebuilt to a standard Welland design: a gabled nave with a bellcote at the west end and separate short chancel; a lean-to robing room on the south and a larger, gabled porch on the north for the congregation.[13] The east window is a curious pattern, which Welland also uses at Laracor, a wide two-light window flanked by single lancets, set rather wide apart, almost like some visual hangover from the Palladianism that had been fashionable a hundred years before. Used in a similar way to the church at Kildalkey, the buttresses at Horetown – here set diagonally at 45 degrees – give bulk to the corners of the church.

The course of the construction of the Horetown church is recorded in a series of photographs taken by Strangman Davis-Goff of Horetown House.[14] He first set up his camera on 29 May 1857, when the foundations had been laid and the walls were already about five feet high (Fig 5). Two features are striking in this first view: the number of fir-tree trunks – thirty-eight in all – which were to be used as scaffolding poles and the quantity of stones, already dressed in blocks to form the single chamfered reveals for the lancet windows, which are laid out in an orderly way on the grass. There is no sign of a masons' lodge or workplace and we must assume that the cut stone was prepared by the contractor off site and brought to Horetown as the building work progressed. Very much in evidence are two long planks, cross-battened to prevent slipping, which would have provided access for workmen carrying the blocks of dressed stone to a platform formed round the walls of the robing room. By November the same year, when the second photograph was taken, the walls of the church stood complete, apart from the chancel gable and the west end. Presumably the work had stopped for the season, since planks are laid over the tops of the walls to protect the exposed masonry from winter weather.

By 7 May 1858 (Fig 6) the masonry work at Horetown was complete. The bellcote of dressed freestone is in place, the chancel gable is finished and the first of the scissors trusses of the main roof is set in place against the chancel wall. The scaffolding has been raised to make a platform above the tops of the lancet windows, from which the builders will construct the carpentry of the roof. Huge piles of sand, presumably to be used for plastering the interior, lie in the foreground. The long cross-battened planks, seen in the first picture, now run at a steep incline to the tops of the building platforms and, for what it is worth, there is not a ladder to be seen. Square slabs of stone, standing proud of the surface of the slopes of the gables, will act as masonry keys for the coping stones to be added once the slating of the roof is in place.

Of all the information, provided by the Davis Goff photographs, what is least expected is the way in which the chancel arch has been constructed. In

Fig 5. Photograph by Strangman Davis Goff of Horetown Church, Co. Wexford, under construction on 29 May 1857

Fig 6. Photograph of Horetown Church, Co. Wexford, under construction on 7 May 1858

Fig 7. Photograph of Horetown Church, Co. Wexford, under construction on 11 June 1858

engineering terms the chancel arch of a rural church by Welland was the only complex part of the structure. What the photographs make perfectly clear is that the support provided for building the arch at Horetown was not formed, as might be expected, by a structure of timber centering but by a temporary masonry wall, roughly-built of rubble stone, which was left standing through the winter of 1857/58 to support the arch while the masonry settled. This wall, which must have been dismantled before the church was opened appears clearly in the photograph of November 1857 and again in the view of May 1858. The large square opening, seen just below the apex of the arch, must have been left to allow access from one side of the gable to the other for the carpenters who were assembling the roof.

The final photograph taken of the building during its construction, (Fig 7) dates from 11 June 1858. Progress has been rapid throughout May: the roof of the church is covered in timber sarking and only the chancel and robing room remain to be roofed. The masonry supporting the chancel arch is still in place and a ladder has been tied against the eaves platform, no doubt for the use of the plumbers and slaters who will have been amongst the last of the tradesmen to work on the exterior of the building. Strangman Davis-Goff took his last photograph of Horetown on 4 May 1860, some time after the church had been completed. It is a view from the south-east showing the bulk of the church in close perspective with the east window lost in deep shadow. The photographer can tell us nothing of the final trade to be considered in the completion of the church, the glazier's, for he seems never to have attempted to use his camera inside the building.

There is however one further rural church by Welland in Co.Wexford, St. John's Kilnamanagh, nine miles south of Gorey, for which there exists an ample documentation in relation to its glass. Kilnamanagh, designed in 1852, is yet another example of a classic type of Welland church. It has a gabled nave with a west bellcote, a south porch, north robing room (with lean-to roof) and a short chancel. At the west end a bell ringer's box projects from the centre of the gable, and the building is given attractive emphasis by a generous supply of diagonal and double-stepped buttresses at the corners with additional lateral buttresses to the sides of the nave (Fig 8).[15] The landowner in this parish was Robert Stephen Doyne of Wells.

Fig 8. Joseph Welland. Design for Church at Kilnamanagh, Co. Wexford: elevation of west gable. Ink on cartridge paper. Not dated

Though Kilnamanagh looks exactly like the richer and more impressive kind of Welland rural church, its history throws an interesting light on the processes of church building which applied in the Church of Ireland in the early nineteenth century. Welland's church replaced a comparatively modern structure, a T-plan church, which had been built in 1813 with a grant of £563 from the Board of First Fruits, the balance of the cost being provided by the Doyne family.[16] In 1843 when the parishioners numbered 315, an appeal was made to the Ecclesiastical Commissioners for money to build a gallery. Significantly, perhaps, that request was refused and within nine years a new church had been designed for the parish by Joseph Welland.[17]

It would appear that the church, as it was first built, lacked the present chancel which was either added or enlarged in the early 1860s. By the autumn of 1863 Robert Doyne had decided to add some stained glass to complete the building, principally as a memorial to his parents. With this in mind he had spoken to Lord Enniskillen, who recommended the London glassmaker, William Warrington, whom he had himself employed for the east window of Enniskillen Cathedral.[18] A correspondence of sixteen letters between Warrington, his son, Robert Doyne and Mrs Doyne charts the progress of this work.[19] On 14 December 1863 Warrington had replied to Doyne's request for information, listing a number of his works in Ireland – Lissadell, Armagh Cathedral, Templemore Abbey 'and very many others' and informing him that he was sending him his book *A History of Stained Glass* 'with a parcel of designs enclosed in it'.[20] Though Warrington was the first English writer to identify the historical sequence of glass design in Britain, the book in fact was illustrated entirely with his own designs and was intended to act as a catalogue of the firm's work. Since it was an imperial folio and 'too large and heavy to send by post', it had to be forwarded by rail.[21]

The book was 'intended to explain principles' and from it Warrington imagined that the Doynes would 'pretty well judge what ought to be adopted in the style of design'. For the windows in the body of the church 'a greenish tint is no doubt desirable but by no means should it be clear as it throws a sickly light into the church and does not arrest the sun's rays. It should be what we technically call matted, ie. uncleared or translucent, and then it produces a quite harmonious colour'. He ends by expressing the hope that he will hear from the Doynes when they have read his book and inspected the drawings.[22]

He did. The Doynes were clearly delighted with Warrington's work, and by the end of January he had been commissioned to provide glass in a geometrical pattern of silver-grey, red and blue with a border of shamrocks, for the triple lancet east window and to provide a vesica-shaped narrative scene of 'The Children brought to Christ' (Fig 9) as the centrepiece of the middle light. By July 1864 he was writing to say that the sizes that Doyne had sent were perfectly clear and that 'the side window (of the chancel) can be done as that at Gorey'. On 29 August he wrote to report that the east window was progressing well and that he expected it to be in place 'in the course of September'. By this time the two lancet windows and the trefoil at the west end of the church had been added to his commission, and on 1 October the same year he sent the design for these as well. Mrs Doyne's approval having been given, all the work for Kilnamanagh was finished before the end of the year and installed by Warrington's son in January 1865. The final bill for the graded lights in the chancel, and the two-light lancets and quatrefoil in the west gable came to £151,[23] a not insubstantial sum in comparison with the likely

Fig 9. William Warrington. Panel of Christ and the children from the central lancet of the east window of St. John's Church, Kilnamanagh. 1864.

cost of the church itself or with the architect's annual stipend of £600. There followed a brief disagreement – misunderstanding might be a better word – between Robert Doyne and Warrington & Sons as to the price of the work, which was paid in two instalments, £100 in February 1865 with the balance, discounted at 5%, of £41 a month later.[23]

It is gratifying, when the documents for this modest piece of Anglo-Irish patronage survive, that the windows themselves are still in place. They are elegant and unobtrusive, designed to create a subdued religious light and, so far as Warrington was able, to recreate an authentic medieval idiom for the interior of the church. In Welland's small churches there is always a strongly volumetric quality, even when they are simple cells, and the Warrington glass with its slivery light and family mottoes is entirely appropriate to this setting. It is very much Protestant glass with no image other than an unexceptional scene of Christ among women and children to disturb denominational decorum.

NOTES

1. All that is at present known of William Welland's career is contained in Anthony P.W. Malcomson. 2002. Archbishop Charles Agar, Dublin, Four Courts Press, pp.370–76. Welland's letters to Brodrick are in the Midleton Papers in the National Library of Ireland, ms. 8871
2. Dublin Builder, Vol. 2, 1 April 1860, p.232. For Monaghan Courthouse, which Welland designed in 1830, see Brett, Charles E.B. 1973. Court Houses and Market Houses of the Province of Ulster. Belfast, The Ulster Architectural Heritage Society. As preparation of this essay, a list of the Welland's known works, with an outline of his biography, has been prepared by Ann Martha Rowan and will form part of the comprehensive database of Irish architects 1720 to 1940 on which she is working for (and from the resources of) the Irish Architectural Archive. Though much work remains to be done on the work and organisation of the Ecclesiastical Commissioners of Ireland, the database provides an invaluable starting point for anyone working on the careers of the Welland family as architects.
3. These are the Disraeli School, Rathvilly, Co. Carlow, 1826, (see Journal of the Royal Society of Antiquaries of Ireland 78, 1948, p.11) and Midleton College, Co.Cork, where the reconstruction was 'completed in 1829 under the supervision of the Commissioners' architect. Mr Joseph Welland' (see JRASI, Vol. 82 (1952), p.23).
4. In this year George Papworth was appointed architect for the Province of Tuam; it would appear that Welland then took over a general responsibility in Dublin.
5. Quoted in Dublin Builder, 1 May 1860, p.245.
6. Men who worked for the Ecclesiastical Commissioners, either in the Dublin office or as District Inspectors, include James Franklin Fuller, John Guy Ferguson, William Fullerton, William Gillespie, William Hagerty, Alexander Hardy, William Hunter, James W. Martin, William Edward Martin, James & Edward McAllister, D.P. McCarthy, John Domville Phillips, William Tinsley and William Welland junior. For these see the Irish Architectural Archive Database of

Irish Architects 1720-1940.

7. Obituary in Dublin Builder
8. Besides his most polemical volume, Contrasts (Salisbury, Privately Printed, 1836), the key publications by Pugin were The True Principles of Pointed or Christian Architecture (London, John Weale, 1841); An Apology for the Revival of Christian Architecture in England, (London, John Weale, 1843) A Glossary of Ecclesiastical Ornament and Costume, (London, Bohn, 1844) and two articles published in The Dublin Review (1843) and subsequently separately reprinted as The Present State of Ecclesiastical Architecture in England (London, Charles Dolman, 1843).
9. Ecclesiastical Commissioners of Ireland, Third Report, 1836, describes the church which preceded Welland's design at Kilkenny West 'an old monastic building, which has been altered and repaired by vestry assessments; but when built or altered, or at what expense, is not stated'. Welland's designs are in the Representative Church Body Library, Dublin, Portfolio 23. They are formed into a paper booklet, 365 by 528 mm, with a bold block-letter title page.
10. Welland's drawing for the churches of Balrath Boyne, Kildalkey and Laracor are in the Representative Church Body Library, Dublin, Portfolio 23. The Balrath Boyne designs are on four sheets of cartridge paper and lack any cover. They are inscribed 'Joseph Welland Archt.', in a rather childish hand, which is presumably the writing of an office clerk and are also countersigned 'J Welland' in the architect's usual hand and dated 'May 17/57'. The designs for Kildalkey, on four sheets, are signed 'J Welland Archt.' and dated 'Feb 55'. The designs for Laracor, on six sheets, are signed 'J Welland Archt.' but are not dated. None of these buildings remain in use as churches: Kildalkey has been demolished and the other two have been converted into houses. Welland's drawings are reproduced by kind permission of the Representative Church Body.
11. The tracing paper books measure 382 by 508 mm and use a paper which was commercially produced rather than one that was made in the office.
12. There is a tantalizing gap in the official record of the Church of Ireland's buildings in the 19th century. The Commission on Ecclesiastical Revenue and Patronage, Ireland, was set up in 1833. The Commissioners met in the Council Chamber of Dublin Castle where, under the guidance of their secretary, John C. Erck, they gathered information on the Revenues of the Archbishoprics and Bishoprics of the country (First Report, 1834), on the Revenues of Deans & Chapters (Second Report, 1835) and on the different Diocese (Third and Fourth Reports, 1836 & 37). These printed volumes, particularly the Third and Fourth Reports, give much detail on the state of church buildings throughout the country and the sums expended on them up to that time. The volumes seem to have been prepared to provide a factual basis for the work of the Commissioners and, for the remainder of the life of the Commission, were not followed up by any further published reports. The documentary and manuscript material, relating to the work of the Commissioners, was destroyed with other public records in the Four Courts fire of 1922. Copies of the Commissioner's four Reports are rare: a full set is held in the Representative Church Body Library in Dublin.
13. The drawings for Horetown Church are in the Representative Church Body Library, Dublin, Portfolio 17. Interestingly they exist in two forms; (i) as an office book, similar to Kildalkey and Laracor, where three pages of tracing paper drawings record the basic scheme and (ii) as five pages on paper, backed by cloth and marked in pencil 'returned by Contractor', with a further five drawings of carpentry and stonework details. The five principal pages are signed 'J Welland

Architect. 'The church was dedicated on 30 May 1862.

14. Copies of the Davis-Goff photographs of Horetown Church are in the Irish Architectural Archive.
15. Four drawings for Kilnamanagh Church, signed 'J Welland Archt.' from an original set of eight are in the Representative Church Body Library, Dublin, Portfolio 17. The Builder for 3 April 1852, p.219, reports that the church was to be rebuilt.
16. Ecclesiastical Commissioners of Ireland. Fourth Report, 1838, p.213
17. William John Hall, ND., c. 1956. St. John's Church Kilnamanagh and a short paper on the Oxford Movement, Printed in Plymouth.
18. William Warrington (1796-1869) is said to have restored some ancient stained glass as early as 1833 though the first windows known to be by him are those executed for A.W.N. Pugin for St.Mary's Chapel at Oscott College, Warwickshire. A manuscript notebook entitles 'A list of some of the Principal Works in Stained Glass by William Warrington . . .' is in the Victoria & Albert Museum Library (86.BB.27). This lists 21 Irish commissions for not less than 34 windows. See also Martin Harris, 1980. Victorian Stained Glass. London, Barrie & Jenkins.
19. In the 1980s this correspondence was in the possession of Mr & Mrs Charles Doyne in Guernsey.
20. Warrington, William. 1848. The History of Stained Glass from the Earliest Period to the Present Time. London, privately printed.
21. Warrington to Doyne, 14 Dec 1864
22. Ibid.
23. On 6 February 1865 the younger Warrington wrote:

    I beg to enclose the account for the Sta. Glass windows in Kilnamanagh Church and must apologise in asking if it is convenient for you to settle the same in consequence of my father having some very heavy payments to meet at this time.

    The cost of the windows at £151, broke down as follows; the east window £73, the west window, £63, wire guards, bars, cases etc., £7 plus £8 to cover the travel for fixing them in place.

    The draft of Doyne's reply reads:

    Dear Sir, Your account furnished so far exceeds what your father's letters, now before me, led us to suppose would be the cost of the windows that I could not settle it without writing to him on the subject in addition to which I have to write to other parties connected with the erection of them, as I was not aware of being called on to pay for them so soon & was subsequently not prepared to do so.

    An additional note reads:

    before leaving this, your son applied to me for the account of the two windows, but as his statement did not agree with what you said the windows would cost I preferred writing to you on the subject.

    On 10 February 1865 William Warrington replies:

    If you refer to my very last letter you will find in reply to Mrs Doyne or you, on your adoption of the last design for the west window after my stating that the price would necessarily [be] *increased from the designs being richer and higher in order, I stated that 60 guineas would be the cost. The East window was of necessity enriched according to make it keep place and balance, therefore the price of that was naturally increased which I did not think you would object to, as to have all satisfactory has been my main object. Under any circumstances the price is moderate and I trust all is satisfactory.*

Brett of Belfast, Scott of Dublin
Mews of Buildings, arts and parts
Feelings, feelings, Georgian ceilings
Landscapes, streetscapes, cattlemarts
Edwin Evans

The Temple of the Winds, Mount Stewart, in its surrounding parkland setting beside Strangford Lough.

Watercolour by David Evans

JOHN NASH AND THE BUILDING OF ROCKINGHAM, CO ROSCOMMON

GORDON WHEELER

THE TORTUOUS RAMIFICATIONS OF the descent of the various estates and titles (knighthoods, baronetcies, baronies, viscountcies, and an earldom) through the senior and cadet branches of the Kings, King-Harmans, Stafford-King-Harmans and King-Tenisons have been amply dealt with elsewhere.[1] Suffice it to say here that the family were masters in the art of consolidating and increasing their acreage by judicious and timely marriages to heiresses, preferably their own cousins. They were also adept at preventing by legal devices their properties falling into the hands of undesirable members of the family; and were not at all diffident about taking each other to court over disputed inheritances. By 1878 the family had amassed 98,395 acres,[2] mainly in Counties Cork, Longford, Roscommon and Sligo, but sales under the various Land Acts up to 1903 had reduced the King-Harman holdings by some 70,000 acres,[3] still leaving several thousand, principally at Rockingham.

The first member of the King family to be associated with Boyle was Sir John King, originally of Feathercock Hall near Northallerton in Yorkshire, who held many Crown offices in Ireland under Elizabeth I and James I and was given the joint lease of the lands of the dissolved Boyle Abbey by James I in 1604. By 1607 Sir John was building 'a great castle' at Boyle and was cultivating much of the surrounding district. Some ten years or so later he received a direct royal grant of the Abbey lands amounting to 4,127 acres, and before his death in 1636 he had been granted lands in twenty-one different counties. At some time between 1643 and his death in 1657, Sir John's eldest son, Sir Robert King, was the builder of what was probably the first separate family house in the town, 'Boyle Abbey'. The younger son of this Sir Robert, Sir Robert King, the first baronet, was given extensive lands around Lough Key outside Boyle by his elder brother, the first Baron Kingston. These had formed part of the ancestral patrimony of the MacDermots, Kings of Moylurg and princes of Coolavin, the remains of whose early thirteenth-century castle stood on Rock (or Castle) Island. In 1673, on the estate later to be known as 'Rockingham', Sir Robert built a 'sumptuous mansion' and a chapel, which were thought at the time to be beyond his means and above his station. This house stood in the neighbourhood of the nineteenth-century estate chapel, of which the shell still remains to-day, about a quarter of a mile south-east of the site of the now demolished Rockingham House.

The town house burned down in 1720, but was rebuilt very soon afterwards by Sir Henry King, the third baronet. This is the splendid brick-vaulted house, known as 'King House', which stands on the riverside at Boyle to-day and which has been given a possible attribution by Maurice Craig on stylistic grounds to Sir Edward Lovett Pearce or to his assistant, William Halfpenny.[4] It was handsomely restored by Roscommon County Council, under the supervision of Maura Shaffrey, in 1995.

Sir Henry was already being referred to as 'of Rockingham' as early as 1727.[5] The fifth baronet, Sir Edward King, inherited the Boyle house in 1755 and, after a wrangle with his brother over a will, came into possession of the lands and house at Rockingham in 1759. When he was elevated to the peerage in 1764, he took the title of Baron Kingston (second creation), 'of Rockingham'. The house was destroyed by fire in the 1760s, and Edward, having become Earl of Kingston in 1768, is said to have considered the position of the town house unsuitable for a great nobleman. He commenced a new house, 'Kingston Hall', at Rockingham, which was ready for occupation in 1771, and moved in in the following year, having lent the town house to his eldest son, Robert, Viscount Kingsborough, and his young family. Kingston Hall was about a mile to the south-east of the final Rockingham House, towards the Ardcarne end of the demesne near the small Lough Keel and roughly in the area occupied later by the early nineteenth-century home farm buildings. It was reached from the Carrick-on-Shannon/Boyle road,[6] and the site would seem to be indicated in the 1837 Ordnance Survey[7] by the pattern of plantings and approach avenues.

Lord Kingston certainly continued to use the town house in later years: when the Rev. Daniel Augustus Beaufort called on him in October 1787, he was entertained at the Boyle house and noted that the earl was still involved in laying out the estate at Kingston Hall.[8] In the latter part of the eighteenth century the Boyle house is frequently referred to as 'Kingston Lodge', but, as the name 'Boyle Abbey' was still being used in mid century, this was probably a change of name dating from the 1770s, to distinguish the house from Kingston Hall. Following the damage caused by yet another fire in 1788, Kingston Lodge was sold to the army at the end of the century and became a barracks, and now 'King House'.

Under the will of the second Earl of Kingston, the Rockingham estate passed in 1799 to his second son, the Hon. Robert Edward King. Robert had joined the army in 1792 with a commission as colonel, fighting with distinction and being wounded during the campaign against the French in the West Indies in 1794. He became MP for Jamestown (south-east of Rockingham) in 1796 and for the family borough of Boyle from 1798 to 1800. Unfortunately, due to the extravagance of his father and grandfather, he had inherited Rockingham heavily encumbered by debts of £119,000 (estimated by A.L. King-Harman to be the equivalent of 5.35 million pounds in 1996 terms), so, when he was proposing in 1799 to marry his cousin, the Hon. Frances Harman (Parsons), daughter and heiress of Lord Oxmantown (later Earl of Rosse), it was only natural that his future father-in-law should initiate some inquiries about his financial prospects. Amongst the terms discussed for the marriage settlement, Robert was proposing to build 'a magnificent mansion'.[9] The marriage went ahead, and Oxmantown set about recommending his son-in-law for a peerage, emphasizing both how well-connected and how well-off Robert was![10] Although the King family had several times voted against the Union, Robert was created Baron Erris of Boyle in 1800 and Viscount Lorton in 1806. He would not appear to have seen any further active service apart from militia and regimental duties at home: he became a Major-General in 1808, a Lieutenant-General in 1813, and a full General in 1830. From 1823 until his death in 1854 Viscount Lorton was a representative Irish peer in the United Kingdom House of Lords; and, from 1831 to 1854, Lord Lieutenant of County Roscommon.[11]

Lord Lorton's portrait by Sir Thomas Beechey[12] shows a military man of decidedly determined jaw, indicative of the hauteur with which he dealt with his architect and clerk of works during the building of Rockingham. His stubborn determination had already been demonstrated in 1797 by his relentless pursuit of his sister's seducer, via a duel in London to a fracas in County Cork which resulted in the death of the malefactor, although Lorton's father, then Lord Kingsborough, actually fired the fatal shot.

Before 1815 Lorton and his wife spent much time in Dublin where their seven children were born in the King family house in Henrietta Street. Nothing more was heard of the 'magnificent mansion' until 1808 when John Nash visited Rockingham for a week in September.[13] Lorton's choice of architect is not surprising, as Nash had already designed Killymoon Castle, Cookstown, County Tyrone, for Lorton's cousin, Colonel James Stewart, in 1802, and Lissan rectory, County Tyrone for Stewart's nephew, the Rev. John Staples, in 1807.[14] Nash was also supervising his additions to Caledon House, County Tyrone, for the second

Earl of Caledon in 1808.[15] The site chosen for the new house commanded a superb view northwards over Lough Key and its islands from a small hill rising directly from the lakeside; and was just above an earlier MacDermot homestead and harbour known as Caladh na Carraige (the landing-place of the Rock).[16] Nash's first plans and elevations arrived in January 1809 and would appear to have met with initial approval, so much so that a contract was entered into with Nash, and copies of the drawings were made by Charles Lilly and a Mr Taylor in Dublin, presumably for quantity surveying of materials required. However, Lorton was originally aiming to have a house costing £20,000, but, when the estimates arrived in February, they stood at £31,500 and had risen by June to £39,000, a not unusual experience for Nash's clients.[17] (From February 1809 until June 1810 various alterations and reductions were made in efforts to bring down the cost, first to £28,500 and finally to £26,500.) Nash spent another week at Rockingham in the early summer of 1809, following which Lorton wrote on July 2 to James Stewart at Killymoon:

> *...I find that the best way forward for me will be to reduce the expense to a certainty and which Mr Nash will engage to do and also to finish the work in the very best manner possible; he has been here and we have made more alterations and a small reduction in the plan and which upon the whole very much improves it...*[18]

In view of the need for economy, it is surprising to find various additional proposals being estimated in September and October – such as a second basement level; second-floor attic turrets on the east and west fronts; an increase from six to eight columns in the semi-circular colonnade of the north front; and the use of stone ashlar instead of stucco. These changes were duly incorporated by Nash in a second set of drawings submitted in December: four elevations 'on a small scale' (Figs 3,4,5 & 6),[19] and five floor plans showing two basement levels (Fig 2), the main floor (Fig 1), of the bedroom floor and a mezzanine floor containing five nurseries and an unusually capacious bathroom (incorporating a large raised plunge bath and a smaller hot bath), inserted over the ground-floor rooms on the south side to left and right of the main staircase.

Probably in continuing efforts to reduce costs still further, all the foregoing was abandoned and a new start made following suggestions which Lady Lorton had put forward as early as January of 1809. These third drawings[20] were ready by March 1810, estimates were agreed, a contract entered into, and the first stone of the house was finally laid on June 4.[21] Nash spent six days at Rockingham to inaugurate the building work, but Lorton had, however, already annulled that part of this second contract relating to the mason work and had taken on himself

Fig 1. Proposed plan of ground floor of Rockingham, December 1809 (Courtesy of Lady Dunn and the Irish Architectural Archive)

Fig 2. Proposed plan of the upper basement floor of Rockingham, December 1809 (Courtesy of Lady Dunn and the Irish Architectural Archive)

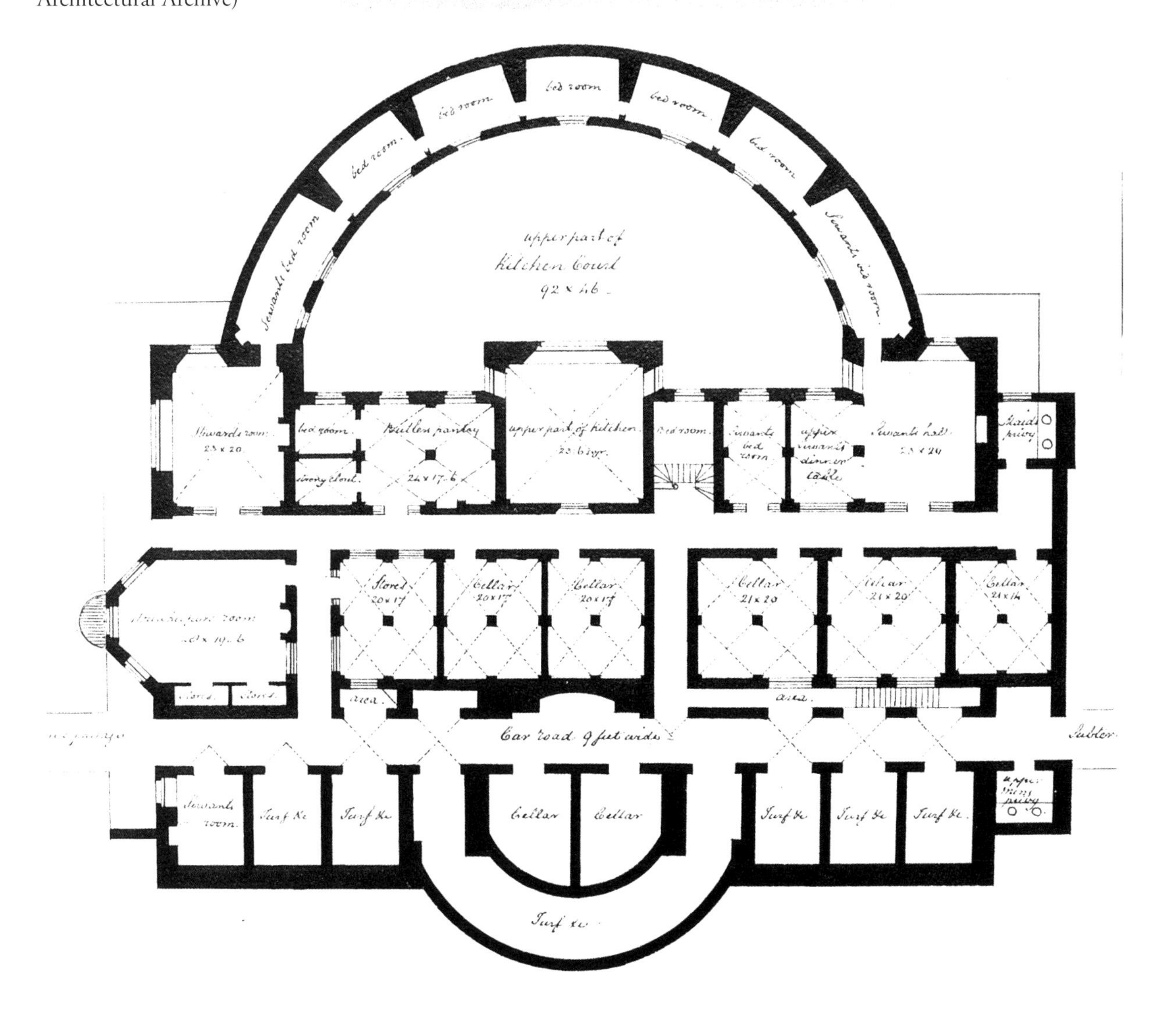

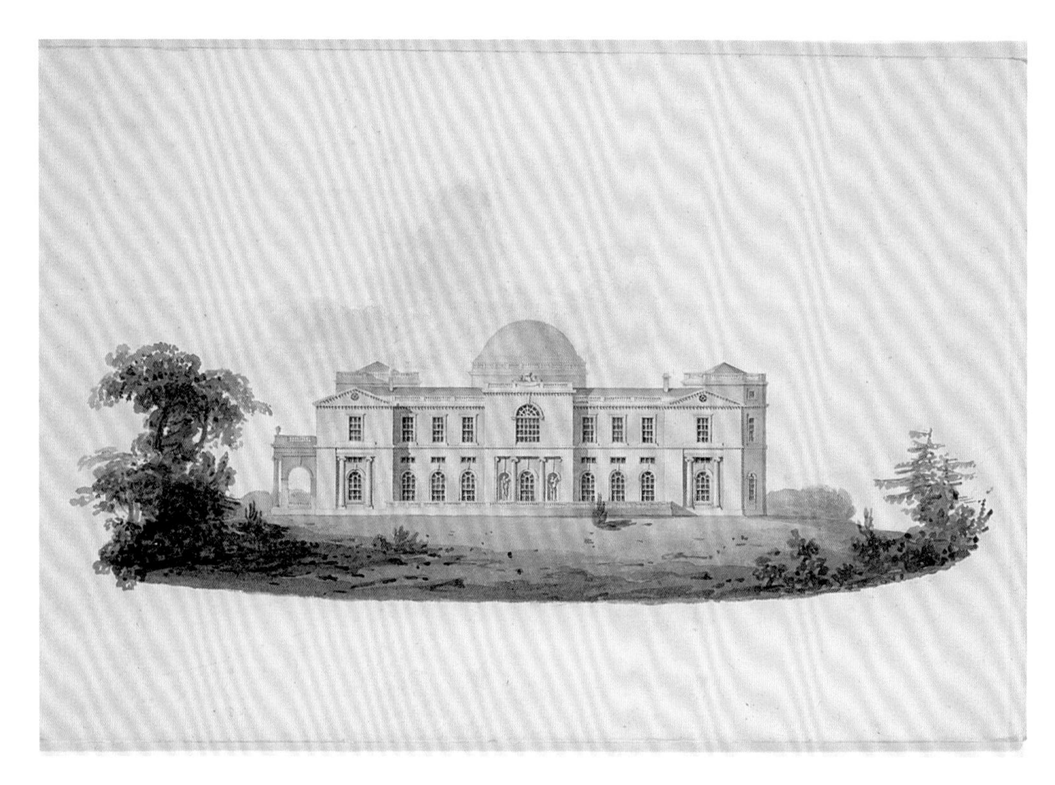

Figs 3, 4 & 5. Proposed south front, west (entrance) front and east front of Rockingham, December 1809. Watercolours by G.S. Repton (Courtesy of lady Dunn and the Royal Institute of British Architects)

Fig 4.

Fig 5.

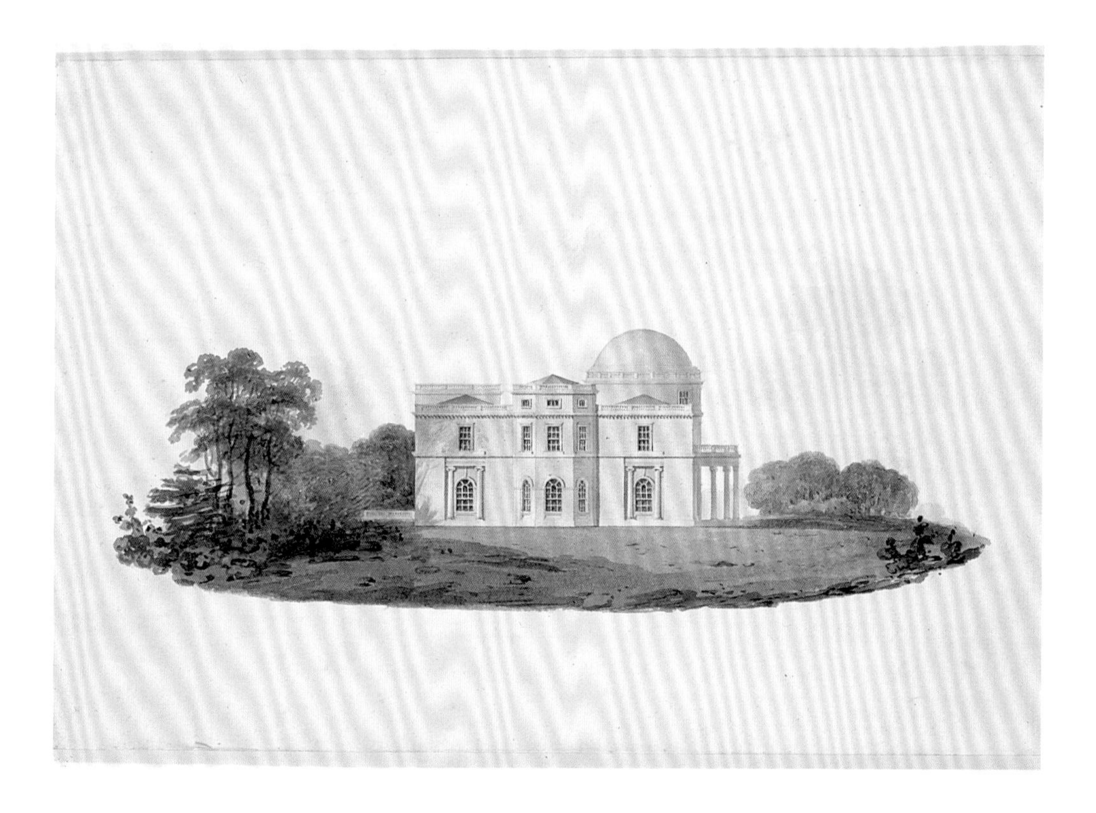

the responsibility for executing and paying directly for the carcase of the house (i.e. quarrying, materials and labour costs for the walls).

A comparison of the second and third[22] designs for the north (or lake) elevation (Figs 6 & 7) shows that economies had been effected by omitting the deep three-storied canted bow at the east end; reducing the height of the attic storey in the drum of the dome; and, most significantly, by running the roofs of the side wings into to the drum, instead of the previous individual hipped roofs which had stood clear of it. Unfortunately, even the third design was to be still further modified before building commenced, as can be seen from the photographs of the ruined house in the Irish Architectural Archive: the small lobbies interrupting the enfilade of reception rooms on the north, together with other small service rooms on the south, were omitted, resulting in a loss of two bays on both the main fronts and a truncation of the total length of the house by some twenty-five feet. A knock-on effect was the return of the colonnade to its original six rather than eight columns. The statuary in the niches, and the engaged columns adorning the window recesses, on the ground floor may well have been a further casualty of economy: they are certainly not present in a later photograph taken in about 1858 by Edward King-Tenison.[23] On the entrance front of the house (Fig 4), James Arthur O'Connor's distant view of 1818 from

Fig 6. Proposed north (lake) front of Rockingham, December 1809. Watercolour by G. S. Repton (Courtesy of Lady Dunn and the Royal Institute of British Architects)

Fig 7. Proposed north (lake) front of Rockingham, March 1810. Watercolour by G. S. Repton (Courtesy of Lady Dunn)

Fig 8. Oil painting of Rockingham and Lough Key from the west, 1818/19 by James Arthur O'Connor (Courtesy of Wellesley Ashe Gallery, Dublin)

the west in a painting of about 1819/1819 (Fig 8)[24] shows still more changes, in that the blocks to either side of the portico were built with pedimented gables rather than straight parapets; and the attic storey over the entrance hall block, which had been retained in the March 1810 drawing of the lake elevation (Fig 7), was omitted.

In the absence of corresponding plans, it is not possible to tell what interior changes were made between the second and third designs, but Father Browne's photographs of the 1940s[25] show considerable alterations to the detailing of the central gallery between the second design and the house as built: doors now give direct and more practical access to the circular drawing-room and to the music room (originally the billiard-room); and the upper flights of the imperial staircase now curve round an apsidal space. Some of this may, however, date from the reconstruction of the interior in the 1860s which is described below.

The most striking element of the design of Rockingham, the central domed tempietto, Nash had used before in two of his English classical country houses, Casino at Dulwich, Surrey (1797)[26] and Sundridge Park at Bromley, Kent (1799)[27] and was to use again in a number of his private and public commissions. The spinal top-lit 'Gallery of Communication' was a favourite device found in many of his house plans. Rockingham was the epitome of all those great houses which sought to conceal the comings and goings of their servants and tradesmen by covered passages or tunnels entering at basement level. Nash here went still further by having his complete two-storey kitchen court sunk below the ground and centrally lit by a vast semi-circular area adjoining the basement to the south. All the normal offices, plus dairy, bakehouse, washhouse, and servants' bedrooms, opened off the inner and outer faces of the area; and from the upper storey of the basement a tunnel led eastwards for a distance of over 86 yards, and another, principally for the supply of fuel, ran down to a lakeside jetty, 120 yards away to the north.[28]

Preparation of the site had commenced in 1809: John Lynn, a carpenter sent over from England by Nash as clerk of works under the first, subsequently aborted contract, began work in August, building boats and constructing a landing-stage and a light railway, so that supplies could be brought in by water via the Boyle River and Lough Key. (The stone for the house came from a limestone quarry on the estate and from quarries at nearby Curlew, Cavetown, Castle Tenison and Drumshanbo.[29] Most other materials, apart from soft timber, had to come from either Dublin to Drumsna via the Shannon canal system or from England via Sligo, and there is no doubt that getting everything to the west of Ireland was extremely expensive.[30]) Excavation of the very considerable basement and foundations started in October.

Nash's accounts also commenced in August 1809, and Lord Lorton's own note of expenses[31] shows more or less uniform quarterly payments via Nash to suppliers and contractors until the summer of 1811. In October of that year Lorton abruptly dismissed Nash, probably because building faults were already coming to light, but possibly also because he may have felt that he himself could handle the finances more efficiently. Lynn, who had been given the contract for the joinery and carpenter's work from the beginning, now found himself acting as supervising architect as well, with responsibility for sourcing materials and paying suppliers, though still only being paid clerk of work's wages![32] Nash's final bill for just over £4,000, covering outstanding balances for his expenses and payments to contractors, and including his own professional charges, was submitted in January 1813. The percentage element of his fees could not be calculated until the measuring (i.e. quantity surveying and labour valuation) of all work done on the house up to September 1811 had been completed by James Pain and Charles Lilly of Dublin. Lorton not only disputed their calculations, sending to London for a second opinion (perhaps he had heard that Pain had been one of Nash's pupils), but also queried other charges and proposed an enormous reduction in Nash's fees, which he considered excessive. The draft of a document summarizing his dissatisfaction is worth quoting in extenso:

> *In consequence of Mr Nash having made the most extraordinary & most exorbitant demand of £2675.12.3 this deduction is made & calculated, from his own Schedule of Professional Charges at the highest, for it must be observed that the original Plan has never been departed from but merely curtailed in consequence of his having exceeded the Sum of £20,000 (that Lord Lorton told him it was his intention to lay out upon a House) by £19,000…*
>
> *In addition to the deductions made [i.e. overcharging for materials, redundant workmen sent over from England, etc, etc] a very strong claim may be made for others such as the various mistakes & blunders which can be ascertained by comparing the working plans with the Building as it stands among the following are some viz: the construction of the Roof & the bad timbers in it, no light whatever to some of the Water Closets & passages, some of the fire places & flues marked where it was impossible to place the former or carry the latter – Jambs of the Hall Door too short etc, etc – all the above with the exception of the roof have been corrected with much trouble and expence; – the expence of carriage of articles sent in waste – If a professional Man should be sent to inspect the House & the plans by which it was intended to have been built, he would find the strongest proofs, either of ignorance or of gross neglect.*[33]

In spite of Nash's detailed explanation of his charges (see Appendix below), the disagreement rumbled on for some time, both client and architect threatening each other with arbitration and court cases, until finally Nash, having turned down a first offer of £1800, settled for £2000 (*including* his overall fees!).

Most of Lynn's surviving 'weekly papers' to Lord Lorton date from the period 1812 to 1815, when he ceased to receive a wage as clerk of works. In the summer of 1813 he is using materials such as lead and flooring from 'the old house', that is Kingston Hall, and reports that the dome is complete. Of the row with Nash he writes, 'I was very glad to hear that Mr Nash was so well Settle[d] with. I never though[t] he would hold out when it came to the Last push'; and adds, rather oddly, 'I am told that he has very Little to Do at this time'. (He cannot have known that Nash was working on Royal Lodge, Windsor and on Carlton House in London, both for the Prince Regent, in 1813 and had already commenced realizing his plans for the development of Regent's Park in 1812[34]). By May 1814 Lorton has cause to complain that Lynn is neglecting his work at Rockingham in favour of his contract at nearby Castle Tenison: he regrets that he had recommended Lynn in the previous year to his aunt's husband, Colonel Thomas Tenison. A year later, Lynn, obviously still under pressure, writes 'I shall not Do anything more to the Sligo job' (his contract for the building of Sligo gaol[35]) 'till next Spring, therefore I have only Castle tenison to attend to and of Corse shall be most at home'. As late as April 1815 all the columns of the entrance portico are ready and are still going up in June. Much work is being done on the farm buildings at this time, but the summer months are largely taken up by a detailed inspection of the timbers in most rooms, following an outbreak of dry rot, and the consequent necessary treatment.[36] By August, final painting and decorating are going on, leading to Lynn fussing about strong paint smells and to Mrs Lynn fussing about damp beds, pending the imminent moving in of the Lorton family. (Lynn is installing steam heating pipes to rectify the latter problem.[37])

The last item in Lorton's own accounts relating to the house is for the library bookcases which were fitted in January 1817, although bills for painting and decorating and for carpets and curtains were still being settled until November 1818. The total cost of the house to Lorton up to February 1817 amounted to £52,048.3.6 Irish, of which £1,139.9.6 was spent on papering and painting and £5,784.5.8 on furniture. The £45,000 odd represented by the fabric and fees was the equivalent of about £42,000 English. Between 1809 and 1816 Lorton had to borrow over £11,000 Irish to help meet these costs.

As has been demonstrated above, the carefully balanced proportions of Nash's two surviving designs had already been weakened, before they were finally completely destroyed in 1822 by the removal of the dome and the substitution of a second bedroom floor around the central light well across the entire length of the house. (The plans of December 1809 had provided for nine bedrooms plus the nurseries, but it is likely that the lateral compression which eventually took place led to a reduction in this number.) Also, Isaac Weld notes, 'at the same time, the ground plan underwent alterations and the building was enlarged'[38]: this would seem to have involved the extension of the entrance portico forwards to form a porte-cochère,[39] and the addition of a large stone-built orangery to the east end. R.D. King-Harman suggests[40] that Nash was recalled by Lord Lorton to carry out this work, but it is highly unlikely that either of them would have wished to become re-involved with the other after their acrimonious break in 1811, or that Nash would have considered being a party to what amounted to the vandalism of his design. Perhaps, more probably, John Lynn might be proposed as the culprit. After the completion of Rockingham and of Castle Tenison in 1815, he had set himself up in Sligo as a building contractor, timber importer and builder's merchant. He had continued as a supplier of materials to Lorton and in 1819 was working for him on the enlargement and reroofing of Boyle church. In 1820 he had finished his refacing and extension of Strokestown Park and the building of Strokestown church, County Roscommon, for Lord Hartland,[41] so he was now plainly something of an architect.[42]

A Scottish tourist, Robert Graham, has left us an account of how the house looked and was laid out in 1836, although his transposition of the rooms identified as library and drawing room conflicts both with Nash's second plan (Fig 1) and with subsequent use of those rooms: it is possible, of course, that such a re-arrangement was incorporated in Nash's final plan, or it may have been part of the 1822 work:

> *...it is not strictly Grecian, nor Gothic; but it makes a splendid and convenient house. It has been fitted up in the French style, with a good deal of Arabesque painting, gilding, &c &c. From a small hall of entry, you proceed into a grand gallery, lighted from above with stained glass, and also from a handsome staircase branching off rectangularly in the middle. At the further end of this gallery is the music room in sequence leading into the conservatory; and parralel* [sic] *& alongside of this line are the Drawing room, circular library and Dining room of the same large dimension with the drawing room. The form of the library admits of separate entrances to these rooms by private stairs and passages for the servants. There are about 25 capital bedrooms upstairs, and an additional set on a floor above that, which was the last improvement .- The house offices are in a sunken court arched & covered over, so as scarcely to be discoverable from without & they are connected by a sunken passage at the stables; and there is a canal of communication with the bog, from which the supply of turf comes, and which is brought in through the lake by a subterranean communication, which ends at a square shaft, by which the fuel may be hoisted up by machinery thro' the interior of the house...*[43]

The interior of Rockingham was almost totally destroyed on Wednesday, April 22, 1863[44] by a disastrous fire in which many King-Harman records also perished, but its restoration was complete by 1871. At some time it is obvious that very considerable changes were made to the south or garden frontage. It is not possible, however, to say with certainty whether the rather dull and featureless, almost completely flat, frontage with Wyatt windows, which is visible in later photographs, dated from the 1822 building work or from rebuilding after the fire of 1863. This is the state of the house which David Thomson was describing when he wrote, perhaps a little unkindly, 'a most splendid house...of the most hideous architecture conceivable...The walls..., hugely solid and built of local limestone, towered above the park like some top-heavy mausoleum in a green graveyard'.[45]

Between inheriting in 1799 and his death in 1854, Lord Lorton is reputed to have spent £400,000 (eighteen million pounds in 1996 values according to A.L. King-Harman's calculations) on the Rockingham estate, including the house. The commission for landscaping the new park had been given to the celebrated John Sutherland,[46] who was already at work in May 1814.[47] Sutherland had previously been employed on garden buildings at Caledon in 1807;[48] and on the landscaping of Shane's Castle, County Antrim, possibly in about 1809;[49] and was subsequently to landscape two more of the houses designed by Nash in Ireland, Lough Cutra Castle, County Galway, and Gracefield Lodge, County Laois, both in the 1820s[50]. At Rockingham the entire demesne was developed as a Brownian landscape park, the main house itself being isolated in a smooth sea of shaven lawns. Narrow canals were cut across peninsulas to create islands reached by handsome bridges. In the words of Robert Graham, 'The general character of the grounds is that of smoothness & beauty, rather than of grandeur. The demesne itself consists of undulating ground, with the most thriving wood tho' not of great age...'[51]

Sutherland was a competent builder[52] and may himself have been responsible for the designs of the series of follies, mock castles, bridges and gate-lodges found throughout the demesne.[53] Mansbridge[54] and local tradition are inclined to assign the majority of these buildings to Nash, but there is no reference to them in his final account of 1813, and, again, it is unlikely that he would have been retained to carry them out after his discharge by Lord Lorton in 1811. Much of this work was in place by the time of the Ordnance Survey carried out in 1837 (Fig 9),[55] but Sutherland had died in 1826, so some of the datable structures, such as the gothick 'Abbey' gatehouse of 1832 over the beech avenue approach from Boyle,[56] and the estate chapel of 1833, which replaced the old church of 1673, the rustic stone Fairy Bridge of 1836 and Cloontykilla Castle hunting lodge of 1839,[57] may have been later realizations of his designs. The circular fishing 'temple' or gazebo, at the end of a causeway and bridge projecting into Lough Key, appears to post-date 1837, but there are no certain dates for the ten acre walled garden[58] with its extensive glasshouses to the south-west of the house, or for the gothick gatehouse over the beech avenue approach from Boyle, or for the particularly fine ice-house, or for the most prominent of all the eye-catchers, the rebuilding and extension of the old MacDermot stronghold on Castle Island as a folly.[59] Of all the buildings in the demesne, the one with the most likely claim on stylistic grounds to have been designed by Nash is the remarkable bow-fronted and colonnaded 'tiara' gate-lodge, which has strong references to the

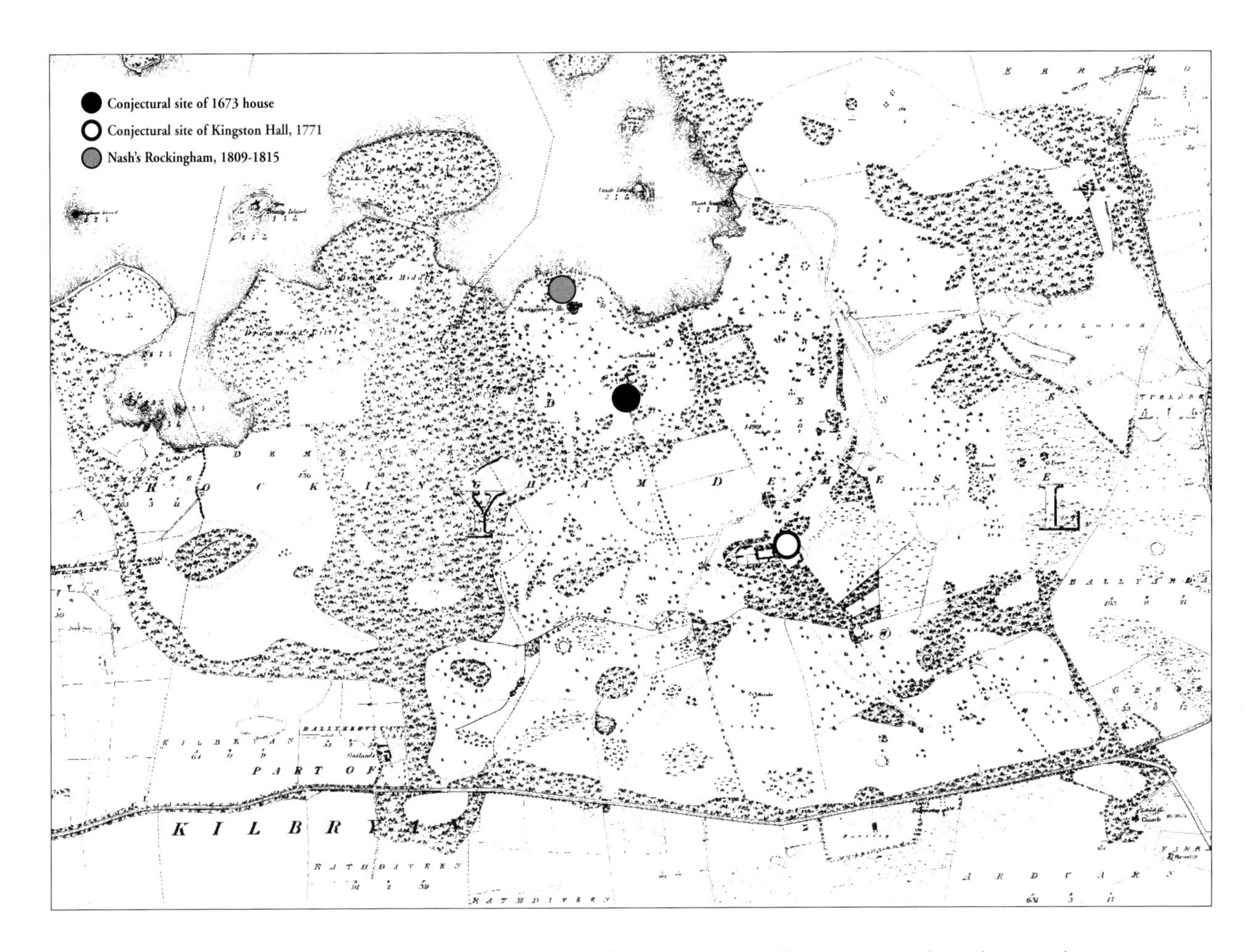

Fig 9. Rockingham Demesne, 1837. From six-inch Ordnance Survey map of 1838.

main house itself, on the Boyle/Carrick-on-Shannon road at the south-western Kilbryan corner of the estate.

A reason may, perhaps, be put forward for the number of later buildings in the demesne so long after the completion of the house. Lord Lorton and his older brother, George, third Earl of Kingston, were in constant competition with each other: George is said to have embarked on the enormous Mitchelstown Castle (1823-1825) in County Cork, at a cost of £100,000 because of his jealousy over the size of Rockingham. Their rivalry culminated in a bitter and protracted legal battle over ownership of the King estates in County Sligo, which Lorton eventually won in 1830 with a very considerable retrospective award of rents.[60]

Sir Bernard Burke, writing in the last years of Lorton's life, described the estate with enthusiasm as 'considered as, beyond all comparison, the finest seat in Ireland', with drives extending for seventy or eighty miles without having to retrace one's path. He thought the house 'a very perfect specimen of an Italian palace adapted to the circumstances of our climate' and gave the roof walk a special mention.[61]

Following the rebuilding of the 1860s and an interior redecoration of 1929, apparently no further changes were made until after the second World War, when Sir Cecil Stafford-King-Harman had the top floor and basement sealed off and the kitchen brought upstairs in the early 1950s by Philip Tilden, an English architect who was well known for his ability to adopt large houses such as Chartwell, Luton Hoo and Clarence House, for modern living and reduced staffing. When fire struck again in September 1957, once more gutting the interior but leaving the walls still standing, Sir Cecil contemplated rebuilding to Nash's original two storeys and replacing the dome, but this proved to be prohibitively expensive. He sold the estate in 1961 to the Irish Department of Lands, who razed the ruin to ground level in 1970 and developed about half of the 2000 acres into the Lough Key Forest Park, selling off the rest as small farms. Fortunately much of the furniture, at least from the ground floor, and most of the King portraits survived the fire and are still with descendants of the family.[62] Some of the larger pieces were acquired by the National Trust and for many years helped to furnish Florence Court in County Fermanagh until the Enniskillen furniture returned there in 1998 (discussed elsewhere in this volume). They are now fulfilling a similar function on loan to Fota House in County Cork. According to family tradition, these are said to have been designed by Nash, although there is no known documentary evidence for such an attribution.

Appendix

Mr Nash justifies his professional charges

[Nothing like the riches of documentation which are available for the practice of Sir John Soane have survived from Nash's office. For such an important architect there is surprisingly little in the Drawings Collection of the Royal Institute of British Architects.[63] He made his pupils make record drawings of all work in hand,[64] but only two such notebooks kept by George Stanley Repton are known.[65] His own collection of drawings was sold at auction after his death in 1835,[66] and as for correspondence and personal papers, nearly everything has been lost: original material on his Irish houses is particularly scarce. The diaries, which might have revealed much about his commissions and movements, were destroyed at his death,[67] with the exception of two volumes for 1832 and 1835,[68] long after his retirement from professional activity. Apart from his official work in London, most of the documents which have survived have been found amongst the papers of his private clients, as is the case with the highly informative statement which follows. The manuscript is the property of the National Library of Ireland,[69] and the transcript appears with the permission of the Council and Trustees]

Professional Charges submitted to Lord Lorton before any designs were made & submitted to writing at the foot of the first estimate dated February 14th 1809 in the following words

Where buildings are carried into execution (viz)

For fair drawings of elevations whatever I pay for drawing them out without anything for design where the building is executed and nothing for drawing out the plans –

For designs plans working drawings and every direction necessary to carry the designs into execution, and settling but not measuring the workmen's accounts 5pr Cent on the total expenditure;[70] *materials found by the gentleman are included in the cost ad valorem, and this 5 pr Cent is the whole of our legitimate charge.*

If an estimate is previously required 1½ pr Cent is charged on such Estimate for making it.

If I am called upon to indemnify the estimate, that is to say to bear harmless the gentleman against any extra charge or any excess in the estimate, I charge 5pr Cent for that indemnification; but this I always wish to decline and only propose it to do away the imputation on architects of their always exceeding their estimates.

For journeys to inspect the business whenever required to do so[71]*, I charge for posting there & back*[72] *as it really is & 3 guineas a day for my time.*

Charges where the work is not executed

For designs and plans of a house under £2000 cost[73]	*20 guineas*
From 2 to 4 thousand £ cost	*30 guineas*
From 4 to 6 thousand	*45 guineas*
From 6 to 8 thousand	*55 guineas*
From 8 to 10 thousand	*70 guineas*
From 10 to 14 thousand	*85 guineas*
From 14 to 20 thousand	*100 guineas*
From 20 to 30 thousand	*125 guineas*
From 30 to 40 thousand	*150 guineas*
From 40 thousand upwards	*200 guineas*

And for the fair elevations of those drawings, whatever I pay for them.

In the case of the building not being executed, I charge 5 guineas a day for my time

Professional account according to the Scedule on the other side

1808 24th Septr to 1st Octr

7 Days at Rockingham, 5 days travelling 350 miles at 70 miles pr Day & 5 days returning making in all 17 days at 5 guineas pr Day the plans not being carried into execution £89. 5. 0

700 Miles posting & expenses crossing & recrossing from Holyhead to Dublin £74. 4. 0

1809 Jan 7

Sent from Ireland compleat designs of a house of the cost from 30 to 40 thousand pounds approved of but not executed £157.10. 0

Paid for drawing four very high finished elevations of the above house at 15 Guineas £63. 0. 0

Febr 14th

Sent to Dublin correct estimates & particulars of the above house

	£31458.10. 1	
June 29th Further estimates	*7571. 5.10*	
	39029.15.11 [at 1½%]	*£585. 8. 1*

N.B. Lord Lorton entered into an agreement to execute the above house, including professional charges and on the terms of indemnification, having previously omitted many articles & inserted others & engaging him to find sundry articles at certain prices the whole being comprized in a bill of particulars finally arranged & including professional charges for £28511.8.1 in which sum the estimating was charged as above at 100£ each but the designs & plan being afterwards abandoned the contract was nugatory & the above & an engagement entered into to perform 5 journeyscharges are made according to that part of the schedule of terms which respects the designs not carried into effect. But if any other had been carried into execution by me I should have charged 3 guineas a day for my time, but Lord Lorton in the house afterwards erected having discharged me as his architect before its completion, I consider myself entitled to 5 guineas a day for my time.

Between February 1809 and June 1810 the plans were altered and reduced, and 3 other plans made for all which I charge £0. 0. 0

Decr 23, 1809 revised and reinstated the estimate on a reduced plan and drew out designs of the plan so reduced £0. 0. 0

A complete set of fair designs on a small scale[74] £0. 0. 0

Between the adoption of the first plan and its final rejection the following other estimates were made

14th Octr 1809

Estimate of Stone Ashler Front instead of Parker's Cement

£1053.16. 2

13th Septr 1809

Estimate of additional range of rooms over Kitchen offices

316. 0. 0

" *of Attic Turret over front entrance*

200.15.8

" *of octagon turret in East front*

211.17. 9

" *of arms etc over principal stairs*

80. 0. 0

" *of extra rough stonework, plastering & flooring over Attics in entrance*

19. 3. 0

" *of the like in the East front*

23. 0. 0

" *of 2 additional columns in the circular portico*

41. 0. 0

£1948.12.7

Commission to estimating at 1½pr Ct 29. 4. 7

Journey 1809

7 days at Rockingham – 5 days travelling and 5 days returning making 17 days at 5 guineas 89. 5. 0

700 miles posting and expenses, crossing and recrossing from Holyhead 74. 4. 0

All the aforegoing designs and estimates were set aside & an entire new plan and designs from a suggestion of Lady Lortons at the end of January 1809 which after various sketches were finally fixed upon and the working plans elevations sections etc etc made and are the designs now carrying into execution –

March 1810

Designs of a new house of between 25 & 30 thousand pounds cost £157.10, but as Lord Lorton executes & pays for the carcasing of the house to me as an architect I only charge half for the designs

£78.15. 0

June 26th 1810

Making complete estimates and particulars of the above designs for the amount of which Lord Lorton entered into a Contract and afterwards broke through £26,543.18.6

Commission on the amount of the same at 1½ pt ct 398. 3. 1

Paid for drawing four highly finished elevations[75] *of the said house* 63. 0. 0

June 1810

Journey – 6 days at Rockingham, 5 days travelling, 5 days returning at 3 guineas per day instead of 5 guineas, the plans being carried into execution, 16 days 50. 8. 0

Posting and expenses as before 74. 4. 0

Commission on £9981.10. 4 being that part of the expenditure made out by Messrs Pain & Lilly at 5 per Cent 499. 1. 6

Commission on that part of the expenditure which did not come under their cognizance such as excavation, Bricks, quarrying Stone, Lime, Carriage, &

the Mason's work and others from the 11th Octr [1809] to the completion of the carcass of the house supposed in the absence of better information at £7000 which at 5 pr Ct *350. 0. 0*

£2,675.12. 3

The commission is charged on the supposed amount of the carcass of the house, the working plans for which (being all the professional labour I was bound to do) being completed. If the amount is wrong, Lord Lorton who alone knows what it has cost him can get it right.

Signed
John Nash
Dover Street
21st Janr 1813

NOTES

1. King-Harman, R.D. 1959. *The Kings, Earls of Kingston. An Account of the Family and their Estates in Ireland between the Reigns of the two Queens Elizabeth.* Cambridge, Heffer; King-Harman, A.L. 1996. *The Kings of King House. The Story of the Descendants of Sir John King of Boyle and their Estates at Mitchelstown, Rockingham and Newcastle.* Bedford, A.L. King-Harman; Power B. 2000. *White Knights, Dark Earls. The Rise and Fall of an Anglo-Irish Dynasty.* Cork, The Collins Press. Unless otherwise indicated, details of King family history are taken from these sources.
2. Hussey de Burgh, U. 1878. *The Landowners of Ireland.* Dublin, Hodges, Foster and Figgis, pp. 251-252
3. Dooley, T. 2001. *The Decline of the Big House in Ireland. A study of Irish Landed Families 1860-1960.* Dublin, Wolfhound Press, p.114
4. Craig, M. 1974. 'Sir Edward Lovett Pearce', *Bulletin of the Irish Georgian Society,* 17, Nos 1/2 (Jan/June), pp.10-14. Although as yet still not authenticated by documentary evidence, Dr Craig has retained King House in a more recent list of 'buildings in some way connected to Pearce'; see Craig, M. 1996. 'The quest for Sir Edward Lovett Pearce', *Irish Arts Review,* 12, pp.27-34
5. Lease, King-Harman papers, National Archives, 90/D14051. Unfortunately the map of Sir Henry's estates in Roscommon and Sligo, which were surveyed by Garret Hogan in 1724 (National Library of Ireland, Sir John Ainsworth's inventories of private collections, PC 105: King papers), excluded Rockingham, so that it is not possible to pinpoint more exactly the position of the seventeenth-century house.
6. Taylor, G. and Skinner, A. 1783. *Maps of the Roads of Ireland.* London, the Authors, p.64; 'A mile beyond Ardkarne church on the R, is Kingston-Hall, a most magnificent and beautiful edifice, with extensive and delightful parks and demesnes …', Wilson, W. 1786. *The Post-*

Chaise Companion ... through Ireland. Dublin, the Author, p.103; '... situate in a valley ..., at a small distance from the public road...', Atkinson, A. 1815. *The Irish Tourist: in a Series of Picturesque Views, Travelling Incidents and Observations ....* Dublin, the Author, p.33. Atkinson was passing by in November 1810. His scanty account and failure to mention the ongoing building work on the new Rockingham would lead one to suspect that he did not actually enter the demesne, although Lord Lorton subscribed for four copies of his book!

7. Ordnance Survey map, 1838. In 1770 Thomas Cuttle produced a set of maps (National Library of Ireland, Ms 21.f.13) of the Earl of Kingston's estates, based on Garret Hogan's map of 1724. This time Rockingham was included but, maddeningly, the relevant folio (53) is missing from the set. However, such surveys as Cuttle's and Hogan's were primarily concerned with acreage, and buildings were rarely recorded.
8. Beaufort, D.A. 'Journal of a tour through part of Ireland ... in 1787', pt 2, 21 October, Trinity College, Dublin Library Ms 4027
9. King-Harman papers, Public Record Office of Northern Ireland, D4168/C/1/1-4; King-Harman papers, National Archives, 90/D13149 – marriage settlement
10. Letter quoted in Malcomson, A.P.W. 1982. *The Pursuit of the Heiress. Aristocratic Marriage in Ireland 1750-1820.* Belfast, Ulster Historical Foundation, pp.23-24
11. [Cockayne, G.E.] 1932. *The Complete Peerage ... By G.E.C.* Vol. 8. London, St Catherine Press, p.144; Johnston-Liik, E.M. 2002. *History of the Irish Parliament 1692-1800.* Belfast, Ulster Historical Foundation, Vol. 5, pp.33-34
12. Reproduced in King-Harman, A.L., *op. cit.*, p.44
13. Stafford-King-Harman papers, National Library of Ireland, Ms 8810 (7,8). This is a considerable archive relating to the building of Rockingham. It falls into two sections: letters and drafts of letters between Lord Lorton, Nash, John Lynn (the clerk of works) and others, together with some work tally-sheets; and about 400 individual bills and accounts. Unless otherwise indicated, the record which follows is derived from this source. One document in particular, Nash's justification of his professional charges, is of such importance, not only for the light it sheds on the development of the plan for the house, but also for the information it contains on Nash's fees and practice, that it has been transcribed as an Appendix to this paper. I have to thank Dr Edward McParland for first drawing this whole manuscript group to my attention in connection with my long-standing pursuit of the career of the Sligo and Downpatrick architect, John Lynn.
14. Mansbridge, M. 1991. *John Nash. A Complete Catalogue.* London, Phaidon, p.104
15. Rowan, A. 1979 *North West Ulster* (The Buildings of Ireland). Harmondsworth, Penguin Books, p.162
16. Mattimoe, C. 1992. *North Roscommon, its People and Past.* Boyle, Roscommon Herald, pp.25-26; Burke F. 1895. *Lough Cé and its Annals, North Roscommon and the Diocese of Elphin in Times of Old.* Dublin, Hodges Figgis, p.17
17. Uvedale Price (1798) to Sir George Beaumont, 'He is reasonable in his charges, but don't trust his estimates but get some other person to execute his designs, and don't say I told you so', as quoted in Summerson, J. 1980. *The Life and Work of John Nash, Architect.* London, Allen & Unwin, p.40; Mrs Stewart of Killymoon (1803) to her husband, Colonel James Stewart, 'I always feared Nash was too moderate in his first valuations. I'm very anxious to know what he now makes it', as quoted from the Clements papers (Correspondence of James

Stewart of Killymoon) in Davis, T. 1966. *John Nash, the Prince Regent's Architect.* London, Country Life, p.50. (There is a microfilm of this correspondence in the National Library of Ireland, n3805.) Nash's overexpenditure at Buckingham Palace has become legendary, although perhaps more the fault of his royal patron than his own.

18. Clements papers, *ibid*, as quoted in Davis, *op. cit.*, p.53
19. Bettley, J. 1988. 'Vignettes of a vanished country house', *Country Life*, 182, No. 46 (Nov. 17), pp.116-117. These watercolour drawings, 7"x10_", Bettley attributes to George Stanley Repton, who was a pupil in Nash's office. The complete set of drawings and plans remains with a member of the King family.
20. Two large monochrome drawings, reputedly from Nash's office, were in Rockingham in the 1940s, but these might have been details or working drawings relating to any of the three designs so far mentioned; see Summerson, J. 1949. *John Nash, Architect to King George IV.* 2nd ed. London, Allen & Unwin, p.97
21. National Library of Ireland, Ms 3775, Lord Lorton's account book, 'The expenses incurred in the building of the new house at Rockingham, the first stone of which was laid the fourth of June 1810.'
22. This fine watercolour, 18½"x26", was for long in the possession of Sir John Summerson, who attributed it also to George Stanley Repton. It was sold at Sotheby's in 1993 and has returned to a member of the King family.
23. King-Tenison, E. Kilronan Castle photograph album, National Photographic Archive: plate 45
24. When O'Connor was undertaking commissions in the West of Ireland; see Strickland, W.G. 1913. *A Dictionary of Irish Artists.* Dublin, Maunsel. Vol. 2, p.180. I am grateful to The Knight of Glin for helping me to trace the present whereabouts of this painting.
25. Some reproduced in MacDonnell, R. 2002. *The Lost Houses of Ireland.* London, Weidenfield & Nicolson, p.183-190, and others in Bence-Jones, M. 1996. *Life in an Irish Country House.* London, Constable, pp.217-219, and in Bence-Jones, M. 1978. *Burke's Guide to Country Houses.* Vol. 1: Ireland. London, Burke's Peerage, p.244.
26. Summerson, 1980, *op. cit.*, p.49
27. Mansbridge, *op. cit.*, p.85
28. These measurements are derived from those given in Casey, C. 1998. 'The Regency house in Ireland' in M. Airs (ed.) *The Regency Great House*, pp.38-48. Oxford, University of Oxford Department for Continuing Education
29. The quality of the limestone in the parish of Ardcarne for architectural purposes is commented upon in Lewis, S. 1837. *A Topographical Dictionary of Ireland.* London, Lewis, Vol.1, p.43. The finely finished ashlar of Rockingham was particularly admired in both Inglis, H.D. 1835. *Ireland in 1834.* London. Whittaker, Vol.2, pp.143-144 and Barrow, J. 1836. *A Tour round ... Ireland ... in 1835.* London, Murray, p.157
30. For more on this, see Casey, *op. cit.*, p.42
31. National Library of Ireland, Ms 3775, 3776
32. Lynn was paid the equivalent of about two guineas a week, the going rate for a clerk of works in England at the time (National Library of Ireland, Ms 3775). There are useful paragraphs on the employment, duties and emoluments of clerks of works in the early nineteenth century in Linstrum, D. 1972. *Sir Jeffry Wyatville.* Oxford, Clarendon Press, pp.25-27; see also Richardson, M. 1992. 'Sir John Soane: the business of architecture' in G. Worsley (ed.)

Georgian Architectural Practice. Papers given at the Georgian Group Symposium, 1991, London, Georgian Group, pp.66-71.

33. Sir John Summerson succinctly summed up Nash's rather slapdash approach in his 'Introduction' to Davis, T. 1960. *The Architecture of John Nash*. London, Studio: 9

    As a man of business, though he was no rogue he moved sometimes a little too fast to be wholly respectable. As a designer he certainly moved much too fast to be respectable at all by the standards of the scholars and critics of his own or any other time. His detailing was terrible. And, what is worse, he knew that it was terrible and did not care. "Never mind" he would say of some egregious misfit arriving from one of his sketches, "it won't be observed in the execution".

    Criticisms, Summerson writes again 'might be directed against nearly all Nash's big houses: superficiality and carelessness in the working out of ideas in themselves original and striking' (Summerson, 1980, *op. cit.*, p.50). In 1815 Nash had another 'furious row', this time with Sir James Langham, arising from structural defects in the house which he was building for him at the top of the new Regent Street in London; see Summerson, 1980, op. cit., p.83
34. Colvin, H. 1995. *A Biographical Dictionary of British Architects 1600-1840*. 3rd ed. New Haven, Yale University Press, pp. 693, 694
35. McTernan, J.C. 2000. *A Sligo Miscellany. A Chronicle of People, Places & Events of other Days.* Sligo, Avena Publications, p.338
36. Attacks of dry rot seem not to have been at all uncommon in buildings which took years to complete. At Corsham Court in Wiltshire, where Nash carried out additions and alterations between 1796 and 1803 'The construction was a calamity: poor workmanship, careless detailing and lack of supervision led to dry rot. The remedial works lasted another ten years, when Nash was paid off' (Mansbridge, *op. cit.* p.77). At Wilton House, also in Wiltshire, where alterations were made by James Wyatt between 1801 and 1811, all the woodwork in the new cloisters was found to be infected with dry rot; see Robinson, J.M. 1979. *The Wyatts. An Architectural Dynasty.* Oxford, Oxford University Press, p.73
37. This was very up-to-date: Pakenham Hall in County Westmeath was the first Irish country house recorded as having steam heating in about 1807; see Girouard, M. 1978. *Life in the English Country House. A Social and Architectural History.* New Haven, Yale University Press, p.263, and Pakenham, V. 2000. *The Big House in Ireland.* London, Cassell, p.54
38. Weld, I. 1832. *Statistical Survey of the County of Roscommon.* Dublin, Graisberry, pp.231-240
39. It is this altered version of the portico which is being described in Lewis, *op. cit.*, Vol. 1, p.43. The porte-cochère had the effect of considerably darkening the entrance hall. This was eventually remedied only in 1902 by the substitution of a more open roof during the preparations for the tenancy of the Lord Lieutenant, the Earl of Dudley (contemporary Dublin newspaper report).
40. King-Harman, R.D., *op. cit.*, p.101
41. Pakenham-Mahon papers, National Library of Ireland, Ms 10, 104(1)
42. 'Mr Lynn was formerly engaged by Lord Lorton in the construction of Rockingham house. He was originally a Carpenter by trade, but the Patronage of the noble Lord has, it would appear, transfused into his mind the theory of his profession, and converted him into an Architect'; see [Bell, T.] 'Rambles Northward in Ireland ... By the Author of the Royal Irish Academy's Prize Essay on Gothic Architecture for the year 1826', National Library of Ireland,

Ms Joly 12, p.72. I am grateful to Ann Martha Rowan for this reference.

43. Graham, R. 1835-1836. 'Diary of three tours in Ireland', Vol. 3, National Library of Ireland, Ms 1658. The figure given for the number of bedrooms probably now includes the old nurseries and some of the former dressing rooms. Isaac Weld, visiting the house in 1830, was also much impressed by the fuelling arrangements and by the ingenious method for tracing flues to chimney-stacks in case of fire; see Weld, *op. cit.*.
44. *Roscommon Herald*, 25/4/1863; King-Harman, R.D., *op. cit.*, pp.176-177. King-Harman says that the house was 'practically demolished', but a photograph taken by Edward King-Tenison not long after the fire shows the smoke-blackened walls of the lake frontage standing full height, although many windows are gaping voids or are boarded up; see King-Tenison, op. cit.: plate 72. According to the *Roscommon Herald*, the house was burnt out within three or four hours, although part of it was still burning two days later. A little of the 'costly furniture' and plate was saved, as must have been a considerable number of the family portraits which were still adorning the rebuilt house in 1902 (see note 39 above).
45. Thomson, D. 1974. *Woodbrook*. London, Barrie & Jenkins, p.68. A Dublin newspaper account of 1902 managed to put it more tactfully, if circuitously: 'The main body of the house is otherwise architecturally not particularly interesting, being of square, massive proportions, and not tapering off into any aestheticisms of artistic fancy'!
46. National Library of Ireland, Ms 3275: folio 16. This is a legal deposition of about 1819, in which Sutherland states that he had been employed by Viscount Lorton from twelve to fifteen years at Rockingham,

    ... laying out ornamental and useful plantations, to the extent of some hundred acres, and in improving and laying out the ground and approaches, and in laying out subterraneous passages, and in altering and improving both the offices belonging to the Mansion-house, and also to the Farm-house.

    The length of time mentioned, together with Sutherland's claim that he had worked for Lorton's father and grandfather, confirm that he was also responsible for the landscaping of the earlier Kingston Hall.
47. May 10, 1814, Lynn reports that Sutherland has been marking trees for felling.
48. Caledon papers, Public Record Office of Northern Ireland, D2433/34/3, D2433/35/3
49. Public Record Office of Northern Ireland, D1470/3
50. For further details of Sutherland's career, see Bowe, P. 1977. 'Mr. Sutherland's elegant taste'. *Country Life*, CLXXII, No. 4176 (14 July), pp.118-19; Bowe, P. 1981. 'Some Irish landscape gardeners' in Jackson-Stops, G. (ed.) *National Trust Studies*, 1981, pp.6-16. London, Sotheby Parke Bernet; Lamb, K. and Bowe, P. 1995. *A History of Gardening in Ireland.* Dublin, National Botanic Gardens, pp.43-49,p.61; Bowe, P. in Jellicoe, G. 1986. *The Oxford Companion to Gardens.* Oxford, Oxford University Press, p.541; and Malins, E. and The Knight of Glin. 1976. *Lost Demesnes. Irish Landscape Gardening, 1660-1845.* London, Barrie & Jenkins, pp.82,89,96
51. Graham, *op. cit.*.
52. He is in fact described as an 'architect' rather than a landscape gardener in the Dublin directories of his time; see Colley, M. 1991. 'A list of architects, builders, surveyors, measurers and engineers extracted from Wilson's Dublin *Directories* from 1760 to 1837', *Bulletin of the Irish Georgian Society*, 34, pp.2-69. At Oakport, the 1200-acre estate to the east

of Rockingham, Sutherland not only laid out the gardens and plantations for Lorton's brother, the third Earl of Kingston, but also designed the hothouses and offices there and the main house itself, 'a large edifice in the ancient or Gothic style of architecture'; see National Library of Ireland Ms 3275 and Lewis, *op. cit.*, Vol. 1, p.43

53. Many of these are described and illustrated in Howley, J. 1993. *The Follies and Garden Buildings of Ireland.* New Haven, Yale University Press, pp. 86,98-101,126,185-187
54. Mansbridge, *op. cit.*, pp.164-166
55. Ordnance Survey map, 1838
56. Built for £1168.4.0 to incorporate a keeper's cottage (National Library of Ireland, Sir John Ainsworth's inventories of private collections, PC105: King papers. These documents were never transferred to the National Library and were probably lost in the 1957 fire at Rockingham)
57. Datestone
58. The 'old garden' wall (?at Kingston Hall) was demolished in 1810, possibly for its bricks; a separate accounting page for the 'new garden' was commenced in 1813 (National Library of Ireland, Ms 3776).
59. The castle is still in its ruinous state in James Arthur O'Connor's view of 1818/1819 (Fig 8) but has been 'renovated' by the time of Robert Graham's visit in 1836 (Graham, *op. cit.*); and is also described in its extended form in Batt, E. 1835. 'Our tour in Ireland in 1835', National Library of Ireland, Ms 16184.
60. Power, *op. cit.*, p.186
61. Burke, J.B. 1855. *A Visitation of Seats and Arms of the Noblemen and Gentlemen of Great Britain and Ireland.* London, Hurst and Blackett. 2nd series, Vol.2, p.46-48
62. Bernadette Foley, visiting the ruin in 1962, saw scorched books still lying on the remains of the library shelves; see Foley, B. 1988. 'Rockingham' in *Boyle. A selection of Articles on Places, Buildings and Events of Local Interest,* pp.151-156. Boyle, Roscommon Herald
63. Royal Institute of British Architects. 1973. *Catalogue of the Drawings Collection.* Vol. L-N. Farnborough, Greg
64. Worsley, G. 1991. 'Architecture and the architectural profession during the Regency' in his *Architectural Drawings of the Regency Period 1790-1837. From the Drawings Collection of the Royal Institute of British Architects.* London, Deutsch, pp. 1-32.
65. One is in the Royal Institute of British Architects Drawings Collection and the other is at the Royal Pavilion in Brighton; see Temple, N. 1993. *George Repton's Pavilion Notebook. A Catalogue Raisonné.* Aldershot, Scolar Press
66. Evans, R.H. 1835. *Architectural and Miscellaneous Library, Prints and Drawings of John Nash to be Sold 15* [-20] *July 1835.* London, Evans. There is a priced copy in the British Library, S.-C.E.52(5)
67. Davis, T. 1965. 'John Nash in Ireland', *Bulletin of the Irish Georgian Society,* 8, pp.55-64
68. Nash, J. 2000. *The Diaries of John Nash Architect 1832 to 1835.* Ed. by Malcolm Pinhorn. Leominster, Pinhorns
69. Ms 8810(8), file 2
70. A 5% architect's commission was being charged as far back as the late seventeeth century. This was James Gibbs's charge in the 1720s, to which, like Nash, he added the costs of special drawings. Travelling expenses would customarily be extra. In his earlier career in

Wales, Nash charged 4½% commission for Hereford Gaol (1792-1796) and during his short partnership with Humphry Repton, lasting from 1795 to 1799, he also took 4½% out of the total 7% of their joint commission for architectural design and landscaping.
Final measurement of work carried out was included in the usual 5% until the first half of the nineteenth century, when quantity surveyors gradually took over this task. Some architects sought an extra 2½% for measuring the completed work, but John Soane was adamant that the 5% was sufficient. The Architects' Club set up a committee to review the matter of charges in 1795, but the dispute over measuring continued for some years: James Wyatt, Henry Holland, Nash and S.P. Cockerell were among the majority in disagreement with Soane. In their evidence in 1828 before the House of Commons Select Committee on the Office of Works and Public Buildings, Nash, Soane, Robert Smirke, Cockerell and Thomas Hardwick all concurred that 5% of the cost of the work was the normal architect's fee for design and superintendence.
In Ireland, in about 1823, the Morrisons, according to their printed rates, were charging 5% for design and superintendence and 1½% for detailed estimates; with travelling expenses at one shilling a mile. The Institute of Architects of Ireland issued a schedule of charges in 1840: still 5% for design and superintendence, but 1% for a detailed estimate.
(See Colvin, H. 1992. 'Architect and client' in Worsley (ed.), *op. cit.*, p.8; Friedman, T. 1992. 'James Gibbs and "This most miserable business of architecture"' in *ibid.*, p.12; Summerson, 1980, op. cit., p.15; Farington, J. 1978-1998. *The Diary (1793-1821).* Ed by K. Garlick [and others]. 17 vols. New Haven, Yale University Press: June 3, 1797, December 12, 1798, February 11, 1803; Kaye, W.B. 1960. *The Development of the Architectural Profession in Britain. A Sociological Study.* London, Allen & Unwin, pp.59, 90; Linstrum, op. cit., p.27; Parliamentary Papers [H.C.1828.iv.446]; Rowan, A.M. (ed.) 1989. *The Architecture of Richard Morrison (1767-1849) and William Vitruvius Morrison (1794-1838).* Dublin, Irish Architectural Archive, p.174.

71. A London architect usually expected to visit his provincial commissions at least once a year; see Colvin, 1992, *op. cit.*, p.7
72. According to Joseph Farington, writing in 1796, James 'Wyatt told me that his professional Journies are so many that He computes he travels 4000 miles in a year'; of Nash he records in 1821, 'He said that ... he ... had travelled in the 3 kingdoms Eleven thousand miles in the year and in that time had expended £1500 in Chaise hire'; see Farington, op. cit.: July 20, 1796, November 11, 1821.
73. Sir John Summerson, citing the Wykeham-Musgrave papers in the Bodleian Library, notes that in 1804 Nash had a set scale of charges for small buildings – cottages 3 guineas each, farmhouses 7 guineas, farmhouse and farmyard 15 guineas, lodges 10 guineas; see Summerson, 1980, *op. cit.*, p.51
74. See Figs 3-6
75. See Fig 7

SOURCES FOR THE HERITAGE GARDENS INVENTORY OF NORTHERN IRELAND[1]

BELINDA JUPP

THE PURPOSE OF COMPILING the Inventory was to discover the past and present stock of parks, gardens and demesnes in the six counties of Northern Ireland. It was commissioned by the Northern Ireland Heritage Gardens Committee and, as the result of the allotted three-years work, was published in 1992 as the *Heritage Gardens Inventory.* The following is a personal account of a sample of the archival material encountered in the survey.

The Committee is an *ad hoc* body representing those with an interest in preserving historic sites and promoting research into the history of gardens and horticulture. It was established in 1980, with the original aim of preparing an inventory of outstanding parks and gardens to submit to the International Council on Monuments & Sites (ICOMOS). This organisation, which had provided the spur to garden history, had stated in article 9 of the 1981 Florence Charter: 'The preservation of historic gardens depends on their identification and listing.' As a result, the booklet *Northern Gardens* was published in 1982, containing an outline history of twenty six identified 'gardens of international importance'. These were reputedly selected with much angst by the founding Committee members. Following this pioneering work, it became clear that a more comprehensive, county-by-county, record of all significant sites was necessary to bring to the public arena what the Committee now realised was a substantial garden and gardening heritage.

The Committee gathered funds to bring this ambition to fruition. Most of the financing was to come from the Department of the Environment for Northern Ireland under the auspices of Dr. Ann Hamlin, who by that time had become a valued member of the Committee. To facilitate the project, a junior fellowship for three years was established in the Institute of Irish Studies at The Queen's University, Belfast. From the outset, the survey was to be as full an historic search as was possible. Under direction from the Committee 'everything' was to be recorded, both extant and extinct. Article 15 of the Florence Charter noted the necessity of '...thorough prior research...' and accordingly the Inventory was to contain not only lists of sites but properly organised reference material collated as an archive. The ultimate aim of the Inventory and archive, apart from bringing the sites to public notice, was to be useful to individuals and organisations who might play a vital role in dictating the way that sites develop in the future. It was planned that those sites of particular merit and which met strict criteria, would eventually be placed on a Register, emulating work already undertaken in England and Wales. These would eventually be given statutory protection and in an ideal world, would be appreciated and conserved.

Garden history is a comparatively new field of study, which has gathered momentum in the last thirty or so years. There are no clear research paths. Source material comes from a wide diversity of disciplines such as history, geography, horticulture, architecture and the pictorial arts. Apart from finding the sites themselves, the creation of the archive was experimental and led down both well-trodden and more obscure routes. The members of the Committee were very helpful from the outset. Dr Charles Nelson recommended sites of horticultural importance, Hugh Dixon provided a list of historic houses with notable grounds, Margaret Garner extended an invitation to use her library and Dr Molly Sanderson made introductions to neighbouring owners.

This record of collected source material is in some ways very general and in others idiosyncratic in the choice of references mentioned. It would be impossible to cover every source but a personal selection hopefully can give a flavour of the background to the assemblage. The subject matter can conveniently be referred to as 'sites' but variously as gardens, demesnes and grounds wherever appropriate.

The starting point was to discover what was, or had been, there. The first task was systematically going through all editions of the six-inch Ordnance Survey County Series maps. The pleasure of looking at the expertly engraved first edition, published from 1833, was tempered by the lack of field boundaries and contours. Nevertheless, extant demesnes were easy to identify and more so in the second revision, published from 1845, where demesne areas were stippled with 'demesne ruling'. Demesne land is that which the landowner held for his own use and would typically include the house at the centre, stables, home farm, and woodland. More importantly, demesnes contained ornamental grounds and often embellishments such as a grotto or summer house. Ordnance Survey twenty-five inch maps were published from 1887, during a time when estate land had started to be transferred from landlord to tenant. New houses and gardens appeared on each edition. Public parks became features on later maps and were duly noted. Time limitations meant that it was not possible to record the numberless town gardens and smaller gardens in this survey. Although the maps were informative, not everything showed up. Many sites were 'lost' before the first edition was made. The former existence of known lost sites or those with scant surviving remnants were nevertheless to be noted.

Gradually the lists of sites grew and other questions had to be answered. For example, in what state were they and their component parts? Site visits became necessary. Historic sites included in the *Inventory* were designed landscapes of all shapes and sizes, encompassing small rock gardens, vast demesnes, nursery gardens and municipal parks. Each was unique and each one survived in different conditions. They ranged from the creation of one person or the result of activity spanning the centuries. Many are excellent examples of a particular acknowledged style; others may contain a notable and well-established plant collection; some may form an integral setting for buildings of historical importance or the creation of a particular designer. The very vibrant nature of gardens, with incessant growth and the changing of the seasons, makes them volatile and difficult to define. However, trees live for a very long time and their distribution within the landscape gives structure and continuity within the sites. Lay-out and land-form can survive for generations, displaying features such as canals, lakes, ponds, walls, paths and garden buildings. These are some of the principal items to be looked for in a site survey. The search also involves looking for what was there at different periods; layer upon layer. Early formal gardens were overlaid with the verdant pastures of the late 18th century 'landscape' style and subsequently overlaid again with multifarious Victorian flower beds or an arboretum of exotic trees. Studying the site, though pleasant in itself (in clement weather), needs a trained eye.

Site visits found owners very hospitable and interested in the project. Many coffees, lunches and teas were consumed in grand dining rooms or kitchens before or after informative tours. Both well-tended and fully-functioning large grounds or abandoned and bramble-filled skeletons were of interest. There were many beautifully maintained ornamental gardens and many that had passed their days of glory but were still essentially intact. It took time to walk miles, take photographs, fill in a pro-forma for each place and discover as much as possible about further sources. However a site survey does not tell the whole story. The usual research repositories had to be combed for documentary evidence to discover how, when and why sites evolved and developed.

At the time that the *Inventory* was compiled, the supply of secondary sources on established sites was small. It was dispiriting to discover that virtually the only book devoted to the topic was *Lost Demesnes – Irish Landscape Gardening 1660 to 1845* by Edward Malins and The Knight of Glin, published in 1976. Its companion, *Irish Gardens and Demesnes from 1830* by Malins and Patrick Bowe was published in 1980. Many of the grander sites in the north are referred to in these innovatory studies. The Ulster Architectural Heritage Society series, *Historic Buildings, Groups of Buildings, Areas of Architectural Importance* begun in the 1960s, was useful in identifying sites and for their analysis of garden buildings. R.M Young's *Belfast in the Province of Ulster in the 20th Century* published in 1909, contains pages devoted to grand and moderately sized houses, which would all have had some degree of ornamental surroundings worth investigating. Though there are few specific references to these grounds, one or two good photographs are included.

The unpublished in-depth historic landscape studies of National Trust properties, Castle Coole, Castle Ward, Florence Court, and Crom Castle[2] by Thomas McErlean and Terence Reeves-Smyth were ground-breaking, to which there was nothing to add, as the work was already done. The guidance of these two experts was invaluable in the compilation of the *Inventory* and the archive. One or two coffee table books provided interest, for example, Sybil Connolly and Helen Dillon edited and published in 1986 *In An Irish Garden*, which consists of contemporary accounts written by the gardeners themselves, either of maintained old gardens or gardens that might turn out to be 'heritage' gardens of the future! No cut-off date had been set by the Committee.

As in all parts of the temperate world, horticulture emerged from agriculture. As far as is known the first organised gardens in Northern Ireland were monastic, in which herbs, fruit, flowers and vegetables would have been grown for culinary and medicinal purposes. These gardens disappeared following the dissolution of the monasteries but during the time of their existence, monks and friars introduced many plants into Ireland, which is not particularly rich in native flora.

The first informative pictorial representation of specific sites dates from the Plantation period. Many of Thomas Raven's picture-maps depict buildings with their surrounding gardens. For example, the Skinners' Building in Dungiven, Co.Londonderry of 1622 (Fig 1) shows a manor house and bawn enclosure, with a garden behind the house laid out in a formal manner in four plots, divided by paths. The garden is adjacent to the house, protected on two sides by walls and by the River Roe on the third side.

Fig 1. The Skinners' Building at Dungiven: detail of a picture-map by Thomas Raven 1622, T510/1, PRONI

Gardening activity is usually associated with times of peace but a curiosity was displayed in the exhibition of Ireland in the 1690s at the Ulster Museum in 1990, entitled 'Kings in Conflict'. A reproduction of 'A Ground Plot ye Strong Fort of Charlemont in Ireland' by Samuel Hobson, reproduced from Story's *Continuation* of 1693,[3] shows the fort surrounded by orchards and gardens both in the town and 'under Command of ye Fort.'

In another much later period of conflict, a plan of the town of Antrim in Sir Richard Musgrave's *Memoirs of the Different Rebellions in Ireland*, of 1801, shows the formation of battle that took place in the summer of 1798 in the clearly delineated 'Lord Massareens's domain' [sic],[4] in which the walled garden is a numbered feature and the woodland is called 'Close Planting'. Demesne, walled garden and wood survive today in much the same form in what is now a public park, Antrim Castle Gardens.

An unusual source is an interior family portrait of the 'Family of Thomas Bateson Esq.,' attributed to Strickland Lowry and painted in 1762. The family wanted to commemorate not only their portraits but their property as well and this was managed by the clever device of displaying topographical paintings on the wall behind the figures. Though small, the picture on the right of their house and demesne at Orangefield, which has now gone, enables the viewer to see a large walled garden close to the house, with fields and woods extending out into the landscape, exemplifying this phase in garden history in Ireland. The portrait exhibits a family in a period of good fortune. As fortunes fluctuated, development and ornamentation of gardens reflected advantageous marriages, successful business ventures, good crops or other reasons that an enabled an owner to follow fashion and improve his house and grounds.

The essential starting point for tracing family history of the owners are the many editions of Sir Bernard Burke's *Peerage, Baronetcy and Knightage* and *A Genealogical & Heraldic History of the Landed Gentlemen of Ireland.* Family and estate papers, available in the Public Record Office (NI) or in private hands, though irresistible, were noted in the archive for future reference for more in-depth studies. However estate maps were easily assimilated. These proliferated from the late 18th century and were drawn up to assist with the management of demesnes and estates during times of increased population and an interest in agricultural improvement.

In the same era that the Bateson portrait was painted, Mrs Delany, wife of the Dean of Down and sometime resident in Co.Down, sketched and wrote descriptions of gardens. On the 1st of October 1758 she wrote from Belvoir about a visit to another property at Hillsborough belonging to her host:

> *The day cleared up; Lord Hillsborough, Mr Bayley and I walked round the improvements, a gravel path two Irish Miles long, the ground laid out in very good taste, some wood, some nurseries: shrubs and flowers diversify the scene, a pretty piece of water with an island in it, and all the views pleasant. D.D. and Sally saved themselves, as the ground was damp, for another walk, which was to a castle that Lord Hillsborough is building.* [the D.D. referred to is her husband, Dr Delany and Sally is her goddaughter, Sally Chapone].

Though not informative in the detail, it is especially interesting as it refers to the grounds of the former house, which are now under the lake. The 'castle that Lord Hillsborough is building', is the present house, Hillsborough Castle. Mrs Delany goes on to describe the gardens at the 'old castle..' (Hillsborough Fort), which had by then:

> *fallen to decay...the court behind it measures just an English acre, and is laid down in a bowling green, and round it is a raised high terrace, at each corner of which is a square of about fifty feet, which are to make four gardens, one for roses only, the other for all sorts of flowers – these on each side of the castle; the other two for evergreens and flowering shrubs.*[5]

These gardens and the bowling green have also gone, so her observations and particularly the measurements, are intriguing. Mrs Delany's sketches included studies of garden sites near the Delanys' homes at Mount Panther and Hollymount.

Coinciding with the demise of the formal lay-out of grounds in favour of the English Landscape style at the end of the 18th century, professional artists were commissioned to produce topographical studies of great houses in their setting. The wonderfully picturesque location of many great houses in Ireland is emphasised and is still appreciated today. A period marked by the highest quality of landscape painting in Ireland provided many insights into the structure and features of individual sites. Thomas Roberts painted a series of views of Upper Lough Erne in the 1770s, which included a painting of the grounds of Bellisle, Co. Fermanagh[6]. John James Barralet's work at Florence Court, Tollymore Park and Glenarm Castle was expertly engraved by Thomas Milton for publication from 1783 to 1793 in his *Collection of Select Views of the Different Seats of the Nobility and Gentry in the Kingdom of Ireland.* Jonathan Fisher also published his engraved drawings in sixty plates in his *Scenery of Ireland* in 1795, including a superb plate of Castle Ward house surrounded by parkland. Both Fisher and the accomplished landscape artist, William Ashford, painted Castle Ward and the pictures still hang in the house. Fisher also included an aquatint of Belleisle (Fig 2) in his book, drawn from the same position as the Roberts' vista. The Belleisle depictions show an informal landscape in which a path meanders through parkland and leads to a gazebo in a sublime position on the lough shore. Other 19th century publications illustrated gentlemens' seats in their surroundings. Specific to the environs of Belfast, *Belfast Scenery,* consists of Edward Proctor's aquatints of Joseph Molloy's drawings, which was published in 1832 as a series of thirty views of houses set in grounds. They are useful in that they show the not-so-grand homes that were being built in increasing numbers at that time but

Fig 2. Belleisle, aquatint by Jonathan Fisher, *Scenery of Ireland* Vol. I 1795 plate 34

their landscape setting, though doubtless in the fashion of the day, is remarkably similar in each site.

Mrs Delany was on her way to the Giant's Causeway when she visited Hillsborough. From the late 18th century an increasing number of travellers journeyed round Ireland and recorded what they encountered and published their memoirs when they returned home. The Giant's Causeway was a must on the Irish itinerary. Many either visited or stayed in houses along the way and wrote of their impressions of the state of the gardens. It was quite usual for strangers (of the right class) to call and view great houses and demesnes and references recall tours of the house by the housekeeper and the grounds by the head gardener. The travellers needed maps. George Taylor & Andrew Skinner's *Maps of the Roads of Ireland* was published in 1778 and was probably a great boon at the time. The maps identify houses on either side of the roads, the names of the owners and surrounding trees, indicating grounds that might be worth further investigation. Some travellers observed with an expert eye, others were amateur and quixotic. Titles such as the *Post Chaise Companion*, which ran to several editions from 1786, *Guide Through Ireland* of 1838 and *A Walking Tour Round Ireland in 1865*,[7] were intriguing and contained useful snippets. The most informative for Inventory purposes was Atkinson's *Ireland Exhibited to England in the 19th Century…*, published in 1823. He showed a particular interest in the grounds and while most observers concentrated on the ornamental parts, he included this rare comment on a productive walled garden:

The garden of Fruit-hill [Drenagh, Co.Londonderry] *is in tolerably good keeping with the other features of this place. It embraces an area of nearly three English acres, walled in, well stocked with fruit trees in full bearing, rather too well stocked with apple trees for the beauty of its appearance, (we speak not here of espaliers, which are ornamental, and are the only bearer of the apple that we would admit into a garden) and included every class of vegetables necessary for the consumption of a house… The demesne contains about 220 Conyngham acres, of a variable soil, all however fertile and productive, and evidently adapted to the growth of plants…*[8]

A German visitor, Johann George Kohl, made the general comment in his 1844 translated publication, *Ireland, Scotland, England, (and Wales)* that 'On the whole way from Belfast to Carrickfergus, the road is bordered by lines of country seats and gardens.'[9] Most travellers' tales are not wonderfully informative, as they deal with a host of subject matter but it is a bonus when they do identify sites because they note their condition at the time of the visit. Much more detail could be gleaned from the Ordnance Survey Memoir.

The Ordnance Survey Memoir, prior to its recent publication, was available in draft form when the garden *Inventory* was being put together. Written in the early 19th century as an adjunct to first complete mapping of Ireland, the Memoirs were compiled between 1830 and 1840. Their recorded comments and drawings provide a glimpse of life into part of pre-famine Ireland through the eyes of both military and civilian surveyors. They were intended to show in words what could not be shown cartographically. For the purposes of the *Inventory*, garden and demesne lay-outs could be analysed on the maps perfectly satisfactorily. Yet entries in the Memoirs described not only houses in their setting but what grew there, the climatic conditions and the state of the soil. However the quality, quantity and regional coverage of the observations are very variable and some areas were not mentioned at all. Where the entries are informative, as is the following on Greenmount, Co. Antrim, they are a valuable bonus for garden history:

Greenmount, the property of the Honourable and Reverend Archdeacon Agar, is situated in the townland of Tirgracey, about 1 mile south of Antrim and near the road leading from Antrim to Crumlin. The house, which is spacious, is a handsome and modern looking mansion, presenting an Ionic front consisting of a portico, and a balcony supported by 6 columns. The house is rather low and the view from it, except from the upper storey, is confined to the grounds. The offices, which are suitable, are near the house. The garden contains 6 acres 3 roods. It is walled and very well stocked. The hot house includes a tolerable grapery and pinery, which however from not keeping up the fires, are going to destruction. The demesne and grounds contain 160 acres, 39 of which are laid out in ornamental grounds and planting. There are three handsome ponds, a very pretty flower garden, many nice walks, a little temple with handsomely stained glass windows, all of which are quite out of order and in a state of neglect and ruin. Greenmount was built in 1820 by Robert Thompson Esquire. The front was added a few years after. In 1835 it came into the possession of Mr Agar and has not since been, nor is likely to be occupied.[10]

The basic lay-out and features at Greenmount have survived this period of neglect and remain to this day, interspersed with buildings for the horticultural college. But for the OSM nobody would ever have heard of the more ephemeral garden at Doraville, Co.Fermanagh, which boasted a '...choice and varied collection of dahlias.'[11] Dahlias had been introduced to Britain from Mexico in 1789 and by 1830 there were nearly 60 garden varieties.

Writing specifically about gardens and gardening increased in earnest at the beginning of the 19th century. J.C. Loudon published his first *Encyclopaedia of Gardening* in 1822, which became extremely influential and was reprinted and re-edited until 1878. The early editions included site reports on gardens, including those in Ireland. Loudon made use of Statistical Surveys and County Guides, which were topographical surveys covering most counties of Ireland and included five (excluding Fermanagh) in the north, published in the early years of the 19th century. In the 1834 edition of the Encyclopaedia, Loudon utilises a descriptive quote on Downhill from the *Statistical Survey of the County of Londonderry*, published in 1802. The part quoted here is easy to envisage for those of us who know the site '...trees and hedges seem to fly from the enemy; their scanty growth sprouts all from the side most distant from the sea, leaving a ragged, wounded, and blighted rear to the destructive pursuer...'[12] and it goes on to describes the condition of the Earl-Bishop of Derry's ambitious planting between 1780 and 1787 of twenty thousand forest trees in the glens around an impossibly windswept site on the north coast headland.

During a time when many new plants were being introduced, Loudon encouraged owners to invigorate their '...neglected arboriculture and landscape gardens..'. In order to compile his eight volume work, *Arboretum et Fruticetum Britannicum*, Loudon sent out pro-formas to local observers and received feed-back from, amongst others, Earl Roden of Tollymore, Lord Viscount Ferrard of Antrim Castle and Sir Robert Bateson, the Batesons having moved by then from Orangefield to Moira. The gardens at Moira had been famous when the property of Sir Arthur Rawdon in the late 17th century. Loudon's correspondents, while reporting on tree species and sizes, gave excellent retrospective accounts of

Fig 3. Cranmore near Belfast, lithograph by A. McQuillan from a drawing by 'E.M.' *Ulster Journal of Archaeology* 1853 p.136

Rawdon's pioneering efforts as a distinguished plant collector. While the exotic plants from Jamaica that Sir Arthur had collected for him failed to thrive even under glass (the first glasshouses in Ireland were at Moira), they reported that John Templeton was successful in his experiments, begun in 1786, in growing camellias out of doors that were formerly always housed under glass. Templeton lived at Malone in Belfast and by was coincidence custodian of trees planted in Sir Arthur Rawdon's generation, 'Crann-more (sic), that is, Great tree, in honour of the very fine chestnut trees which are in front of the house, and which were probably planted in the 17th century.'[13] Two enormous sweet chestnut trees (Fig 3) still grow in front of the (now ruinous) house. Moira Demesne is a public park today and few venerable trees survive. The very equable climate of most parts of the north of Ireland enables a vast range of plants from the temperate world to be successfully grown.

A curious and individual source, discovered on a site visit, is a tablet of stone in a field at Holestone in Co. Antrim, on which is engraved '2,500 forest trees planted by William Owen on this farm from the year 1791 – 1802'. Very fine stands of beech survive at Holestone and can thus be accurately dated. This is a clue to the intense tree planting at that period. Ireland was (and still is) seriously lacking in tree cover and this was acknowledged in seventeen Acts from 1698 aimed at encouraging planting. An Act of 1765 required that if all trees planted were registered with a Justice of the Peace, a tenant could claim the trees or their value when the lease expired. Amongst these ledgers in the Public Record Office is a section published in 1984 in *A Register of Trees for Co. Londonderry 1768-1811* that contains numbers and species of tree, by whom they were planted, year of planting and the townland in which they were planted.

Many arboreta were planted during the 19th century and a spate of interest in collecting plants from overseas increased at the beginning of the 20th-century, headed by Lord Annesley of Castlewellan Castle. He published a limited edition on his own collection, '*Beautiful and Rare Trees and Plants*', in 1903. The existence of both this and Sir John Ross of Bladensburg's '*List of Trees and Shrubs Grown in the Grounds of Rostrevor House, Co.Down*' of 1911 were noted in the archive. Sir John amassed a superb collection, which grew to perfection in the clement climate of Rostrevor. Alas, it has all but gone but is remembered from his limited publication. When Lady Edith Londonderry came to Mount Stewart in the 1920s, she sought advice from Sir John. No garden survey can ignore the wonderful gardens at Mount Stewart but like other renowned and well-recorded gardens there was not much new to discover.

Detailed descriptions of Mount Stewart and Rowallane are to be found in Country Life. Specialist magazines and journals, though mainly interested in plants and design details, proved a fruitful source. A long-lasting journal *Irish Gardening*, was published from 1906 to 1922 and in Vol. III, 1908, there is a delightful photo of an idyllic cottage garden at 'The Orchard' in Enniskillen. (Fig 4) The photo inspired a visit, but alas the place had gone. Some years ago the late owner had grubbed up all his orchard trees because he had been driven to distraction by boys from nearby Portora (Royal Grammar School) stealing his apples. Articles in journals were the major source of information on 20th-century gardens.

All the well-known collections of photographs, the Lawrence Collection and those by Welch, Hogg and Green, are collated and available to view. They have all provided a rich source of images captured at specific moments in time. They belong to a era which was a hey-day for gardens, when they were maintained to the highest standard and gardeners were plentiful. Surprisingly, few family snaps turned up in owners' albums, though amateur paintings are treasured.

Fig 4. The 'Orchard' Enniskillen, The Cottage Home of Mr T. Maguire, *Irish Gardening* Vol. III 1908 p.151

Watercolours by a member of the Close family are the only remaining memory of the lovely early 20th century gardens at Drumbanagher, Co.Armagh. The house (but for the porte-cochère) and garden have completely disappeared. Nancy Jury captured the garden at Brooklands, Co.Antrim in full glory, which was designed to compliment her father's 'Arts and Crafts' house, built in 1909. The then fashionable Italianate terrace at Drumcairne House, Co.Tyrone, was painted in 1914 by, 'a female member of the Caulfield family' and is now in the collection of the Armagh County Museum (Fig 5). In spite of always having to be wary of artistic license when interpreting a painting or drawing on the ground, in the last two cases the remnants of the gardens, as see today, show that they were convincingly represented.

The few examples quoted here are intended to give an impression of the type of evidence that can be collected for research into our garden history. In common with all research topics, the subject was open-ended and the project in question had a time-limit. Most of the documentary and pictorial material is well-known but in this particular survey anything extant was looked at in conjunction with site surveys, although early gardens that are no longer evident on the ground are only remembered through paper searches. It is obvious from the small sample quoted here that the quality and quantity of material taken, site by site, varied enormously. The sources offer inconsistent coverage of individual sites and (with the exception

Fig 5.
Drumcairne Formal Garden (1914) by a member of the Caulfield family. Photograph Reproduced with Kind permission of the Trustees of the Museums & Galleries of Northern Ireland

of the OS maps), as a whole over the six counties. By the time the research project came to an end, over 600 sites had been recorded. There is a brief description of each in the publication, in which they are uneasily categorised to ICOMOS European standardisation. The archive is in the Monuments and Buildings Record held by Built Heritage, Environment and Heritage Service, Department of Environment (NI). The information is there to be processed, both as 'avenues to the past' for further research or to look to the future, should enhancement plans or threats involve any of the parks, gardens or demesnes.

NOTES

1. Most full titles of books and dates of publication are given in the text. Where they are not, they and unpublished works are cited in the endnotes.
2. McErlean, T. 1985. *Historic Landscape Survey of Castle Coole Demesne*, 2 Vols; McErlean, T and Reeves-Smyth, T. 1986. *Castle Ward Demesne*, 2 Vols; Reeves-Smyth, T. 1989; Reeves-Smyth, T. *Crom Demesne*, 2 Vols; Reeves-Smyth, T. 1987. *Florence Court Demesne*, 3 Vols. Reeves-Smyth, T. All National Trust, Unpublished.
3. Black, E (ed.) 1990. *Kings in Conflict, Ireland in the 1690.* Belfast, Ulster Museum, plate 148, p.157.
4. Musgrave, R. 1801. *Memoirs of the Different Rebellions in Ireland from the arrival of the English.* London, Stockdale & Dublin, Milliken.
5. Llanover, Lady (ed.) 1861. *The Autobiography and Correspondence of Mary Granville. Mrs Delany.* London, Richard Bentley, Vol. III, pp.511-13.
6. Crookshank, A and Glin, Knight of, 1978. *The Painters of Ireland.* London, Barrie and Jenkins, p.132, plate 26.
7. Wilson, W. 1784. *Post Chaise Companion or Traveller's Directory through Ireland*, Dublin, Author; Fraser, J. 1838. *Guide Through Ireland descriptive of its Scenery, Towns, Seats, Antiquities*, Dublin, William Curry; Barry, W.W. 1867. *Walking Tour Round Ireland in 1865.* London, William Bentley.
8. Atkinson, A. 1823. *Ireland Exhibited to England in the 19th Century.* London, Baldwin, Cradock and Joy. 2 Vols, p.211.
9. Kohl, J.G. 1844. *Ireland, Scotland and England.* London, Chapman, p.99.
10. Day, A., McWilliams P and English, L (eds.) 1993. *Ordnance Survey Memoirs of Ireland Parishes of County Antrim XIII, Templepatrick & District 1833,1835,1838.* Belfast, The Institute of Irish Studies, Vol 35, p.62.
11. Day, A and McWilliams, P (eds.) 1992. *Ordnance Survey Memoirs of Ireland, Parishes of County Fermanagh II, 1834-5, Lower Lough Erne.* Belfast, The Institute of Irish Studies, Vol. 14, p.34
12. Loudon, J.C. 1822. *Encyclopaedia of Gardening.* London, Longman. Re-print 1834, p.513 quoting Sampson, G.V, the elder. 1802. *Statistical Survey of the County of Londonderry*, Dublin, p.424.
13. Loudon, J. C. 1844. *Arboretum et Fruticetum Britannicum*, Vols. 1-VIII. London, Longman. Second edition. Vol. I, p.111.

THE PALINGENESIS OF FLORENCE COURT

IAN B MCQUISTON

SETTLED IN THE STUNNING south-west Fermanagh countryside lies Florence Court, ancestral home of the Earls of Enniskillen since the early 18th century. The mansion, which has undergone various enhancements over the years, stands on rising ground overlooking an expansive park towards a perimeter of mature trees, a setting which has remained largely unaltered over many generations of the Enniskillen family (Fig 1).

Inside the mansion, however, matters have been a little less settled. Florence Court was gifted to the National Trust by Michael, Viscount Cole, son of the 5th Earl of Enniskillen, in 1954, and the family continued to live in the mansion sharing the relatively modest rooms with National Trust visitors during the public

Fig 1. The main front of Florence Court

Fig 2. David Lowry Cole (late 6th Earl of Enniskillen), and Nancy Henderson MacLennan marry in London, 7th May 1955.

season. Lord Cole died in 1956 at the early age of thirty four, unmarried; through his will he left his Florence Court estate, including the contents of the house, to his first cousin, David Lowry Cole who owned and managed a ranch in Kenya at the time. Only on the death of his uncle, Lord Cole's father in 1963, did David Lowry Cole become the 6th Earl of Enniskillen, and return to Florence Court with Nancy, his second wife (Fig 2). Nancy Henderson MacLennan was a somewhat formidable American lady who had been US Vice-Consul in Cairo, Nairobi and Tokyo following a period as a Washington and United Nations correspondent for *The New York Times*. Co-existing with the National Trust, particularly inside the mansion where privacy and public access were often in conflict, became increasingly difficult and finally with differences irreconcilable, Lord and Lady Enniskillen departed from Florence Court in 1973, leaving an empty house behind, never to return.

The National Trust for the next 25 years presented Florence Court as a grand country house furnished with furniture and paintings on loan, together with some good pieces of Irish furniture specifically purchased for the house; none of this material had any connection with Florence Court or the family.

In 1997 all this changed and the palingenesis of Florence Court began; this essay charts the intriguing story of how, from those dark days of 1973 and the echoing despair of empty halls, visitors to Florence Court can once again enjoy a property with its soul restored following the return of much of the material accumulated by many generations of the Enniskillen family.

The First Break

The letter which arrived in early January 1997 with a Scottish postmark immediately stood out; addressed to Professor Ronald Buchanan (Regional Chairman of the National Trust Northern Ireland Committee) and endorsed 'Private and Confidential', the handwriting style was large, bold and assertive. But who was the writer?

Nancy, Dowager Countess of Enniskillen, then residing at Kinloch House near Dunkeld in Perthshire, had seen a copy of the 1992 Visitor Guide to Florence Court and wrote to the Regional Chairman with an extensive critique highlighting a considerable list of 'errors', not least that the National Trust had got the donor of the property wrong! The Regional Chairman and the author immediately realised the opportunity this unexpected contact created. Over a period of some 25 years the Regional Committee of the National Trust had from time to time mused about the fate of the contents of Florence Court and of the possibility of getting them back. It was also obvious that Lady Enniskillen's critique was largely valid; the timing of her intervention was also fortuitous because a new guide was in preparation along with a series of interpretive panels for the property. The Regional Chairman wrote immediately welcoming her help, indicating that the changes would be made and that she would see proofs for approval.

The Regional Chairman was also due to travel presently to Scotland and he and the author agreed that this provided an opportunity to meet Lady Enniskillen discreetly and to try and establish a personal relationship; the initiative worked, and over ensuing weeks there was more correspondence about the new publications, until on 26th April 1997, Lady Enniskillen wrote:

> *In a few weeks I hope to be able to write to you – or contact you in person – re an idea/suggestion close to my heart; but presently, relatively confidential.*

In the same letter she expressed her delight at the progress with the new guide book and panels, and enclosed a cheque for £1000 as a contribution towards the costs of publication.

In various telephone discussions and in further correspondence, which Lady Enniskillen always copied to the National Chairman of the National Trust in London, it emerged that her idea had been to leave a large bequest to the National Trust. The true nature of this bequest and the imperative to move matters along, which had become increasingly obvious, came in a letter from the Dowager on 24th May 1997. With the letter was an extract from her will, extending to 15 pages, listing some 250 items which: 'are of historic interest concerning Ireland, my dear husband Captain David Lowry Cole MBE the sixth Earl of Enniskillen, his family and their seat of Florence Court'; she further revealed:

> *My doctors have given me – statistically speaking – at the outside, five months. I hope of course to be an exception and live a little longer (to finish my work for my late husband, Lord Enniskillen: his papers, his archives, etcetera, etcetera). But – it is a somewhat strange and some-what incurable disease (myelodysplasia) and I might go much sooner – possibly.*

And then suggested:

> *It has occurred to me that for expediency and for the security of the items of the bequest itself – and also for the help* (sic) *to the National Trust and for the pleasure and peace of mind it would give me, if the National Trust were to accept my bequest, and under the provisoes* (sic) *inherent in it, I should give these things now, while I am still alive. (No one know better than I, what and where they are, etcetera, etcetera).*

Time was of the essence and a further visit to Kinloch House was quickly arranged; as with the correspondence, the Countess stressed that the visit should be made in complete confidence.

The Visit

Kinloch House nestles on a wooded site in grouse moor country some 10 miles west of Dunkeld, at Amulree in Perthshire. The Regional Chairman and the author arrived promptly at 10.00am on 17th June 1997 to be welcomed on the doorstep by Nancy, Dowager Countess of Enniskillen. Lady Enniskillen was the perfect host, charming, extremely easy and interesting to talk to, generous with her time and hospitality; she very readily autographed the author's copy of her Florence Court – My Irish Home; it was evident though that the effects of her illness meant that she tired noticeably after a few hours. She clearly had a deep love for Florence Court and her late husband the 6th Earl of Enniskillen, who had died on 30th May 1989, and this emerged as the party progressed around Kinloch House admiring the many items which Lady Enniskillen had decided to return to Florence Court. She was emphatic that she had taken the decision to return the items without any influence or duress from other parties. She believed it was what the late 6th Earl would have wished had he still been alive.

Lady Enniskillen then confirmed that the gift of the 250 or so items in advance of her death was subject to three conditions, viz:

- That the National Trust would accept the list in full, and not select from it
- That the National Trust would display all the items in the public rooms at Florence Court at an early date
- That the National Trust would acknowledge that the items had been gifted to it according to the wishes of the 6th Earl of Enniskillen.

The two visitors, mindful of the momentous opportunity to recover such a comprehensive range of items accumulated over many generations, indicated that it should not be difficult for the National Trust to accept the gift and the three provisos, and so it was that Charles Nunneley, the National Chairman, wrote to the Dowager Countess on 26th June 1997 gratefully accepting the gift with the three conditions. The National Chairman was later to call on Lady Enniskillen on 17th August 1997 while on a grouse shoot at a nearby estate.

Before leaving Kinloch House on that day the author agreed to put in place arrangements to have the items removed from Scotland and installed in Florence Court before 10th September 1997, a symbolic target date being the 6th Earl's birthday. A further thought was left with the Dowager Countess, and that was that she might agree to be interviewed as part of the National Trust's oral history project, especially in view of her first hand experience of living at Florence Court and in Kenya prior to and through the independence period and in which the 6th Earl had played such an important role. She politely declined in a letter of 6th July 1997, saying: 'the fact is that the written word, not the spoken word, is for me, the more trusted and more satisfying medium; and the one to which I am accustomed'.

The Move

It was clear that Lady Enniskillen wished to be centrally involved in the planning of the move and its execution, and so it was that on 3rd July 1997, Peter Marlow (Historic Buildings Representative of the National Trust in Northern Ireland), the author, and Andrew Reeves of the removal firm Reeves of Petersfield gathered at Kinloch House. The planning was covered in minute detail, from the size of lorry which could access her driveway to the provision of lavatory facilities for the staff from Reeves. A tour of the house allowed each item on offer to be seen and photographed, but this exercise caused Lady Enniskillen to become increasingly agitated, ostensibly on security grounds, but also because items not on her bequest list might have been recorded. It was thought that the team would need three days to complete the packing; Lady Enniskillen would make herself available throughout and wished to be present when each item was being removed from its room and taken to the packing area in her garage.

As on previous occasions this visit ended on a positive and pleasant note; Peter Marlow presented Nancy with two half bottles of bubbly, and she was later to write, 'Thank you again for the bottles of champagne, a favourite drink, and from a fellow New Englander!'. All parties were now working to a timetable which would see packing begin at Kinloch House on 18th August and the items arriving at Florence Court on 21st August.

An obvious problem at Florence Court was what to do with all the contents so generously loaned by various people, and which had enabled the house to be presented in an appropriate style for some 25 years. Carefully drafted letters went to the various lenders explaining the situation and offering a range of options, including storage on site, redistribution to other National Trust houses, or return to the lender. Storage was going to be a problem and joiners were immediately recruited from McAleer & Teague, local contractors well used to working with the National Trust, to provide racking in the second floor rooms at Florence Court. Arrangements were also put in place to advise visitors that for 6 days full access to the mansion would not be possible, even though it was at the height of the visitor season.

The Reeves of Petersfield van arrived fully laden at Florence Court on 21st August as planned, and the local staff led by Jim Chestnutt (Property Manager), together with the joiners and conservation specialists, set to immediately to install the items in their former home. This was made a little easier due to outline schemes having been prepared, based on the photographs taken earlier by Peter Marlow in Scotland, and local research by Jim Chestnutt. The work was completed with time to spare. Photographs of the new installation were sent to Lady Enniskillen on 30th August, and she replied on 2nd September 1997, saying:

> *I think you have done an excellent job of placing and hanging all these items; notably, of course, the pictures. I am deeply pleased you have placed my late husband, the sixth Earl's portrait by Wraith in the Florence Court drawing room. And I am charmed by your decision to place Florence Wrey – for whom the house was named – over the fireplace in the grand hall.*

Fig 3. The Drawing Room at Florence Court showing two of the three large Irish landscapes (Belleek on the left, Enniskillen on the right) and a portrait of Charlotte Baird (4th Countess of Enniskillen) over the mantle piece, gifted by Nancy, Dowager Countess of Enniskillen.

The portrait of the 6th Earl, painted posthumously, was commissioned by Lady Enniskillen and executed by Robert Wraith, a student and assistant of Annigoni, and depicts the Earl standing in front of the mansion with the distinctive outline of the local mountain, Benaughlin, behind.

As a result of the generous gift from Nancy, Dowager Countess of Enniskillen, among the many items repatriated to Florence Court are portraits of six Earls of Enniskillen, three magnificent 18th century large Irish landscapes of Enniskillen, Devenish and Belleek, pencil and watercolour drawings by members of the family, several display cabinets filled with medals and miniatures, Irish 18th century silver trays and cups, wine coasters and cigarette boxes. There are historical items illustrating the 3rd Earl's association with the Orange Order including a large marble bust of William III, a rare and important 17th century silver gilt mustard pot which once belonged to William III, and cannon balls from the Siege of Derry. Two large cannon, said to have been won in a wager from the 2nd Earl of Belmore by the Lord Enniskillen of the day, which adorned the front steps at Florence Court once again stand defiantly overlooking the park in front of the house.

Death of a Countess

The inevitable consequence of Lady Enniskillen's bone marrow disorder occurred on 24th February 1998, nine months to the day from her letter telling the National Trust that she had perhaps five months to live; she managed a further four and died aged 81. *The Times* on Monday 2nd March 1998 included the entry:

Enniskillen – Nancy Henderson, Dowager Countess. At home on 24th February 1998. Beloved wife of the late Captain David Lowry Cole sixth Earl of Enniskillen. Funeral in Northern Ireland at 2pm on 4th March, St John's Church, Florencecourt. No flowers.

A small congregation of perhaps 20 gathered for the Service; Nancy's remains were flown by private aircraft to St Angelo airfield, near Enniskillen, accompanied by three friends including her Housekeeper. Among the congregation was Lady Linda Muir, the 7th Earl's sister, and her husband, the only family members present. The Scottish visitors flew back to Scotland immediately after the funeral proceedings. Interment was in the Enniskillen family burial ground, adjacent to the church. The distinctive tomb in a dark green slate had been sourced by Nancy in the Lake District; she had had the stone shaped and engraved in Oxford and following an introduction by Roland Paxton, a Professor of engineering history, asked Gordon Millington of the Belfast firm of Consulting Engineers Kirk, McClure and Morton, to arrange shipping and installation at St John's. The choice of professional engineers was to alleviate Lady Enniskillen's concern about subsidence and she wished to ensure that the foundations were secure. The local contracting firm of Tracey Bros carried out the work installing the tomb where Nancy would join her late husband; the engraving was complete apart from a blank for the date of her death to be filled in. The engraving which Lady Enniskillen had chosen for the 6th Earl caused the Rector some concern; it read:

He who was all wisdom, courage, joy and truth
With his sheer life had made this a happier and better world
For he had grace and in him dwelt the spirit of God

Following consultation with the Bishop the engraving was allowed to remain unaltered!

The Dowager Countess of Enniskillen's Estate

As this chapter closed attention now moved to the administration of the late Dowager's estate. Aside from individual personal bequests the major beneficiary was Cambridge University which was bequeathed her chattels thus exempting the estate from inheritance tax. The Univerity's primary interest was in the extensive library; its Keeper of Rare Books visited Kinloch House and arranged for the transfer of about 1000 volumes. Peter Fox, Cambridge University's Librarian, later explained that about half these would be retained to form a small permanent memorial to the 6th Earl and to Lady Enniskillen; those retained were virtually all pre-1850 imprints. In a letter he described the Kinloch House collection as a reasonably typical country house library of its period. It had an Irish flavour, a number of 18th and 19th century books had Irish imprints, some had Irish subject matter, but there was very little material printed before 1700. There would be much more on books in the months ahead.

In August 1998, Christopher Shepherd of Christie's Heritage and Taxation Advisory Service, wrote to Peter Marlow to say that Christie's had been appointed by the Executors of the late Countess of Enniskillen to dispose of all the chattels and books not retained by Cambridge University. There was to be a continuing correspondence between Messrs Shepherd and Marlow , who clearly established a good rapport, for the next two years until Christopher Shepherd retired in July 2000. By a strange coincidence he was succeeded by Anastasia Tennant who had previously been working in the National Trust's Legal Department.

It transpired that following the death of Michael, Viscount Cole in 1956, a large number of chattels at Florence Court were listed as being exempt from estate duty, the significance of which was that for certain purchasers the agreed market value of such items are reduced by approximately three quarters of the potential capital tax liabilities. Chrisitie's were now approaching the National Trust to discuss a possible private treaty sale of these exempt items, which were valued at around £560,000; to a qualifying body the amount payable after a 50% discount would be around £287,000. Christie's believed that the National Arts Collection Fund (NACF) or similar body would have to 'front' the purchase for the National Trust, not realising that the Trust's status under Section 40 of the Finance Act 1930 had been clarified following prolonged correspondence with the Inland Revenue during 1995-1996; Christopher Shepherd was delighted to receive this confirmation from Dudley Dodd (Deputy Director of Historic Buildings) at the Trust's London head office.

The inventory of 150 exempt items supplied by Christie's included 56 relating to furniture, 47 to silver, 27 to porcelain, 15 to paintings, 2 were clocks, and there were single entries for textiles and sculpture. It was pointed out that this list needed further research against the original 1956 inventory prepared by John Ross & Son of Belfast, so that some items might have to be added or deleted; there was a particular problem with some of the books in the library which may not have been exempted at that time. Much of the research on exempted, and indeed on non-exempted, items was pursued quietly and thoroughly behind the scenes by Jim Chestnutt using every available publication and photograph of Florence Court he could lay his hands on. Jim Chestnutt in no small way smoothed the way for a great deal of what was eventually to return to Florence Court.

On Christmas Eve 1998 Christie's issued a complete inventory of all the items in Lady Enniskillen's estate, exempt and non-exempt. These had now been removed from Kinloch House and were stored at the warehouse of Shore Porters in Aberdeen, with the exception of silver and porcelain pieces which had been removed to Christie's premises in Glasgow. Plans were prepared to visit Aberdeen to view what was on offer by private treaty sale and what might be of interest among the non-exempt items. During a bitterly cold spell of weather an intrepid team, including Simon Jervis (Historic Buildings Secretary), David Oosterman (Historic Buildings Assistant), Peter Marlow, Jim Chestnutt, Alastair Laing (Adviser on Pictures and Sculpture), Jonathan Harris and Bruce Lindsay (independent antique dealers), assembled in Aberdeen on 3rd February 1999.

A final selection of the exempt items was made and agreed with Christie's, together with a wish list of non-exempt items. The National Trust wrote to Christie's in early March to suggest that the Executors might wish to extend the private sale to include those non-exempt items which were of low monetary value but which had an intimate association with Florence Court; this list, substantially compiled by Jim Chestnutt, was valued at some £17,000. Confirmation was received at the end of April that, subject to Inland Revenue approval, the Executors and Cambridge University had agreed to the private sale of 85 lots of exempt items for the net price of £206,415, together with 16 lots of non-exempt items to the value of £5,360. A pair of stone elephants to which Jim Chestnutt had taken a liking were not included, but Jim's disappointment would be overcome before the story's end! Inland Revenue approval was given in May 1999.

On 23rd June 1999, the National Trust became responsible for the storage charges of all the exempt items it had purchased and which were still held by Shore Porters in Aberdeen, pending removal to Florence Court.

The Auctions

Christie's planned to dispose of the remaining non-exempt chattels by auction, one at its South Kensington premises for the better items on 22nd September 1999 and one in Glasgow at the premises of Kerr and McAlister on 7th October 1999, for the lesser or mostly household items. A further complication arose when Christie's withdrew a few particularly valuable pieces to be placed in auctions at its London, King Street premises on 11th and 12th November and 17th December 1999. The National Trust planned to attend all the auctions and to bid until money allocated to the campaign ran out. There was still no word about the books.

South Kensington

Preparation for the first auction in September was intense and detailed. The catalogues were cross checked against the inventories, preferred items identified on the basis of their proven provenance and their intrinsic historical and art historical significance, valuations noted (bearing in mind Christie's usual practice of suppressing maximum/minimum estimates in order to encourage buyers), and a four point rating scale applied to each item – A to D. The intention was to allow the bidding team flexibility to make decisions on the day, depending on how quickly the available funds were spent. The South Kensington auction offered 600 lots, from which the Trust had shortlisted 54. Bidding on behalf of the Trust was in the capable hands of Bruce Lindsay, of the dealers Harris Lindsay, supported by a Trust team comprising Dudley Dodd, and David Oosterman from Head Office and Peter Marlow and Jim Chestnutt from Northern Ireland; the support team's job was to record each sale, to monitor the available funds – given buyers and sellers premiums – and to decide quickly when to drop out of a bidding process in favour of a higher rated item due later in the proceedings.

The auction room was barely half full for the morning session, with even fewer attending in the afternoon, and even though telephone bids were being received, the low attendance may have influenced the successful outcome for the Trust. As Jim Chestnutt reported in an e-mail to the author the following day:

> *Wonderful news. It was a very exciting day. The Trust secured the purchase of 3 lots. The purchase included 25 picture lots. We have the 3 Ducros, 9 out of the 10 Keisermanns, 8 out of the 9 old masters; in fact we practically swept the board with the pictures; significantly they hammered well under the bidding maximum, and in general sold at much less than we had been led to expect... The remaining 12 lots*

included flatware, chairs, the club fender, walking cane, the sideboard, and the bookcase.

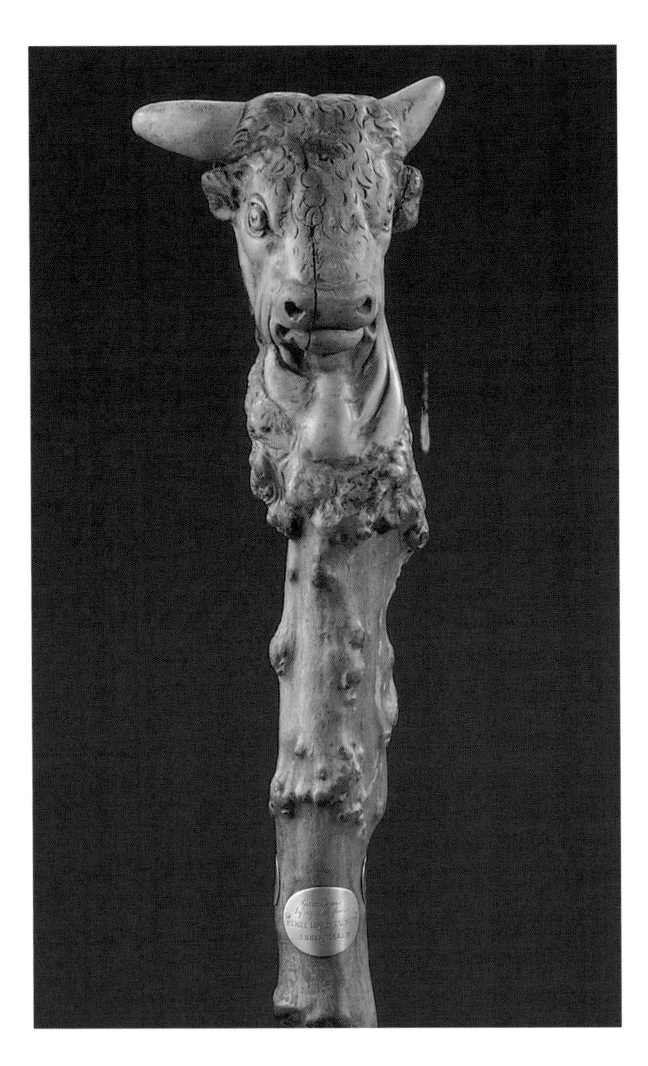

Fig 4. A late 19th century burr fruitwood walking cane, with the handle modelled as a bull's head: Lot 399 in the Christie's 26th September auction in London

Also included was Lot 406, a pair of Indian black-painted model elephants carved all over with scrolling flowersprays and shells on rectangular bases, which no doubt enhanced Jim's delight! Expenditure at South Kensington, including commission and VAT, was £104,000.

John, Viscount Cole, subsequently 2nd Earl of Enniskillen (1768-1840), undertook the Grand Tour, as was the fashion in the 18th century, in 1792. Among his many purchases were three glamorous watercolours by Louis Ducros of *The Tombs of Metellus*, *The Colosseum*, and *The Arch of Titus*, and a substantial group of sepia-wash drawings by Franz Keisermann for which there was a marked taste in 18th century Britain; these were a missing element from the late Countess' gift and from the purchases by private treaty with the executors which the Trust was able to make on favourable terms thanks to the operation of the tax *douceur*. Because they were a rare survival by direct descent from their original owner the National Trust was particularly satisfied that it had succeeded in ensuring their return to Florence Court.

The Trust did not bid for Lot 98, described as a Group of Sundry Silver, but one item from that Lot made its way to Belfast and then to an antique dealer in Lisbellaw. Heather Hamilton (Senior Guide at Florence Court) spotted the inscribed silver guilt key which the 5th Earl had used to open the County Buildings in Enniskillen in 1960; a quick visit by Jim Chestnutt secured the key for £90 on 15th January 2000.

Glasgow

The National Trust's sights now turned north to Glasgow and to a very different auction. Proceedings kicked off at 5.45pm on 7th October and such was the unruly excitement of the customers that the local constabulary had to be called twice to contain the enthusiasm of the over exuberant assembly! Overheard was the comment, 'There's a lot of junk around here tonight', which elicited the reply, 'Aye, but it's upper class junk'! Peter Marlow and Jim Chestnutt were holding the purse strings for the Trust on this occasion, and no doubt it was Peter that another punter was referring to when he wryly remarked, 'Who the h**l is that rich b*****d who is buying everything?', because at the end of the evening the Trust had successfully bid for 21 lots. These were smaller, personal items generally – pictures, framed photographs, rougher furniture, boxes of linen. Due to some confusion over a lot number the Trust was outbid by a member of the Conservation Department of Kelvingrove Museum for a large number of Lord Enniskillen's hats. Subsequently, a deal was done and the hats acquired, including a busby which belonged to the 6th Earl's father in its original tin box inscribed, 'Hon G Cole 10th Royal Hussars', black silk top hat, grey top hat and a bowler all in their original Lock & Co boxes, 7 trilbys and a Patt steel helmet. The bold *Mount Blanc* fountain pen which Lady Enniskillen had used in all her correspondence with the National Trust during 1997 was to elude the Trust bidders; it fetched in excess of £200.

Also attending the Glasgow auction was Tobina Cole, wife of Arthur Cole, a brother of the late 6th Earl of Enniskillen. Due to the improving relationship between the National Trust and the Enniskillen family, Tobina gifted nine books in her possession which had belonged to Charlotte Enniskillen, the 4th Countess. These mid to late Victorian volumes, all with Charlotte's bookplate, arrived at Florence Court on 26th November 1999, with a covering letter from Tobina Cole which explained that Charlotte was:

> *Arthur's grandmother; but she was very old by the time he knew her; by that time living in London with two Italian servants she had brought back from Florence. I think she was rather like Linda, slim, red headed, vital with a quick wit. When she was old she used to mourn that Africa had stolen her children and certainly with she found her husband's renowned bad temper hard to live with so spent most of her time in Florence – but she loved music, was very artistic and social too, so perhaps she found Florence Court too cut off.*

King Street

Three items had been withheld by Christie's for its specialist King Street auctions, a *Portrait of Field Marshall George Ferrar 1st Marquis of Townsend (Lord Lieutenant of Ireland)* from the Studio of Sir Joshua Reynolds, a *Still Life with*

Flowers and Parrot by Astolfo Petrazzi, and a very fine marble specimen table.

Because it was a condition that the National Trust accept all the items in the late Dowager Countess' gift, only necessary and appropriate Regional Staff were involved, perhaps to the annoyance of excluded Head Office staff and the many specialist advisors. But now, when it came to dealing with the remainder of the Dowager Countess' estate, and an element of choice came into play, the full wagon train circled for the kill; opinions varied, passions flared, memos and e-mails whizzed.

Peter Marlow had opened the debate with Alastair Laing as early as 21st July 1999 in the wake of the freezing February foray to Aberdeen. He wanted to debate with Alastair the question of the 'Reynolds' and the large Italian flower picture. He saw no need to spend money on the 'Reynolds'; it was he felt yet another portrait, not a good picture and 'Nancy didn't want us to have it'. It had in fact been listed in the Will to come to the Trust but was deleted by Nancy before the deal was struck. He noted that the large flower picture had no Enniskillen label, was in very poor condition, had a high estimate without the benefit of being exempted, and would he felt be hard to place in Florence Court. The debate ebbed and flowed over succeeding months, with Alastair plugging away in support of the two pictures. As the auctions came and went, and still no word on the book front, priorities had to be struck as available funding diminished. Although opinion was warming to the 'Reynolds', there was greater enthusiasm for the marble specimen table and it was agreed that on 11th November Bruce Lindsay would again bid for the Trust up to £45,000 plus one, on the table which had an estimate of £10,000 - £15,000. On the day the Trust was outbid by a dealer, and attention moved to the 12th November when it was agreed that another dealer Christopher Foley would bid for the Trust up to £10,000 plus one, on the 'Reynolds' which had an estimate of £3000 - £5000. On this occasion the Trust was successful and acquired the much debated picture for £3058. Alastair Laing was to record:

> *Excellent news that we got this, and so cheap! But, an important factor in going for it having been that it is visible in an old photograph of the Drawing Room, where we ought to try to reinstate it.*

The loss of the specimen table to a commercial dealer who was likely to seek maximum profit raised the prospect that it could leave the country, so Simon Jervis (Historic Buildings Secretary) wrote immediately to Christopher Wilk, Head of the Furniture and Woodwork Department at the Victoria and Albert Museum, seeking an Export Stop if the need arose; there were follow up

Fig 5. A Roman specimen marble with mosaic marble top on an Irish ebonised stand. Acquired by private treaty in December 1999, shown here in the Entrance Hall with a bust of William III in the niche behind, before its removal in 1973.

discussions with the V&A, which was asked to deal with the case, and which now sought additional evidence of any Grand Tour link, but the Trust could not add to the old *Country Life* photograph showing the table at Florence Court. There was no alternative but to await developments, and if the opportunity arose to try for the table again as a separate project with separate funding.

But, as the saying goes, 'you cannot keep a good man down', and Alastair Laing now popped up again and made a further impassioned plea for the Petrazzi *Still Life*; he wrote to Peter Marlow on the 22nd November 1999, two weeks before the final auction:

As you will remember, I – but not you – was keen on obtaining it when we saw it in Aberdeen. I am now all the keener, because the exercise of doing a paper hang for Florence Court has made me aware of how much we need large pictures, particularly for the Drawing Room . . . I fully accept that the specimen table should be the prime object of our efforts; but, if David Oosterman's inquiries reveal that it is effectively beyond our reach for a long time to come, could you be persuaded to divert its funds to an equivalent bid of £45,000 (plus a bid, if caught on the wrong foot)?

This was indeed the agreed strategy for the 17th December auction, when the Trust would bid up to £45,000 plus one, for the Petrazzi Still Life which had an estimate of £30,000 - £50,000. Perhaps David Oosterman's report of the auction best sums up the action:

The sale-room was very crowded, buoyant, and competition keen. A fair number of lots failed to sell, but generally prices were well in excess of estimates. Christie's obviously were aware of considerable interest, and began the bidding at £50,000. So effectively we were unsuccessful from the start. Bidding in the room continued up to £180,000 and the final two bidders were both via telephone. We tried. If only it had been conditionally exempt…

The hammer price at the auction was £310,000!

As a very hectic 1999 drew to a close there was to be an unexpected Christmas surprise for Florence Court. It is not recorded why, or in what frame of mind, Jonathan Harris was walking along Pimlico Road on 23rd December 1999. Perhaps he was still reflecting on the failure of his partner Bruce Lindsay to bid successfully for the marble specimen table as he wandered into Christopher Hodsoll Ltd; he could not believe what he saw but there was the Florence Court specimen table on sale by the man who had outbid the Trust at Christie's. An immediate phone call to the National Trust brought Simon Jervis, about to depart on Christmas leave, to examine the table and to conclude a deal there and then for £76,000, £50,000 payable immediately and the balance within two months. An e-mail to Peter Marlow confirming the deal simply said, 'What a wonderful way to start the holiday season – Merry Christmas to you'.

The Christopher Hodsoll Invoice described the table as:

A Roman specimen marble and mosaic marble top on an Irish ebonised stand. The mosaic centre panel includes circles and flower shapes, with outer borders and brocatelle moulded edge, above a plain frieze, on turned entasied legs and a plinth base.

Fig 6. The Dining Room at Florence Court with its original contents reinstated.

The Books

As the new century opened there was still no information on the extensive library of books which had been removed from Florence Court to Kinloch House, except for the 500 volumes retained by Cambridge University almost two years previously.

Although there had been sporadic attempts to get information on the books from Christie's over many months it was a letter to their Deputy Chairman from Peter Marlow in November 1999 that finally loosened the logjam. Peter, believing that the books were tax exempt, also copied the letter to his friend Christopher Shepherd in the Heritage and Taxation Advisory Service at Christie's. A response two weeks later indicated that Christie's had now catalogued 180 lots of books for auction, had set aside 12 boxes of 'decorative bindings' for the Trust, and had about 100 boxes of hardbacks – mostly 19th century fiction – paperbacks and other miscellaneous books which they proposed to transfer to Roseberry's auction house in South London for a lower value sale room dispersal. The 'decorative bindings' had been set to one side in response to a request in April 1999 from the Trust for 450 linear feet of books, ideally Irish imprints, in calf bindings and with family bookplates, to help reinstate the library at Florence Court.

The mists began to clear in early February 2000 when Christie's explained that although some 3000 books had been exempted in 1956, they had not been accurately listed. The Trust now had to decide which individual books it wished to acquire from those held by Christie's and from the residue held by Roseberry's. This daunting task was carried out by Mark Purcell (Libraries Advisor), Peter Marlow and David Oosterman, and by early April 36 lots had been selected and were being held in Christie's Fine Art Services Store in Vauxhall, together with the 12 boxes of selected bindings. A selection, filling some 12 boxes, was made from the miscellaneous books at Roseberry's. These were withdrawn from the auction arranged for 18th April and set to one side for direct sale to the Trust.

Christopher Shepherd, now approaching his retirement from Christie's, had one final task to complete and on 22nd May 2000, having received clearance from the executors and Cambridge University, he put the case to the Inland Revenue for tax exemption on the Enniskillen library. He explained that the John Ross & Co 1959 inventory indicated that 3000 volumes were tax exempt, but with only a few exceptions none were specifically named. These 3000 volumes were in Lady Enniskillen's possession when she died; Cambridge University took 500 volumes as a beneficiary under her Will; Christie's selected approximately 1400 of the better books; and the balance of approximately 100 boxes consigned to Roseberry's.

He explained that the National Trust wished to acquire 430 of the volumes held by Christie's at an agreed price of £18,037, including the highly topical Report on the navigation of the River Shannon, Dublin 1837 – a book which had almost slipped through the scrutiny net due to a catalogue listing error. The Trust also wished to purchase approximately 500 less important books, for furnishing purposes, at an agreed price of £6000.

Shepherd asked the Inland Revenue, Capital Taxes Office, to consider that the books retained by Cambridge University, the books selected for sale by Christie's and the boxes of books which the National Trust would like to purchase, should be treated as having been exempted in 1956. He confirmed that no individual book or set of books which the Trust wished to purchase had a value exceeding £6000 so Capital Gains Tax would not apply. If accepted, the total value of the

Fig 7. The Library at Florence Court with a portrait of the 5th earl of Enniskillen over the mantle piece.

books at £24,037, less notional estate duty at a rate of 48.75%, would give a special price of £12,319 to be paid by the National Trust.

Happily, the Inland Revenue accepted Christopher Shepherd's proposition on 14th June 2000, and 10 months later on 17th April 2001, Delivery Services of Belfast deposited 38 crates of books from Christie's Fine Art Services Store, with Jim Chestnutt at Florence Court, closing metaphorically a significant chapter in the story.

Money Matters

In the 18 month period from June 1999 to the end of 2000, excluding staff time, travel and interim conservation services, the National Trust spent almost £420,000 in recovering the contents of Florence Court.

The front of house team which was spending the money relied heavily on the support and ingenuity of Andy Copestake (Director of Finance) and Mike Wilson (Treasury Controller), both based at the Trust's finance headquarters in Heywood House, Wiltshire. Andy Copestake fully accepted the unique opportunity which existed to reinstate the mansion at Florence Court, but he expected maximum effort to be applied in seeking grant support from outside the Trust, at Head Office and in the Region, before committing internal funds. During a Management Board visit to the Northern Ireland Region in early 1999 he suggested that the exposure of the Trust should not exceed £300,000.

An obvious candidate for support was the Heritage Lottery Fund, and the National Heritage Memorial Fund. Dudley Dodd put an initial case to these Funds for support to acquire chattels for Powis Castle and Florence Court in early December 1998. In the case of Florence Court the request was for £215,000 to help acquire the tax exempt chattels. In its response the Heritage Lottery Fund stated:

> *We are looking to the Trust to prioritise its applications to NHMF/HLF. We know of several other capital projects in the pipeline, including Thurgarton, Gibside stables, Godolphin and Llanerchaeron. These are a formidable shopping list on their own, quite apart from the long list of other priorities listed in your recent Annual Report. Where these acquisitions fall within this pecking order is not clear.*

Somewhat subdued, Dudley Dodd advised the Heritage Lottery Fund, on 22nd December 1998, that as far as the Florence Court chattels were concerned the Trust would resort to its own funds and any other sources which could be identified. He immediately challenged the Northern Ireland Region to make an appropriate contribution; the figure of £36,000, or roughly 10% of the estimated total, was mentioned.

While this challenge languished in the pending tray in the Regional Office at Rowallane House, Dudley Dodd with renewed vigour in the New Year 1999, was considering support from the National Arts Collection Fund (NACF). Peter Marlow strongly concurred, noting that this would be the first time the National Trust had sought NACF support for Northern Ireland. An application submitted in August seeking help to acquire the Ducros watercolours and Keisermann drawings at the South Kensington auction was successful and realised a grant of almost £14,000.

Meanwhile in Northern Ireland the author had arranged to meet Jim Lamont, a former colleague and now Acting Chief Executive of the Environment and Heritage Service, to explore the possibility of Article 106 (2)(c) of The Planning (NI) Order 1991 being used to support the acquisition of Florence Court chattels. This Article gives the Department of the Environment for Northern Ireland specific powers to make grants or loans to the National Trust towards the cost of acquiring any objects ordinarily kept in any listed building – it had never been used before. Following confirmation from the Inland Revenue that the National Trust had received approval to purchase the exempt chattels by private treaty, and on production of an inventory of the objects in question, Jim Lamont created the precedent and got approval for a 25% grant, almost £52,000. This was confirmed on 25th October 1999 on condition that 'these chattels will return to Florence Court for display'. Head Office was well pleased.

The National Trust contribution of £376,000 – not too far in excess of Andy Copestake's original suggestion – came primarily from the Goodman Bequest (£222,000) and a collection of assorted Defined Purpose Funds which Mike Wilson had adeptly identified and utilized.

Tailpiece

And so with the palingenesis of Florence Court complete it seems appropriate to give the last word to Nancy, the late Dowager Countess of Enniskillen, who wrote to the Regional Chairman on 15th July 1997:

With family portraits again in the house and with the return of some of its historic, Irish memorabilia, I believe that the public and the family and our friends will take no little joy and pride in the existence per se of the National Trust's Florence Court. Florence Court belongs to everyone. Whatever family and historic spirit shines from the house is lit by the Trust's ever-enhancing maintenance and showing of it. I applaud this truth and give you and all concerned my hearty congratulations.

ACKNOWLEDGEMENTS

I would like to thank Ruth Laird, current Director of the National Trust in Northern Ireland for permission to borrow the many files connected with this story, and to former colleagues and friends – Professor Ronald Buchanan, Diane Forbes, Peter Marlow, Jim Chestnutt, Gordon Millington – for the help and patience they have afforded me in my researching and writing of this essay. Any surviving errors are attributable to the author.

A CONTEMPTIBLE HABITATION[1]: SOME CONTEMPORARY VIEWS OF IRISH CABINS FROM THE SIXTEENTH TO THE NINETEENTH CENTURIES

NESSA ROCHE

DURING THE TWENTIETH CENTURY an increase in interest in the social and material circumstances of all members of past societies led to research in subjects once considered too mundane for serious historical attention. Among such subjects is that of the humblest cabin habitations of our forebears, a topic that includes strands of architectural, social, ethnographical and geographical interest. Most of these huts or cabins have left no visible trace (though many were still inhabited when pioneering geographers and ethnographers started their fieldwork), and even archaeological excavation provides few clues due to the impermanence of the materials used.[2] However these dwellings elicited some commentary through the centuries by the writers of travelogues, diaries, economic tracts or estate records. Documentary sources, therefore, give us personal, partial and statistical information on the ubiquitous Irish cabin and its inhabitants.

The subjective viewpoint

From our standpoint the term cabin almost invariably means a wretched roadside hut barely sheltering people struggling in poverty, however it is clear from trawling through written sources that the description cabin was loosely applied to all sorts of small dwellings ranging from hovels to farmhouses. It appears that writers have always used the term cabin from the perspective of their own society or class, leaving open the likelihood that the writer's intended impression is misread by readers of a different class, country or time. This essay aims to show, through airing contemporary descriptions, that the term cabin applied to a far broader standard of dwelling than may now commonly be assumed.

Origin and use of the term cabin

Seeking an etymology

The etymology of the word 'cabin' is of interest. Although it was in common usage in Ireland by the end of the sixteenth century (and perhaps earlier), and is usually confined to descriptions of rudimentary dwellings of the 'mere' Irish by foreign as well as Irish commentators, it is not of Gaelic Irish extraction.

The early eighteenth-century English traveller John Loveday assists with the etymological search. His first guess is the 'French *Cabane*, a Cottage, a Thatched House'; he also notes that 'it occurs in [Edward] Lhuyd's *Irish-English Dictionary* thus – "a Caban and Cabain, *a Cottage, – a Cabbin*"'.[3] Wyatt Papworth's seminal nineteenth-century *Dictionary of Architecture* lists 'cabin' as a word employed by old English writers for a dark lodging or small room, distinguished as a dwelling from a cottage or bothie by consisting of a single room, and from a hut by having a regular roof, and being turfed or thatched on the sides and top.[4]

Archaism or accurate description?

The passages repeated here and elsewhere indicate the continued use in Ireland of the word cabin after it had died out at some time before or during the seventeenth century in England.[5] Many eighteenth-century authors preface their use of the word cabin with an explanation, such as the Englishwoman Mary Delany, who wrote in 1744 'we were invited and dined at Mr Baylis's but a small mile from hence. They live in what is called in this country '*a cabin*' - that is a house of one floor and thatched. The writer John Bush explained the word to his readers in 1764, when describing the dwellings of beggars 'who live in huts, or cabins as they are called'. Arthur Young also prefaced his detailed observations, writing that 'the cottages of the Irish ... are all called cabins'.[6]

Differing applications of the term: cabin as hut, house and episcopal haven

Distinction between hut and house

Although in writings of every period the use of the word cabin was freely varied with the terms cottage, cot, hovel and hut to describe the same basic structures, Kinmonth notes that their inhabitants almost always preferred the word house, regardless of size and status, to lend their homes some small semblance of dignity.[7] While often used to describe a more or less permanent structure (usually intended as a family dwelling) cabin could also describe a booleying hut or *creata*, a temporary shelter erected and removed or reconstructed when and where desired during the grazing season.[8]

Gailey cites several documents in which the words cottage, creata and cabin were freely interchanged, these 'having in common a smaller size and perhaps less permanent nature than what were being described at the same period as 'houses'.[9] However, by the end of the seventeenth century a common distinction between structures defined as house and cabin – the presence or absence of a chimney – was beginning to break down.[10] In 1698 John Dunton, the London bookseller who made a prolonged visit to Ireland in the late 1690s, reported coming on 'a contemptible habitation' of 'a little Irish town of about nine cabins' in north Co. Dublin, which had, he noted, 'two chimneys each'.[11]

Mark Elstob, an Swedish visitor who travelled to Kilkenny in 1778, picked up on the difference between the two sub-classes of peasant housing – those of the small tenant farmer and of the landless day labourer:

> *The houses are very low, some of them are extremely low, which latter, in Ireland, are denominated cabins. [...] The peasant houses are, in general, but little better than the cabins. The difference consists in the former having a chimney, or a hole in the roof – a window of at least a foot square, in the front, and a whited outside, in imitation of their tyrannic lord's.*[12]

Despite a general increase in living standards in the latter decades of the eighteenth century the boundaries between house and cabin remained difficult to discern. In his *Statistical Survey of County Meath* (1802), Robert Thompson terms the dwellings of tenants 'cottages' (in contrast to the 'cabbins' of the landless labourers), but states that:

> *few of them [tenant cottages] have chimneys and fewer still have any other means of admitting the light, than by opening the door or a small hole in the wall, stopped up occasionally with a bundle of straw etc.*[13]

John Curwen, visiting Ireland some years later, found that he 'became taught that there existed gradations [in housing standards]; and possibly as many in the scale of necessity as that of superfluity.'[14]

Stretching the bounds of the cabin sub-class: the cabin orné

Several eighteenth-century references are indicative of a usage of *cabin* in a manner not unconnected with the emerging fashion for cottages *orné* and picturesque landscapes.[15] Early descriptions tantalise by their elusiveness. Bishop Richard Pococke, an indefatigable traveller in Ireland as elsewhere, was impressed with a dwelling at Altadore in Co. Wicklow he saw in 1752, which was 'the retirement home of the late General Pearce, who affected to build it as

Fig 1. 'The Cottage', pencil drawing by Mary Delany, 1766. Courtesy of the Hon. Desmond Guinness. Mrs Delany recorded her impressions of Irish life in a candid manner, including detailed comments on the basic habitations of those met in the course of travels with her husband, Dean Delany. While she described many such houses as cabins, this one seems from the content of poem accompanying the picture ('*A sweeter spot on earth was never found*') to perhaps be sited in her beloved garden at Delville, Co. Dublin as a place for carrying on craft work. [in 'the cabin orné']

a thatched cabin'. On the roof Pearce 'erected a tower to make it look like a village with a church to it'.[16] In 1757 Lord Chief Baron Edward Willes, whose diaries indicate a cultured outlook, took as his summer retreat a thatched cabin at Rockfield, six miles from Dublin.[17] His was not a lone fancy, as earlier in the century Bishop King commented disdainfully on the behaviour of his peers that 'an Irish bishop chuses to live in a cabine' in spite of official repairs to glebe houses. (Fig. 1).[18] The word cottage is also used imaginatively. For example, the *Ordnance Survey Memoirs*, in describing the temporary dwelling of a Monaghan landlord, calls it a cottage, despite the fact that it had 'no less than 27 bedrooms'.[19]

The well-to-do cabin dweller

As evidenced by such descriptions, cabin dwellings were not necessarily the preserve of the sub-tenant, cottier or spalpeen.[20] The impoverished eighteenth-century rural Catholic gentry and their co-religious leaseholders (the rising class of middle men), also dwelt in cabins, partially through cultural preference and partially from conservatism or caution at raising their profile. In the 1830s Amlaoibh O'Súilleabháin wrote:

Fig 2. Labourer's Hut, Gweedore, Co. Donegal. Lawrence Collection. Courtesy of the National Library of Ireland. Such images, which encapsulate the poverty of peasant life, recur in photographs taken in all parts of Ireland in the nineteenth and early twentieth centuries, but especially those on the geographical fringes where the land was barely capable of sustaining life.

Snug is a low, sheltered cabin, on which the thatch is laid on thick, and in which are food and fire. No house is so comfortable as a thatched, mud-walled cabin, with a solid door, small windows, a big fire and plenty of provisions.[21]

That persons of substantial income would choose the humblest sort of dwelling clearly astonished outsiders. In 1732 Mary Pendarves, on a visit to Killala, Co. Mayo with her prospective husband Dean Delany, described visits to several cabins, including one which belonged:

to a gentleman of fifteen hundred pounds a year, who spends most part of his time and fortune in that place; the situation is pretty, being just by the river side, but the house is worse than I have represented [she did not describe it]. He keeps a man cook, and has given entertainment of twenty dishes of meat! The people of this country don't seem solicitous of having good dwellings or more furniture than is absolutely necessary – hardly so much, but they make it up in eating and drinking![22]

The physical appearance of the Irish cabin

Worse than the kraals of the Hottentots or huts of the Laplanders…[23]

Fig 3. 'Armagh City and a fort on the Blackwater' (two excerpts) after July 1601, by Richard Bartlett. Courtesy of the National Library of Ireland. The clumps of cabins depicted near the ruined cathedral contrast with the right angles and windows of those in the (English) fort. The former are like those described by Luke Gernon in 1620, 'The baser cottages are built of underwood, called wattle, and covered some with thatch and some with green sedge, of a round form and without chimneys, and to my imagination, resemble so many hives of bees, about a country farm'. (From *A Discourse of Ireland*, in Falkiner, C. L. (ed.,) 1904, *Illustrations of Irish History.* London; 355)

First impressions

To sixteenth- and early seventeenth-century settlers and visitors who came from the relatively prosperous countries of England, France and Spain, the ubiquity of rounded clumps of rudimentary cabins throughout the land must have reinforced the notion of the Irish as wild savages. The English official Fynes Moryson who was posted to Ireland in the 1610s, described Irish huts:

Like the Nomads removing their dwellings according to the commodity of pastures for their cows, [they] sleep … in a poor house of clay, or in a cabin, made of the boughs of trees and covered with turf, for such are the dwellings of the very lords among them.[24]

When William Lithgow arrived in Ireland in 1619 he found that:

The vulgar Irish, I protest, live more miserably than the undaunted or untamed Arabian, the idolatrous Turcoman, or the moon-worshipping Caramans … . Their houses are advanced three or four yards, high, pavillion-like, incircling, erected in a singular frame of smoke-torn straw, green long-pricked turf, and rain-dropping wattles.[25]

Richard Head wrote in *The Western Wonder* (1678) of the basest constructions, that:

the cots are generally built on the side of a hill, not to be discerned till you just come upon them. The cottage is usually raised three feet from the eaves to the ground on the one side, and the other side hath a rock for a wall to save charges, in regard carriage is dear and money but scarce especially to such who never see it but once in seven years.[26]

Numerous eighteenth- and nineteenth-century accounts reinforce these descriptions, best summarised perhaps by Arthur Young, the agriculturalist and agent:

The cottages of the Irish, which are all called cabins, are the most miserable looking hovels that can well be conceived. They generally consist of only one room. Mud kneaded with straw is the common material of the walls. These are rarely above seven feet high, and not always above five or six. They are about two feet thick, and have only a door, which lets in light instead of a window.[27]

Landlord improvements

In *The Political Anatomy of Ireland* (1672) the politician William Petty urged 'reformation' of the 'nasty cabbins', the 'lamentable sties' of which there were, he

Fig 4. 'An Irish Cabin', engraving in Arthur Young, 1780, A Tour in Ireland (part II). Courtesy of Jacqueline Donnelly. Though Young used the term relatively freely to describe dwellings of both moderate and humble size, his drawing of a cabin - one of the few illustrations in this lengthy treatise - illustrates graphically the poverty which his readers may not have wished to see reproduced.

estimated, above 160,000 around the country with one or no chimney, and their replacement by 'building ... 168,000 small stone-wall Houses with Chimneys, Doors, Windores, gardens, and Orchards, ditch'd and quicksetted ... the which [sic] may cost 3l each in all'.[28]

Positive steps made by landlords to raise standards of habitation and sanitation are rarely recorded in contemporary notices. Many members of this much-maligned group were genuine in their attempts to house their tenants (although day-labourers and other migratory workers had no such benefactors). Arthur Young related in 1780 an instance of good works. One landowner, Sir William Osborne, built a cabin for a beggar and set him up as a small farmer. This man succeeding, Young wrote that Osborne then housed many others, the cabins 'done on contract at six pounds each', with the tenants then raising 'what little offices they want[ed] for themselves'. Young noted that in some cases where there were no cabbins on the land, the farmer built them on garden plots, while in others the labourers raised them themselves and the farmer 'only assist[ed] them with the roof, etc'.[29]

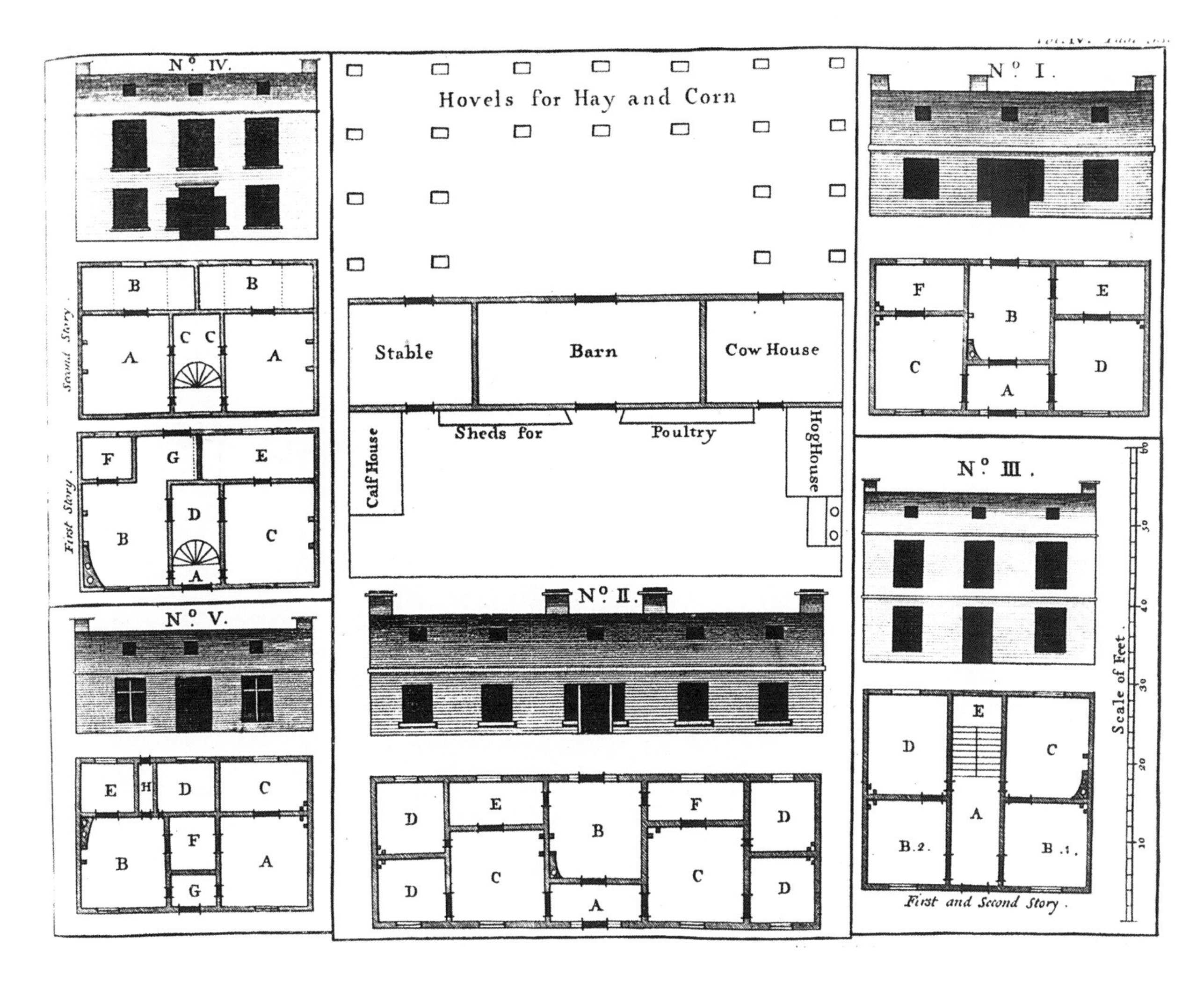

Fig 5. Sheet of designs for farmhouses and cabins, from *A Compleat Body of Husbandry* (Dublin edition, 1757), vol. iv, 383. Courtesy of the Irish Architectural Archive. It may be that the absence of the term cabin from English eighteenth-century writings could indicate that this Dublin edition was revised in Ireland to suit local conditions. It is the earliest known didactic illustration of a tenant dwelling, predating by nearly fifty years the similar efforts of authors such as Robert Thompson in the *Statistical Survey of Co. Meath* (1802).

The Archbishop of Armagh housed his tenantry with care, as related by a visitor, Mrs Montagu, in 1793.

> *His Grace shew'd me the plans of Farm Houses and Cottages he had erected on his estate near Rokeby [Co. Louth] in such a manner as will give prosperity to his tenants and comfort and subsistence to the cottagers; to all these he has restricted the Rent, that the avarice of a future Landlord and the extortions of stewards may not encroach on his benevolent institutions.'*[30]

Improved cottage plans were proposed by the Irish Society in Ulster, when in 1836 the Deputation instructed William Tite to prepare designs of a cottage and of a small farmhouse.[31]

Differences in Ulster

A number of visitors made comments on the cleanliness and

industry of Ulster cabin-dwellers, who in general enjoyed better security of tenure, however exceptions are also noted. Edward Willes, in the middle of the eighteenth century, saw neat cabins from Monaghan to Carrickmacross, 'and what adds greatly to the beauty, every little cabin has an orchard and garden belonging to it', the inhabitants occupied with spinning or weaving.[32] John Wesley, the noted preacher, wrote in the 1770s that 'no sooner did we enter Ulster than we observed the difference ... the cottages not only neat, but with doors, windows and chimney'.[33] Sir Charles Coote, in his *Statistical Account of Co. Armagh* (1804) noted that 'the meanest house has something to recommend it; almost in every one the exterior is whitewashed, and the roof well thatched, with a neatly enclosed little garden'. The best were of stone, not mud, and were remarkable for their comfort and cleanliness.[34] The provincial difference remained apparent to travellers even on the eve of the great famine. James Johnson wrote in 1844 that 'we see as we enter Ulster that the cabins become more substantial, comfortable and water-tight'.[35] Not every observer was impressed, however. Dean Swift stated in 1729 that the cabins of the Scotch in Ulster were as dirty and miserable as those of the wildest Irish, while according to reports done for the Irish Society, even in the nineteenth century housing in some areas was deplorable.[36]

Fig 6. 'A Northern Cabbin 1745', pencil drawing by Mary Delany. Private Collection. Courtesy of Ruth Hayden, author of *Mrs Delany: Her Life and her Flowers* (1980) and *Mrs Delany and her Flower Collages* (1992). While many who visited the planted counties of Ulster, including Mrs Delany, were impressed by the general standard of tenant dwelling, it is clear that not all of the poor were housed well. The assortment of household goods stored on the roof of this cabin indicates some strength in the trusses, while there is a makeshift chimney (but evidently no windows).

Urban cabins

The cabin was not confined to rural areas. From the first growth of urban centres until late into the nineteenth century towns and cities were ringed by such dwellings. *Advertisements for Ireland* (1623), encouraged their removal; 'in the heart of the best towns, cities, boroughs, there stand many poor cottages of straw, chaff, and clay to the eyesore of the whole town'.[37] Of Clonmel and other towns, Loveday wrote 'long rows of cabins make large Suburbs here'[38]. Dr. Richard Twiss, no lover of Ireland, wrote in the 1770s that 'the outskirts of Dublin consist chiefly of huts, which are termed cabbins; they are made of mud dried, and mostly without either chimneys or window'.[39] Some town cabins had a loft storey, as building ground was expensive or impossible to for cabin-dwellers to acquire.[40]

Private houses were not the only lowly buildings encountered by travellers; some were driven to stay in inns, both urban and rural, that they described as cabins. One such 'filthy, one-roomed cabin' was located by the gate to Adare Manor, before the village was demolished to construct the present settlement, which is, ironically, composed of cottages orné.[41] Arthur Young was rarely reduced to taking shelter in inns; one he stayed in at Ratoath, Co. Meath in 1776 elicited this exclamation – 'preserve me, fates! from another'.[42] 'Dry' lodgings, commonly advertised by roadside cabins, offered bed without food. Thomas Reid wrote of 'the erroneous boast of dry lodgings, as should rain descend, there is nothing scarcely to prevent its visitation'.[43]

Descriptions of cabin interior layouts and character[44]

Living in one room

Most often alluded to by contemporary visitors, but not particularly descriptive of the cabin interior, is the single living space, or apartment, to give it the common term. In very many instances the writer notes the dual purpose of the cabin, housing both humans and animals. So commented William Lithgow in 1619: 'Their several rooms, hall, parlours, kitchens, barns and stables are inclosed in one'.[45] Rudimentary divisions could be erected where space allowed. The *Report of the Commissioners Inquiring into the Conditions of the Irish Poor of 1836* describes a common makeshift division of the cabin into two rooms –

> *There is usually a dresser, which answers a double purpose, for the cabins being often built in one room, the dresser is placed across the house by way of a division,*

thus making a second room, the less important one facing the backing boards.[46]

The diarist Dorothea Herbert wrote a graphic description of falling foul of this mode of wall building, in her stay in a cabin in Co. Waterford in 1791:

As I was knocking a nail in the partition of my bedchamber to hang up my wardrobe a most dreadful clatter of delft ware convinced me that the kitchen dresser parted my dormitory from the common refectionary'.[47]

Very few writers refer to the 'outshot' bed projection most common in the north and west; in 1802 McParlan calls this recess a 'hag', divided from the room by straw mat curtains.[48]

The inclusion of animals

As noted by most observers (in expressing their abhorrence of the practice), those who could afford animals usually dwelt with them. William Petty evoked a dismal and wretched impression of such 'nasty' rural cabins:

in which neither butter nor cheese, nor linen, yarn nor worsted, and I can think no other, can be made to the best advantage; chiefly by reason of the soot and smoke annoying the same; as also for the narrowness and nastiness of the place; which cannot be kept clean nor sage from beasts or vermin, nor from damps or musty stenches, of which all the eggs laid in or kept in these cabins do partake.[49]

Thomas Campbell wrote in the 1770s:

the manner in which the poor of this country live, I cannot help calling beastly. For upon the same floor, and frequently without any partition are lodged the husband and wife, the multitudinous brood of children, all huddled together upon straw or rushes, with the cow, the calf, the pig, and the horse, if they are rich enough to have one.[50]

The animal was not necessarily a year-round inhabitant, however; the village of dirty cabins in which Dorothea Herbert and her sisters spent a summer also 'served in the winter for cowhouses and pig styes'[51]. Smell and dirt are, however, relative: those who possessed animals were better off than those who did not, while smoke did not necessarily seize the occupants with asphyxia. When Bishop Pococke entered a cabin in 1752:

the man observing that the smoke was very troublesome to me, he made me a low seat near the fire, and I found it was not so inconvenient, the smoak [sic] rising up and condensing above.[52]

Fixtures and furnishings

The paucity of furnishings was noticed by almost every visitor who stepped inside a typical cabin. The Jacobite soldier John Stevens was not enamoured of those he had to sleep in, as:

> *in the better sort of cabins there is commonly one flock bed, seldom more, feathers being too costly ... That they have no locks to their doors is not because there are not thieves but because there is nothing to steal.*[53]

However the absence of worldly goods was not always an indication of destitution, as gradually realised by Mrs Delany and other perceptive chroniclers. Arthur Young wrote that:

> *the apparent poverty … is greater than the real. … I was in the cabins of dairymen and farmers, not small ones, whose cabins were not at all better, or better furnished, than those of the poorest labourer.*[54]

Although the sparsely furnished cabin was always the norm, more salubrious cabins could be stocked with respectable furnishings, as these were houses belonging to people of some standing or wealth. Mrs Delany visited Magillan, Co. Derry in 1758 and wrote of the house of Archdeacon Golden that:

> *the cabin is a lowly one, but elegantly neat, and decorated in a pretty taste with some very fine pieces of china; very good tea, very good supper, and above all very good instructive conversation.*[55]

Bishop Pococke – as inquisitive a chronicler as Mrs Delany – remarked on the inventiveness of the occupants in forming articles out of the materials at hand. Near Lough Conn, Co. Mayo he visited a cabin 'where they had clean straw and clean blankets', as well as wood vessels, stools and a table.[56] Arthur Young visited 'a multitude of cabins that had much useful furniture, and some even superfluous; chairs, tables, boxes, chests of drawers, earthenware'.[57]

Two and more rooms: larger cabins

The *Georgian Society Records* transcribes an advertisement in 1739 for 'a neat cabin' at Larabryane, Co. Kildare, in an instance of the term cabin being applied to a salubrious building more like a small villa. It contained 'three rooms wainscoted, a large kitchen, cellar, and some closets on the 1st floor, ship-cabins above stairs… and as much of the furniture as the buyer wants'. Included with the property was a 'large coachhouse, stables, car house, barn, cow house, brew and bake house, granary, dairy, pigeon house, and several other convenient offices.'[58] Of a cabin at Mount Panther, Co. Down, Mrs Delany wrote in 1744 that:

it is situated very near the sea, with a pretty neat court before it; the outside promises very little, but the inside is quite elegant, as much as I saw of it, which was the hall, a large parlour, drawing room and bed-chamber.[59]

Gabriel Beranger, the noted antiquarian artist, wrote a passage on labourers' cabins in Wexford in 1780, which describes small but well furnished houses:

The inside of the cabins is [sic] divided into two parts; the first serves for kitchen and parlour, and inside are the beds. There is also a loft for a storeroom, and all is neat and clean, and the furniture kept in good order. I have seen in these cabins bureaus of oak so clean that they shone like polished mahogany.[60]

The travel writer Charles Bowden's comments make plain his admiration for the cabin (and person) of one Charles Dunroche he was brought to visit near Clonegal, Co. Carlow in the 1790s:

It is but a small cabin, however it is laid out with great taste, and divided into six apartments. On the right, as I entered, his shop is situated, in which I perceived a number of common vial bottles, containing medicines of different colours.[61]

Summary

These few remarks provide a short pen picture of the social and physical environment of the cabin-dweller, and may broaden a little the common perception of the term. Many other references show that, although beneath official notice until the early nineteenth century, and still of more social interest than otherwise, cabins have long been the subject of passing comment for diverse reasons.

ACKNOWLEDGEMENTS

My thanks are due to a number of people for their ready assistance and interest such as David Griffin, the late Leo Swan, Audrey Horning, Seán Kirwan and most notably to Dr. Edward MacParland of Trinity College Dublin for freely sharing all of his accumulated references to cabins.

NOTES

1. Fifth of six English bookseller John Dunton's letters (1698), appendix B of MacLysaght, E. 1939. *Irish Life in the Seventeenth Century: After Cromwell.* London, Longmans, Green, p.379.
2. A number of Irish researchers and writers have researched the ethnographical, social, and art-historical view of the lowest class of housing. For an overview see the following (other publications are noted below). *Artica: Essays Presented to Ake Campbell* 1956. Vol. 11 of *Studia Ethnographica Upsaliensia.* Uppsala; Evans, E. Estyn. 1942. *Irish Heritage: the landscape, the people and their work.* Dublin; Evans, E. Estyn. 1957. *Irish Folk Ways.* London; Gailey, A. 1984. *Rural Houses of the North of Ireland.* Edinburgh; O'Conor, K. 1998. *The Archaeology of Medieval Rural Settlement.* Dublin, RIA/Discovery Programme; Horning, A. 2001. '"Dwelling houses in the old Irish Barbarous manner": archaeological evidence for Gaelic architecture in an Ulster Plantation village' in Duffy, P. Edwards, D. and Fitzpatrick, E. (eds.) *Gaelic Ireland: land, lordship and settlement c.1250-1650.* Dublin, Four Courts Press.
3. Loveday, J. 1890. *Diary of A Tour* [in 1732]. Edinburgh, p.27. In 1695, some decades before Loveday, the French-sounding 'cabinet' is found in a phrase entered in the Kinsale town records in a reference to some inhabitants 'having only Irish cabinets to dwell in'. See O'Sullivan, F. 1916. *History of Kinsale.* Dublin, p.152.
4. Papworth, W. 1852-92. *Dictionary of Architecture.* London. 8 vols, *C*, p.5. Papworth gives another possible explanation for the Irish dwelling under cabinet: an open summerhouse, which may be of a square or round form.
5. The term cabin is absent from accounts by English travellers in Britain. Celia Fiennes and Daniel Defoe, who avidly described their surroundings, including occasional remarks on humble rural habitations, did not use the word. Morris C. (ed.) 1982. *The Illustrated Journies of Celia Fiennes, 1685-c.1712.* London, MacDonald & Co and Webb and Bower; Furbank, P. N. Owens, W. R. and Coulson, A. J (eds) 1991. Daniel Defoe *A Tour through the whole island of Great Britain.* New Haven and London, Yale University Press.
6. Day, A. (ed.) 1991. *Letters from Georgian Ireland.* Belfast, Friar's Bush Press, p.202. Mount Panther, Down, 10 September 1744. Bush, 1764. *Hibernia Curiosa*, excerpted in Harrington (ed.) 1991. *The English Traveller in Ireland.* Dublin, Wolfhound Press, p.159; Young, A. 1780. *Tour in Ireland.* Dublin. Part II, p.25.
7. See Kinmonth, C. 1993. *Irish Country Furniture.* New Haven and London, Yale University Press, p.5. Kinmonth draws on opinions voiced in Day and Williams (eds), 1990. *O.S. Memoirs of Ireland, County Tyrone.* Belfast, I.I.S./R.I.A. Vol. 5, p.124.
8. Edmund Spenser wrote in *A View of the Present State of Ireland* (1633) that it was the peasant 'custom of Bollyng' to 'keep their cattle and to live themselves the most part of the year in Bollies pasturing upon the mountain and waste wild places'. See Harrington (ed.) 1991, *op cit.*, p.62; Gailey, 1984, *op cit.*, p.197) states that *creata* is an Irish word for a timber framework – the ribs of a house or roof.
9. Gailey, 1984, *op.cit.*, pp.197-8 reports that in 1703, a Thomas Ashe referred to 'some Crates or Cabbins' at Plaister in Tyrone. Public Record Office of Northern Ireland [PRONI]. T 848/1, f.32.
10. Gailey, 1984, *op cit.*, p.198), notes that a survey of the manor of Castledillon, Co. Armagh, c.1700, refers to a brick chimney in both a stone-and-clay-wall house and a mud-wall cabin.
11. MacLysaght 1939, p.379.

12. Elstob, M. 1778. *A Trip to Kilkenny from Durham.* Dublin, p.56 & p.164. While not expressly stated by Elstob, the appearance of each type may have resulted from use of different construction methods, one superior to the other enabling higher and straighter walls.
13. Thompson, R. 1802. *Statistical Survey of Co. Meath.* Dublin, Dublin Society, p.72.
14. Curwen, J. C. 1818. *Observations on the State of Ireland.* London, p.105.
15. The cottage orné was very popular in England during the reign of the Picturesque in the eighteenth and early nineteenth centuries, however 'most Irish gentry lived too close to the land and saw too much of the miseries of rural life to want to play at it', as explained by Brian de Breffny and Rosemary Ffolliott, 1975. *The Houses of Ireland.* London, Thames and Hudson, p.178. Nevertheless images of idyllic landscapes with contented rural peasantry proved to be popular subjects in Irish painting in the late eighteenth and early nineteenth centuries. The reader is directed to Brian P. Kennedy, 1993. 'The Traditional Irish Thatched House: Image and Reality, 1793-1993', in Adele M. Dalsimer (ed.) *Visualizing Ireland, National Identity and the Pictorial Tradition,* pp.165-179. Boston, Faber and Faber.
16. Stokes G. T. (ed.). 1891. *Bishop Pococke's Tour in Ireland.* Dublin and London, p.161.
17. Kelly, J. (ed.) 1990. *The Letters of Lord Chief Baron Edward Willes to the Earl of Warwick, 1757-1762.* Aberystwyth, Boethius Press, p.21 & p.70.
18. British Library [BL] Add 6116, Wake Letters, Bishop Nicholson of Derry to Bishop Wake, 3 May 1720. Reference from Dr. Edward McParland.
19. Day A. and P. McWilliams (eds) 1998. *O. S. Memoirs of Ireland, Counties of South Ulster.* Belfast, I.I.S./R.I.A. Vol. 40, p.138.
20. Spalpeen is used by Arthur Young in the 1770s; 'many of the poor here have no cows; there are cabbins on the road side that have no land; the inhabitants of them are called spalpeens, who are paid for their labour in cash, by the month etc'. Young, 1780, *op, cit.,* I, p.374.
21. Extract from *Cinnlae Amhlaoibh Uí Shuilleabháin,* 1831, translated by Kevin Whelan. Whelan, K. 1996. *The Tree of Liberty.* Cork, Cork University Press, p.29.
22. Day (ed.) 1991, *op. cit.,* p.124. Newtown Gore, Co. Mayo 12 June 1732. A few days later she wrote again of a similar instance. 'We ... took shelter in a cabin as poor as that I described to you some time age. The master of it ... is absolutely worth two thousand pounds a year'. Killala, Co. Mayo 21 June 1732; Ibid, p.125.
23. Paraphrase of the Rev. James Hall who wrote 'the kraals of the Hottentots, the huts of the Laplanders, and the caves and holes of the natives of New Holland, seem preferable, in many points of view, to the hovels of the poor Irish'. Hall, Rev. J. 1813. *A Tour through Ireland in 1807,* excerpted in Hadfield A. and J. McVeagh (eds) 1994. *Strangers to the Land.* Gerrards Cross, pp.253-4.
24. Moryson's itinerary is partially reproduced in H. Morley (ed.) 1890. *Ireland under Elizabeth and James the First.* London, this quotation on p. 430. Note that here Moryson calls the clay structure a house, while the cabin is a rough erection of underwood.
25. Lithgow's *Travels* are reprinted in Hall. 1813, *op cit.,* pp.312-324).
26. Head is quoted in MacLysaght, 1939, *op cit.,* p.110). John Barrow saw similar scenes over one hundred and fifty years later near Maam in Connemara. 'We passed a few cottages on our route, which were very wretched; some were built, or rather cut into the sloping of a hill, so that one wall in front, with the roof, was all that was required for their completion'. Barrow, J. 1836. *A Tour Round Ireland.* London, p.246.

27. Young , 1780, *op cit.*, II, pp.25-6.
28. Petty, W. 1691. *Political Anatomy of Ireland 1672.* London, 9, p.14, p.79.
29. Young, 1780, *op cit.*, I, p.326. He provides many statistics; near Mount Mellick he found that cabins cost 3*l* 3s, while five to six pounds was more usual. (1780, II, p.20). Masonry cabins in the same place came to 20l. (Young, 1780, *op cit.*, II, p.41).
30. Quoted in de Breffny and Ffolliott, 1975, *op cit.*, p.178. To aid income, there were large rooms for the purpose of spinning and weaving, and each cottage had a garden and field. However John Bush, author of *Hibernia Curiosa* (1764), wrote that the majority of Anglo-Irish and English property-holders were 'petty and despicable landlords, third, fourth and fifth from the first proprietor (of which inferior and worst kind of landlords this kingdom abounds infinitely too much for the reputation of the real proprietors, or the prosperity of agriculture)'. Bush is quoted in Harrington (ed.) 1991, *op cit.*, pp.158-9.
31. As reported in Camblin, 1951. *The Town in Ulster.* Belfast, Mullan; 66. The cottage contained two rooms with a piggery at the rear. Occasional didactic cottage designs such as those of Thomson in the *Statistical Survey of Co. Meath* (1802) may have reached a wider audience, as eventually did the works of J. C. Loudon, the English architect and author, principally his 1833 *Cottage and Villa Encyclopaedia.* London.
32. Kelly (ed.) 1990, *op cit.*, p.31.
33. Camblin 1951, *op cit.*, p.65.
34. Coote is quoted in Maxwell, 1949. *Country and Town in Ireland under the Georges.* Dundalk, Dundalgan Press, p.128. This contrasts with the bleak findings of many of the authors of the Statistical Surveys of other counties.
35. Johnson, 1844. *A Tour in Ireland.* London, p.327.
36. Camblin 1951, *op cit.*, p.65. Although many visitors to Ulster did not observe the presence of hovels as found elsewhere - or chose not to comment upon them - in the 1820s Thomas Reid did refer to the countryside around Ballygawley in Co. Tyrone as 'strewed with miserable hovels'. Reid, 1823 *Travels in Ireland*, excepted in Hadfield and McVeagh (eds) 1994, *op cit.*, p.200.
37. O'Brien G. (ed.) 1923. *Advertisements for Ireland, 1623* Dublin, Royal Society of Antiquaries of Ireland, p.36. The tract is attributed to Sir Henry Bourgchier.
38. Loveday, 1890, *op cit.*, p.36
39. Hadfield and McVeagh (eds.) 1994, *op cit.*, p.253.
40. Thompson (1802) opined that lofts were found only in 'town cabbins' as there building ground had more value. Extracted in Jack Fitzsimons, 1990. *Thatched Houses in County Meath.* Meath, privately printed, p.58
41. de Breffny and Ffolliott 1975, *op cit.*, p.179.
42. Young 1780, *op cit.*, I, p.94.
43. Reid, 1823, *op cit.*, p.206. Dr. Twiss - not wanting to share with hogs - avoided several inns he saw in Dunleer, Co. Louth in the 1770s, which had over the door a 'board with the words "good dry lodgings"'; Twiss, in Harrington (ed.) 1991, *op cit.*, p.171.
44. Authorities such as Ake Campbell, Estyn Evans and Alan Gailey have thoroughly investigated internal house layouts for construction and materials, regional variations and traditional customs. See note two above.
45. Lithgow, in Hall 1813, *op cit.*, p.312.

46. This excerpt from the report concerning Corbally, Co. Tipperary is quoted by Kinmonth, 1993, *op cit.*, p.118). Source, House of Commons Parliamentary Papers: *Report of Commissioners* (II) 1836, Supplement to Appendix E. xxxii. Co. Tipperary, p.241. According to Kinmonth similar descriptions are given in counties Cork, Kerry, Clare, Kilkenny, Longford Meath, Offaly, Wicklow, Limerick, Donegal and Down.
47. Herbert, D. 1988. *Retrospections of Dorothea Herbert 1770 - 1806*. Dublin, p.300.
48. McParlan's 1802 *Statistical Survey of Co. Mayo*. Dublin, Dublin Society is quoted by Gailey A. 1987. 'Changes in Irish rural housing 1600-1900', in P. O'Flanagan, P. Ferguson and K. Whelan (eds) *Rural Ireland 1600-1900: Modernisation and Change*. Cork, Cork University Press.
49. Petty, 1691, *op.cit.*, p.79. Several writers refer to floors being excavated and therefore vulnerable to damp, such as John Barrow, who wrote of 'there generally being a step *down* from the door' into the room. Barrow, 1836, *op cit.*, p.193. A sad detail of this arrangement is reported by Thompson, 1802, *op cit.*, p.71; he had often 'seen a hole dug in the floor, to receive the water coming in at the door, or under the foundation, from whence it might be pailed out with the greater ease when it collected'.
50. Campbell, Rev. T. 1778. *A Philosophical Survey of the South of Ireland*. Dublin, p.146.
51. Herbert, 1988, *op cit.*, p.300.
52. McVeagh, J. (ed.) 1995. *Bishop Pococke's Irish Tour*. Dublin, p.81.
53. Stevens, 1691. *A Journal of my Travels in Ireland since the Revolution*, excerpted in Harrington (ed.) 1991, *op cit.*, p.129 & p.134.
54. Young, 1780, *op cit.*, II, p.26 Young found this approach on the whole to be a more sensible custom than that prevalent in England, where 'a man's cottage will be filled with superfluities before he possesses a cow … a hog is a much more valuable piece of goods than a set of tea things' (ibid.). Young's opinion echoes that of Mary Delany (see above).
55. Day (ed.) 1991, *op cit.*, p.153.
56. McVeagh, J. (ed.) 1995. *Bishop Pococke's Irish Tour*. Dublin, p.81.
57. Young, 1780, *op cit.*, II, p.26. The articles described in the better sort of cabin, Young found upon enquiry, had all been purchased within the previous ten years (ibid.). Both Pococke and Young may have cause to have remarked on the exceptions rather than the rule.
58. The advertisement is reprinted in Georgian Society, 1969. *Georgian Society Records*. 1909-1913. Shannon, Irish University Press. 5 vols., vol. 3, p.20. There were also an orchard, gardens, ponds and good farming land.
59. Day (ed.) 1991, *op.cit.*, p.202.
60. Wilde, W. (ed.) 1880. *Memoirs of Gabriel Beranger*. Dublin, p.152.
61. Bowden, C. 1791. *A Tour Through Ireland*. Dublin, p.113. The full episode is interesting; save if Bowden was misled, Dunroche was a remarkable man, a self-taught surveyor, carpenter, cabinet-maker and upholder, as well as a quack or herbalist.

SPACE, TIME AND CONSERVATION

RICHARD ORAM

SIGFRIED GIEDION DELIVERED THE Charles Eliot Norton lectures of 1938-1939 at Harvard University, on the subject of a new tradition in architecture. In his foreword Giedion writes – "Space, Time and Architecture (his title) is intended for those who are alarmed by the present state of our culture and anxious to find a way out of the apparent chaos of its contradictory tendencies." The published version of these lectures was a great inspiration to me as an architectural student, since Giedion managed to place contemporary architecture into an historic perspective that I had not before experienced. Although he never refers directly to conservation as such, he continually makes historical references. Again, he writes "our period has come to consciousness of itself --------- this consciousness is relative to a sense of history." Necessarily, that consciousness is impossible without a direct reference to the legacy of history and for that legacy to be a tangible experience in our every day lives, buildings must be conserved. Giedion's thought process goes on to guide the reader along an historic progression of creative architecture through time always paralleled by a similarly evolving attitude towards the past and so it is that the inspiration of Giedion's writings has led to this title.

Current writing on the subject of building conservation often leaves the impression that there is only one correct approach. In fact it has taken a very long period of evolution and development to arrive where we now find ourselves and it is unlikely that the story is over. The standards that are accepted today have not been long established, however the idea of conservation in the broader sense has been with us since time began. There would seem to have been moments in history when there had been a unity of culture and in those brief periods, conservation does not surface as an identifiable element in cultural philosophy. By contrast, those periods when meaning had to struggle for existence, conservation is brought into sharp perspective. It was a cultural issue for the Assyrians and later for the Greeks then the Romans. Greek and Roman attitudes contrasted strongly. The Greeks gave serious prominence to authenticity, authorship and social and geographical context, when assessing cultural value. The Romans, on the other hand, rated the aesthetic values at the expense of contextual considerations. They were happy to move and re use beautiful objects. The triumphal arch of Constantine incorporates sculptures taken from earlier works for Trajan, Hadrian and Marcus Aurelius all re-displayed without any qualms about their origins. The same is true of Constantine's Christian basilicas, all, with the exception of S. Paolo Fuori le Mura in Rome, are blatant examples of recycling from earlier pagan structures.

This essentially late empire attitude is one that has characterised western thought throughout the first millennium and beyond into the region of modern history. The Venetian reuse of artefacts sourced from Byzantium and Alexandria is well known. At home, here in Ireland, there are similar examples; the mediaeval windows in the plantation Church at Castlecaulfield of 1680 (Fig 1) or the antique carved stones built into the 1750 building works at Tynan Abbey or the Romanesque doorway removed to adorn Beresford's new Cathedral building at Kilmore as late as 1860. There are of course many, many more examples but these are enough to give a flavour of a once popular view of the antique. The

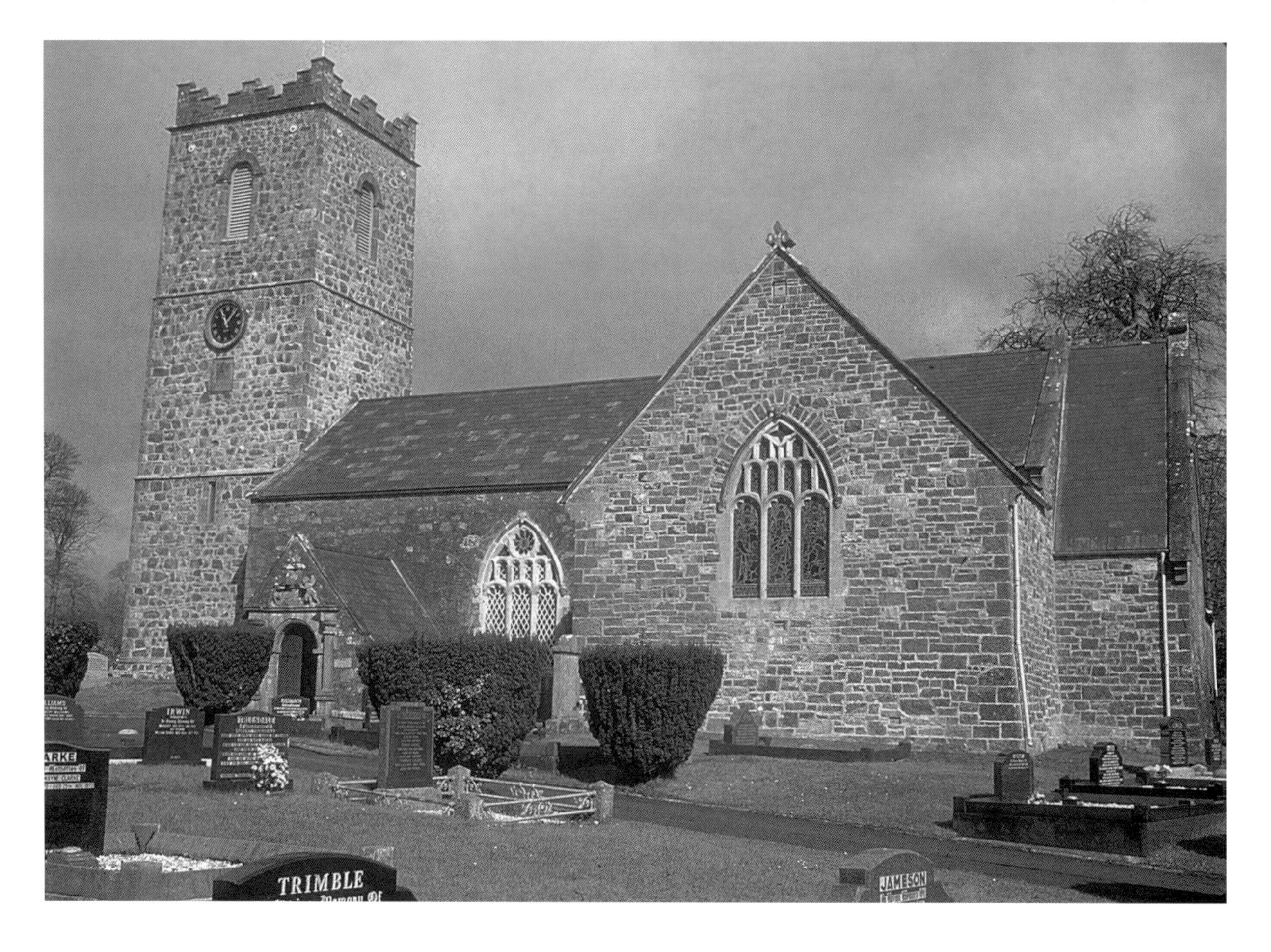

Fig 1.
St Michael's Church, Castlecaulfield, County Tyrone

current version of this debate is now focussed on the future for the Elgin Marbles.

It was the Spirit of the Renaissance that sowed the seeds for all modern views on the conservation theme. The first identifiable point of change is signalled by Pope Pius II in his decision to protect the remaining fragments of pagan Rome. Never before in recorded history, had a society ever looked over its shoulder and formed the view that what had gone before was at least as good, if not better than, the present. From this critical decision there developed the most modern and most beautiful capitol city in all of the western world, reaching perfection under the direction of Sixtus V. In this visionary scheme the past and the present were conjoined in total harmony. The echo down the centuries has found voice again in Minister Tessa Jowell's report "A Force for the Future".

Once awarded an honourable place in history, the monuments of Imperial Rome and elsewhere, began to attract international attention. This interest transformed into the notion of the "Grand Tour". A whole chain of ideas and initiatives emanated from this, such that a knowledge of the ancients became the only accepted cultural measure of the age. This classical epidemic was not limited to matters architectural but reached into every branch of learning, arts and science. The Roman Empire had never wielded such influence even at the very height of its military power.

A consequence was the creation of a two tier society in Europe. One tier championing an international neo-classicism and the other holding to local

Fig 2. The Forum in Rome showing the wall of the Curia Senatus and the Temple of Julius Caesar in the foreground and the Arch of Augustus and the House of Vestals in the background.

vernacular standards and traditions that had been the rule for society from its beginning. This dichotomy remains with us today. Gradually the vernacular was sidelined and its influence slipped lower and lower down the social scale. This trend is clear to see in the development of building forms through to the early years of the 20th century when the vernacular becomes virtually extinct as a creative force. As always architecture has acted as a social barometer. The same forces are to be seen at work throughout society. In government and in religion as well as the arts and learning.

Fig 3. The interior of the Colosseum in Rome

The thirst for the classics and all things antique led to the founding of British Schools in Rome and Athens. A network of antiquarian studies and trade routes, spun a web that reached into every corner of the civilized world. Christian relics were eclipsed by antique collectables. The new light shone out as every ruin and remain was meticulously measured and recorded often to be copied in designs of new buildings for the educated classes. For some it was a hobby or a past-time, for others it was a lucrative business. Classical institutes of learning were founded of which Northern Ireland had its share. The most famous survivor is the Royal Belfast Academical Institution, housed very suitably in a very fine classical building designed by Sir John Soane. Soane's classical studies are legendary. His amazing antiquarian collection can still be viewed in the context of his own wonderfully idiosyncratic creation at 13 Lincoln's Inn Fields, very much a phenomenon of its time and quite unlike anything that would be conceived of today.

The emergence of the culture of the nation state now set people to look more critically at historical objects and sites closer to home, A murmur passed around that perhaps our own ruins of past glories might be every bit as important as those to be seen in Rome. An Hibernian Antiquarian Society was founded in

Fig 4. Cottages on Mullalelish Road, Laurelvale, Co. Armagh

Fig 5. The ruins of the Franciscan Priory in Armagh, County Armagh

1779. Although it was short lived, the attitudes and ideas that it embraced were developing into a serious force in society. Illustrative of these changing standards is Richard Robinson's incorporation of the ruins of the Franciscan Priory in Armagh as a picturesque incident in the landscaping of his new archiepiscopal demesne (Fig 5), where as, half a century earlier, in the same city, the remains of the abbey of S.S. Peter and Paul were openly used as a quarry for building the new meeting house nearby. The changing attitude found its way into print when Francis and Daniel Grose published and illustrated "The Antiquities of Ireland" followed in 1829 by Thomas Bell's "Gothic Architecture in Ireland".

In 1821 the Belfast Natural History and Philosophical Society was founded and as the century rolled on, the membership became increasingly "hands on" in their attitude to the historic sites of the North; so much so that under the leadership of Francis Joseph Bigger, a wide range of historic buildings and archaeological sites were excavated and actively conserved. The results of their work can be seen today at the Giants Ring, Nendrum, St. Tassagh's, Jordan's Castle, the Middle Church of Ballinderry and many others. The mood for conservation was given a boost by historically destructive works on many of our most important buildings, for example the old Cathedral in Armagh during the 1830s and Christ Church Dublin as late as the 1870s. Such works certainly

Fig 6. St Patrick's Church of Ireland Cathedral, Armagh

saved the buildings in question but at a price. It was in this context that the Society for the Protection of Ancient Buildings had been inaugurated in 1877, under the guidance of William Morris and his colleagues. These new developments brought the conservation debate closer to the people and everyone could see and enjoy the results.

Now government became involved in the protection of our heritage. By 1874 fourteen historic sites in Ireland were in state care and by 1877 that number had risen to 119. The public entry onto the stage of conservation was next marked by legislation, beginning in Ireland with the 1882, Ancient Monuments (Ireland) Act. The context of major historical sites was by now being seriously considered as a factor in their authenticity and cultural importance.

A rash of new organisations with specific interests were a phenomenon of the inter war period. The Ancient Monuments Society of 1924, the Georgian Group of 1937. Victorian interests had to wait until after the war when in 1958 the Victorian Society was founded. Tourism was reaching an ever wider public and heritage became a major quest for all. By the outbreak of World War II, the modern attitude to heritage and conservation was well developed and it was now to be severely tested ; destruction of cultural sites was to be on a scale never before imagined. The catastrophe to come had been foreseen by many people, recording institutes had been set up all across Europe and contingency plans had been made for the safe removal and storage of a significant volume of artefacts; so when finally the war was over there existed a data bank for reconstruction for most of the more significant sites. Central and Eastern European states had been hit the worst. Here governments saw in restoration and conservation a means to help in the rebirth of nationhood. Vast sums of money were poured into these schemes and state institutions were created to provide the professions, skills and technical backup.

There were enormous problems to overcome starting with the sheer extent of the undertaking not to mention the shortage of skills and materials. Some of the unsung heroes of this era are worthy of mention, Kazimerz Macur, in 1945 handed the task of rebuilding Gdansk from a heap of rouble, Major Kedrinsky who, in 1943 took over the command for the conservation of the Zarskejo Selo complex on the outskirts of St. Petersberg and Romauld Chankz who set to work at the incredible Templar fortress city of Marlbork in 1946 where he sorted through the wreckage and tried to pick up from where Konrad Steinbeck had left off. These men dedicated their entire professional lives, each to one single conservation project, there were many others like them.

Fig 7. Warsaw in ruins in 1944

Fig 8. District heating schemes and historic reconstruction at Elblag, Poland

These projects gradually developed technical and research excellence that has been a mainstay to present day conservation throughout the world but the subsequent break up of the communist system is now taking its toll. The flow of money and resources is drying up as the new capitalist governments redraw political agendas. Even in the West there seems to be a growing perception that our heritage is now secure and no longer needs the public support it once enjoyed but anyone who is involved in the heritage industry knows this is delusion. Heritage will always need a watchful eye and a caring hand, if it is to be passed on to the next generation.

The British Isles were relatively sheltered from the extremes of World War II. Accordingly, post war conservation took a slightly different turn. New legislation of 1944 empowered the government to carry out an audit of historic buildings in England and Wales. In 1946 a revision obliged government to do this and thereby the notion of "listing" had arrived but was not to reach as far as Northern Ireland until 1972. In the Republic the Planning and Development Act 2000 is the first enactment to oblige government departments to act in favour of the nations heritage.

Legislation parcels out powers and duties but it does not establish philosophies and so legislation must be backed up by policies. The earliest source of policy was the Athens' Charter. An international conference was held in Athens in 1931 to discuss principles for the protection of historic sites and buildings. The findings of this conference were endorsed by The League of Nations and recommended to member states under the title of the "Athens Charter" and so another chapter in the history of conservation was opened.

Following the World War II, UNESCO took up the banner for conservation in the international field. Another landmark meeting took place in Venice in 1964. From this conference a charter was published that is now at the heart of practically all current European legislation for conservation. Equally important was the creation of ICOMOS (International Counsel on Monuments and Sites) by those delegates who considered it important to maintain the contacts made in Venice with a view to policing the implementation of the Venice principles in the future. The Council of Europe has also accepted a conservation remit. The most direct experience of this in local terms is the European Open Days when owners open buildings to the public that would normally be closed to view.

The international charters have been very influential even if individual nation states do not often openly acknowledge their lead. Necessarily these basic guidelines have to be translated into the local context. In the British Isles, England and Wales were the first to go into print with Planning Policy Guidance; Note 15; 1992. This was followed in Scotland with a Memorandum of Guidance 1993 and in Northern Ireland in 1999 with Planning Policy Guidance No 6. Statutory Guidelines and Advice Notes: Architectural Heritage Protection for the Republic, are now in final draft stage. Last but by no means least, in this list of conservation guidance, is British Standard 7913 – "A Guide to the Principles of the Conservation of Historic Buildings": This standard was a complete departure for B.S.I. who had never before issued a document concerned primarily with a philosophy of approach.

Conservation in the British Isles is now, generally speaking, regulated by government but implemented by the individual or corporate owners sometimes with the encouragement of grants and tax concessions. Conservation has travelled a long way over the centuries, developing out of the interests of individuals and by stages, into a vast international network. There have emerged a whole range of new threats to our built heritage that must be matched by further development and research on the part of conservators. Ethnic conflicts have brought about massive destruction to heritage sites in recent years. Naturally enough, what is treasured by one section of a population becomes a target for their enemies. Then there are changes in our society that have left many historic structures without a use; and movements in population leading to serious changes in the settings of historic structures. Legislation for health and safety, against toxic substances, to accommodate people with disabilities, green issues, sustainability and sophisticated theft; all these issues have an impact on conservation, so no one can sit back and claim the battle is over.

Now, what of the future? Supposing no new major catastrophe befalls us the old heresies will continue to resurface. For this reason it is necessary, periodically, to reinvent the wheel and because, "Tis time that stays and we that goes". (Thomas McCarrie, memoirs, Portaferry). Those who have an interest in conservation must always be vigilant, especially since government, at least in the North of Ireland, seems to be ever more content to be a processor of the law and to leave the pro active and promotional work to others. As ever, there is a great deal of educating to be done. Take building owners and professionals; well tried and accepted principles must be regularly revisited and refreshed. This is at least as important as the dissemination of recent conservation experience and research. Slightly more challenging is to meet the educational needs of the building industry. Here with most obvious deficiency is training in traditional skills; another is the application of new technologies without harming the quality of the product. If new technologies are ignored there is a very real risk that conservation costs could rise to limit serious work to the elite section of the market.

Before bringing this paper to a close it is worth reflecting that a consequence of conservation being a creative activity is that it involves an element of selection. Resources are almost always limited with the result that the first decision to be made is what to conserve and what to leave to its ultimate fate. After the initial selection has been made the next consideration is likely to be the extent of intervention. Intervention work may be relatively minor and aesthetically insignificant like lightning protection but it may need to be quite radical, think of the extension work at the Linenhall Library or at the Ulster Museum. It is now extremely rare for there to be no requirement to comply with some additional statute or regulation. Which ever way you look at it and whether you like it or not, whenever conservation is carried out, a unique mark is left by that work such that, for better or for worse, that building will never be the same again. Some works of conservation have been sufficiently characteristic of their time to be dateable by eye. Even quite practical works like repointing and cleaning can illustrate fashionable trends of a particular age. Most people agree that the ideal is for conservation work to leave no trace but this is extremely difficult to achieve. If we cannot leave the building as we found it, we must, at least, be respectful in what we do. Carrying this principle a stage further, a similar respect should be shown when building in close proximity to a building of historic value. There used to be a slogan for safely crossing the road – "Wait, watch and listen". Something like it could be appropriate advice to architects and developers working on or near historically sensitive sites. The present setting of Robinson's Bar in Great

Fig 9. The interior of the Synod Hall of the Roman Catholic Cathedral, Armagh, during conservation

Victoria Street Belfast is a case in point.

Good conservation always requires a long term view. Regular planned maintenance and repair must go hand in hand with contingency plans, to be ready to make use of additional resources at short notice, for example grant aid. Many historic buildings have survived periods of serious neglect only to be born again but many more have been lost by the same means. The role of government is changing with everything else. The department with direct responsibility is being replaced by agencies and in other instances, duties are contracted into the private sector. The role of the watch dog committees, the Historic Buildings Councils, is also being challenged. In this climate of change the independent voluntary societies become particularly important. They can provide for continuity at the local level and at the other end of the scale the policy making international committees take on an additional significance in the campaign to achieve acceptance of standards of excellence. Money is not always the sole answer to conservation problems although it is undeniably a key factor for success.

I will end as I began by quoting from Giedion – "History is not simply a repository of unchanging facts but a process, a pattern of living and changing attitudes and interpretations. As such it is deeply a part of our own natures". Who could disagree?

IRELAND'S FIRST BUNGALOW?

PRIMROSE WILSON

ROGER NORTH, WHO WROTE *Of Building* in 1698, said that an interest in architecture 'is a sober entertainment and doth not impeach but defend health. Other pleasures which are less despised, as wine, women, gambling, etc., have a sting which this hath not. And it is also an exercise of the mind as well as of the body ...he that hath no relish for the grandeur and joy of building is a stupid ox and wants that vivacity of sense and spirit that seasons humane life and makes it less insipid.'[1] North, had he been alive today, would have found much to relish in Irish architecture except, perhaps, the modern bungalow! It is not a subject to excite many people, but the story of the man who built the first one in Ireland is of interest from a social history perspective as well as an architectural one. Through an extraordinary set of circumstances an up to the minute style from California was introduced into a remote corner of Ireland; the tragedy is that it was not the exemplar chosen when bungalows spread across the country decades later.

William Calwell was born in Ballycarry, County Antrim, in 1863 and emigrated to California in 1881. His uncle, Robert Wisnom, who lived in San Mateo, took William on as an apprentice in his building business. He prospered and in due course ran his own business designing and building houses in the San Mateo area. In 1907 he was diagnosed as suffering from a terminal illness and decided to return to end his days in his native Ballycarry. On discovering that the diagnosis was incorrect William decided not to go back to California and he lived on in Ballycarry until the age of ninety.

In c.1908 William Calwell built a house for himself at 54 Main Street in the 'Shingle style' sometimes known as the 'Californian bungalow'. This distinctive brand of domestic architecture was all the rage at the time with architects and speculative builders on the West Coast of America.[2] The chief exponents of this style in the early years of the twentieth century were the Greene brothers, Charles and Henry, who were based in Pasadena, California. 'The individual character of their work evolved from a study of timber craftmanship, an appreciation of

Japanese design and a love of nature and natural materials.'[3] The style had its origins in the English Arts and Crafts movement and was characterised by low pitch gabled roofs, roughcast or shingle walls, verandahs and sash windows, often with geometric glazing. They were located as single dwellings in suburban blocks and the garden was integrated into the design. Charles Greene (1868-1957) and Henry (1870-1954) were contemporaries of Frank Lloyd Wright (1867-1959) but as J.M. Fitch points out while there was 'a superficial resemblance to Wright's houses of the same period, there seems to have been no connection whatever between them. Their similarity springs directly from the fact that both were strongly influenced by the Japanese.'[4]

The Greene's clients who were mainly 'wealthy Midwesterners of liberal Protestant or Quaker background'[5] wanted comfortable, unpretentious houses. During the rapid development of California in the early years of the twentieth century many wealthy and educated people who were prepared to be innovative had moved from the East to the West Coast of America. Fitch says 'they belonged to that segment of opinion which supported national parks, woman's suffrage, progressive education, factory reform. They were involved in new theories of love and marriage, of birth control and child care, of diet and hygiene. At the practical level, these interests are more of less directly expressed in the twin beds, sleeping porches, children's rooms and well-planned kitchens of the Greene houses.'[6]

The early photograph of 54 Main Street, Ballycarry, shows a one and half storey building with basement, shingle clad walls and roof, canted bays,

Fig 1. Photograph of the house front c.1910 (Monuments and Buildings Record: EHS: Built Heritage)

Fig 2. Watercolour of the house by J.W. Carey dated 1914 (Monuments and Buildings Record: EHS: Built Heritage)

verandah, sash and casement windows. The boundary to the road is of chain link fencing between short piers of rounded river stones with a small lattice timber gate for pedestrians and a larger one for the pony and trap. A model of US West Coast suburbia, popular from the turn of the century to the outbreak of the First World War, had arrived in Ballycarry by 1908! The bungalow has undergone a number of changes in the intervening years. The setting has changed as trees have matured and other houses were built nearby; a diagonally slatted fence was added at the side and the piers have been painted. The building was re-roofed with asbestos slates and a pair of suspended timber slatted garden seats were added to the verandah. The internal layout is unchanged except for a small rear extension and the original parquet floors, six-panelled doors with metal finger plates and knobs remain. The large basement has a billiard room. Despite the exterior alterations it retains its essential characteristics and was listed[7] in category B2 when Ballycarry was resurveyed in 1999.[8]

The Californian bungalow style was introduced to Australia in an article in Building in 1908 entitled 'The Building of a Bungalow: A Style that Should be Popular in Australia'. This was further reinforced when a full-size bungalow was featured at Sydney's Ideal Home Exhibition in 1916. The style spread rapidly with some regional variations across Australia and to Tasmania. As Maisy Stapleton points out 'one of the most interesting aspects of the Californian style was the development of a set of standard details for bungalow houses giving remarkable consistency despite different plans and sites.'[9] The style remained popular in Australia until the 1940s largely due to the influence of and

Fig 3. Photograph of the house front in 2002 (Primrose Wilson)

admiration for the culture of the United States promoted through films, mass-circulation newspapers and international magazines.[10]

William Calwell designed and built other houses in the area around Ballycarry and they can still be seen though many have been altered subsequently. Mr Calwell had other interests as well as house-building. In 1910 he set up a co-operative dairy in Ballycarry though its success was hampered by a shortage of milk. In California he had encountered Friesian cattle and he felt this breed were the answer for the Irish milk trade. Initially he was unsuccessful in importing stock from Holland but with the help of the British Friesian Society he and others established herds in Ireland. William Calwell was also an amateur poet and many of his verses were written about Friesian cattle. In 1944 his family published his later poems and in the author's forword he put forward his personal philosophy:

> *'I believe in the fundamental principle that Jesus taught and of which Burns sang - the brotherhood of man. Not cut-throat competition and national rivalry which lead inevitably to periodic wars, but co-operation with all men for the good of all men.'*[11]

This remarkable man, whose return to his native land was brought about by a quirk of fate, contributed much to life in Ballycarry. He had a pioneering role in

Fig 4. Detail of the house front in 2002 (Primrose Wilson)

bringing Friesian cattle to Ireland and setting up a co-operative dairy.[12] Unfortunately William Calwell seems to have been forgotten except in his native county. Perhaps because bungalows are considered by many to be a blight rather than a blessing 54 Main Street, Ballycarry, has been largely ignored too. But the sturdy little house which he built for himself with such care will soon be a century old and he cared enough about quality to use shingles brought all the way from New Orleans!

ACKNOWLEDGEMENTS

The author would like to thank the owner of 54 Main Street, Ballycarry for helping with information in the writing of this paper.

NOTES

1. Apperly A, Irving R and Reynolds P. 1998. *Identifying Australian Architecture.* Sydney, Angus & Robertson, p.9 (Irving)
2. Gossel P. Leuthauser G. 1991. *Architecture in the Twentieth Century.* Koln. Taschen; Peel L.

Powell P. Garrett A. 1989. *An Introduction to 20th -Century Architecture.* London, Quintet Publishing Limited.

3. Apperly A, Irving R and Reynolds P. 1998. *Identifying Australian Architecture.* Sydney, Angus & Robertson, p.118 (Apperly)
4. Fitch J.M. 1966. *American Building 1:The Historical Forces That Shaped It.* Boston, Houghton Miflin Company Boston, p.232
5. *Ibid,* p.232
6. *Ibid,* p232
7. Environment & Heritage Service: Historic Buildings Second Survey notes. 1999
8. Historic Buildings Reference: 06/05/049 (Grade B2). Listed 12/09/01. Forthill Townland.
9. Apperly A, Irving R and Reynolds P. 1998. *Identifying Australian Architecture.* Sydney, Angus & Robertson, p.119 (Irving)
10. Stapleton M. 1985. 'Between the Wars' in R. Irving (comp) *The History and Design of the Australian House.* Melbourne. Oxford University Press.
11. In forward of Calwell. W. 1944. *Forty Years of Topical Rhyme.* Published privately.
12. Dowlin A. (comp.) 1963. 'Breeding Friesian Cattle' from Town and Country Life, London in *Ballycarry in Olden Days.* Belfast. Graham & Heslip Ltd.

IRISH TOWNS. THEIR HISTORIC CENTRES

PATRICK SHAFFREY

TODAY IRELAND IS EXPERIENCING an era of physical and social development unparalleled in our history, greater perhaps than the late 18th and early 19th century and much greater than during the 1960's. A combination of financial incentives, European Union investments and demographic patterns, have all generated great changes and nowhere more obvious than in our urban areas.

In 1975 it was anticipated that Irish towns would grow more over the next twenty-five years than they had in the past 100 years. "The Irish Town – An Approach to Survival"[1] attempted to define the architectural and civic character of Irish towns as they then existed and suggested guidelines for their development, which might add to, rather than detract, from their character. Growth did take place but was more uneven than anticipated, with major recessions during the 1980's.

However, the massive growth in recent years is now indicating that the targets anticipated previously will be achieved, if not surpassed. The huge growth in cities and towns throughout the country is proof of this with the Dublin region anticipating a population of 1.5m by the year 2010, cities like Galway envisaging populations of 150,000; and regional county towns such as Navan growing to 60,000.

Northern Ireland is one of the fastest growing regions in Europe. The regional population growth rate is twice the current United Kingdom rate and exceeds that of the Republic of Ireland. The population of Northern Ireland is expected to continue to grow and reach 1.835 million by 2025.[2] This may generate a regional need for up to 250,000 additional dwellings by 2025. In addition the cultural complexities of our population are more varied with significant inward migration from other countries and changing household structures.

Despite any future interim recessions, which undoubtedly will happen from time to time, Ireland, with the peace settlement gradually establishing strong roots, and as a member of the European Community, is geared to play an important role in the multi-faceted relationship between Europe, America and the Third World. It is likely therefore that the next century will see a pattern of continued physical growth.

What form will this growth take? Ireland is a small island, still sparsely populated compared to other parts of Europe and the World. We could have a population of up to 10 million by the end of this century and perhaps much earlier. If present settlement trends were to continue the population could be scattered throughout the island in one essentially suburban form. In the process, large parts of the environment, which makes the country so distinctive, would change.

There are areas where natural conditions will always prevail against increasing urbanity, for example, mountain tops, bog lands, exposed coastlines. However, with increased means of communication, in its many diverse forms, there is an in-built tendency towards a dispersed settlement pattern, which will pose great challenges. There is also a varied and widely distributed range of historic settlements, from small crossroads villages to the major regional towns and cities. The current emphasis on 'sustainable development' will focus more attention on the existing settlement patterns and hopefully provide a blueprint for the future national planning strategy.

Therefore, there are great environmental challenges in the years ahead, not least to protect, and, where opportunity occurs, add to the civic qualities of existing towns and villages. There is an inherent aesthetic in all forms of human settlement which should never be lost sight of. How we might approach this is the subject of this essay with particular regard to the historic centres.

Irish Towns Today

There is a discernible pattern to the development of Irish towns. From the mid-18th to the mid-19th century there was considerable growth which shaped the form and character of most towns and is still clearly evident today in both the larger cities and small rural settlements (Fig 1). This is principally a classical layout with Georgian and Victorian style architecture which attained high environmental standards in the larger cities and towns. It is also inherent in the many everyday town buildings.

The 1850s to the 1960s was a time of political unrest and changes, two world wars and periodic economic depressions. There was relatively little physical

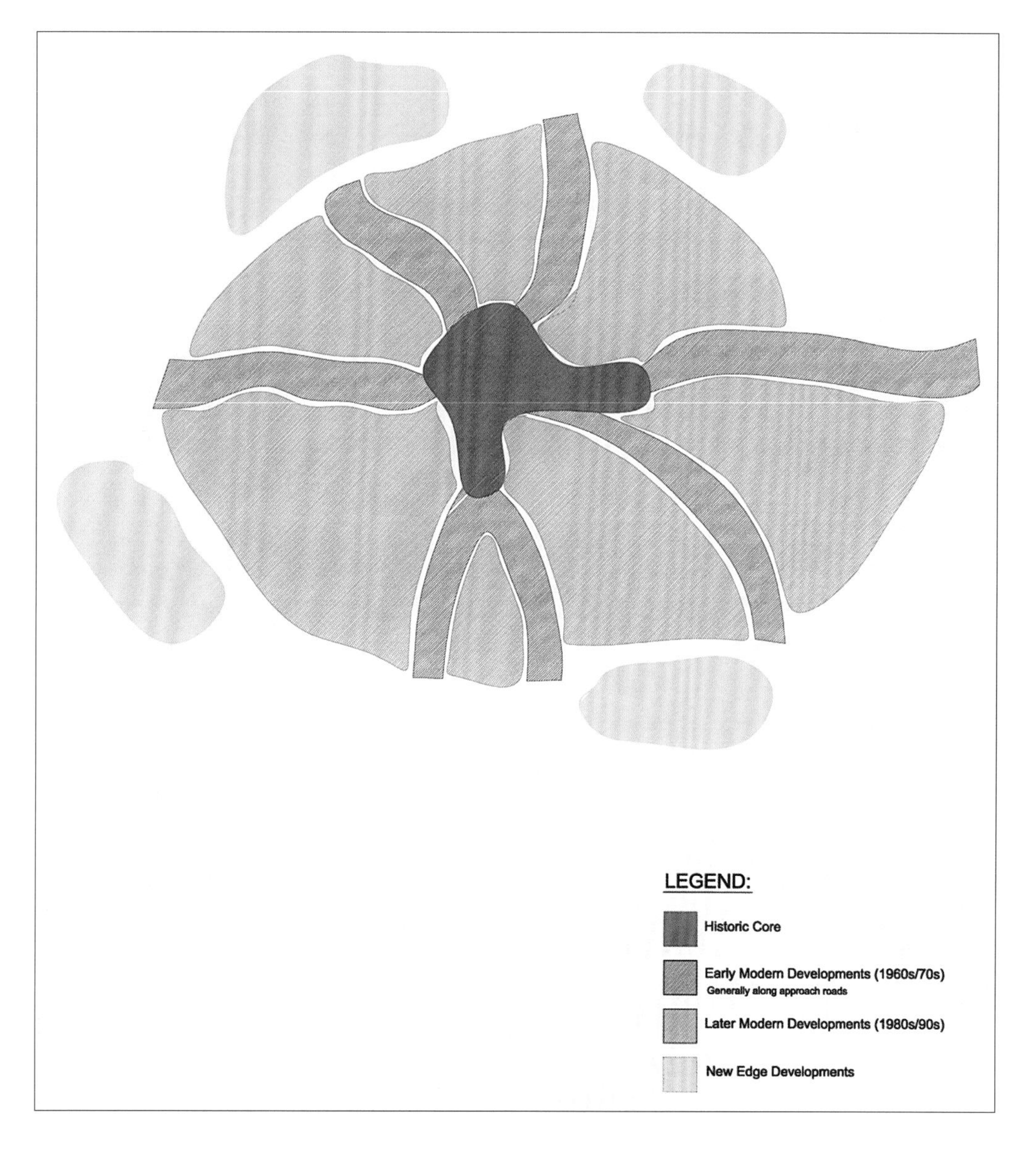

Fig 1. Diagram showing the emerging physical structure of towns today. All the different elements require sensitive planning, but it is the historic centre which gives a town its distinctive character and personality.

growth except in the cities, some provincial centres and the industrial towns of the north-east. It was also a period of massive emigration not only from the countryside but from the smaller country towns, where there were extremely dense and sub-standard living conditions.

The 1960s marked the first phase of modern expansion. It consisted mostly of suburban development on the edge of towns, facilitated by the growth of private transport. It was marked by a decline in the importance of the historic centres where there was little or no investment, except for relatively isolated office development in the larger towns and cities. The period was marked by phases of growth and recession – the '60s and '70s growth; the '80s and early '90s generally recession.

However, since the mid-1990s there has been a period of continuous growth, not only in the suburbs, but in the historic centres also. This modern phase of development has greatly exceeded anything ever experienced before even in the late 18th century. The various Urban Renewal Acts[3] provided a series of financial incentives to encourage the development of parts of cities and towns which had been underused and often derelict for many years. The Urban Development grants, the International Fund for Ireland Urban Development Programme/the Community Regeneration Programme assisted urban renewal in Northern Ireland.[4]

However, the great thrust of recent developments, despite the financial incentives, has been on the peripheries of cities and towns, and this has been mostly in the form of low density housing (Figs 2 & 3). In the past most new housing was for owner/occupiers or social/public housing for those in need. Today, the private rental sector is an important component of the market. Housing is widely considered as an investment commodity, rather than the physical fabric for emerging communities.

There are now clearly defined development patterns in cities and towns and they all have special visual and aesthetic characteristics.

Firstly, there are the historic centres, including developments up to the 1950s –

Fig 2. Aerial Photograph of Athy, Co. Kildare.

Fig 3. Aerial Photograph of Moira, Co. Down. The historic centre with its close-knit structure of buildings, streets, public spaces, contrasts with the emerging conformity of the modern suburbs.

generally its physical structure is close knit and compact and with a variety of building forms and land uses. The important public, community and commercial buildings are located here – churches, town halls, courthouses, schools, shops - those uses at the hub of social life. Housing is generally terraced and at relatively high densities, characterised by long, narrow, deep plots with outbuildings and gardens, now generally unused and derelict. Much of it has been converted for commercial uses – shops and offices.

Lurgan, Co. Armagh, is a particularly good example of a large town with many underused back areas of significant heritage interest and economic potential (Fig 4). How to match these possible conflicting situations represents a real challenge in urban renewal and regeneration.

Secondly, there are the early modern suburbs, a much looser structure located on the main roads outside towns – a mixture of individual houses, factories,

Fig 4. Lurgan, Co. Armagh. Such back areas, if improved with sensitivity, will also strengthen the town's social and economic structure.

garages and estates. Densities are low; uses predominately residential. There is a singularity of use and layout compared with the older centres that were of mixed use. Neighbourhood/shopping centres are essentially single use entities.

Thirdly, and beyond these early suburbs, are the new development areas fuelled by the current economic growth. The cities and larger towns are expanding considerably beyond the older suburbs and in many cases engulfing adjacent villages. Once again the predominant land use is residential, mostly in the form of individual estates with little or no connection with adjacent uses or other housing estates. More often than not there is a single, often gated, entrance from main distributor roads. The location of these is haphazard and bears little relation to the historic centre. The buildings forming the edge of these developments turn their backs on their neighbours and the countryside beyond instead of integrating and sharing.

Fourthly, and most recently, has been the growth of business parks and new industrial areas. Their visual expression are in contrast with the industrial areas of the past – extensively landscaped grounds, high-tech bright and airy buildings, generally with a single controlled entrance and with little or no connections to adjacent uses. Those working in such new developments come from different districts and are highly dependent on private transport. These form the beginnings of the "edge city", a new urban concept.

These patterns are now clearly identifiable and repeated throughout the country from cities to small villages, the scale varying depending on the size and importance of the settlement - the historic centres with a variety of uses and building forms; in contrast, the suburbs and outlying areas are mostly single use entities and extremely dependent on private transport. Neither are static elements. They are still changing in response to social and economic needs and both require specific planning and design approaches. The historic centres contain most of the architecturally important buildings. They evolved in a gradual way, over many centuries, and so represent a precious legacy which must be conserved and handled with care. In particular, they attract tourists and visitors which are an important economic resource, not least for the smaller settlements.

Today, our historic centres, be they cities or small villages, require a policy of repair and renewal, rather than extensive redevelopment. We need to recognise and improve the existing aesthetic characteristics, rather than make wholesale changes to create new patterns.

Earlier approaches in the 1960's, with their emphasis on comprehensive single use developments – mainly offices, were on the whole unsatisfactory. There is little point in returning to such approaches, particularly when there are alternative opportunities to create new urban forms in the peripheral areas. The Local Government (Planning and Development) Act 2000 provides a legislative framework to underpin the conservation of historic centres. There is much stronger protection for important individual buildings, whether they are a great public edifice or merely a more modest vernacular type. The legislation also allows for the protection and improvement of essential characteristics of entire neighbourhoods which are deemed worthy of conservation. The legislative framework therefore is in place but the challenge of informing and enthusing the general public to the importance of our historic centres still remains.

Although towns and cities generally have undergone great changes in the last 20 years or so, many historic centres are still substantially intact. In the context of the great changes ahead it is important to keep that balance.

The 1972 Planning Order Northern Ireland updated in 1992 has for long provided for the designation of Conservation Areas in cities and towns throughout the province. However, the ongoing "troubles" did not create a satisfactory context for urban conservation policies to work in a creative fashion. The situation now is much more conducive. Planning is in the hands of the new Assembly, but will they make the regeneration of cities and towns a major priority.

Historic Centres

Form

The main aesthetic components of historic centres are firstly their general form and character, which is influenced by their topographical context. A town or village built on a hilly site will by its nature influence the layout, the atmosphere and the form of the buildings. There will be views and vistas over the surrounding landscape, narrow winding streets, which are full of surprises and intimacy. Conversely, settlements developed in the context of flat landscapes, generally have a more spacious and formal layout (Fig 5). The view from the single main street village to the countryside has less surprises. Its essential character is immediately recognisable. Many large cities and towns may combine elements of both. It is these essential forms which give cities and towns 'their personality' e.g. Ennis, Co. Clare, is different in "personality and character" from

Fig 5. Beragh, Co. Tyrone. The architectural character of this one street village, with its simple buildings and long burgage plots, sits easily in the landscape.

Fig 6. Inistioge, Co. Kilkenny.

Fig 7. Castlecomer. Co. Kilkenny. Contrasting visual character influenced by topography and historical background.

Nenagh, Co. Tipperary, though both are county towns and provide the same function as administrative, regional and residential nodes. On a smaller scale, Inistioge, Co. Kilkenny, with its narrow winding streets and access ways, is different in personality to Castlecomer, also in Co. Kilkenny, with its broad and spacious treelined streets (Figs 6 & 7); Rathfriland, Co. Down, with its spacious market place on the hilltop is different in personality to its county's neighbour (Fig 8), Portaferry, stretched along the coastline (Fig 9). In the cities, Rathgar

Fig 8. Aerial Photograph of Rathfriland, Co. Down. Formal layout on a hilltop with potentially great public spaces.

and Donnybrook in Dublin, the Malone and Ormeau districts in Belfast with their larger houses, tree lined roads, are different in character to the narrow dense residential streets of Phibsboro, South Circular Road, or the Shankill/Falls Roads.

It is this essential 'personality' or 'character' which needs to be identified and protected in the context of future development/improvement policies. This totality of elements fused together within a compact space and influenced by local topography, create an aesthetic which, in its distinctive form, is personal to each town or village, but, in its generality, shares a distinctively Irish common

Fig 9. Portaferry, Co. Down. The town provides a distinctive backdrop to Strangford Lough.

theme with historic centres everywhere. Combined with these physical characteristics is the vitality and energy generated by the mixture of land uses, shops, houses, churches, schools, all closely intertwined, and the tradition of historic settlements. The mixture of uses is an essential defining characteristic of historic centres and their general compatibility with each other is essential for a vibrant and culturally strong community.

Temple Bar in Dublin is perhaps the most significant example of urban renewal to date in the country. In the physical sense it is quite successful – it respects the historic grain of the area and the architectural qualities of many of the new buildings are high. It has added to the City's public space network with new squares and streets which can accommodate a variety of cultural, economic and amenity uses. However, the predominance of large pubs, night clubs and restaurants, has slowed down the emergence of an indigenous local community and is in danger of becoming another single use entity, i.e. a night-time entertainment hub.

Old towns and villages are like old buildings, we have to treat them carefully; retain their intrinsic characteristics; repair, rather than replace, like we do the elements of an historic building – windows, doors, plasterwork. Above all, we should avoid making them all look the same, as is tending to happen, with bollards, paving, tree planting, tree lighting, flower baskets, etc., and the latest, perhaps more garish fad, the stripping off of original renders, thus exposing stone that was never meant to be exposed and, over time, causing serious damage to the building structures. The essential visual quality of the Irish town is unfussy, simple, with a certain ruggedness. There is generally no need to "tart them up".

We must retain the historic streets and laneways (Fig 10), vistas, especially those with an eccentric form, building lines, the general ambience of squares and market places. For example, the main square or diamond, is essentially the community's main living room. It should be a place for public gatherings, activities, recitals, meetings, etc., supporting the life in the town as it evolves and develops and not just function as a glorified car park. Ideally, in all towns and villages, traffic, and all the signage that goes with its control, in the main square should be significantly reduced, so that its civic qualities can be better appreciated. If a start was made in this respect it would have a beneficial effect on the rest of the town.

The major emphasis of new development in the future will be residential of varying sorts – starter homes, larger homes and apartments, shelter and affordable housing. It should be possible to provide a variety of living accommodation within the context of old towns imaginatively reusing empty or underused buildings, back areas, outbuildings, inserting sympathetic new buildings in old yards, small fields, etc., gradually knitting together the fabric of the town. New developments need not be "pastiche or copyist". Contemporary architectural expression, which respects the grain and scale of the town, can bring a fresh and stimulating feel to an

Fig 10. Borris, Co. Carlow. Old laneways are a precious asset in towns. They should never be taken for granted.

old town. Even disused factories and institutions can be converted to residential and cultural uses. There will be opportunities to add to a town's network of public spaces, streets and linkages of different types, complimenting the particular character of the town. It is possible that as the larger towns become more stressful to live in, the environmental potential of the smaller centres will be more appreciated. However, developments must be handled with care. A large new housing scheme will change the social fabric of a small village and does create concerns for the existing communities.

Buildings

These can range from a small single dwelling to the grandiose church or other public building. They all have their own particular characteristics derived from their history, architectural style and design, nature and type of materials used and their general state of maintenance. Individual buildings may be quite simple in appearance, but, collectively, they make an important contribution to the overall character of a street or town. Then there are buildings which form part of a group, because they are dependant on each other while being quite insignificant individually, for example, commercial street buildings, originally constructed with living accommodation on upper floors, and street houses, sometimes to a similar design or of varied appearance and with other building types mixed in. One of the important aspects of towns is that buildings are observed in the context of the other buildings. The coherence of a town is derived from the relationship between the various architectural expressions, construction techniques and proportions of the buildings.

There are many factors today which are shaping the character of our historic centres – social and demographic changes often contributed to a decline in population and with this a consequent decline in the need for certain building types. There are new philosophies emerging from recent experience in dealing with architecturally important buildings. In some cases the architecture of the building may be so significant that the retention of its essential characteristics will limit the scope of any proposed new uses and that this use will have to accept these limitations in deference to the architectural character of the building. In other instances it will be acceptable and indeed necessary to adapt historic buildings for new uses, which, while respecting their character, will involve significant changes and intervention. For example, an old mill would traditionally have been built with cast iron columns, heavy timber floors and low ceiling heights. In particular, low ceiling heights might not be acceptable in the context of the new use so adaptation would be required. In many instances new uses may be the only way to secure the long term future of the building, adaptation will often be necessary.

Churches are among the important architectural treasures in most towns and may become redundant and require new uses if they are to be saved in any meaningful way. To date, there is a growing number of examples of churches and other public buildings being adapted for new and currently more relevant uses. This is a trend which will continue in the future.

Convents and monasteries are another common building type in many towns. Generally they were built towards the end of the 19th century, a period of great ecclesiastical renewal, but the modern process of change and decline has been swift and dramatic. Today comparatively few religious/institutional buildings are being used for their original purpose and quite a number have been demolished completely. They were however, buildings of presence, well crafted and always well maintained. In most cases the settings included gardens, grounds, sometimes entire farms, which, over the years, were important elements in the urban landscapes.

However, too often the urban context of these religious institutions has been ignored or compromised in the changing situation. Fine gardens have been needlessly destroyed to be replaced by standardised housing estates. Opportunities to create new urban landscapes have too often been ignored. Farms, which had the potential to be precious open lands for future generations, are being built over. This indeed is a tragic loss in the cities and larger towns and occasionally in small towns and villages. For example, the great swathe of open farm lands between Dun Laoghaire and Dublin, formerly owned by "St. Mary's School for the Blind' – a truly precious asset in the overall urban context, is shortly to become another business park and housing estate. The Presentation Convent in Carlow with its orchard, gardens, graveyard and, together with the adjacent College and Cathedral, formed an historic open area in the centre of a busy county town, was developed as a typical town house, apartment complex, now common in many towns.

Adapting old buildings and open lands require sensitivity and skill, knowledge of the building's significance and imaginative design approaches that will produce a satisfactory aesthetic and historically appropriate solution if they are to continue to contribute to the environment, life and heritage of our towns.

Civic Spaces

These are the streets, squares, incidental spaces, playing fields, graveyards and demesnes, which are formed by the disposition of the buildings, sometimes in a planned way, as a great city square or street, or, in an informal incidental manner, which has evolved gradually over the years in response to changing social and economic habits and subject to the requirements of the often simple vernacular town buildings which form them. In the smaller towns, the market place and its adjacent commercial streets, which were often the *raison d'être* for the town's establishment, have been important in a commercial and community sense for generations. Today, there is a fundamental conflict between the character of old towns and the demands of modern traffic.

For many years however, streets and squares have been considered specifically as traffic and service arteries to the buildings and all changes and improvements have been designed to cater for the needs of transport. Important historic streets have become urban freeways; great squares, parking lots; residential roads used as 'rat runs' to escape congestion elsewhere in a town. Streets have been widened and buildings demolished to cater for this obsession. For example, in the 1960's, the Dublin Quays were designated as a potential urban freeway; most quayside buildings were earmarked for demolition and so all maintenance and improvements effectively ceased. There was however no money to finance such a project and so this architecturally important element of the City became underused and potentially derelict. It is only recently being revitalised and restored to something approaching its civic importance. Modern planning has also left a bad civic legacy in centres such as Carrickfergus, Newry and Armagh.

In recent years there has been a growing awareness of the importance of public spaces, which is very welcome. The concept of extensive widening of existing streets has been largely discredited. In the cities and larger towns there has been a welcome trend in giving more preference to pedestrians within the major shopping areas. This has been a long time coming and has been greatly resisted by trade organisations and individual owners. Private transport assumed such an important place in the community psyche that people considered that removing cars from streets would be bad for business. Traders often live outside towns and see the old centres as merely economic units; the views of residents, for example, parents with young children are rarely heard. However, experience to date has demonstrated that trade does not necessarily decrease with pedestrianisation, in fact the opposite is most often the case and now this argument has largely been won. In some instances it is not a case of removing cars altogether, indeed some movement in areas can add to a certain vitality and security. The aim is to provide a proper balance and a respect by all people, but especially car drivers, to abide by civilised codes.

The physical implementations of traffic calming and control require new approaches, particularly at entrances to villages on main roads. The Northern Troubles resulted in the forced reduction of traffic and parking in the historic centres of many towns – an environmental benefit which should be retained in the years ahead, but unfortunately this sense of calmness is already being slowly eroded. Ideally, it should only be necessary to have the minimum of signs to regulate traffic without a whole plethora of ramps, bollards, yellow lines, road markings, etc. This new type of street furniture in many ways is eroding the essential quality of pleasant spaces. What should be informal spaces to walk around are turned into regimented and highly controlled areas.

Providing for traffic can destroy the character of a town, even off-street car parks must be handled with care. Old walls and boundaries should be retained in the context of providing additional parking facilities. Car parks should be considered as potential civic spaces and cultural venues. We must plan for traffic in a positive and imaginative manner. The car can serve our needs, but not dominate the environment, or more importantly that of our neighbours.

However, this new interest in public spaces and improving their settings, has not always been successful. There has been a rash of public area improvements throughout the country and there is a danger that all towns and villages are beginning to look the same with brick paved footpaths, incongruous public art works, rows of bollards, without any sense of the essential personality and aesthetic qualities of the town.

The importance of cycling as a means of personal transport and recreational activity has been largely ignored. There are some ad hoc cycle-ways generally along existing roads in the cities, but there is no integrated and comprehensive network. In the smaller towns and villages the concept of cycle-ways is rarely considered as of any significance whatsoever.

Conclusion

If the historic centres of our cities, towns and villages, are handled with care and sensitivity, are considered as minor works of art which they undoubtedly are, are repaired and updated rather than comprehensively altered, they will provide a pleasant living context for future generations. In addition, because of their rarity value, they will provide a strong cultural foundation for future society. Therefore, it makes good sense both culturally and economically that their development is environmentally and aesthetically acceptable. Local communities must, above all, be fully involved and must be made aware of the intrinsic merit of what makes their particular town or city district different, but not necessarily better, than their neighbours. The Governments, Planning Authorities, Professional Bodies and voluntary organisations like An Taisce, Irish Georgian Society and the Ulster Architectural Heritage Society must continue to lead and influence the wider community. Any further financial incentives must be tied in much more effectively to both architectural and social objectives.

Schools can play a significant role. Geography, civic and art classes should use their own town or district as a teaching resource. If local communities appreciate fully the intrinsic character of their town, its civic future will be bright indeed. If they don't understand or care and allow economic forces alone to dictate policies the outlook is bleak. The challenges over the next decades will be immense and society will require more people in the mould of Charlie Brett – not that easy to come by.

ACKNOWLEDGEMENT:

Thanks are due to the following: Peter Barrow – Photography; Herma Boyle, Photographer; Esler Crawford, Photographer; and in particular the late and much missed Hugh McKay, Department of the Environment, Planning Service Northern Ireland

NOTES

1. Shaffrey, P. 1975. *The Irish Town – An Approach to Survival.* Dublin, The O'Brien Press.
2. Department for Regional Development. September 2001. *Shaping our Future, Regional Development Strategy for Northern Ireland 2025* and *The Family of Settlements Report.* Belfast, Department for Regional Development.
3. *Urban Renewal Act* 1986-1988 (this provides for urban renewal tax incentives in the cities and large towns).
   Town Renewal Act 2000 (this provides for town renewal in small towns).
   Temple Bar Area Renewal and Development Act, 1991.
   Dublin Docklands Developments Act, 1997.
   4. Social Need (Northern Ireland) Order 1986.

CLONACHULLION CONNECTIONS

DAWSON STELFOX

IN 1986, MY (SOON TO BE) wife, Margaret Magennis, bought a semi-derelict two room cottage on the upper slopes of Clonachullion Hill, on the flanks of the Shimna Valley, one of the most distinctive parts of the Mournes.[1] For us the motivation was a base for continuing to explore the mountains, but whilst that continues to provide endless pleasures, gradually other values and qualities of the place have seeped into our consciousness.

It was only later that we realised that Margaret was returning to her ancestral lands, for from the 12th century onwards this area was in the hands of the Magennis Clan, the territorial Lords of Iveagh. The New Castle was built by Felix Magennis in 1588.[2] The Schedule of Freeholders of Iveagh, 1609, shows this immediate area – 7 townlands out of the parish of Kilcoo – to be under Brian McHugh McAholly Magennis as part of his much larger estates. Like many of the Irish Lords he took advantage of the English policy of 'surrender and regrant' and in 1610 surrendered to King James, to be regranted his lands – 7½ townlands, comprising 2000 acres, in 1611. He later disposed of Ballyfofanny.

Following Brian McHugh Magennis' death in 1619 there are conflicting records of how his lands were distributed. He was succeeded by his son Phelim who died in 1628 leaving his son Bernard. The *Book of Survey and Distribution* records that six townlands of the lower Shimna valley, around Tollymore – Ballyhafry, Tullybranigan, Tollymore, Aghacullion, Clonachullion and Burrenbane were held by Bernard (Bryan) Magennis in 1640. Tollymore was the only Magennis land not to be forfeited under the Commonwealth following the 1641 rebellion. Bryan died unmarried circa 1660 and the estate passed to his aunt Ellen who, in 1685 married a William Hamilton from Ayrshire. Their grandson, James Hamilton, was created Lord Limerick in 1719 and the following year established Tollymore estate as a deer park. James Hamilton also bought most of Dundalk in 1695 and both estates were laid out in a romantic manner, with Thomas Wright engaged as architect in 1746-7.[3]

The first 'big' house at Tollymore was started c.1750, with the old bridge of 1726 and the Clanbrassil barn of 1757.[4] The curious stone towers along the road from Bryansford are still known as Lord Limerick's follies and mark the boundary with Downshire land to the north.

> *"Upwards of two miles north west of New-Caftle ftands Briansford or Tullamore, near which on the ftirts of Sliev-neir and Sliev-fnavan (Mountains fo called the Lord Limerick has two Deer Parks (remarkable for excellent Venifon,) or rather one divided into two by a Wall carried through the middle of it, finely wooded, cut into Ridings and Viftoes, and watered by a River running through it in a channel of Rocks and precipices, which paffes under a Bridge of hewn Stone, from whence are beautiful Profpects of the Sea"*[5]

Lord Limerick's son, again James Hamilton, enlarged the house and added the two fine entrances – Barbican Gate (1780) and Bryansford Gate (1786). As he died childless in 1798, the estate passed to his sister Anne, who had married Robert Jocelyn, created Earl of Roden in 1771. Those same townlands, (with two others – Foffanybane and Foffanyreagh) already formed part of the Roden estates in this area. The name Roden, rather than Clanbrassil, henceforth became the family name associated with the estate.

In the 1960's Lord Roden let some of his outbuildings be used to start an outdoor pursuits centre, which later became established as Tollymore Mountain Centre at a new purpose built timber cabin in the forest, constructed from trees cut on the estate. It was through Tollymore Mountain Centre that I learnt many of the skills that were to encourage me to travel to the world's mountains.

In 1993, on the walk into the cold and barren Rongbuk valley on the north side of Everest, I was joined by a Robert Jocelyn, part of a group trekking in to support the first Irish Everest expedition. The name didn't immediately mean anything to me, until the fireside stories of Tollymore brought us both to a realisation of a shared history and values from two different viewpoints; Robert's view outwards from the big house at Tollymore, mine looking down on the Deer Park from one of his family's former tenant's cottages, both of us fascinated and absorbed by the interconnections and how the present patterns of habitation and environment have been formed. Robert is now living in Connemara and is currently writing his own history of the Tollymore estate.

This essay seeks to trace these patterns, concentrating on the Clonachullion townland, marking how people have lived in the Shimna Valley, to demonstrate how important it is and to make a case for its protection.

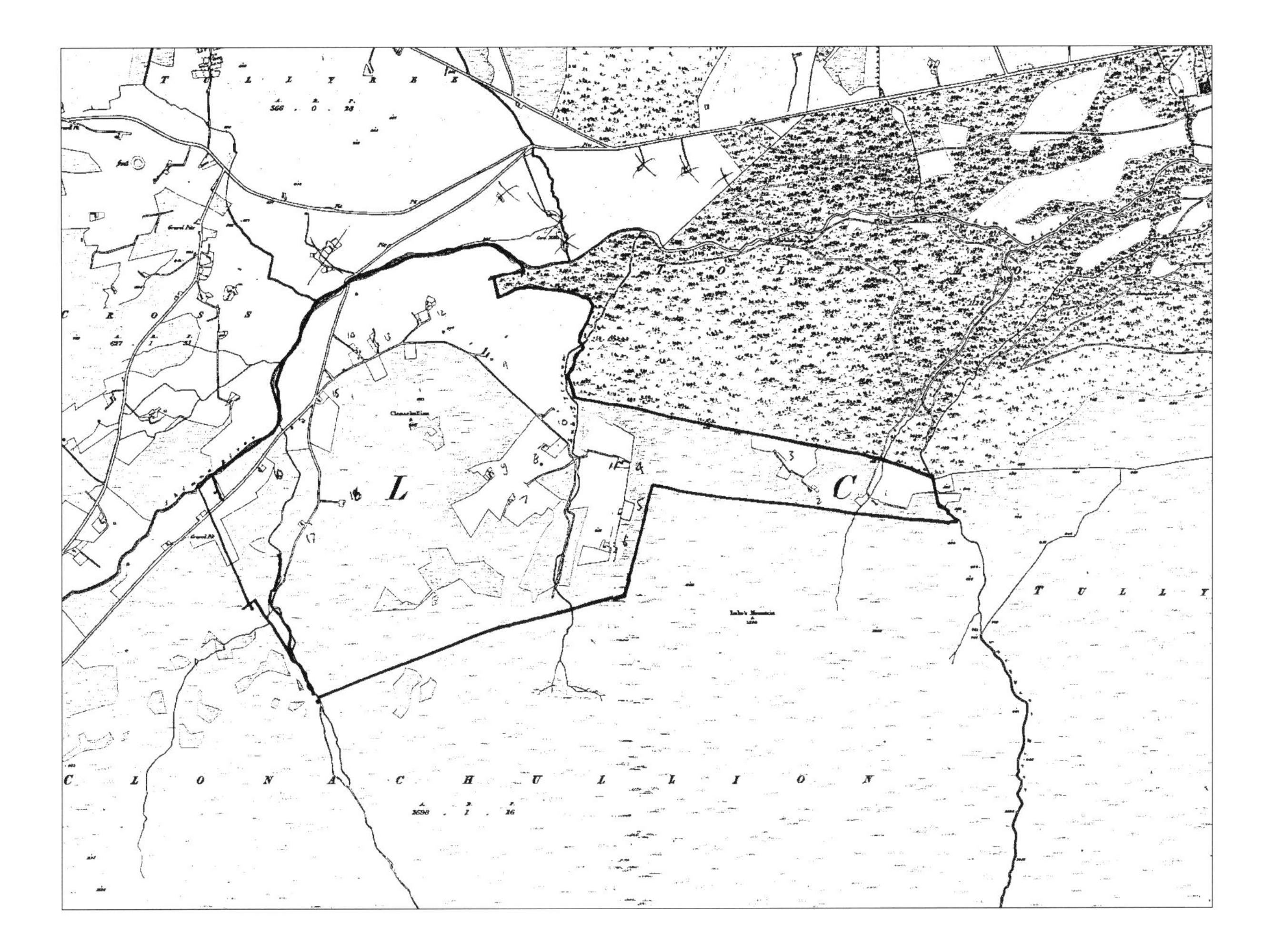

Fig 1. Ordnance Survey, Sheet 47 Co. Down (1834)

A History of change in the Shimna Valley

The earliest surviving signs of human habitation are the raths and cashels of the early Christian period from the 6th to the 9th centuries. These are circular stone (cashel) or earth (rath) banks usually 20m-40m across, enclosing round timber or, more likely in this area, rectangular stone houses, acting as centres of habitation for an extended family living around. The White Fort in Tollymore Park is the closest surviving cashel, but curiously not marked on early estate or OS maps, until the 1938 edition.[6] Possibly the trees obscured it from the early surveyors, but it is noticeable that the 1938 edition charts considerably more detail than earlier editions – wells, lime kilns etc are all specifically named and marked.

The land was relatively sparsely populated and there was little habitation above 500 feet in height. Land and farms were totally bound up with status and hierarchy, with the tenant free farmers and bondsmen, linked to the nobles and kings by clientship relationships. It is thought that these original family groups or

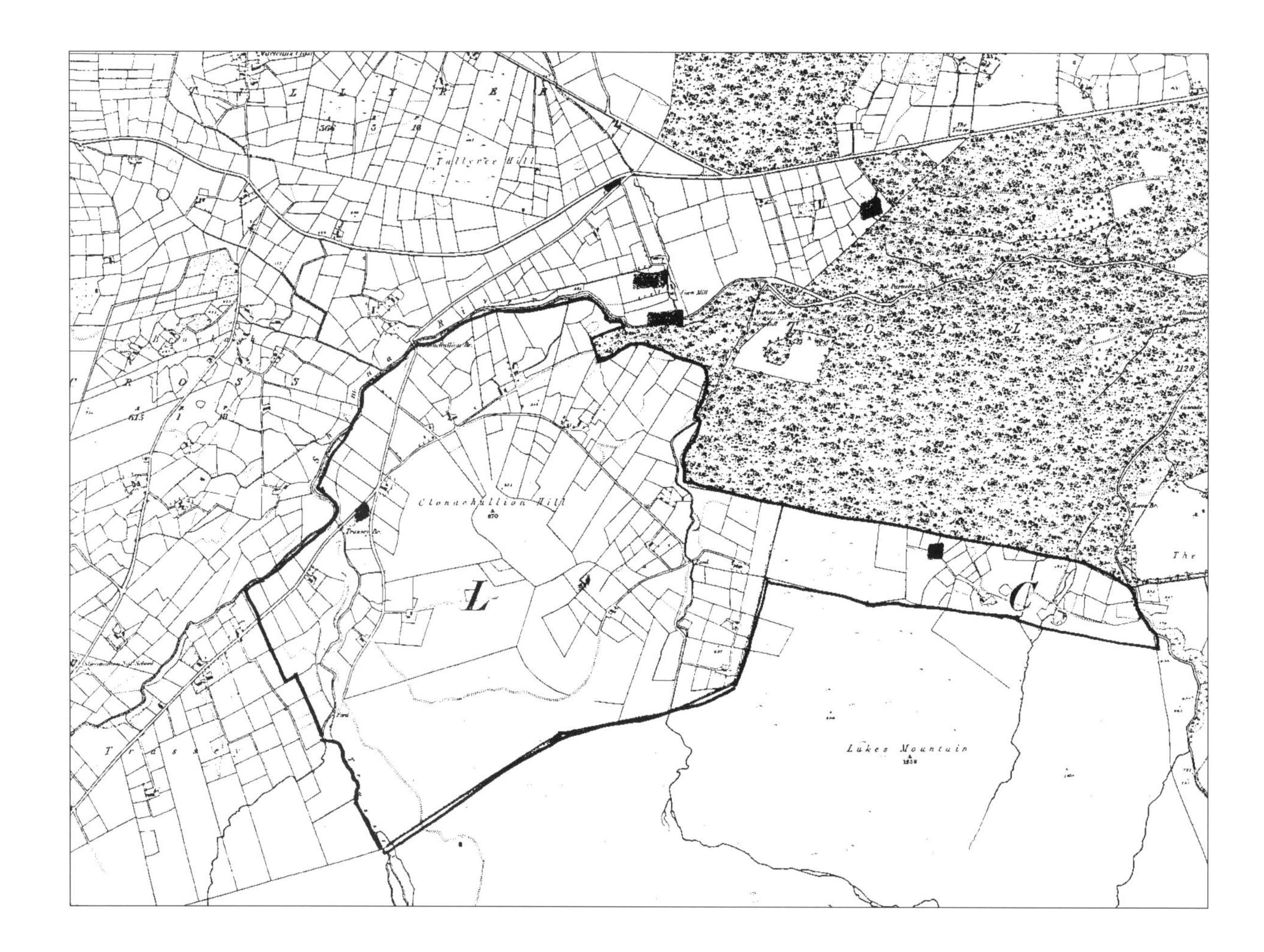

Fig 2. Ordnance Survey, Sheet 47, Co. Down (1859)

clachans, given the name 'bally', anglicized as 'town', gave rise to the townlands – originally the land of one extended family, and the former 'kingship' areas became the parishes.

This has a resonance in Clonachullion, where the earliest Tollymore estate records, from 1743 right through to 1800, record the whole townland (720 acres), all under one (albeit changing) family name. Is this the written evidence of a much older tradition, long since broken down by rising populations in the fertile areas, still in place on the marginal hill land of the edge of the mountains?

The 9th and 10th centuries saw the Viking arrive and the building of Round Towers – the nearest being at Maghera. The Vikings were defeated by the local kings who acquired new powers and by the 12th century the Magennis clan had established themselves throughout County Down. However, as Estyn Evan remarked in 'Irish Folk Ways':

The crafts of arable farming, of animal husbandry and the home industries have

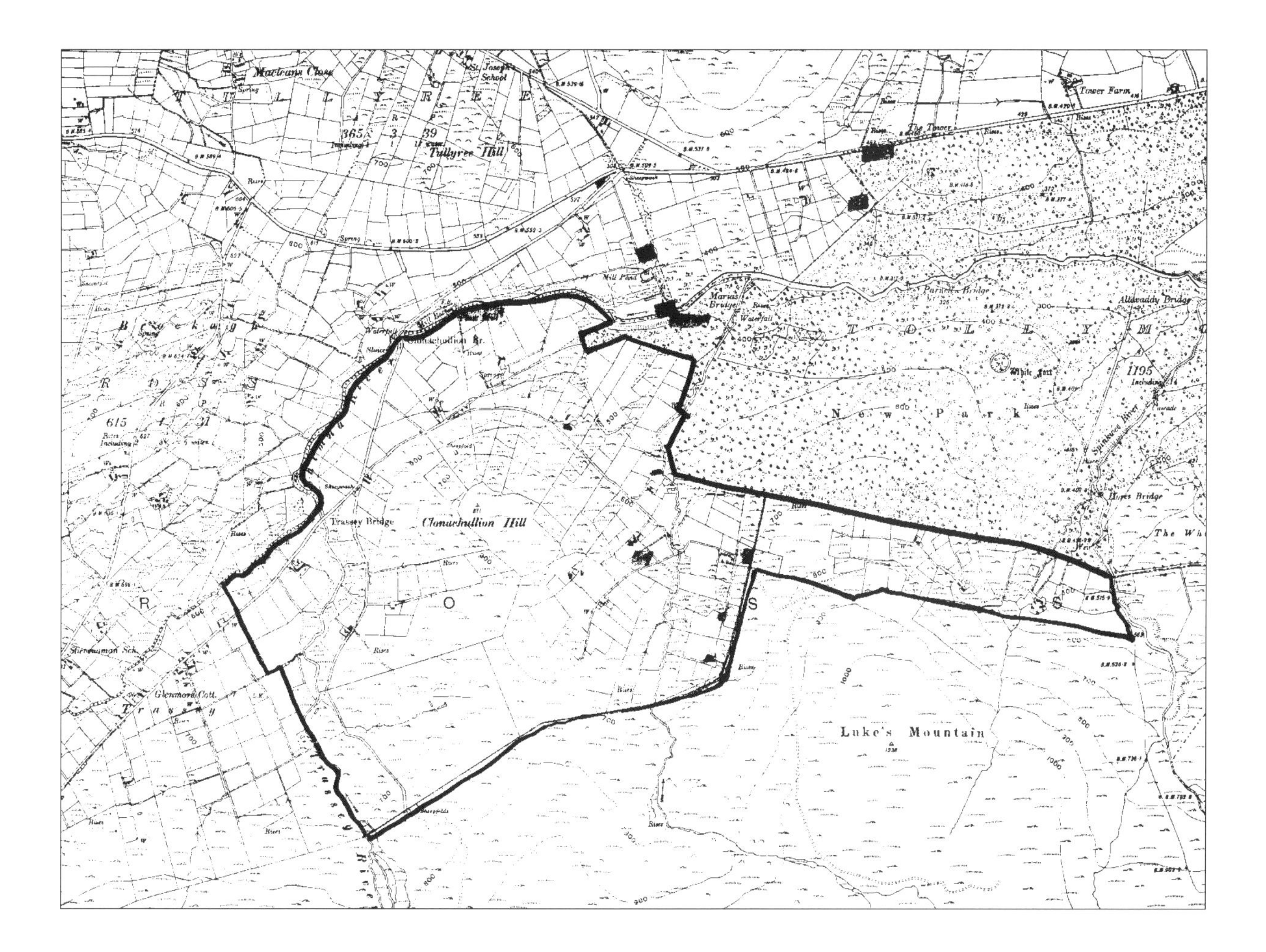

Fig 3. Ordnance Survey Sheet 47, Co. Down (1938 partial revision)

done more to shape our instincts and thoughts than the trampling of armies or the wrangling of kings which fill the documents from which history is written[7]

It was of course the tenantry who created much of the wealth used to build the great houses and demesnes. In the 17th Century there was a shortage of tenants, so landlords had to offer long leases and low rents. By the 18th century, however, the population was rising, and the landlords shortened leases and raised rents. Farms were subdivided and the population became dependant on the potato for sustenance.

Marginal areas of the Tollymore estate contained some of the least productive land in County Down. The result was an expansion of cultivation onto progressively less fertile upland soils. The developing practice of liming the thin mountain soils contributed to their productivity, and at least one lime kiln survives in the townland, high on Clonachullion Hill, miles away from any source of limestone.

In the bofom of the Mourne Mountains, there is a place called the Deers Meadow and by some, the King's Meadow (because people have their grazing in it free), extending fome miles in Breadth and length, to which great numbers of poor people resort in the Summer Months to graze their cattle. They bring with them their Wives, Children and little wretched furniture, erect Huts and live there for two Months and fometimes more, and often cut their Turf to ferve for the next returning Seafon : which done, they retire with their Cattle to their former habitations.[8]

The old rundale system of farming around the nucleated clachan settlement, with infield and outfield enclosures and the practice of transhumance to the summer boolying grounds at the Deer's Meadow,[9] gave way by the early 1800's to individual houses on their own land enclosures, and the characteristic ladder strips stretching up the hill.

The Shimna valley still offers evidence of these radical changes written in the enclosure patterns. Low down in the valley around McCleans Close there is an irregular jumble of field boundaries – small around the clachan infields, larger outfields beyond. However, on the elevated slopes of Clonachullion, substantially populated for the first time in the early 1800's, the narrow strips radiating up and around the hill, testify to the new system, all the settlements enjoying a strip of better low land and progressively poorer strips up the mountain.

This is born out by the Tollymore estate records. The 1745 rent roll only names 'Mr Harrison's late farme' at a half yearly rent of £10.10s. In 1769 it is recorded as 'A Grant and Partners' for a yearly rent of £22.1s 1d. By 1800 the townland is recorded under 'heirs of Rowland Savage' on a yearly rent of £70.12s.

It is not until the first edition OS map in 1834 that there is substantial settlement with almost all the farmsteads that were to exist for the next century and more already established. Unfortunately the rent rolls between 1800 and 1857 do not survive and the early estate maps show only the Deer Park itself, so it is not possible to date every individual farm, but it is clear that most date from between 1800 and 1834, with the possibility that one or two may predate that, such as Mr. Harrison's farm.

The maps record the location and general size, while the rent rolls list the valuations, but what were the houses actually like? In 1759, Chief Baron Willes likened the difficulty of journeying between Downpatrick and Newry, through the Mourne mountains to that of travelling through the Alps:

..it is the wildest and most mountainous country I have seen. The cabins one sees on

Fig 4. Abandoned lazy beds on Clonachullion Hill (Site 28 on 1910 Map)

> *the sides of the hills are the most miserable huts I ever saw, built with sods and turf – no chimney, the door made of a hurdle, the smoke all goes out through the door and the cocks and hens, pigs, goats and if perchance they have a cow, inhabit the same dwelling* [10]

The Poor Law inquiry of 1836 gives more factual detail as to construction methods when most of the houses in Clonachullion were being built. They record that most houses in the Mournes as being built of 'stone and earth' – limewashed stone walls with sod packing at gables and roof. The majority were thatched and chimneys were by now the norm, with a few better houses having slate roofs and brick chimneys. 20% were only one room, measuring only 15 x 20 feet on the outside. Sash windows were only just being introduced, and floors were of earth. The peat fire was never allowed go out, the mountain bogs providing a plentiful fuel supply. The OS Memoirs also record the houses of Kilcoo parish as:

Some of the habitations in the wilder parts of the parish are very wretched. Those in the more cultivated districts are, however, more comfortable. They are built of stone, mostly one storey in height and generally thatched. The windows are of glass and the number of rooms varies from one to four.[11]

The period immediately before, during and after the famine is of immense interest. There are excellent records both in the form of the rent rolls from Tollymore and the OS maps, though there are gaps in the crucial period from 1800 to 1834.

Although County Down was free from the extreme effects of the famine witnessed in other parts, there were areas of serious deprivation, concentrated on the more marginal areas. As a whole, County Down lost 45% of its population of 1841 by 1911, the majority moving to Belfast or emigrating.

The tenants of Tollymore estate benefited from a caring landlord and the Bryansford Relief Committee. In the earlier part of the famine Lord Roden funded relief work, notably wall building and drainage, but this later gave way to food relief through the poor law system. The most visible legacy of this relief work is the southern boundary wall of Clonachullion townland running around Clonachullion Hill towards Luke's mountain, not shown on the 1834 OS, prominent on the 1859 edition and the 1857 estate maps. This is a well built wall, quite unlike the rough stone field boundaries, with a characteristic top coping detail.

Of the 27 houses shown in the townland on the OS map of 1834, only one was abandoned by 1857, while there was one new house, and a further two had been extended. However, by the time of the 1863 Griffiths Valuation six of the highest houses had been abandoned, of which only a few walls and traces of the lazy beds survives. This remains the strongest evidence of the effects of the famine in Clonachullion with the highest and most marginal holdings proving unsustainable and amalgamated into larger farms. Local tradition has it that the stone and slate from some at least of these abandoned farms was used to extend or rebuild the surviving settlements, which explains why in some cases there are few traces remaining of the abandoned houses.

As John Mogey recorded in nearby Hilltown in the early 1940's:

Farmsteads never climb above 500' on the barren granite slopes and there has been a tendency for the limit of settlement to move downhill. At the head of every valley is a series of abandoned farms reverting rapidly to heather and bracken, and almost indistinguishable from the open sheep pasture of the hill slopes.[12]

Fig 5. View of upper Tullyree from Site 30

A comparison with the valuations of 1863 and 1907 reveals a pattern of small holdings, turbary rights and mountain access, with a stable number of dwellings. However a significant rise in rents shows a pattern of extensions, improvements or rebuilding, giving evidence of the next radical period of change by the start of the 20th century.

The Land Acts spelt the end of most of the great estates in Ireland and of the prosperity of the families that owned them. Until that time land was rented on short leases and tenants could be displaced without warning. The Land Acts provided for the selling of the land to the tenants.[13] Bit by bit the estates were sold off to the tenantry until nothing was left but the demesne land – in this case Tollymore Park.

The Settled Land Acts 1882 – 90 were the basis of this radical change and came in three progressive stages. In 1882 the three 'F's, long sought by reformers, were passed into law – Fair rent (set by land courts if not agreed and usually reduced), Free sale and Fixity of tenure – protection against eviction.

The 1903 Wyndham Land Act encouraged landlords to sell estates, the money being advanced to tenants by the Treasury to be repaid over sixty-eight and a half years by annuities at the rate of 3.25%. But it was the final Bill, in 1909, which compelled landlords to sell, based on fixed Valuations derived from Judicial Rents, that brought land sales to tenants to a conclusion.

At Tollymore, this process is recorded in the Judicial Rent Book of 1910, accompanied by an annotated OS map with all tenants named (though confusingly different reference numbers between book and map). In most cases the judicial process reduced the rents. The selling process was slow, delayed further by the outbreak of the First World War and it seems it was the 1930's before all the agreements were signed. The tenants had up to 25 years to pay and so it was not until the 1960's that all the former tenants had bought out their farms, though most were completed long before then.

John Mogey recorded in the Hilltown area, in the 1940's:

The land hereabouts as everywhere else in Northern Ireland is in the process of becoming the property of the farmers[14]

This security of tenure and a post war agricultural boom, combined with a growing stone trade, triggered a remarkable upsurge in farm improvements, with many of the houses being extended, raised to two storeys and slated, or even rebuilt, during this period. The old rent system gave no incentive to improve at the tenants expense as it only raised the rent without any security. The effect of these legal changes seems to have been immediate and dramatic, substantially improving the living conditions of the people within a very short period of time.

Photographic evidence exists of one such improvement. In 1890 R.J. Welch recorded the classic view over Clonachullion Bridge (known now popularly but incorrectly as Trassey Bridge), looking up towards the Hares Gap. In the middle distance at the start of what is now known as the Trassey track is an extended cottage, gable to the road. In 1920, WA Green 15 recorded the same view, this time capturing the new two storey house now built on the same site, facing square onto the road, with the former house now confined to outbuildings. The changes are faithfully recorded on the OS maps.

By the 1940's, when J.M.Mogey was conducting his survey into rural life in Northern Ireland for the NI Council of Social Service, he was able to record this change:

Thatch has almost entirely gone, probably because of high winds but also because of money made outside the region enabling the change to take place...80% of the houses are slated.[16]

Fig 6. Ruins of house on Site 29, on slopes of Lukes Mountain

The Shimna Valley Today

Caroline Maguire's important 1999 study – 'A Changing Vernacular Landscape', looked at five areas around Northern Ireland, studying the patterns of change in vernacular houses over the last century.[17] Amongst the areas were five townlands in the Shimna Valley, including Clonachullion. Over these five townlands, the key findings were:

- 29% of buildings occupied in 1908 have disappeared – replaced or lost without trace
- 37% are unoccupied or are lying derelict
- 34% remain occupied – mostly substantially remodelled

If the new buildings on new sites are added in then 16% of the total occupied building stock in 1999 are new buildings on new sites, while 23% are replaced on a traditional site and 61% are traditionally occupied.

In the estate records of Clonachullion, the townland is divided into two parts – the long strip of land on the south side of the Shimna River and the higher land stretching around and over Clonachullion Hill. In Appendix One I have charted in detail the changes to the farmsteads of this latter half townland, based on estate records, Ordnance Survey maps and family history.

Occupied dwellings in this area are:

1834	1857/9	1904/7	1938	Current
18	17	13	13	10 – 5 Full time (2 farmers)
				1 Vacant
				4 Holiday homes

Some key facts emerge from these statistics. Only one new building has been constructed, although many of the houses have been enlarged and altered. One house (No. 24 Trassey Rd) is 'listed' and all but one retain their essential vernacular character.

Eight, (44%) of the houses occupied in 1834 are now gone or derelict – most going in the immediate post famine period. In the last ten years, many of the remaining house have become holiday homes or have passed from farming families to those of other occupations – some commuting to work, others working locally. Only two houses (11%) remain occupied by those engaged in full time agriculture.

Looking to the Future

Clonachullion townland epitomizes the long, slowly evolving tradition of building and living in the Irish landscape, shaped by the changing relationship with landlord and tenant and the major national events and changes in economic fortune. The houses are but one part of a landscape where every field boundary tells its own story.

That relationship changed forever at the start of the twentieth century when tenants became freeholders, precipitating a major building boom. But despite this new found wealth the houses were extended within the local traditions and used local materials, so that the overall effect is one of harmonious and seamless transition, proving it is possible to create better living conditions without destroying the character of the landscape.

Fig 7. Ruins of house on Site 19,on side of Clonachullion Hill

The Shimna Valley, and in particular the Clonachullion townland, has to date escaped the worst excesses of the bungalow blitz which has so devastated most of the Irish countryside. Whilst the threat from poorly designed and insensitively located bungalows may have receded due to increased intervention from Planning Service, the current trend is for very large two storey houses, equally insensitively placed. The slow erosion of character of the Shimna Valley is already underway, and whilst there are encouraging signs of higher expectations coming from Planning Service, they are restricted in their powers of intervention by current designations and policies.

The Shimna Valley is one of the most scenic parts of the Mourne Area of Outstanding Natural Beauty (AONB). Photographers ever since the era of Welch and Green have captured the classic view of the hills from the edge of Tullyree, looking across the Shimna Valley and Clonachullion Hill to the high Mournes. It is one of the most frequented areas for walkers and car borne tourists. The inhabited landscape of the Shimna Valley, Clonachullion and Slievenaman is equally as important to these visitors as the mountains themselves. It is a landscape shaped by the historical patterns of habitation and landscaping – stone walled enclosures and shelter belts, and most crucially of all the vernacular farmhouses, surrounded by outbuildings and barns, each tailored to their purpose and as important as the houses themselves.

The challenge of how to recognise the importance of vernacular houses and offer them statutory protection has exercised the statutory and voluntary bodies for many years. The best examples can be and are listed, but it is not enough just to preserve a few special cases – part of the value of the vernacular tradition is that it is the normal method of building in any particular locality. It thus follows that the statutory areas plans should recognise what the local vernacular traditions are and put in place measures to protect them. Sir Charles Brett, in his County Buildings series, has drawn attention to the importance of the vernacular by including them alongside the castles, churches and mansions of the county. That recognition should act as a guide for increased protection.

Environmentally Sensitive Area (ESA) grants through the Dept of Agriculture have greatly influenced the upkeep of traditional boundary walls, farm buildings, shelterbelts and gates, but do not extend to the farmhouse – resulting all too often in a modern bungalow jarring with well kept traditional walls and gates.

Yet apart from the three listed vernacular houses, none of these buildings has any protection against summary demolition on the whim of the owner. The traditional farmer would not entertain this – any building was far too valuable to be demolished without thought, but there are fewer and fewer farmers left in the Shimna valley, a pattern repeated in the hill land everywhere. In their place are generally people who want to live in this magnificent countryside, but they have other priorities, such as views out from picture windows and double garages, perfectly valid in themselves, but so easily destructive of vernacular character.

AONB designation carries no built heritage policy and no enforcement powers. The current debate on National Parks is welcome but the focus remains on landscape designation, not on planning powers as the UK National Park model. A National Park designation will only be meaningful if it brings with it a serious reappraisal of planning policy and a statutory plan for the National Park area.

In the meantime, there is one designation that would provide such protection – Conservation Area. This has not to date been used outside of urban areas, but the Roe Valley Country Park near Limavady is the first proposed rural Conservation Area, there focused on the industrial heritage of the area.

I would submit that the Shimna Valley is the prime candidate for a rural Conservation Area based on vernacular heritage. There is an easily contained area, shaped by the natural features of the surrounding hills. There are already three listed vernacular buildings (and others equally worthy). The relationship and proximity of the Tollymore estate and estate village of Bryansford provides an extra dimension which so well tells the story of changing landlord/tenant relationships through history. The vernacular landscape is still largely intact and there is a growing awareness of its value.

For the last two years I have conducted walking tours around the valley as part of European Heritage Open Days. Some of the owners have opened up their houses and people came from all over Ireland to absorb the rich history and legacy of the area. Some, like me, had been visiting the Mournes for years to take in the pleasures of climbing the hills and were now discovering the immense social and cultural history of the surrounding areas, the history of the farmers, turfcutters and quarrymen who shaped the landscape to what it is we know and love today.

It would be so easy for this rich tradition to be slowly eroded without care and thought and Conservation Area status can bring that thinking space between the intentions of owners and the wishes of the wider society. Conservation Areas are not about stopping change, certainly not about stopping traditional farming practices that have shaped and changed the land in the first place, but they are about managing change – and in many cases bringing in extra resources to ensure changes are compatible with the existing landscape.

Little of the Irish countryside is wilderness in any true sense – almost all has felt the influence of man, and the layers of each succeeding generation are still there to be seen for those who care to look. Even the highest point of Northern Ireland, Slieve Donard, has the remains of an early cairn; the 6th century cell of St Domengard; the 19th century surveyors cairn and the 20th century wall and tower of the Belfast Water Commissioners, so expertly built in the harshest of conditions by the skilled Mourne masons.

These human interventions do not diminish the value of the hills, but instead add other dimensions to their power over our lives. The hills and valleys of the Mournes have not been destroyed by these historical interventions, but shaped into a delicate balance between man and nature, stretching back over generations. It is that balance that is so much under threat today.

We have the technical ability to place a house of any size down on top of the landscape, regardless of prevailing winds or topography. We have the economic resources to build houses of 3000 sq ft or more, in the most sensitive of areas. We have the selfish arrogance to ignore the effects of such buildings on the character of the countryside and those who both live in it and who come to visit and enjoy it.

This attitude would be understandable in the immediate aftermath of the breaking up of the estates when for the first time the ordinary people owned their houses and land. But at least a generation has passed since then and although ownership of land will continue to be a crucial issue, it is time to start considering the interests and values of wider society in how land, in at least the most special and scenic areas, is managed.

The restoration of Hanna's Close, on the southern side of the Mournes, for the locally based River Valley Development Association, showed that traditional vernacular houses could be restored to offer high quality accommodation without destroying their character. This though was for visitors – self-catering accommodation – and although it has proved very popular and created a thriving local business, it has not convinced local people that the same principles could apply for full time residences.

The Mourne Homesteads programme hopes to do just that. The project was originated by the Mourne Heritage Trust – the community based management body for the Mourne AONB, and supported by the Pilgrim Trust, the Northern Ireland Housing executive and the Heritage Lottery Fund. A first phase of ten traditional houses has been identified, of a variety of types, spread throughout the Mournes, to be restored for local people to live in, with the funders supporting the 'heritage deficit' – the additional cost (including VAT) of restoring a house over the zero rated demolish and new build popular option.

The Mourne Homesteads project also undertook a comprehensive audit of the surviving traditional buildings in the Mourne AONB, carried out by Harriet Devlin and Dick Oram. This has shown that there are still a vast number of traditional buildings within the area, but also that they are disappearing at an ever increasing rate. It is not yet too late to address this loss, but it very soon will be.

Both the 1999 ICOMOS Charter on the Built Vernacular Heritage and the 2000 Oxford Declaration on Landscape stress the interconnections between landscape and cultural heritage and recognize the existence of 'cultural landscapes'. *The 1996 Ecovast 'Traditional Rural Buildings – A strategy for Europe'* document, firmly placed importance on the local vernacular.

The Shimna Valley is, in my opinion, a special cultural landscape that requires protection. Conservation Area status would be a good start, a National Park for the Mournes with appropriate planning powers would set it into a wider context, but what is needed most is a rejection of the selfish 'anything goes' attitudes and a rediscovery of the respect and understanding of the character of the countryside.

NOTES

1. Clonachullion means 'meadow of the holly'. See O Mainnin, M. B. 1993. *Place Names of Northern Ireland. Volume 3. County Down III. The Mournes*. Belfast, The Institute of Irish Studies, p.107.
2. Jope, M (ed.) *An Archaeological Survey of County Down*. Belfast, HMSO, p.262.
3. Malins, E. and The Knight of Glin. 1976. *Lost Demesnes. Irish Landscape Gardening 1660-1845*. London, Barrie and Jenkins, p.118.
4. Richard Pococke visited Tollymore in 1752 and said that Lord Limerick had 'begun to build a pretty lodge, two rooms of which are finished, designing to spend the summer months here'. See Stokes, G.T (ed.) 1891. *Pocockes Tour of Ireland in 1752*. Dublin, p.9.
5. Harris, W. 1744. *The Antient and Present State of County Down. Dublin*, Exshaw [First Edition], p.81.
6. Jope, op.cit., p.178
7. Evans, Estyn E. 1957. *Irish Folk Ways* London, Routledge and Kegan Paul, pp.xiv.
8. Harris, *op cit.*, p.125.
9. Evans, Estyn E. 1951. *Mourne Country* Dundalk, Dundalgan Press (W. Tempest) Ltd, p.128.
10. Crawford and Trainor (eds) 1969. *Aspects of Irish Social History 750-1800*. Belfast, Public Records Office of Northern Ireland. Quote taken from passage in Elliot, Marianne. 2000. *The Catholics of Ulster*. London, Allen Lane.
11. Day, Angelique, & McWilliams, Patrick. 1990. *Ordnance Survey Memoirs*. Belfast, The Institute of Irish Studies, Volume 3, p.44.
12. Mogey, John M. 1947. *Rural Life in Northern Ireland. Five Regional Studies Made for the Northern Ireland Council of Social Service*. London, Oxford University Press, p.88.
13. Proudfoot, Lindsay (ed.). 1997. *Down, History and Society* Dublin, Geography Publications
14. *Ibid*, p.90
15. *Ibid*, p.95
16. Hamond F & Porter T. 1991. *A Tour of the Mournes*. Belfast, The Friar's Bush Press, p.81.
17. Maguire, C. 1999. A Changing Vernacular Landscape. Belfast, Institute of Irish Studies

Appendix 1
Change in Upper Clonachullion 1834-2002

House No	Family Name	Area A R P	OS 1st 1834	OSRev1859	OS 2nd 1904	OS Rev 1938	Today
1857 50 1910 15	Sarah Kane Mary Kane	0 0 6	3 small bdgs	2 small bdgs	1 small bdg	same	derelict 1 room bdg
20 Trassey Rd. 1857 37-41 1910 20	Michael Kane M. Kane	17 1 5	2 bdgs, either side of lane	1 longer bdg along lane 1 new at rt	1 extra bdg	same	remains in original family and full time use. 2 storey angles to lane. extended house in unaltered state
22 Trassey Rd 1857 42-43 1910 21	Patrick Kane P. Kane		1 bdg and 1 small outbdg	1 larger bdg 1 extra bdg	same	same	vacant 1 storey 2 room cottage unaltered
24 Trassey Rd (LB) 1857 58-64 1910 24A,B	John McAlister James Devlin	34 0 27	1 small bdg	1 new bdg on 2 storey house site and other along access road	Building on road gone	same	restored 2 storey house and 1 storey return. Full time use
28 Trassey Rd 1857 46-49 1910 23	Pat Kane Jnr Mary Kane	16 2 1	2 bdgs parallel to each other	1 longer bdg - 2 small outbdgs	1 longer bdg only down the slope	same	large new extens. built to end of original hse, across slope
30 Trassey Rd 1857 72-75 1910 24A,B	Felix McAleavy Felix McAleavy	21 2 14	1 small hse and small outbdg	1 additional outbdg	same	1 small outbdg	2 storey hse altered twice
32 Trassey Rd 1857 32-36 1910 27	William Keane (sic) W Kane	19.3.2	house with lane as current - no outbdgs	1 outbdg	same	1 additional outbdg	remains in original family and full time use. 2 storey extended house in unaltered state
1857 100-02 1910 28	Michael McCaherty Dan O'Hare	7.2.12	1 small bdg and enclosure	2 bdgs and enclosures	ruined	same	remains of walls

House No	Family Name	Area A R P	OS 1st 1834	OSRev1859	OS 2nd 1904	OS Rev 1938	Today
1857 98-99 1910 28	Roger McCaherty Dan O'Hare	7. 0 15	1 small bdg and enclosure	2 bdgs and enclosures	ruined	same	remains of walls
1857 133-6 1910 29	John Turner William Turner	20 . 2. 8	1 small house (other bdg could be house for adjoining plot let to Robert Turner)	hse and outbdgs other bdgs close	same 1 extra outbdg	ruined	ruins remain
1857 127-32 1910 31	Alexander Turner William Skillen	20 . 4. 35	2 small bdgs	3 small bdgs	same	same	1 storey cottage attached outbdg
1857 76-78 1910 19	Peter McKeon Dan O'Hare	16 . 1. 13	2 small bdgs broken lane	1 larger bdg 1 smaller	same	same	substantial ruins remain
1857 103-106 1910 19	John O'Hare Dan O'Hare	13 . 3. 10	2 small bdgs no access lane	enclosure only no bdg	same	same	enclosure walls
34 Trassey Rd 1857 65-68 1910 27	Widow Dan McClean W Kane	23 1 0	house with lane as current 1 small outbdg lime kiln marked	longer hse 2 outbdgs	same	same Well and Lime Kiln named	restored cottage and outbdgs
42 Trassey Rd 1857 5-13 1910 15	Robert Dalzell Mary Kane		old hse rt angles to road	old hse and small bdg to rear	same	new front hse old hse as outbdg	2 storey front house well restored and original hse used as outbdgs
1857 53-54 1910 15	James Leslie occupied by John Turner Mary Kane		1 small bdg in enclosure	2 small bdgs in enclosure	ruin	ruin	ruined walls remain in forest
1857 79-81 1910 15	Roger McPolin Mary Kane	8 .0 .30	1 small bdg	same	not marked	not marked	no trace remains
Trassey Rd 1857 16-22 1910 12	James Fitzpatrick P Fitzpatrick	27 .0 .29	1 small bdg gable to road	2 bdgs gable to road	larger bdg facing road and original	same	modern bungalow no trace remains of original bdgs

WELL WORTH A VISIT. KNOCKBREDA PARISH CHURCH AND ITS ARCHITECT

HUGH DIXON

"IT'S WELL WORTH A VISIT," said Charlie, replying to my enquiry about a church with an odd-shaped spire in the distance. With their usual generous hospitality Joyce and Charlie had included me, a newcomer to Ulster in 1969, in a family picnic expedition to County Down. After a happy day we were returning to Belfast down the Carryduff Road. Brett outings tend to partake of the architectural, and after a diet of churches with few and narrow spires, this one seemed unusual. It was contained rather than soaring, and on closer inspection broached from a tower with a proper moulded cornice. Glimpses between mature yews suggested walls that were both straight and curved. It seemed in a class of its own; and so it proved. It was Knockbreda Parish Church. Fundamentally it is a hall-and-tower church but the integrity of its design, the neatness of details, the interrelation between its parts, and the interior spatial complexity, mark it out as a building of more than ordinary consequence, and as the work of an accomplished designer. It was built in 1737, during a lean time for church building, and designed by Richard Castle whose reputation is based on great houses and public buildings. It has been noticed by many, and praised, if briefly, in passing; but does closer inspection reveal more about the origins of its architecture or its designer?

Knockbreda was built for Anne, the Dowager Viscountess Middleton on land made available by her son Arthur Hill, later Viscount Dungannon, whose house, Belvoir, stood just to the west. This aristocratic origin and location give it something of the air of a private chapel which may account also for its rarity among Church of Ireland churches in having no dedication[1]. The church has been described and illustrated many times in the last generation but always in wide-ranging studies which allow little more that a recitation of the building's origins and a few general sentences about its architecture. The variations are on a central theme. The most detailed and objective description[2] allows itself no flights of stylistic fancy, nor discussion of its designer. Brett[3] in 1967 thought it 'modest and rural externally; the interior pleasing but not greatly distinguished'.

Fig 1. Knockbreda Parish Church, exterior from the south west. (A.E.P. Collins for *An Archaeological Survey of County Down*, HMSO 1966).

A harmless attempt[4] to relate the building's sophistication to current architectural developments found support from Craig[5] who, underlining the paucity of noteworthy Church of Ireland churches in the whole of Ireland in the eighteenth century – 'one or two of importance in every decade' – placed Knockbreda first in his discussion. Curl[6] found it 'assured ... in its detail and massing... The squat broach spire determinedly classical in feeling'. Larmour[7] notes 'its tidy plan and crisp classical detailing'. Walker[8] points to the possibility of influence from St

Anne's Church, Dawson Street, Dublin (started 1719)[9] the first post reformation church in Ireland to have an apse. Oram[10] points to the comparative rarity of classical Church of Ireland churches and mentions the apsidal transepts as 'unusual features'. Almost all fall for the temptation, firmly resisted here, of moving attention swiftly from the church itself to the fascinating burial monuments which surround it.

Improbably, it is earlier sources, paying closer attention, which provide a key to understanding Knockbreda. Over a century ago Lavens Ewart[11], struggling to reconcile Knockbreda with his Christian gothic world mentions its 'peculiar architectural features that seem to have been suggested by the plans of the early Basilicas, which were much studied at that time'. This is a worthy mid-Victorian stumble towards the light of Palladian enthusiasm in the early 18th Century. The basilican form was studied by Palladio himself, and hence by generations of his followers; essential to it was the dominant (in churches eastward) axis with its focus towards an apse. Often there were several parallel axes each with its apse, and usually such multiplication led to a hierarchy of apses with the central being largest and most elaborate. Rarely in the west are apses placed at right angles to the main axis.

The earliest description, however, is also in many ways the most useful. It is curious that attention has usually been paid to only part[12] of it. Walter Harris and Charles Smith[13] were preparing their The Antient and Present State of the County of Down, published in 1744, in the years just after Knockbreda was built. The new building[14] evidently made an impact:

About half a Mile East of Belvoir, on an Eminence commanding a Prospect of Belfast, the Bay and Town of Carrickfergus, and the County round it, appears the Parish Church of Breda, a Building the neatest and most compleat perhaps of this Kind in the Kingdom. It is, exclusive of the Chancel, 50 Feet by 25, and 25 in Heigth [sic]. From the middle of the Church on each side springs a Semicircle of 18 Feet Diameter, which besides enlarging the Room, adds greatly to the Beauty of the Building. The Steeple, with the Spire, built according to the exact Proportions of Architecture, catches the Eyes of all Travellers. This Church was executed under the Direction of Mr Castell, at the sole Expence of the Right Honourable the Lady Viscountess Dowager Middleton whose Charities, both publick and private, have been very extensive. This Parish, together with those of Knock and Kirkdonell, are at present Episcopally united.

The church retained its simple proportions for over a century and a half. Then in 1883 the square-ended chancel was extended and given apsidal form, and a

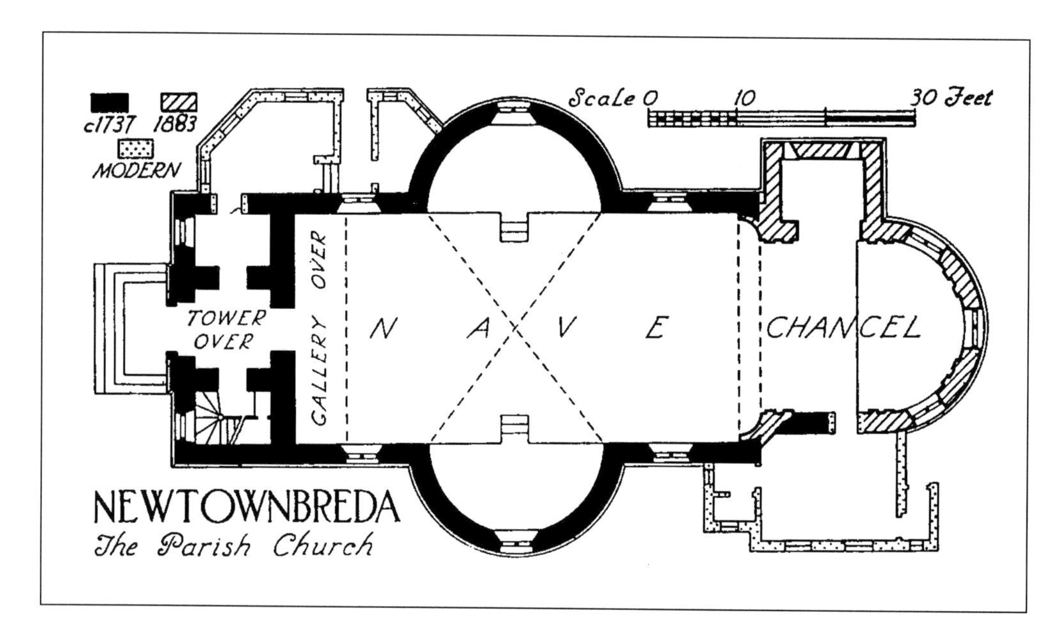

Fig 2. Knockbreda Parish Church, ground plan (drawn by D.M.Waterman for ASCD, HMSO 1966)

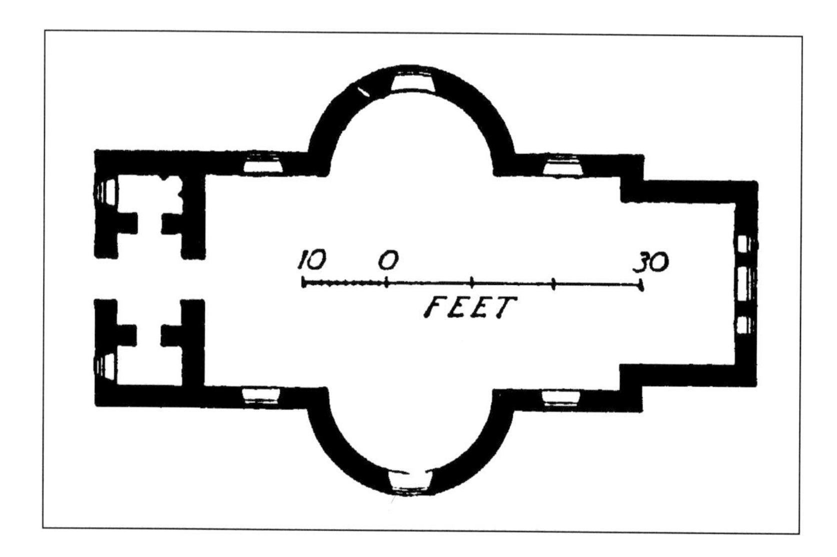

Fig 3. Knockbreda Parish Church, ground plan of 1855 (redrawn for ASCD, HMSO 1966)

northern organ chamber, to designs by Thomas Drew. At the same time stained glass was introduced into the new chancel windows. While Drew's work is generally approved as being sympathetic, the effect of these changes was dramatic. Originally there was a Venetian window[15] in the chancel with an unusally tall central arched element.

Through this, especially during morning services, the light must have streamed in over the shoulders of the preacher in the central pulpit. Drew's more ecclesiologial arrangement emphasises the eastward axis and its focus on the central importance of the altar, but it also compromises the effectiveness of the original space for preacher and congregation. Drew also added a rather cramped western gallery which has an uncomfortable relationship with the nave's western windows. Its staircase was inserted neatly into one of two small vestry or store rooms which flank the tower. This enhanced the need to extend the vestry accommodation, and so is partly the reason for accretions which, though decently done, spoil the external neatness which the Georgians admired. Such, so often, is the fate of classical designs which pass into an age when organic growth seems right and natural. Nevertheless, if we mentally subtract the additions (or take the least changed view from the south west) we have a building of such unusual integrity that we can begin to understand why Harris and Smith thought it 'perhaps the neatest and most compleat of its kind in the kingdom', and wonder about its designer.

'Mr Castell' was, of course, Richard Castle[16] the most successful Palladian architect in Ireland, then approaching the height of his reputation and success. There is much that remains uncertain about his origins and training. In recent research Angus Fowler[17] has shown that much of the accepted knowledge about Castle's early years needs questioning, and in particular, that the continental origins of his style deserve more detailed study. He was born about 1690 possibly in Germany where later he certainly had family connections. His later expertise suggests that at least part of his training was as a navigation engineer. It seems likely that he was living in London when he subscribed to the third volume of Vitruvius Britannicus in 1725, and if so, he was almost certainly associated with the Palladian group there. He is believed to have been invited to Ireland by Sir Gustavus Hume to build his new house at Castle Hume[18] in County Fermanagh. What is certain is that by 1728 he was employed as draughtsman by Sir Edward Lovett Pearce in his designs for the Parliament House in Dublin. Pearce's recommendation (as well as his early death) set Castle on a highly successful career designing country houses and public buildings. 'Mr Castles was remarkably ready at drawing', wrote his earliest biographer, 'and so clear in his directions to workmen, that the most ignorant could not err… He was a man of the strictest integrity, and highly esteemed by the nobility and gentry not only as an artist but as an agreeable companion'. In 1733 he was married in the Huguenot Church in Dublin to Anne Truphet from Lisburn. There were no children and she died in 1744. In later life the lack of home company may have encouraged his habit of drinking late with friends. 'He sacrificed much to Bacchus' said his first biographer. 'Esteemed as an honest and amiable man' said Sadleir, 'yet, in an age when excess was countenanced, he was considered to exceed'. He died aged about sixty at Carton in 1751 while writing to instruct a carpenter employed at Leinster House.

Although he preferred to call himself 'Castle' and used this on official documents, it has long been known that his real name was of Italian form. 'De Ricardi' and the anglicised version 'De Richardi' both appear. Two brothers[19] who administered his will (a casuality of the Four Courts fire, which survives only in transcribed form) combined 'Castles' with De Richardi, one before the other after. Angus Fowler believes that the one who was then living in Dresden was a royal theatre painter, and one of the Castelli, a dynasty of stuccodores from the Tessin area on the border of Italy and Switzerland. Like many families from that area, they brought their craft skills northwards to seek commissions. The Castelli were particularly active in central Germany. With such connections Richard Castle, or Ricardo Castelli, could draw on a wide range of sources in developing his own brand of Palladian building.

Castle designed comparatively few churches, and their survival rate has not been good. Yet they all have, or seem to have had, remarkable features. The earliest, of about 1732, was St.John's at Sligo 'a distinguished Greek cross design'[20] for Robert Howard, Bishop of Elphin, who described it, modestly, as 'a stately building chiefly erected by my means'. Bishop Pococke, making his tour through Ireland in 1752, makes special mention of the roof of the church, which he calls 'a curious piece of work… in every way one of the best designs I have seen'. The church was remodelled in perpendicular revival style in 1812. Pococke also ascribed to Castle the church at Castlebar, County Mayo. This was entirely rebuilt in 1828, but De Latocnaye, preparing his Rambles through Ireland (1799), saw the earlier church, and thought the steeple looked like a syringe. Sadleir dismissed this as simply facetious, but it would be possible to think of the Knockbreda spire in a similar way with the broaching relating to the part of the syringe where fingers hook to resist thumb pressure.

From Carton[21] there is also an unexecuted design for a church by Castle, apparently slightly later than Knockbreda[22]. Superficially conventional, with tower, hall and chancel, it has several curiosities which might repay closer study in relation to Knockbreda. The tower starts square and of such hefty walls as to suggest that there was to be an option of building it higher. Its second stage is octagonal, as is the unbroached squat spire which it supports. The tower has a dummy west door, the actually entrance being on the (ecclesiastical) north. Perhaps this related to the peculiarities of a possible site at Carton. The space inside the tower is circular, and a spiral stair in the thickness of the wall in one corner gives access to a narrow (choir?) gallery. This, with a vestibule below, occupies the west end of the hall space. In the main part of the hall a central pulpit faces an island block of seating. Access aisles run along both walls, and there are box pews in the eastern corners. Behind the pulpit a raised chancel is set in an apse lit by a Venetian window. Curiously, the apse is not expressed externally. A result of this is extremely thick blocks of wall on the eastern corners of the chancel with dummy windows to north and south. This arrangement is difficult to explain. Either the state of the proposed site required massive eastern buttressing for the church, or this is poor planning. The huge proportion of access space suggests the latter, and it is hard to understand how the same architect could have been responsible earlier for the sophisticated planning at Knockbreda.

The contrast is striking. There is a careful relationship of parts to each other and to the whole. At Knockbreda the hall nave is, as Harris and Smith noted, a double cube, the volume favoured for grand domestic interiors by the Palladians, by Inigo Jones and his circle, and by Palladio himself. The geometry of the plan suggests similar ancestry. It can hardly be a coincidence that the external diameter of the apses is the same as the width of the hall, or that the internal diameter is the same as the width of the chancel. Similarly, the depth of the original chancel was the same as the portion of hall wall left to each side of the apse. Even so what looks simple can be complex. For example, the ease with which the plaster vault of the hall is groined with those reaching out to cover the apses is deceptive. They are the same height but not the same width.

The most extraordinary features of the church, however, are the apsidal transepts themselves. They are raised above the main body of the church by three steps which gives the spaces status. No doubt this was intentional; from the church's origins they seem to have been occupied by the local landed families. The most obvious local parallel for this is at Hillsborough where the raised transepts relate in some measure to the presence of the Hill family burial vault on the north side. Nevertheless the principle of privileged seating set above and slightly apart from the main congregation has the same social significance and can be paralleled in the English squire's box, the Scottish laird's loft, and further afield in Europe.[23] At Hillsborough the transepts are deep enough for many seated there to be invisible from most of the nave, and the rectangular shape is intrinsic to the church's cruciform plan. At Knockbreda there is no such intention. The raised apses are wide and shallow enough to have much more of the character of theatrical boxes. In apsidal form they appear to be unique in Ireland, and have few parallels anywhere. The arrangement is not without echoes in contemporary baroque churches in Europe,[24] but the simple serenity is entirely different. In their precise relationship to the wider hall they seem to have a much earlier exemplar in hall and exedrae of Vitruvius, whose work was much

Fig 4. Knockbreda Parish Church from the south east. Watercolour drawing by Andrew Nicholl c.1830. (Ulster Museum; reproduced with the kind permission of the Trustees of the Museums and Galleries of Northern Ireland).

studied at this time. One group of churches, however, do have apsidal transepts. The great Churches of St Giorgio Maggiore and Il Redentore, both in Venice, have them, and the Chapel at Maser not far away also has a similar though embryonic form. While in most ways the comparison is ludicrous, this feature they have in common. The architect of all three was, of course, Andrea Palladio himself. The scale of the apses at Knockbreda imparts to the interior a quality which sets it quite aside from the progress of church building in Ireland.

Finally there is the steeple. It is not very Italian, nor Irish either. With the heavily expressed broaching, and limited height of the upper part, the spire has something in common with spires and tower finials of middle Europe. Allow for an onion projection above the belfry stage (admittedly quite an allowance!) and the kinship is more convincing. Yet, while its character is odd, or inconclusive in style, its proportions relate very well to the rest of the church. The conclusion of Harris and Smith that it is 'built according to the exact proportions of Architecture' seems justified, though exactly which proportions they had in mind is less clear. This was not a great age for spires, and those that were built tend to consist of layers of classical apparatus. Many nevertheless have a marked broach from broad tower to narrow spire. While the London churches of Wren and Gibbs provided a generating centre, there is a distinct lack of assurance in late 17th-century provincial towers and spires. Wren's invention and ability were rarely matched by others, but that did not prevent attempts. At Knockbreda, however, Castle, firmly against the elaborate decoration of the ebbing baroque tide, yet adopted Wren's fundamentals of proportion and the relationship of parts to each other and to the whole. On this occasion it seems, whether by accident or not matters little, that there may be a shadow of substance to Samuel Lewis's ambitious and incorrect assertion that the church was 'a small but elegant edifice in the Grecian style, erected … from a design of Sir Christopher Wren's under the direction of Mr Cassels'.

Is it possible that Richard Castle, whose oeuvre was overwhelmingly unecclesiastical, and who had little current church building to examine in Ireland, was looking back to his sojourn in England, or back to Germany, or even to Italian family origins, and used a synthesis of ideas to produce the extraordinary originality of Knockbreda. Such a question[25] is easier to ask than to answer, but it seems time, at least, to ask.

Anyway, it was well worth a visit, and others, too; and Joyce and Charlie were there on a soft September day twenty-five years ago when Jill and I were married.

NOTES

1. Although it has been accorded one occasionally, borrowed from the neighbouring Presbyterian Church which is correspondingly unusual in having a saintly dedication.
2. Described with plans and exterior photograph in Waterman, D.M and Collins, A.E.P. 1966. *An Archaeological Survey of County Down.* Belfast, HMSO, pp.333-4. The account includes a redrawn plan of the church of 1855 without noting the location of the original. I am particularly grateful to Gail Pollock of the Northern Ireland Environment and Heritage Service for assistance with photographic prints from the Monuments and Buildings Record of Northern Ireland; and to Nick Brannon for approval to use the views and plans in this article.
3. Brett, C.E.B. 1967. *Buildings of Belfast 1700-1914.* London, Weidenfeld and Nicholson; Revised Belfast, 1985, p.9; this account is brought up to date, with much quotation from others, and a characteristic attack on the placing of wires in C.E.B.Brett. 2002. Buildings of North County Down. Belfast, UAHS, pp.36-7, published during the preparation of this piece.

4. Dixon, Hugh. 1975. *An Introduction to Ulster Architecture.* Belfast, UAHS, p35.
5. Craig, Maurice. 1982. *The Architecture of Ireland from earliest times to 1880.* London, Batsford, p213.
6. Curl, James Stevens. 1980. *Classical Churches in Ulster.* Belfast, UAHS, p.8.
7. Larmour, Paul. 1987. *Belfast: An Illustrated Architectural Guide.* Belfast, The Friar's Bush Press, p.105.
8. Walker, Simon. 2000. *Historic Ulster Churches.* Belfast, The Institute of Irish Studies, p.53.
9. Loeber, Rolf. 1981. *A Biographical Dictionary of Architects in Ireland 1600-1720.* London, John Murray, p.54
10. Oram, Richard. 2001. *Expressions of Faith: Ulster's Church Heritage.* Newtownards, Colourpoint, p.58, and perhaps rather underestimating the strength of the fundamental classicism in so many 'toy gothick' churches where gothicity extends no further than pointed openings and thin battlements.
11. Ewart, Lavens. 1886. *Handbook to the United Diocese of Down and Connor and Dromore.* Belfast, p.53
12. Until Brett quoted it in full in *Buildings of North County Down* in 2002!
13. Harris, Walter, and Smith, Charles. 1744. *The Antient and Present State of the County of Down.* Dublin, Exshaw, pp.72-3
14. The date of the church has been a matter of unnecessary dispute. Samuel Lewis in his *Topographical Dictionary of Ireland,* (London 1837. 2nd Ed. 1846, II, pp.200, 399) states flatly in two places that the church was built in 1747. The evidence of Harris and Smith in 1744 shows this must be wrong. The confusion may have arisen from a bequest made by Lady Middleton (incorrectly recorded as 'Midleton' by Lewis) to the poor of the parish in 1747. Brett followed Lewis; and Dixon and Curl followed Brett. Happily, all later authors have followed Harris and Smith (reprinted 1977). Larmour, op. cit. without citing his authority, is most precise: *'this church was built by the Dowager Viscountess Middleton at her sole expense. Her offer of a church was made and accepted in 1733 and the completed building consecrated in August 1737'.* Greater harmony has been achieved over the date and authorship of the extended chancel, 1883 by Thomas Drew, and the date of the vestry, 1910, to which Larmour adds its designer, R.I.Calwell, C.E.
15. The window appears on the 1855 plan (see note 2 above) and in three views of Knockbreda by Andrew Nicholl of the 1830s which also show that Drew adopted the original form of tracery for his new chancel. I am very grateful to Martin Anglesea and Pat McLean of the Ulster Museum for allowing access to, and arranging photographs of, Andrew Nicholl's views of Knockbreda.
16. The standard accounts of Castle's career are an anonymous account in *Anthologia Hibernica* II, 1793, pp.242-243; Sadleir Thomas U. 1911. 'Richard Castle, Architect' in the *Journal of the Royal Society of Antiquarians of Ireland,* Vol. 41, II, pp.241-245; The Knight of Glin. 1964. 'Richard Castle, A Synopsis' in *Quarterly Bulletin of the Irish Georgian Society,* Vol. VII, No.1, pp.31-38. For the best recent comments see McParland, Edward, 2001. *Public Architecture in Ireland 1680-1760.* New Haven and London, Yale University Press, especially pp.14-15, p.185, pp.191-6.

17. I am most grateful to Angus Fowler for sharing his expertise on Germany in the early 18th Century. It is his work, contained in a paper entitled 'Some thoughts on Richard Castle, architect (ca.1690-1751) [Copy in the Irish Architectural Archive] sent to me with a letter dated 11th August 2001, which has cast doubt on the origins of Castle in Kassel, and indeed on whether the family was German at all.
18. Rowan, Alistair, 1979. *The Buildings of Ireland: North West Ulster.* London, Penguin, pp.184-5.
19. The Knight of Glin, *op.cit.*, p.38
20. McParland, E. *op.cit.*, p.44. Craig, Maurice, and Glin, the Knight of, 1970. *Ireland Observed: A Guide to the Buildings and Antiquities of Irelands.* Cork, The Mercier Press, p.98. The Church of St.John was remodelled in Perpendicular Gothick-revival style in 1812. Even in its present state this church, with its Greek cross plan, deserves more detailed study for what it might reveal of its original Castle form.
21. I am most grateful to David Griffin for drawing my attention to this design, which is now in the Irish Architectural Archive, and for his generous help with Castle. It is to be hoped that his own work on Castle, together with that of Jaqueline Eick of Lubeck, will be published soon. Clearly, more is now known of Castle and his family.
22. Castle was busy remodelling the Carton for the Earl of Kildare between 1739 and 1745. The Knight of Glin. 1964, *op. cit.*, proposes a date of about 1743 for the church design.
23. Drummond, Andrew Landale, 1934. *The Church Architecture of Protestantism: An Historical and Constructive Study.* Edinburgh, T & T. Clark, pp.28-9: 'screened boxes (Hoflogen) for the grandees' at Dresden; p.43 'principle pews spacious like parlours'.
24. For example see Meek, H.A. 1988. *Guarino Guarini and his architecture.* Newhaven and London, Yale University Press, especially pp.163ff on Guarini's legacy north of the Alps.
25. Nowhere with more parallel poignancy than by Albert Rechts in his *Handbook to a Hypothetical City* (1986. Gigginstown, Lilliput) *passim sed nota bene* p.43: 'So: what then? If this is a story, has it an ending? If this is a riddle, has it an answer? If this is an enigma, has it a solution?

AN ELIZABETHAN REVIVAL HOUSE IN IRELAND EDWARD BLORE AND THE BUILDING OF CROM, CO FERMANAGH

TERENCE REEVES-SMYTH

IN SPRING 2001 CHARLIE and I embarked upon an exciting venture to the Crimea, a land whose rich architectural heritage is still little known outside the borders of the old Soviet Union. Our destination was the extraordinary palace of Alupka, built in the 1830s on the shores of the Black Sea by the Anglophile, Count Mikhail Vorontov, to designs of the English architect Edward Blore. It's difficult not to be impressed by the opulent eclecticism of this remarkable building, its masterly amalgam of Jacobean, English Castellated, Moghul and Tartar styles, or with it's wonderful silhouette of cupolas, chimneys and pinnacles, which dreamily follow the shape of the mighty mountain crags behind. Alupka is a work of genius and surely unrivalled as an essay in the picturesque tradition of architecture.[1]

Genius is not normally a word associated with Edward Blore. Although he was one of the most successful architects of his generation, his reputation suffered a serious decline after his retirement from practice in 1849 and he is still held in low esteem by many architectural historians. Howard Colvin, for example, believes that 'a dull competence pervades all his work',[2] while Goodhart-Rendel declared that he doubted 'if Blore ever did anything original in his life'.[3] Alupka hardly supports these views; but what of his other buildings? Sadly, many of Blore's more important country houses no longer survive, while many others have suffered drastic later remodelling. However, one building which does remain intact, albeit with some later 19th-century alterations, is the great Elizabethan-style house at Crom, Co. Fermanagh, built at the same time as Alupka.

Idyllically located on the shores of Upper Lough Erne, Crom was Blore's largest Irish commission and is one of only a few *de novo* houses by Blore that remains occupied by the family who built it. An extensive body of documentary material survives relating to the building of this house and its ancillary buildings, including hundreds of beautifully crafted architectural drawings in the hand of Blore himself.[4] This tribute to Charlie offers the opportunity to reassess this material and in the process evaluate its place in the context of the period.

Background

The house at Crom, commonly known as Crom Castle, is a large and imposing 'Elizabethan' or 'Tudor Manor House' style building of blue grey limestone with sandstone dressings, situated on a low hill with commanding views of the surrounding landscape.[5] It was built to a design by Blore between 1830 and 1838 and comprises a south facing rectangular block of 2.5-stories over a basement, with two deep wings enclosing a court to the rere. The entrance front on the east side incorporates a porte-cochère tower, while the west side overlooks a garden terrace with an attached conservatory built at various stages between 1838 and 1851. Much of the house was burnt in 1841, but was rebuilt to its original specifications. Subsequent additions to the castle, which are not discussed in this paper, were made by William G. Murray in 1861 and by William Hague in 1873-1880, while internal alterations were made in 1885-1856 and more recently by Nicholas Johnson in 1979-1981.

Although the mansion designed by Blore was built on a new site, unencumbered by an earlier building, the surrounding demesne was an old one, having been originally established in 1610 after the lands had been granted in the Plantation to Michael Balfour. A Scottish-style fortified house, known now as 'Old Crom Castle', was subsequently built close to the lough shore, strategically sited amidst the enchanting wooded islands and peninsulas of Upper Lough Erne. The property fell into the possession of the Creighton family in 1655, who subsequently successfully defended the castle in two Jacobite sieges in 1689. In the 1720s plans were put in place to build a new mansion here, including a hexagonal gazebo designed by Sir Edward Lovett Pearce; but these were never realised.

The old castle was left as a ruin after being burnt in 1764 and the Creighton family took up temporary residence at nearby Knockballymore.[6] Eventually, in the 1780s John Creighton, who became the first Earl Erne in 1789, built an elegant single-storey lodge on the island of Inisherk and enclosed it with a small park. This was used during the summer months when the family came down to Crom from their Dublin residence. However, following the Act of Union in 1800 most members of the Irish aristocracy no longer had political reasons to retain a Dublin house. The Earl Erne, who voted for the union, decided to build a more substantial residence at Crom, but for reasons unknown, this was not achieved during his lifetime. However, in his will, dated 1820, and proved in

Fig 1. The house and its setting as viewed from the south. Old Crom Castle and its sham ruin additions lies in the foreground of the picture (Aerial view 1987, Courtesy of the School of Archaeology, Queen's University, Belfast)

1828, he bequeathed a sum of £22,711 in consols 'to replace the ancient castle [at Crom] which was consumed by accidental fire in 1764'.

The responsibility for building the new house fell upon the first Earl's grandson, Colonel John Creighton. Unfortunately, the Earl's eldest son, who held the title as second Earl Erne from 1828 to 1842, had been declared legally insane in 1799 'owing to cold bathing in a course of mercury, which disordered his head'. The hapless man was incarcerated in Brooke House, Clapton, where he was allowed a modest maintenance grant of £780 per annum by the 'committee of the lunatic', who controlled his financial affairs. Meanwhile his nephew, Colonel John Creighton, who became the third Earl of Erne in 1842, embarked upon the task of fulfilling his grandfather's wishes and started to seek an architect for the new house at Crom.[7]

Fig 2. Lithograph of Blore's house at Weston, Warwickshire, built between 1826 and 1830. This house appears to have served as a model for Crom.

Edward Blore: The Cheap Architect

The Summer Exhibition of the Royal Academy was a recognised place for ambitious architects in the 19th century to publicise their work. Edward Blore, who relied on personal contacts for his business throughout his life, only submitted designs on three occasions, namely for Goodrich Court in 1826, Weston Park in 1828 and Alupka in 1836. It seems almost certain that Colonel Creighton, when searching for an architect for Crom, saw Blore's exhibited drawings for Weston at the Royal Academy. Indeed, an engraving of Weston was found in the Erne papers and this house, with its porte-cochère, its symmetrical garden front and its roof bustling with turrets, cupolas and chimneys, is very similar to Crom, albeit in a Jacobean-style.[8] Creighton was obviously impressed, for in spring 1829 he called into Blore's office at 62 Welbeck Street, London, to discuss his plans. Blore was duly given the contract for a new house in July 1830.

At the time of the Crom commission in 1830, Edward Blore had been in practice for only six years. Yet, already by that stage he was in considerable demand as an architect and by the mid-1830s was commanding one of the most successful architectural practices in Great Britain. Although he is often thought of as an architect 'who kept mainly or entirely to country house work',[9] in fact Blore was wonderfully versatile and was prepared to do almost anything that he was asked. When he retired in 1849, having practised for only 25 years, he had designed no less than 21 new churches, enlarged or restored 21 churches (including work on six cathedrals), at least six schools, five University buildings, three royal houses, (including a major rebuilding of Buckingham Palace), two town halls, two almshouses, a hospital, the London Charterhouse, plus 21 years of additions and alterations to Lambeth Palace.[10] His country house work included 34 houses, either *de novo* or with major alterations and 18 houses with minor additions or alterations.[11]

Blore's success was, in part, based upon a reputation for trustworthiness and an ability to keep within his estimates. Indeed, the Duchess of Sutherland in 1830 famously dismissed Blore as the 'cheap architect',[12] though this didn't stop her brother-in-law from using Blore to build his great house at Worsley.[13] One notable contract Blore gained through his ability to keep within his estimates was the completion of Buckingham Palace in 1832, following criticisms of John Nash's extravagances. Although the quality of Blore's work here was well below his normal standards, he certainly lived up to his reputation by completing the work for a sum considerably below that voted for the purpose by Parliament.[14] Such cost-effectiveness would have appealed to Creighton with his comparatively modest budget and his notably penurious attitude to household finances, so evident from the Erne papers.

A contributory factor to Blore's ability to keep projects within budget was his practice of taking great care in preparing working drawings, which he did superbly, and in drawing up detailed specifications to avoid errors. He appointed competent clerk-of-works and was constantly travelling, usually by horse or coach, to inspect building progress, sometimes visiting a site over 60 times.[15] Such attention to detail, characteristic also of Robert Smirke and William Burn, was in contrast to the previous generation of architects, notably Wyatt and Nash, who so rarely bothered visiting their building projects it was a wonder they achieved anything. His visits to Ireland were, however, rather more irregular, due to the distance involved. Crom was visited only eight times between 1830 and 1838, each round trip lasting about eight or nine days, while Ballydrain and Castle Upton, both in Co. Antrim were visited three times between 1836 and 1838.[16]

Failure to inspect work in progress on a regular basis could result in difficulties on site, as it did at Crom in 1833 when a serious dispute erupted with the building contractor. Such problems could also be reduced by employing one main contractor for a building operation, working to a fixed estimate drawn up by quantity surveyors with fixed penalty clauses inserted. In most cases, Blore followed this practice, which at that time was starting to be adopted in place of the old cumbersome and unreliable method of day labour combined with small separate contracts, all co-ordinated by the clerk-of-works.[17]

At Crom, a local Lisnaskea limestone was used by Blore for the house. As a rule, he used local materials wherever possible for his buildings, partly because this was within the picturesque tradition of harmonizing architecture with the landscape, but also because it was usually cheaper. He was also prepared to use cheap artificial materials, as at Canford in Dorset, where the 'stone' used was a sandy white clay formed in moulds, and was not averse to using putty or paper mâché for internal decoration, notably ceilings, to cut costs.[18]

In addition, Blore frequently used the same design components for different houses to enable him to increase his output. Ceiling and frieze designs were often repeated and many stone and joinery details standardised. The fittings of some of the bay windows at Crom, for example are identical to ones at Alupka, while an identical chimney design was used for Lodsworth in Sussex and Ballydrain in Co. Antrim.[19] Likewise, stable blocks and gate lodge designs were often alike; for example, the main gate lodges at Crom and Ballydrain are remarkably similar. This may have caused many of Blore's country houses to look much the same; but the formulae was widely adopted by other successful architects of the period, such as Smirke and Burn, and was central to their ability to produce numerous buildings at the same time.[20]

Undoubtedly, many clients were won over to Blore's practice by the quality of his architectural drawings and by the delightful and evocative watercolours he produced of proposed houses.[21] His great skill in the medium and his ability to successfully exploit the contemporary demand for native historical styles lay in his background as a topographical and antiquarian artist. From the age of 17 he had provided illustrations for his father's antiquarian publications and for 20 years had travelled throughout Britain producing drawings and engravings to illustrate numerous popular architectural and topographical books, whilst also publishing a number of his own, notably *The Monumental Remains of Noble and Eminent Persons* (1824-1826). He produced a vast collection of antiquarian drawings and in Colvin's view, had a 'knowledge of medieval precedent' that 'was probably quite as extensive as Pugin's'.[22]

Blore's extensive knowledge of 15th – and 16th century architecture brought him to the notice of Sir Walter Scott, who in 1816 asked him to present proposals to extend his house at Abbotsford in Roxburghshire.[23] Nothing came of Blore's scheme as Scott commissioned the more experienced architect William

Atkinson; but he was so impressed with the ability of this 29 year old artist that he promoted him widely as an architect. The fact that Blore had 'no regular education as an architect,[24] was no barrier to success at that time and through Scott's recommendations he won a number of important early commissions, such Corehouse in Lanarkshire (1824), Freeland in Perthshire (1825) and the remarkable castellated house at Goodrich Court (1828). By the time of the Crom commission in 1830 he was well established as a highly competent master of a huge range of styles.

The Choice of Style

The architectural style adopted for Crom was no whim on the part of Colonel Creighton, but was highly predictable, as was his choice of architect. Although Blore used a whole range of styles for his houses, well over a half of his oeuvre was in the Tudor Manor House style.[25] This reflected the fact that Blore, like his rival William Burn, relied heavily on the patronage of old and substantial landed families, such as the Creightons of Crom rather than the nouveau riche who invariably preferred the opulent Italianate *palazzo* style, championed by Charles Barry in Britain and by Charles Lanyon in Ireland.

Contemporaries would have used the term 'Elizabethan' to denote the style chosen for Crom, though the word tended to be used rather indiscriminately. Humphrey Repton, the landscape gardener, was the first to embrace the idea of resurrecting the architecture of England's great Elizabethan Age in 1799 as an alternative to the romantic 'Castle Gothic' and 'Abbey Gothic' that then dominated country house architecture.[26] By the 1820s however, this alternative had developed into a much broader stylistic model embracing 'Tudor Gothic', 'Elizabethan' and 'Jacobean' revivals, all of which often tended to merge into one another.[27] Architectural purists such as Pugin hated this form of eclectic mix; but it should not be forgotten that architects of Blore's generation, though more scholarly than Nash and his contemporaries, still worked within the romantic picturesque tradition and absolute archaeological authenticity was never their objective.

For aristocratic clients at this time, of whom Colonel Creighton was typical, there were considerable attractions in choosing the Tudor Manor House style. Aside from offering a picturesque appearance, it facilitated flexible planning at a time when country houses were becoming larger and more complex in their layouts. It was cost effective, as the amount of decoration employed could be

Fig 3. View of Crom Castle from the south-east, c.1840, with the Green Lake in the foreground.

adapted to suit the financial means of the client. In addition, it blended in well with the many existing 15th- or 16th-century English manors, permitting alterations rather than the erection of new houses, and was unobtrusive as a style, offering houses that were agreeable without being showy or ostentatious.

Most of all, perhaps, the Tudor Manor House style had a powerful symbolic value for a privileged social class whose position for the first time was being threatened both by the increasing power of manufacturers and by the rise of the middle classes. In an age of political turbulence and heightened national consciousness, this architectural style offered a retreat into a imaginary world of Merrie England and Good Queen Bess, when the peasants were contented and the aristocracy was benevolent – an imaginary world that was powerfully expressed in Joseph's Nash's influential book *Mansions of England in Olden Times* (1839-1849). Significantly the houses illustrated were Elizabethan and Jacobean, not medieval or classical.[28]

In Ireland the revival was started by William Morrison, whose early work at Kilcolman (1819) and Kilruddery (1820-1829) incorporated quite an amalgam of styles, though with a dominant Jacobean flavour.[29] In spirit these houses were still based in the classical castle-style tradition, differing mainly by the use of curvilinear gables and ogee turrets in place of castellations. By the 1830s however Morrison was producing a number of Tudor-Manor-House style houses of real distinction, though by this time his competitors were successfully exploring the style, notably John. B. Keane, Thomas Duff, the Pain brothers and

Daniel Robertson.[30] An early and rather unconventional example in the style is Thomas Rickman's large house at Lough Fea, Co. Monaghan, begun in 1825.[31] Famed for his expertise on gothic architecture, Rickman was a close friend of Blore's, and it may have been the success of this venture that encouraged Blore to accept a large Irish commission for himself.

The First Building Contract 1830-1833

In January 1830, Edward Blore produced a small scale pen-and-ink plan of the three floors of the house at Crom.[32] In general terms, the proposal was similar to what was built, though with some differences. The main block was to be square rather than rectangular in plan, being three rather than two rooms deep and was to have had a large top-lit galleried hall in the centre, flanked on the south by a saloon and on the north by a modest staircase. The porte-cochère tower on the east side was present, but significantly, the Burghley-type towers, which are such a dominant feature of the south front, are absent, while the flanking bay windows are canted rather than rectangular. It would seem that Creighton, presumably to cut costs, got Blore to shorten the house length and in the process, the stairs were moved into the central sky-lit hall and re-designed as a magnificent imperial staircase.

In July 1830, Blore was asked for his terms and was commissioned to build the new house. Preparations subsequently moved rapidly and detailed specifications were produced within a few months, together with working plans and elevations. A clerk-of-works, Mr. Lelam, was appointed and the contract for building the house was awarded to 'an experienced builder', Mr. Henry of Harrington Street, Dublin.

The site chosen was in an area of woodlands on the north side of the townland, over 700m north-west of the ruins of the Old Castle, with a commanding view of the demesne and Lough Erne. Work on excavating the foundations began in November 1830 and by March 1831 the sum of £408 had been paid towards these. In all, a total of £1861 was eventually paid for 'digging foundations and terrace wall', the labourers being paid 1 shilling a day. This was separate from Henry's contract of £12,000, a copy of which does not survive. The laying of drains was also treated separately, for Mr. Lelam was paid £101.10.3d in four instalments for drains between October 1831 and January 1832. By October 1831, Mr. Henry had been paid the full amount of his contract in five instalments.

In reality Henry's work had not been completed by late 1831 and the fulfilment of his contract was far from finished. Evidently he had grossly misjudged the true cost of the contract in his tender, but continued working regardless for another year and a half. However, when he presented a bill of £2,087.16.11d for what he claimed was 'additional work' in 1833, full payment was refused. Henry then rather optimistically 'actively commenced proceedings at law to enforce payment of it'. The full sorry affair, with its claims and counter claims as to who agreed to what, was spelled out in a 'statement of case with Council's opinion' in September 1833. As Henry had no written agreement for the claimed extra works and as the contract specifications signed by Henry had not been changed, Henry lost his claim and ended up being paid only £680.

The Second Building Contract 1834-1838

Following the termination of Mr. Henry's contract in 1833, it would appear that the castle's masonry fabric had been nearly completed, together with the roof and some of the joisting of the 'principal and chamber floors'.[33] The contract to complete the house was advertised early in 1834 and the work was successfully tendered for by Charles McGibbon of Edinburgh, then working for William Playfair at Brownlow House in Lurgan, where he was 'contractor of the whole works'.[34] In April 1834, he offered to:

Complete the mason, carpenter, joiner, glazier, plumber, plaster, painter, iron mongery and Smith works required for furnishing of Crum Castle...for the sum of £8,550 stirling.

The following month he wrote to Blore in London, stating that he would undertake to complete the house by the end of October 1836. He added that:

I might do it in less time, but having until then it gives me the whole summer of 1836, which from being the driest season of the year is the best for fitting up joiners work and from the whole material being still to season. I do not think it would be doing justice of the work to finish it on more quickly – the nature of the work renders it impossible that it be paid by instalments as particular portions of the work are completed, as all must go on gradually together.

The timber for the building was imported, 'there being nothing of the kind required to be had in Ireland', such as 'oak, yellow battens and deals and Baltic Lathwood'. This was laid down during in July and August 1836; but

Fig 4. A gathering of the tenantry on the east terrace in August 1838 to celebrate the completion of Colonel John Creighton's new house. The ruins and sham towers of old Crom Castle can be seen in the background.

McGibbon's work at Crom continued on until 1838, partly because of a whole series of 'extras' that Creighton required. These included lowering the height of the terrace walls, installing 'plunge and shower baths', cisterns and sinks, a 'heat air stove' and other items. A more substantial addition to the original plan was a conservatory that Blore designed to be added onto the end of the east range. This was built in 1837-1838 for £700, with the final floor flagging being laid down in the summer of 1838. This resulted in McGibbon charging £3015 for additional work, bringing the total value of his undertaking to £11,671.15.8d, the last and ninth instalment being paid in August 1838. The completion of the house that month was marked by the presentation of a piece of silver plate to Colonel Creighton by his tenantry, as illustrated in a watercolour currently hanging in the castle.

Interior Furnishing Contracts 1836-1838

The contract to furnish the new house went to the important Edinburgh interior decorating firm of William Trotter, based at 9 Princes Street. This work included everything from paper hanging and painting to the supply of grates, chimney pieces, curtains, carpets and other furnishings. It's perhaps no surprise that Trotter was chosen for the task, considering that Charles McGibbon was himself an Edinburgh man and was already working with the firm at Brownlow House in Co. Armagh.

The Trotter firm's reputation had been established from the early 1770s when they opened their first ware room close to Edinburgh's New Town, thereby catching the district's fashionable trade.[35] After William Trotter assumed control in 1808, the firm became the pre-eminent interior decorators in Scotland, a success that owed much to Trotter's friendship and collaboration with the architect Gillespie Graham. Pugin worked for Graham and Trotter in the 1830s, notably in the furnishing of Taymouth (1838-1842), and it is not insignificant therefore, that in the Erne papers there is a drawing of an elaborate sideboard which is almost certainly by Pugin.[36]

A fascinating bundle of correspondence survives in the Erne papers dating from December 1836 to December 1838, relating to Trotter's work at Crom, together with sketches of chairs, sofas, mirrors, curtain hangings and other furnishings. The Trotter correspondence, signed by George Potts, the firm's manager and representative at the time, is unusual since most of the kind of furnishing details discussed would normally have been dealt with face-to-face on site. Fermanagh, however, was a difficult journey from Edinburgh and visits by Potts could only be occasional.

A total of £4500 was paid to the Trotter firm in two instalments during 1837 and 1838; but, unfortunately, a copy of their original estimate of £3,602.7.6d has not survived. We know from the correspondence however, that it was calculated on a room-by-room basis using copies of Blore's plans, with the drawings of the proposed furniture being attached, together with prices. Though there were some of Trotter's joiners on site, most of the fittings, such as the library bookcases and chimney-pieces were made in Edinburgh, and then sent over. Evidently, not all shipments arrived safely and there was at least one major accident when a large mirror broke. However, the estimates included 'the charge for packing, conveyance and insurance' which amounted to '£180 or five per cent'. The firm charged 5 shillings a day for the men on site doing the paper hangings, plus an allowance of 8 shillings a week, and when questioned on this matter stated that the firm had 'no other mode of charging it than by the time the men are employed', though added that 'in some cases the charge is made by the price of the paper according to its exchange'.

Potts made all the recommendations for the style of furniture and the colours for each room, mostly rather bright by modern standards, while Colonel Creighton and his wife were invited to comment at each stage. Sketch plans showing the furniture positioned in the principal rooms were produced (only one survives), though Potts commented that 'care has been taken not to overload the rooms with furniture as you can judge much better what to add and where when you see the effects of them in their places'. Colour was all important to Potts and when preparations to furnish the principal rooms were being made in spring 1837, he brought to Crom 'abundant patterns of damask' with the idea of having 'green for the library, blue or blue-violet for the saloon, gold colours or amber for the drawing room'. Later he commented that the carpet 'for the saloon is particularly calculated for blue furniture – the [blue] Drawing Room carpet is very splendid and I think now as I did before that that amber or gold will look best with it'.

Work on papering the walls of the principal rooms was undertaken in the spring and summer of 1837. The main paper suppliers appear to have been Robson (drawing room) and Duppa and Collins, while Sewell and Cross of London supplied satin for the boudoir walls.[37] Many of the carpets were also supplied by Sewell and Cross, while Carling of Cheapside supplied the dining room tables and 'damask furniture'. The Jacobean-style library bookshelves arrived from Edinburgh in early 1838; their design is remarkably similar to some of William Manser's 'Ancient Furnishing' products.[38] Soon afterwards the Jacobean-style carved oak chimney piece in this room arrived; this had cost £150 and was designed by Blore, incorporating the family coat of arms in the overmantel. Blore also designed other oak chimneypieces for the house, including the drawing room (£42) and morning room, as well as the neo-rococo carved mirror overmantel frames. The size of some of the plate glasses were very large for the period, reflecting advances being made in manufacturing techniques at the time; the drawing room glass was 7 feet 6 inches high by 4 feet 9 inches wide (£100) and the one in the morning room was 8 feet high and 4 feet 9 inches wide.

Some of the furniture was assembled or made *in situ* at Crom by Trotter's firm, though Creighton grumbled that all pieces 'should have come ready made and properly stuffed and fitted'. Creighton also complained to Potts that the cabinet

Fig 5. Photograph of the library chimney-piece designed by Blore. The room's fittings were moved to the former drawing room in the 1880s (Courtesy of the Irish Architectural Archive)

makers 'had positively more than half their time taken up with the repairs and damages sustained in the carriage over'. There were also problems with the furniture and decorators arriving before the builders had completely finished their work, so that furniture had to be carried 'out of the way of masons', while dampness in the house was 'injuring the furniture, particularly the polish'.

Other than fixtures such as chimney-pieces, it is not clear how much input, if any, Blore had on the type of movable furniture selected. The woodwork for the doors, windows, screens, staircase and wainscotting were all designed by Blore and made by joiners on site working to McGibbon directly. Their names are not known, though we do know that the delicate gothic woodwork in the hall cost

£111. All the woodwork in the house was subsequently painted or varnished by the firm of 'Hog and Lithgow' and completed in October 1837 for £271. The ceilings of the principal rooms, with their simple, rather mechanical, Jacobean designs, though now painted in an off-white colour, were originally painted with 'one coat of oil paint', after which the rib mouldings and cornices were delicately picked out in reds, yellow-browns and greys.[39] Ornamental ceilings in the whole house cost £850.17s.

Thomas Willement was commissioned to provide stained glass panels for the bow window at the foot of the staircase overlooking the courtyard in 1836. He was heraldic artist to George IV and later artist in stained glass to Queen Victoria, and was perhaps the most significant of a group of stained glass craftsmen working in the 1830s and 1840s, who were preparing the ground for the Gothic Revival immediately before Pugin.[40] Although he provided stained glass for a number of other Blore houses, for example Capesthorne in Cheshire (1843) – it seems that Blore was opposed to his working at Crom, which may explain why William Cooper and Co, Picardy Place, Edinburgh, also became involved. For his work at Crom, completed in December 1837, Willement was paid £120, while Cooper was paid £42. After the 1841 fire Willement was again contracted to replace the stained glass in this window.

In common with William Burn, but unlike many other contemporary architects, Blore was usually very concerned to provide adequate conveniences in his houses. The number of WC's installed in Crom during the 1830s is difficult to determine as a few were added after the original plans were drawn up – for example, one for the housemaids – but the total number seems to have been six. Bathrooms were also a feature of Blore houses and at the north end of the family wing on the principal floor there was a room with a 'bath apparatus' with 'hot and cold taps, India rubber and brass plates' fitted in 1836. The room was painted with an imitation of wainscot 'with two coats of copal varnish on shower, bath and cover of plunge 12s.2d'. The 'apparatus' cost £47 including the 'expense for fitting up plunge and shower baths, the former of copper lined and japanned with …for heating and all the necessary pipes'. One assumes that the hot water was heated in the room below. Normally Blore employed a specialist to install such fixtures and while there is no direct evidence for the maker, it its noteworthy that the Bramah company was paid a sum of £47 around this time. At a number of his houses – for example at Worsley in Lancashire, Blore tried to supplement the coal fireplace heat by installing hot air flues and in this respect it may be noted that £70 was spent at Crom for a 'heated air stove'.[41] Gas was not installed in Crom until 1854-1855.

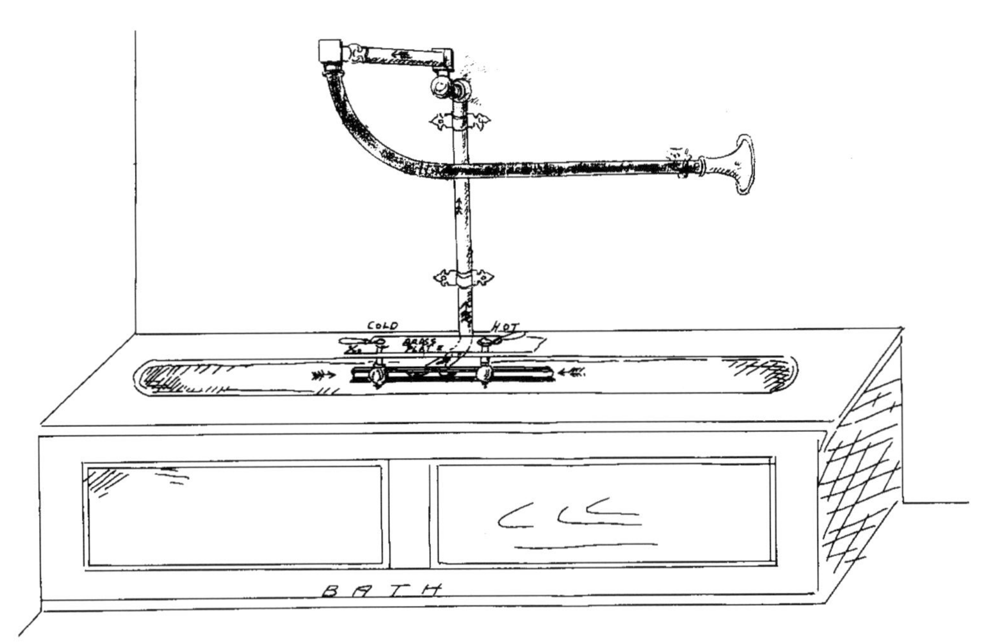

Fig 6. Sketch of the 'bath apparatus' with 'hot and cold taps, India rubber and brass plates' fitted in the west wing in 1836 (PRONI-Erne Papers)

Exterior Composition

The house is composed of quarry-faced Lisnaskea limestone with rectangular windows, all with sandstone dressings, a steeply pitched slated roof and castellated parapets broken by the occasional gable. As with many Tudor revival houses built by Blore and, indeed, Burn, the building incorporates the favoured picturesque device of having one symmetrical façade, behind which the building recedes in a progressive sequence of smaller stepped units, punctuated by towers, turrets and chimneys.

Typically at Crom, the symmetrical façade accommodates the main reception rooms *en suite* and faces south, though not across a garden, but overlooking the park with its wonderful prospect of Lough Erne and the old castle, whose crumbling walls had been picturesquely extended with a sham ruin in 1831-1832, possibly to a Blore design.[42] A massive four-storey central tower with slender octagonal turrets accentuates the symmetrical façade and, despite its castellations and corbel table, is perhaps reminiscent of Burghley's entrance front, which Blore knew well.[43] Crom's tower has no entrance, however, but contains three stories of canted bay windows, outside of which are two-storey gabled bay rectangular projections, also with large mullioned and transomed windows.

On the south and west elevations of the house the basement is entirely concealed by raised terracing, enclosed by a low castellated wall and supported by impressive battered revetments. Among other things, this device ensured that the garden or family side of the house was physically separated from the entrance

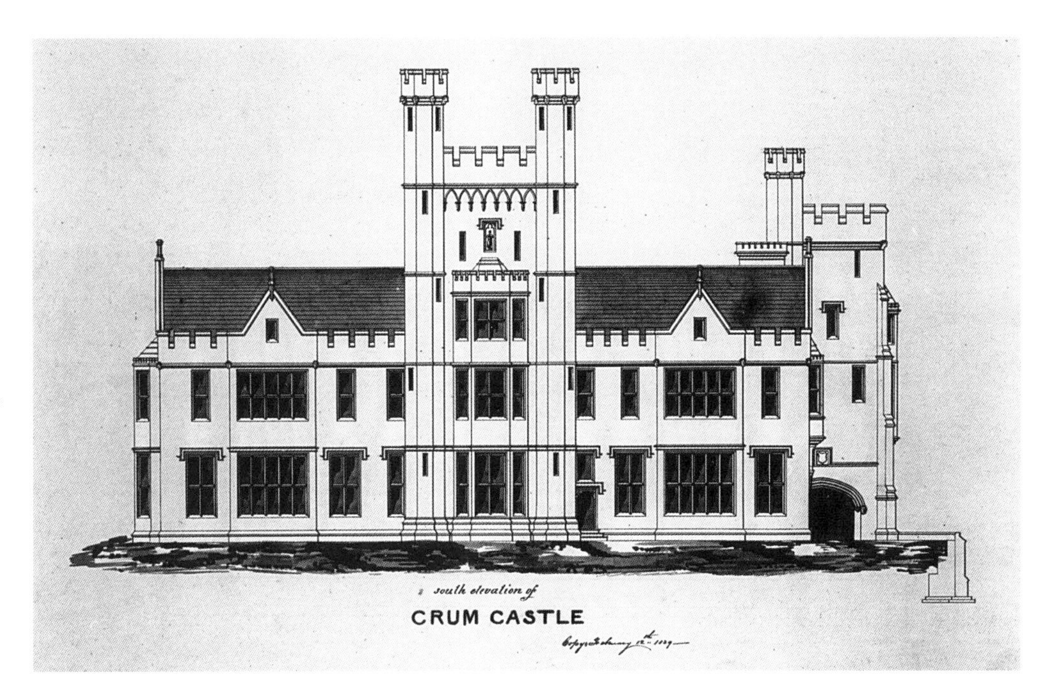

Fig 7. South elevation of the house. An 1839 copy of one of Blore's drawings (Courtesy of the Irish Architectural Archive)

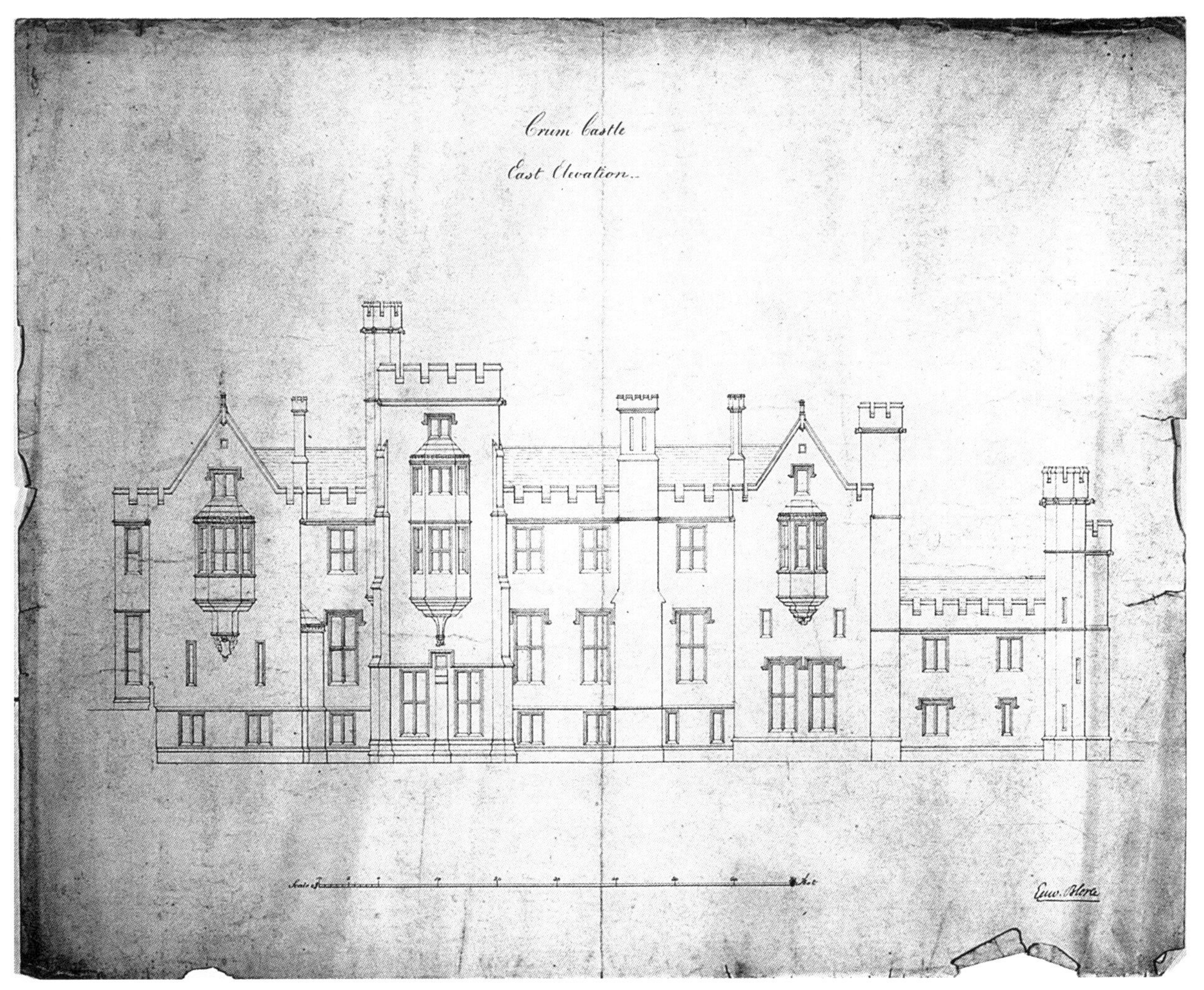

Fig 8. East or public elevation of the house with port cochère. Drawing by Edward Blore (Courtesy of the Irish Architectural Archive)

Fig 9.
Photograph of the east front looking from the north-east.

front whose basement is the ground floor. The entrance or public façade was given picturesque asymmetry by large projecting gable bays, each with an oriel at principal floor level and by a boldly projecting four-storey battlemented tower, known as the Valet's Tower. This has clasping buttresses, a two-storey corbelled oriel and a porte-cochère at base. It's oriels have decorative base carvings, while the porte-cochère arch terminals are enlivened with delightful figures of leprechauns – evidently Blore's concession to the Irish location of this house. Sadly, the gradually receding stepped composition of this façade was unbalanced by additions at the north end in 1861 and 1873, giving it a much more forbidding appearance than was intended by Blore.

The west or garden front, with its array of different-sized mullioned and transomed windows, is comparatively undistinguished. As was customary, Blore designed a conservatory that joined the house at the north end and like other Blore conservatories, it was given a stone framework of ashlar piers. However, due principally to cost-cutting measures, the structure was built in various stages between in 1837 and 1851-1852, with the octagonal pavilion being added last.[44] This overlooks a rectangular terrace, which prior to 1914 was covered by a parterre, possibly designed by William Nesfield, who worked with Blore on quite a number of projects.[45]

It has sometimes been wrongly maintained that the parterre was designed by William Sawrey Gilpin. In fact he had little knowledge of flowers and their

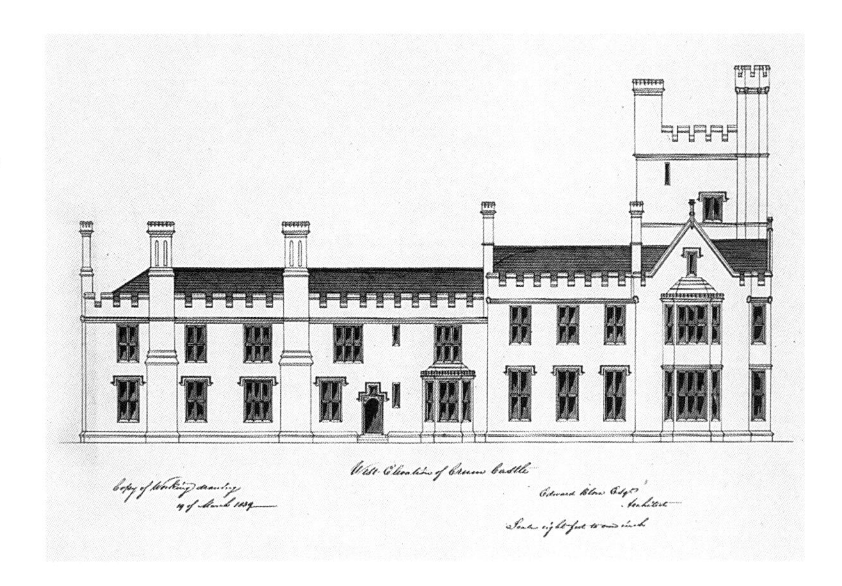

Fig 10. West or private elevation of the house. An 1839 copy of one of Blore's drawings (Courtesy of the Irish Architectural Archive)

Fig 11. Crom Castle as viewed from the south-west. The shadow marks of the parterre are clearly visible (Aerial view 1987, Courtesy of the School of Archaeology, Queen's University, Belfast)

Fig 12. The parterre created at Crom circa.1838-42. This photograph was taken around 1890 (Earl of Erne's Family Albums)

varieties and came to Crom in 1834 to create a suitable parkland setting for the new house. He was a nephew of William Gilpin, the great pioneer of the Picturesque, and his work at Crom, for which he was paid £28.8s, involved planning new avenues, opening vistas and planting trees, all in accordance with picturesque theory, of which he was one of the foremost practitioners of the day.[46] His work at Crom survives as one of the best examples of this style of landscaping in the British Isles.

Interior Plan and Style

Blore's country house plans are sometimes thought to have been a bit old fashioned for their period; but the layout of Crom reflected some of the very latest ideas in country house planning. Most notably, it utilized some of the rationalist principles of practical planning that were then being developed by William Burn in Scotland to meet the changing needs of the day. As houses became larger and more staff were being employed, a key demand was for more privacy, 'the foremost of all maxims' as Robert Kerr remarked.[47] A desire for comfort was also important, while there was an increasing insistence on the segregation of the different ranks and sexes of the occupants. In consequence, houses become more compartmentalised with separate self-contained areas for the family, the various categories of servants and the public rooms.

At Crom, Blore devised a U-shaped plan to accommodate Colonel Creighton's

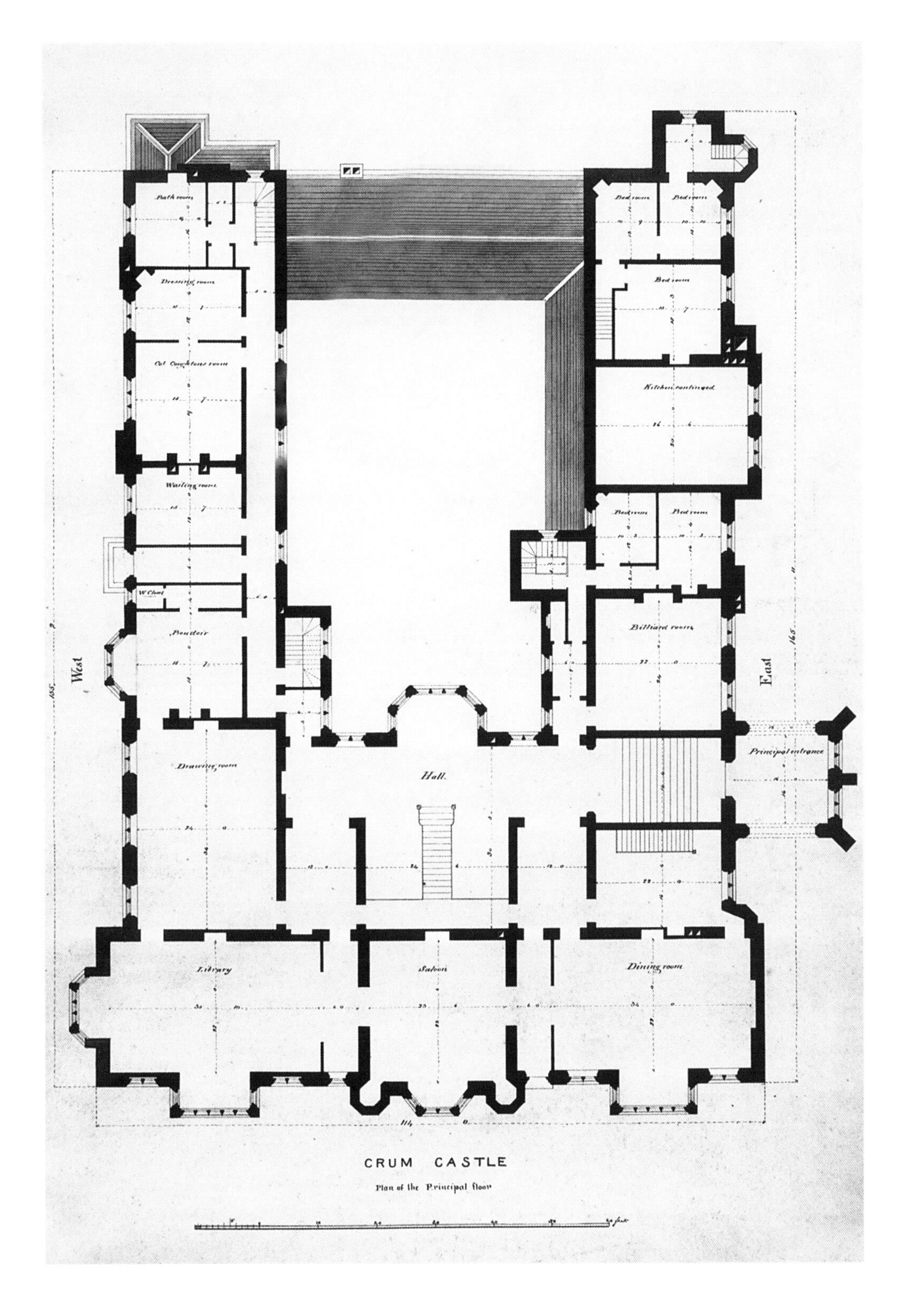

Fig 13. Plan of the principal floor of Crom Castle. An 1839 copy of one of Blore's drawings (Courtesy of the Irish Architectural Archive)

requirements. The main rectangular block contained the public rooms, while a service courtyard to the rere was flanked by a family or private wing on the west and a kitchen wing on the east. The arrangement of the public rooms followed a plan type first devised by Robert Smirke at Newton Don (1815-1818), where the main entrance was placed on the side of the main block, leading to a long axis that provided access to a symmetrical façade of three reception rooms on one side and to private areas at the end. William Burn, a former student of Smirke, refined this layout at Camperdown (1824-1826), by placing a separate family wing at right angles at the far end of the axis. This was the plan solution adopted at Crom; indeed, there are such striking similarities with Camperdown's layout, its seems clear that Blore was already quite familiar with Burn's revolutionary new ideas in country house planning.[48]

The main reasoning behind placing the entrance at the eastern end elevation was to ensure privacy. It offended Victorian sensibilities that visitors arriving at the front door should be able to peep into the house windows. By positioning the main entrance at right angles to the principal suite of reception rooms, callers were kept at a distance. At Crom, this distance was given even greater emphasise by the clever device of placing the entrance at basement level and separating this side of the house from the south and west elevations by raised terracing.

The location of the entrance at basement level had the additional advantage of allowing a staircase to be built in the entrance hall up to the principal floor. This provided added drama for visitors as they approached into what must, perhaps, be the most splendid and theatrical 19th-century staircase hall in Ireland. This remarkable room, which Rowan has suggested recalls Smirke's hall at Lowther Castle,[49] is dominated by a fine double-return imperial staircase, rising behind a perpendicular arcaded screen crisply detailed in timber and plaster. The first flight is tapered to give still greater illusion of depth and monumentality, while above there is a galleried landing lit by an octagonal 'Elizabethan' roof lantern.[50] Further light is provided by a bay window at the foot of the stairs, filled with Willement's stained glass armorial panels and screening the view into the service yard.[51] This opaque glass, together with Minton's encaustic tiles on the floor, the great screen and the relative darkness, all contributed to giving this room a wonderful cathedral-like atmosphere.

The three reception rooms on the symmetrical south front were arranged in an en suite sequence linked with big double doors, which could be thrown open for entertaining. The saloon took pride of place in the centre, the library at the west end and the dining room at the east end to avoid the evening sun and to be near

Fig 14. The staircase and perpendicular arcaded screen (Courtesy of the Irish Architectural Archive)

the kitchen. This tripartite formulae was familiar to many other houses by both Blore and Burn, though often the drawing room was placed in the centre. At Crom, however, as the gardens lay on the west side of the house, Blore placed the drawing room to the west of the staircase hall, where it linked with the library and the boudoir. All of these rooms were given a Jacobean flavour with ribbed ceilings whose patterns varied slightly from room-to-room, though as a cost-cutting measure, the cornice, studded with quatrefoils, was the same throughout. The inter-connected arrangement of the rooms was designed to aid separation from the servants as it enabled family members to pass through from the dining room to the library, drawing room and boudoir and into the family wing without

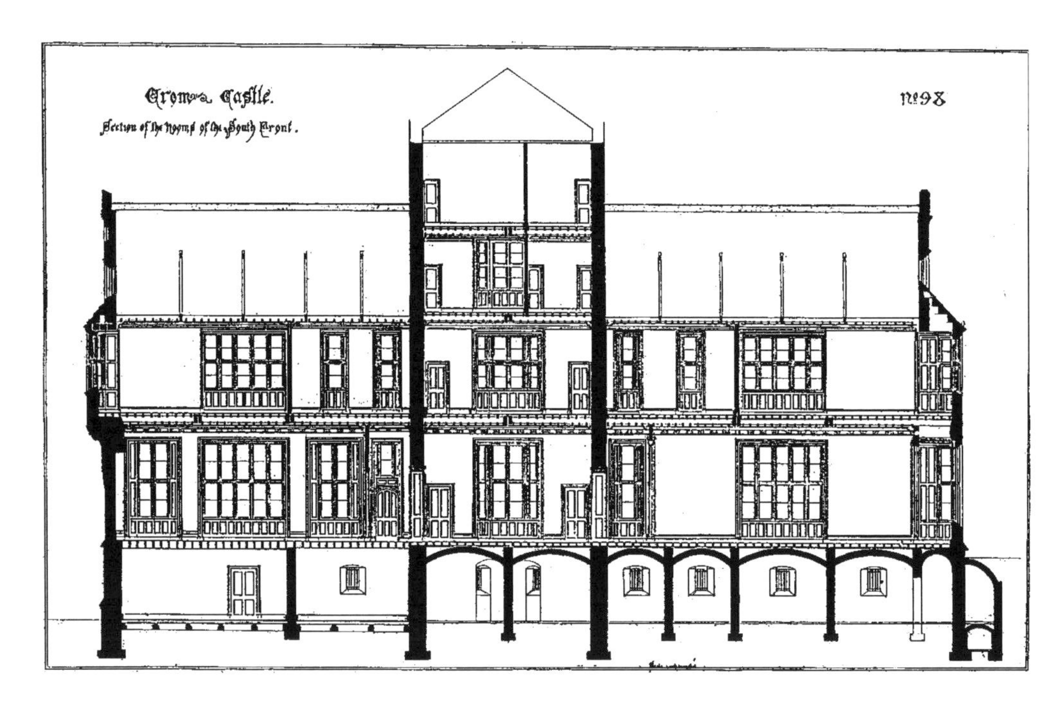

Fig 15. Section through the south front showing the principal rooms. Drawing based on Edward Blore (PRONI-Erne Papers)

ever having to appear in the staircase-hall.

The rooms of the family wing were linked by a service corridor on both floors with a connecting private staircase. Colonel Creighton's bedroom and adjacent dressing room together with a bathroom lay on the principal floor, while the other bedrooms, plus a children's room, lay on the chamber floor. Following 18th-century practice, most of these rooms had adjacent dressing rooms. Guest rooms were placed in the main block, while the servants quarters were confined to much more cramped rooms in the least favourable east side of the house.

Following the formulae seen at Camperdown and at many later Burn houses such as Muckross (1839), the two-storey kitchen was placed on the entrance front and linked to the dining room's servery by a basement passage under the hall.[52] This arrangement ensured that kitchen smells did not enter the kitchen apartments, though the distance involved meant that it did not always make for hot meals. One solution to this problem was to place the dining room on the north side of the hall and thereby nearer the kitchen; but this compromised the privacy of family meals. Consequently, at Crom, as at Camperdown and many other Burn houses, this room north of the entrance hall was occupied, instead, by the billiard room, with the servant's hall below. Most of the other basement rooms, such as various larders, scullery, dairy and butler's room, were grouped around the service court, while much of the area beneath the main block, being unlit, was filled with cellars.

Outbuildings

In conjunction with the house, Blore was also engaged to design some of the ancillary demesne buildings of which some brief mention should be made. Foremost among these was the stable block, which Blore located out of sight, some 120m directly north of the house. As a rule, Blore's stable yard designs, which usually matched the style of the house, were more concerned with convenience and cost, rather than producing magnificent architectural displays.[53] This was the case at Crom, where it followed a standardised plan of a quadrangle with arched entrance containing accommodation for 20 horses in loose boxes and stables, plus carriage houses, harness and cleaning rooms, fodder stores and staff quarters. The yard was built in 1833-1835 by John Clarke of Clones, Co. Monaghan, at a cost of £2,230.12.7d, though to cut costs a number of features in Blore's original plan, notably a cupola, were never built.[54]

Fig 16. Plan of the basement of Crom Castle. Drawing by Edward Blore (Courtesy of the Irish Architectural Archive)

On the south side of the demesne close to the shore of Lough Erne a large

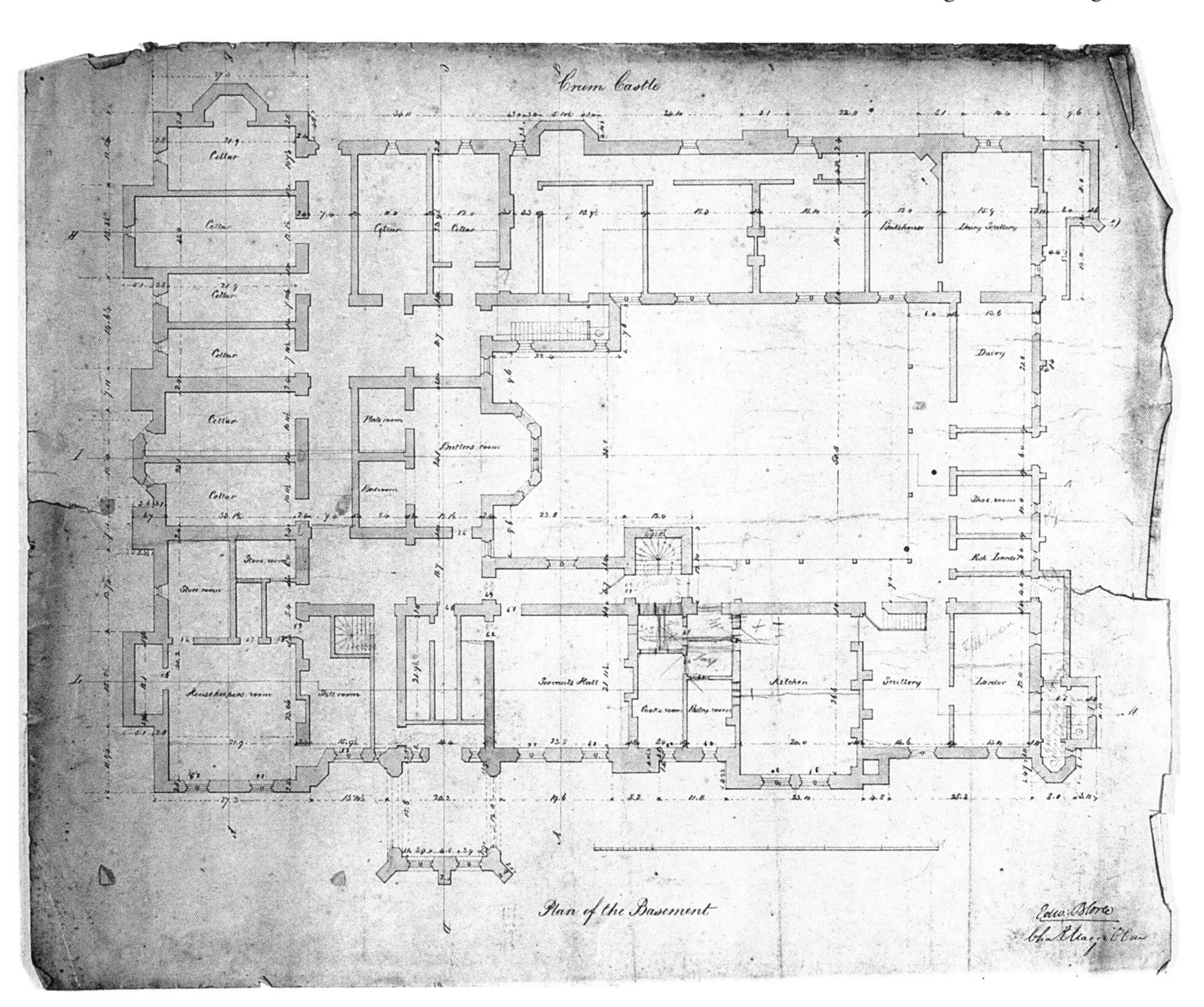

rectangular farm yard was also designed by Blore and built in 1835-1837. It's front façade closely resembles the stable yard, but being a farm yard this complex has witnessed many subsequent alterations, notably in the 1850s when it was converted into a showpiece model farm. Elsewhere a gable-ended turf house with round-headed openings along one side was built in the late 1830s to Blore's design. He also designed two gate lodges, one being at the main entrance and the other across the other side of the lough at Mullynacoagh. The latter is a pretty Tudor-style building with an unusual L-shaped plan, whose the entrance porch projects at 45 degrees from the internal corner. Elaborate wooden gothic gates were also designed by Blore for this lodge, but these have long gone. The main gate lodge, which is identical on plan to a lodge Blore designed for Ballydrain, Co. Antrim, is an irregular 1.5-storey picturesque cottage with two main gables and serrated bargeboards.[55] Both lodges cost £600 to build, but none of Blore's original drawings or specifications have survived.

The 1841 Fire

Blore's great house at Crom had been finished for just about two and half years when tragedy struck. Due to 'an insufficiency of mason work around the flue of a stove to protect timber' a fire took hold of the building on 11 January 1841 and reduced much of the house to a shell.[56] Colonel Creighton was summoned from England and found when he arrived that 'providence had been pleased to leave me a sufficient portion for a dwelling'. That surviving portion was the family or west wing, while the remainder suffered 'almost total destruction'.

When Edward Blore heard about the fire he set about gathering all of his drawings, no doubt in the expectation that he would be asked to rebuild.[57] In the event, Blore's tender was rejected in favour of a relatively unknown Dublin architect, George Sudden.[58] The reason was undoubtedly based on cost, for Sudden charged only £100 for his work over two years, much less than the 5 per cent commission that Blore normally charged.[59] However, the rebuilding followed Blore's original specifications exactly, with only a few modifications, such as the building of two large water tanks in the service yard. Charles McGibbon returned with a contract for £9980, while the Trotter firm was again engaged to supply the furniture, though their bill this time around was only £1,997.13.4d, perhaps suggesting that much of the original furniture had been saved from the fire. The prominent Dublin firm of William Jones also supplied furniture, valued at £256,[60] while Willement replaced the lost 'painted glass' in the staircase hall bow for £268 – rather more than his original bill. In all the total bill for rebuilding and furnishing came to £14,843.[61]

During the rebuilding a row erupted over the financing of the work. A sum of £10,000 was expected from fire insurance; but it was clear at an early stage that this was not going to be enough. Colonel Creighton, it would appear, decided to make an application to the 'committee of the lunatic' for money out of the 'lunatic' second Earl's funds. This provoked an angry response from some members and his application was rejected. Shortly afterwards in 1842 the 'mad Earl' died and his assets were divided among the family. Colonel Creighton accordingly became the third Earl of Erne and in the following year work on his house at Crom was finally completed.

Conclusion

The principal challenge for a country house architect in the 1830s was to achieve a balance between the requisite early Victorian demands for comfort, privacy and social segregation with the aesthetic requirement for a romantic exterior that embraced the qualities of picturesque design. There is little doubt that Edward Blore brilliantly mastered this objective at Crom. He successfully combined the rationalist principals of practical and rectilinear planning as developed by William Burn, with a dramatic castellated Tudor Manor House-style composition of towers, turrets, gables, bays and oriels, whose contrasting masses of light and shade beautifully integrates with Gilpin's surrounding picturesque landscape.

Blore's country house practice in Ireland was largely confined to Crom, though he did accept two smaller commissions at the same time.[62] As a rule, British-based architects tended to limit any involvement in Ireland prior to the advent of the railways. Travel problems aside, there was a belief that an Irish workforce could be, as Blore himself stated 'very difficult people to deal with'. It's possible that Crom did influence some local architects, for example at nearby Castle Saunderson – but, in truth, the house needs to be understood more in the context of the evolving demands of English and Scottish country house building and, in particular, against the background of Blore's other works. Unfortunately, few of his houses have yet to be analysed in any detail and no comprehensive study of his work has been undertaken. From the evidence at Crom and indeed Alupka, it is clear that Blore's rather poor reputation as an architect needs to be reassessed.

ACKNOWLEDGEMENTS

This paper is based on material assembled during a detailed study of Crom Demesne in 1987 for the National Trust. I am grateful to the Earl and Countess of Erne for allowing access to the family papers at that time (since deposited in the Public Reference Office Northern Ireland).

NOTES

1. See Brett, C.E.B. 2000. 'Alupka Palace, Crimea'. *Country Life*, Vol. 196, No.30 (July 25th), pp.74-79; Brett, C.E.B. 2001. 'Letter from Alupka'. *Times Literary Supplement*, No. 5144, p.19.
2. Colvin, H. M. 1995. *A Biographical Dictionary of British Architects 1600-1840.* New Haven and London, Yale University Press for the Paul Mellon Centre for Studies in British Art, p.130.
3. Goodhart-Rendel, H.S. 1963. in Peter Ferriday (ed.), *Victorian Architecture. An Age Revisited.* London, Jonathan Cape, p.57.
4. The main body of material exists in the Erne Papers, deposited in the Public Records Office of Northern Ireland (D/1939). This includes 211 architectural drawings, of which 111 are by Blore himself. There are further drawings in the British Museum, Add. Mss (BM.42027, ff.101-2 and 42029, f.117); the Cambridge University Library, Add. Mss (CUL 3954, f.51,59,56, ff.15,67) and in the Collection of the Royal Institute of British Architects, (RIBA, J2/4, ff.1-8). There are some 24 drawings, of which 4 are by Blore and 16 copies of Blore drawings, in the Irish Architectural Archive, Dublin; this batch came from the office of William G. Murray (Nos. 270-288) who undertook work on the house in 1861. For the Murray drawings see Goslin, B. 1990. *A History and Descriptive Catalogue of the Murray Collection of Architectural Drawings in the Collection of the Royal Institute of the Architects of Ireland.* Dublin, National University of Ireland, M.A. Thesis
5. The late Gervase Jackson-Stops published two well written articles on the house in 1988 titled 'Crom Castle, Co. Fermanagh – 1 & II' in *County Life*, 182: 26th May and 2 June, pp.182-5, 144-147. Data for these papers derived from a detailed survey of the demesne undertaken by the present author for the National Trust in 1987, see Reeves-Smyth, T. 1989. *Crom Castle Demesne.* 2 Vols. National Trust, Unpublished.
6. Knockballymore, built by the Ward family post 1718, was inherited by the first Earl Erne in 1792.
7. Crom was spelt 'Crum' until the mid-19th century and is still pronounced Crum. The Creighton family changed the spelling of their name to Crichton around 1870. The third earl, who succeeded in 1842, was the first to use the title 'Earl of Erne', as opposed to 'Earl Erne'.
8. Weston Park in Warwickshire was built between 1826 and 1830 for Sir George Philips, a Whig M.P whose family made their fortune in textiles. Weston was demolished in 1934.
9. Girouard, M. 1971. *The Victorian County House.* London, p.12. Statement not included in second edition, 1979. *The Victorian Country House. Revised and Enlarged Edition.* London and New Haven, Yale University Press.
10. Blore began rebuilding Lambeth Palace in 1828 – a contract won on the recommendation of the second Earl Spencer. This work continued until 1848 (C.U.L Add. Mss 3928-34). There are some striking similarities between his work here and Crom, especially in use of embryo machicolations.
11. In addition there were numerous rectories, town houses, farm and stable blocks, lodges and

monuments. Blore also advised on a further twenty-four country houses where he was never awarded the commission. These figures from Mellor, H.D. 1974. *Blore's Country Houses.* Thesis submitted to the Courtauld Institute, London, pp.2-3. A number more Blore buildings can now be added to Mellor's useful lists, so this figure can be revised upwards by at least ten per cent. The figures compare not unfavourably with William Burn's remarkable output prior to his partnership with Bryce in 1841.

12. Leconfield, M and J. Gore (eds.) 1955. *Three Howard Sisters. Selections from the Writings of Lady Caroline Lascelles, Lady Dover and the Countess Gower 1825-33.* London, John Murray, p.156. See also Cornforth, J. 1968. 'Trentham, Staffordshire, IV'. *Country Life*, Vol. CXLIII, p.120.
13. Worsley in Lancashire was built for Lord Francis Egerton between 1840-5. It was demolished just after the Second World War.
14. The costs, partly covered by the sale of the Brighton Pavilion, were reduced from £150,000 to £106,000. The major part of this work was the east wing completed in 1847, though its famous façade facing down the Mall had to be refaced in 1913, as the French stone that Blore used was deteriorating in the London air. See Harris J. 1968. *Buckingham Palace.* London, Nelson. Blore was offered a knighthood on completion of his work at the Palace, but declined., see his obituary in the *Proceedings of the Society of Antiquaries*, Vol. 8, p.347.
15. Worsley was visited sixty-one times between 1839 and 1843. In 1838 he inspected work in progress on sixteen country houses, quite apart from visits to other projects, see Meller, *op.cit.*, p.20. In a letter to Creighton dated 9th July 1830, Blore stated that 'allowance for travelling expenses is currently at the rate of posting, but I have made it practice to charge only half that amount, that is 9d per mile to cover all expenses'. In the same letter Blore insisted that 'I cannot now too thoroughly press the point' that 'the workforce in great measure depends upon the efficiency and honesty of the person placed in charge' and argued that his chosen clerk-of-works at Crom should receive £2.12.3d a week, as he had proved to be intelligent and honest and 'should consider his services worth more than that particularly in such a case as the building of Crum Castle where he will have very difficult people to deal with' (Erne Papers).
16. *C.U.L. Add.* Mss. 3954, f.51; 3956, ff.15, 40 & 41. Round trips to Crom, estimated at 860 miles, cost £32.5.0d.
17. There were occasions however, when Blore used the old day labour system, for example at Haveringland Hall in Norfolk, see Wilson. R. 2000. 'Building two Victorian country houses: Haveringland and Brodsworth' in Airs, M (ed.) *The Victorian Country House.* Oxford, Oxford University Department for Continuing Education, pp.106-115. For the importance of the new contract system, see also Girouard, 1979, *op.cit.*, p.17.
18. Meller, *op.cit.*, p.30. Canford (Wimborne) was built in 1824-1836 for William Ponsonby, created Lord de Mauley. Afterwards, much altered and enlarged by Barry for John Guest, the Iron King.
19. The chimney-piece design is in the Print Room of the V & A (8752, f.1).
20. In Ireland the Morrisons also often repeated designs from one house to another. For example, the gate lodges and or gates at Ballyfin, Fota, Langford Lodge, Killruddery, Castle Coole (unexecuted) and Baronscourt (unexecuted) are all much the same. McParland, E, Rowan, A and Rowan, A.M. 1989. *The Architecture of Richard Morrison and William Vitruvius Morrison.* Dublin, The Irish Architectural Archive.
21. Many examples of which are in the RIBA Drawings Collection. His watercolours of Goodrich

Court in Herefordshire are good examples. See Harris, J. 1985. *The Architect and the British Country House 1620-1920.* Washington, The American Institute of Architects Foundation, pp.204-6; Worsley, G. 1991. *Architectural Drawings of the Regency Period 1790-1837. From the Drawings Collection of the Royal Institute of British Architects.* London, Deutsch, p.56.

22. Colvin, 1995. *op.cit.*, pp.129-135. Edward Blore's father, Thomas Blore (1764-1818) was a Derby solicitor, who published eight books between 1807-18.
23. Abbotsford is wrongly attributed to Blore in his obituary published in the *Builder*, Vol. 37 (13 September 1879), p.1019. He produced elevations for the house, now lost, but a watercolour of his proposal still survives at Abbotsford.
24. See Eastlake, C. 1872. *A History of the Gothic Revival. An Attempt to show how the taste for Medieval architecture which lingered in England during the last two centuries has since been encouraged and developed.* London, Longmans, Green & Co. Reprinted Leicester University Press, 1970 & 1978, p.138.
25. Meller, *op.cit.*, p.111.
26. See Girouard, M. 1968 'Attitudes to Elizabethan architecture 1600-1900' in Summerson, J (ed.) *Concerning Architecture. Essays on architectural writers and writings. Presented to Sir Nicholas Pevsner.* London, Allen Lane, The Penguin Press; Pevsner, N. 1972. *Some Architectural Writers of the Nineteenth Century.* Oxford, Oxford University Press, p.83; Brooks, C. 1999. *The Gothic Revival.* London, Phaidon, pp.186-193; Mowl, T. 1993. *Elizabethan Jacobean Style.* London, Phaidon, pp.195-226.
27. The term 'Jacobethan' was invented by Sir John Betjeman to cover the stylistic range (*Ghastly Good Taste*, 1933). However, there are dangers with this term, not least that it implies some stylistic unity for the whole period, see Mowl. 1993., *op.cit*, p.195.
28. Mandler, P. 1997. *The Fall and Rise of the Stately House.* New Haven and London, Yale University Press, pp.40-54; 64-6.
29. McParland, Rowan and Rowan, 1989, *op.cit.*
30. Aside from the Morrison's work, the earliest attempts at Tudor Manorial revivalism in Ireland would appear to be J.B. Keane's Belleek Manor (1825), Castle Irvine (1831), Magheramena (1835-39), Camlin (1838); Thomas Rickman's Lough Fea (1825-7); the Pain brother's Castle Bernard (1833); Thomas Duff's Narrow Water (1836); Daniel Robertson's Carrigglas (1837-42), William Playfair's Brownlow House (1833-42); Frederick Darley's Coolbawn (c.1835) and Thomas Cobden's Ballykelly (c.1835).
31. Built in collaboration with the owner, the famous antiquarian and genealogist Evelyn Philip Shirley (1812-82).
32. Projects with both Blore and Burn seem to have began with such small scale pen-and-ink sketches, usually without elevations. A watercolour perspective was usually also supplied at this stage. They served as the basis for discussion with the client before final instructions were issued.
33. The roof frame used was the Queen Post truss with 'best duchess' slates.
34. For a useful account of Brownlow see Brett, C.E.B. 1999. *Buildings of County Armagh.* Belfast, Ulster Architectural Heritage Society, pp.100-102; see also Gow. I. 1991. 'William Playfair's design for a "Roman Villa" at Lurgan'. *Architectural Heritage*, Volume 2, pp.79-83. Charles McGibbon continued working at Brownlow until it was completed in 1842. He was subsequently engaged with his brother John by the architect William Murray as the contractor

for Castle Dillon in Co. Armagh, see Brett, 1999, *op.cit.*, pp.109-110.

35. Bamford, F. 1983. A Dictionary of Edinburgh Wrights and Furniture Makers 1660-1840. London, Furniture History Society; Gow, Ian (1988) 'New light on late Trotter', in *Country Life*, 182: 100-103 (No.32); Wedgwood, A. 1994. 'Domestic Architecture' in Atterbury P and Wainwright C (eds.) *Pugin. A Gothic Passion*, London and New Haven, Yale University Press and The Victoria and Albert Museum, pp.43-61.
36. Unfortunately it lacks the 'ACP' initials so frequently found on Pugin's drawings.
37. Sewell and Cross were a well known firm of London drapers at the junction of Old Compton Street and Frith Street. James Duppa was a London based 'paper stainer'.
38. The firm of William Manser was based at 27 Wardour Street, London. Established in the late 18th century it made a wide range of Tudor and Jacobean style furniture, mostly in oak.
39. Drawings of the ceilings and their delicately coloured patterns survive for the library, dining room and saloon in the Erne papers. The library (now the drawing room) ceiling has been removed. The colouring scheme appears to have derived from Blore's office.
40. Thomas Willement (1786-1871) had his workshop at Green Street, Grosvenor Square. Other work by him in Ireland includes oriels in the gallery at Adare Manor and widows in both the village's Protestant and Roman Catholic churches.
41. Meller, *op.cit.*, p.71, notes that the Worsley drawings in the R.I.B.A show the bathroom hot water was heated in the room beneath it and had the additional luxury of a cane seated vapour bath attached.
42. The old castle was extended on both flanks in 1831-2 by sham ruins, incorporating two towers and walls with loop holes, all clearly intended to be seen as an eye-catcher from the house It was given an entrances with blocked surrounds and the whole ensemble was incorporated into a newly built terraced garden facing the lough. The sham ruins were further enlarged in 1853.
43. He illustrated his father's book *A Guide to Burghley House, Northamptonshire* published in Stamford in 1815.
44. Although Blore had retired in 1849, he was still in correspondence with the third Earl of Erne on this matter in 1851.
45. Significantly he had just designed the parterre for Weston, a very similar house to Crom. Some other examples include Merevale (Warwicks.), Crewe Hall (Cheshire), Latimers (Bucks.), Worsley (Lancs.) and the Grove (Herts.). Nesfield was also closely tied to the work of William Burn and Antony Salvin, his brother-in-law, see Elliott, B. 1996. 'Nesfield in his Victorian Context' in Ridgeway, C (ed.) *William Andrews Nesfield. Victorian Landscape Architect.* York, The University of York, pp.9-14. Nesfield's only positively known work in Ireland is at Lyrath, Co. Kilkenny, see Nelson, C. 1985. *Garden History.* Vol. 13 (2), pp.156-8.
46. Piebenga, S. 1994. 'William Sawrey Gilpin (1763-1843): Picturesque Improver'. *Garden History*, Vol. 22. No. 2 (Winter), pp.175-196. Gilpin would have understood Picturesque to mean: *'roughness of texture, irregularity, asymmetry, variety, partial concealment, the unexpected and particularly the impression that everything was of natural occurrence, even though it might be artificially contrived.* Appleton, J. 1986. 'Some thoughts on the geology of the picturesque'. *Journal of Garden History*, Vol. 6, p.279.
47. Kerr, R. 1864. *The Gentleman's House. How to Plan English Residences from Parsonage to Palace.* London, John Murray, p.67.
48. Walker, D. 2000. 'William Burn'. In Airs, M (ed.) *The Victorian Country House.* Oxford,

Oxford University Department for Continuing Education, pp.32-50.

49. Rowan, A. 1979. *North West Ulster.* London, Penguin Books, pp.222-3.
50. The device of staircase tapering was used by Blore in other houses, for example in the hall at Great Moreton (1840-6) in Cheshire. The staircase lantern fenestration and ceiling appear to have been based on a plate XIV in T.F. Hunt, 1830. *Exemplars of Tudor Architecture. Adopted to Modern Habitation,* London, Longman, Rees, Orme and Green.
51. Most of the glass panels were removed in the 1960s, but are kept safely in the house.
52. Walker, *op.cit.*, p.42.
53. Meller, *op.cit.*, pp.61-2.
54. Blore's original plans do not survive. Two tenders for the yard were submitted in March 1833, one being from Mr. Henry of Dublin for £3,569 and the other from John Clarke of Clones for £2,172.9.4d. The adjacent forge yard was built in 1837-43, but not to a Blore design.
55. Dean, J.A.K. 1994. *The Gate Lodges of Ulster.* Belfast, Ulster Architectural Heritage Society, p.106. Dean reproduces Blore's drawing of the gates at Mullynacoagh.
56. *The Enniskillen Chronicle and Erne Packet,* January 14th, 1841; Erne Papers (PRONI).
57. At least one working drawing was sent by McGibbon in Edinburgh to Blore in London on April 6th 1841.
58. George Sudden apparently designed the boat house at Crom, showing him to have been an accomplished architect. It's possible he also designed the church at Crom, which as consecrated in 1842. A few years after the completion of his work at Crom in 1844, Sudden was recorded as working at Lough Fea, Co. Monaghan. A number of buildings often wrongly accredited to Blore, notably Castle Saunderson, Co. Cavan, are possibly by Sudden.
59. In 1835-7 Blore was paid £1,000 'for plans & &', plus an additional £169, presumably for expenses.
60. There are at least forty furniture drawings in the Erne Papers, mostly of good quality, signed by Arthur Jones of Stephen's Green. For a brief summary of the firm's history, see Glin, Knight of. 1985. Dublin Directories and trade labels' in *Furniture History,* Vol. 21, pp.258-82.
61. Other expenses included £223 for 'French silk paper'; £116 to the furniture makers Miles and Edwards of Oxford Street; £72 for a billiard table; £50 for 'Binnie iron doors'; £37 for 'McCullagh marble'; £165 for 'blinds and bells'; £244 to an Edinburgh painter and £830 for a 'plate glass ceiling'.
62. Blore's other Irish works include the building of a house and gate lodge for Hugh Montgomery at Ballydrain, Co. Antrim, 1836-8 on the site of an earlier dwelling. It's a variation of the Tudor-Cotswold style that Blore pioneered at Corehouse in 1824 (R.I.B.A Jul. March 1945, 3rd Series, No.5; C.U.L. Add. Mss. 3956, f.40; V & A, 182r; PRONI-D1954/7/2; Black, E. 'Ballydrain, Dunmurry – An estate through the ages', Vol. 5, *Lisburn Historical Society*); At Castle Upton, Co. Antrim, Blore remodelled the house and added a grand castellated gatehouse in 1836-8 for 1st Lord Templetown (B.M. 42028, ff.35-36; C.U.L, Add. Mss. 3956, f.41; V & A. 8713, ff.1-9); Blore also designed a central tower for Mallow Castle, Co. Cork for D. Jephson in 1837 (C.U.L. Add. Mss. 3956, f.49). It's also possible that Blore was responsible for the Jacobean style stable block c.1838-40 at Antrim Castle.

TWO KINDS OF KNOWLEDGE: SOME INFORMATION RESOURCES FOR ULSTER ARCHITECT USE

KAREN LATIMER

ON TUESDAY 11 APRIL 1775 the indefatigable Dr. Johnson was dining with James Boswell, Sir Joshua Reynolds and Richard Cambridge at the latter's 'beautiful villa on the banks of the Thames, near Twickenham'.[1] No sooner had Dr. Johnson arrived (late) than he rushed across the library to pore over his host's collection of books. When Mr. Cambridge commented on this slightly odd behaviour, Johnson answered:

> *Sir, the reason is very plain. Knowledge is of two kinds. We know a subject ourselves, or we know where we can find information upon it. When we enquire into any subject, the first thing we have to do is to know what books have treated of it. This leads us to look at catalogues, and the backs of books in libraries.*[2]

Although no doubt there have long been individuals with immense knowledge of Ulster architecture, it is only relatively recently that a body of published material has come into being and even more recently that any serious attempt has been made to provide useful finding tools to ease the way of researchers into Dr. Johnson's second kind of knowledge.

Charles Brett[3] recounts that when, in 1956 and at the age of twenty seven, he was invited by Lord Antrim to join the Northern Ireland Committee of the National Trust, he eagerly asked what books on Irish architecture he should read to equip him for the task. When a rather astonished Lord Antrim told him that there were no books, the young Brett resolved to write them himself. As can be seen from the select bibliography of his work (elsewhere in this volume), this he has indeed in large measure done.

Some ten years later an architecture student, Marcus Patton, embarking on a course of architecture at Queen's University was discovering from his studies 'that [in Northern Ireland] we had no architecture, that medieval cathedrals only occurred in France or Italy, Wren churches happened in London, and that Georgian architecture came no closer than Dublin'.[4] When he returned to Belfast to continue his studies after his 'year out' in Oxford, he discovered that Brett's

Buildings of Belfast [5] had been published and 'the novel idea that there might be any architecture in grimy old Belfast'[6] had been well and truly planted. By the time Marcus Patton settled permanently in Ulster in 1978 as Director of Hearth, the body of literature on local architecture had expanded considerably, and he himself was to make a valuable contribution to it.

The year 1967 was important for dissemination of information on Ulster architecture, both because of the publication of Brett's *Belfast* and also because it was in that year that the Ulster Architectural Heritage Society (U.A.H.S.) was founded. The publishing programme of this all-purpose pressure group has been impressive indeed. Its surveys and lists of buildings of architectural and historic importance not only shamed Government into introducing legislation[7] to identify, protect and provide grant aid for buildings, but also formed the basis for the early official lists. (These lists are, in themselves, a very useful source of Ulster architecture and are now available online.[8]) In addition to over thirty lists and surveys, the U.A.H.S. has published numerous books on various aspects of architecture in the Province. Subjects covered include building types such as schools, classical churches, gatelodges and workhouses; studies of individual buildings such as Malone House, Ballywalter Park and Parliament Buildings Stormont; the work of individual architects and patrons such as Roger Mulholland, J.J. McCarthy and the Earl Bishop of Derry and more wide ranging treatises on the history of architecture in Ulster and specifically on modern architecture. The band of authors who have been published by the U.A.H.S. certainly qualify as possessors of Dr. Johnson's first kind of knowledge: Charles Brett, James Stevens Curl, Kimmitt (Dixie) Dean, Hugh Dixon, David Evans, Paul Larmour, Dick Oram, Marcus Patton, Peter Rankin, Alistair Rowan and Jeanne Sheehy have all contributed hugely to an understanding of the history of buildings in Ulster.

What of the second kind of knowledge? Where are the finding tools, the secondary sources that lead researchers to the information they need? International and national bibliographies and databases such as APId[9] and Avery[10] rarely include more than the most obvious references to Irish material. Hayes's *Sources for the history of Irish civilisation*[11] is a very useful but highly selective reference tool. In 1988 Dr. Edward McParland published 'A bibliography of Irish architectural history' in *Irish Historical Studies*[12] which included items published between 1900 and 1986 covering the history of architecture in Ireland between the late 17th and early 20th centuries. It is a mine of information with an interesting introduction in which the author examines the growth in the number of publications per decade. He points out that this doubles every decade. As the trend appears to be continuing, this could make the publication of a supplement a somewhat daunting prospect. The Architecture and Planning Library at Queen's University, Belfast maintained for some years a select bibliography of books in stock on Irish architecture. It also keeps lists of postgraduate dissertations carried out by students of the Schools of Architecture and Planning which can be useful guides for researchers. These have now been superseded to some extent by PADDI, Planning Architecture Design Database Ireland, described below.

One way of tackling an enormous task is to break it down into more digestible chunks, and this is what Carol Bardon[13] has done in her extremely useful index of references to the work of Barre, Drew, Jackson, W.H. Lynn and the practice of Lanyon, Lynn and Lanyon which were published in the *Dublin/Irish Builder* between 1859 and 1909. The *Irish Builder* is an invaluable source of information, but is poorly indexed. Apart from Bardon, Hayes and McParland, the most concerted attempt to index the *Irish Builder* has been made by the Irish Architectural Archive.

The diligent thirster after knowledge will ferret out sources of information on Ulster architecture from many sources – the catalogues and calendars of the main libraries and holders of archive collections, north and south of the border; the bibliographies included in the growing number of books and journal articles on the subject; and some or all of the tools described above. But in the post-Johnsonian era, rushing across the room to examine the backs of books in the libraries of one's acquaintances (however pleasurable a pursuit) is not enough. The modern researcher wants to have access to all the necessary information without having to move from his or her desk. To Dr. Johnson's list of 1775, we in the 21st century can now add looking at electronic information sources. But, of course, there are myriads of these, and the aforementioned modern researcher wants the definitive one-stop shop database.

In the early 1990s the architecture and planning libraries at Queen's University Belfast and University College Dublin (hereafter referred to as Q.U.B. and U.C.D.) decided to collaborate on a project to pool resources on Irish architectural information. The full story of the project has been told elsewhere[14,15] although perhaps the unexpurgated version has still to be unveiled. In the early days, what is now the PADDI database existed as two stand-alone Filemaker Pro databases located at Q.U.B. and U.C.D. The databases were extremely popular with students, researchers and practitioners, but there were obvious problems. The main one, of course, was access. In the era of desktop use of electronic resources, it was no longer good enough to provide access only to people who could come into the two participating libraries. Also, the creators of the database were aware that there was a great deal of duplication of effort in identifying and entering material. A third factor in moving on to a new phase in the development of the resource was the need to bring in other key organisations to contribute both material and expertise to the project.

Appropriately enough it was in the first year of the new millennium that the new project – to establish PADDI as a web-based resource for Irish architectural and planning information – got under way. The Ulster Architectural Heritage Society, the Irish Architectural Archive, the Environment and Heritage Service, Planning Service, the Royal Society of Ulster Architects and the Royal Institution of the Architects of Ireland agreed to contribute to the project and nominated representatives to join the Board. PADDI[16] was launched in the newly restored Great Hall at Queen's (and subsequently in the Memorial Hall, U.C.D.) in June 2002.[17]

The database already contains more than 17,000 entries referencing books, parts of books, journal articles, reports, theses, planning documents and other material on all aspects of architecture and planning in Ireland. In addition to the bibliographic database, there are links to other useful sites and a directory of collections in Ireland relevant to researchers in the field. These include amongst others the Belfast City Council Building Control Archive, the Environment and Heritage Service Monuments and Buildings Record, the Irish Architectural Archive, the Public Record Office of Northern Ireland and the photographic collections of the Ulster Museum.

Dr. Johnson may have 'shewed upon all occasions an aversion to go to Ireland'[18] and dismissed the Giant's Causeway as 'Worth seeing? yes; but not worth going to see'[19] long before the current controversy began.[20] Had he had access to some of the books in print today or been led to them by the information tools available to the researchers of the 21st century, he might perhaps have changed his mind and toured Ireland after all.

NOTES

1. Malone, E. and Boswell, J. 1811. *The Life of Samuel Johnson*, 6th ed, Vol. 2, p.686. London, Marshall Hamilton Kent & Co. Ltd.
2. *Ibid*, 689.
3. Brett, C. E. B. Autobiographical literary and autobibliographical notes. Private

communication.

4. Patton, M. 1998. 'Conservation in Northern Ireland since 1969'. ASCHB: *Association for Studies in the Conservation of Historic Buildings Transactions*, 23, pp. 3-14.
5. Brett, C. E. B. 1967. *Buildings of Belfast 1700-1914*. London, Weidenfeld and Nicholson.
6. Patton, *op cit.*, p.6.
7. Great Britain. Northern Ireland. 1972. *The Planning (Northern Ireland) Order 1972.* Statutory Instruments, 1972, No. 1034 (N.I. 7). Belfast, HMSO. (Now updated by the 1991 Order.)
8. http://www.ehsni.gov.uk/BuiltHeritage/
9. *Architectural Publications Index on disc.* RIBA Publications, 1978 –
10. *Avery Index to Architectural Periodicals.* G.K. Hall, Getty Art History Information Program, 1994 –
11. Hayes, R. 1970. *Sources for the History of Irish Civilisation: Articles in Irish Periodicals*, 9v. Boston.
12. McParland, E. 1988. 'A bibliography of Irish architectural history'. *Irish Historical Studies*, 26, No. 102, pp.161-212.
13. Bardon, C. 1998. *An Illustrated Index of References to W.J. Barre, Thomas Drew, Thomas Jackson, Lanyon, Lynn and Lanyon and W.H. Lynn in Dublin Builder 1859-1866 and Irish Builder 1867-1909.* Unpublished diploma assignment, Queen's University Belfast.
14. Barrett, J. and Latimer, K. 1998. 'PADDI: the development of a joint database on planning and architecture in Ireland'. *ARCLIB Bulletin*, No. 8, pp.8-10.
15. Latimer, K. 2000. 'The Irishness of Irish architectural provision: the PADDI database'. *Art Libraries Journal*, 25, No. 3, pp.25-28.
16. http://www.paddi.net
17. 2002. 'Cross-border venture puts PADDI on the web'. *Perspective*, 11, No. 4, p.10.
18. Malone and Boswell, *op cit.*, Vol. 2, p.353.
19. *Ibid.*
20. 2002. 'Conflict over Causeway future coming to a close'. *Newsletter*, 5 February, pp.16-17.

SELECT BIBLIOGRAPHY OF WORKS BY C.E.B. BRETT 1964-2003

KAREN LATIMER

THE BIBLIOGRAPHY IS ARRANGED in chronological order within four sections – books, contributions to edited works, journal articles and unpublished documents. Where a work is jointly authored, Brett has been listed first in order to maintain the chronological sequence. The only exception to this arrangement is the pseudonymously authored work by Albert Rechts which appears, in alphabetical order, at the end of the books section.

In addition to the publications listed in the following bibliography, Charles Brett has written articles for the Northern Ireland Labour Party's monthly journal *The Rising Tide*, as well as being the author of, or contributing to, numerous NILP leaflets, policy statements and election addresses. He has also written occasionally for *The Tribune* and *The Guardian.* While serving for a long period on the Northern Ireland Committee of the National Trust, he was the author (unattributed) of many of its leaflets and guides. In addition, this indefatigable author has written poetry and contributed reviews and comments to many local and national newspapers and architectural journals.

The following bibliography does not contain such unattributable work as is described above but includes all major publications.

Books

Brett C. E. B. 1967. *Buildings of Belfast 1700-1914.* London, Weidenfeld & Nicolson.

Brett C. E. B., Lady Dunleath, Oram R. and Rowan A.J. 1968. *List of Historic Buildings, Groups of Buildings, Areas of Architectural Importance in the Vicinity of Lurgan and Portadown.* Belfast, Ulster Architectural Heritage Society.

Brett C. E. B. and Rowan A. J. 1968. *Ulster Architectural Heritage Society List of Historic Buildings, Groups of Buildings, Buildings of Architectural Importance in the*

Vicinity of the Queen's University of Belfast. Belfast, Ulster Architectural Heritage Society.

Brett C. E. B. and Lady Dunleath. 1969. *List of Historic Buildings, Groups of Buildings, Buildings of Architectural Importance in the Borough of Lisburn.* Belfast, Ulster Architectural Heritage Society.

Brett C. E. B. and Lady Dunleath. 1969. *Ulster Architectural Heritage Society List of Historic Buildings, Groups of Buildings, Areas of Architectural Importance in the Borough of Banbridge.* Belfast, Ulster Architectural Heritage Society.

Brett C. E. B., Bell G. P. and Matthew R. 1969. *Ulster Architectural Heritage Society Survey: With Lists of Historic Buildings, Groups of Buildings, and Buildings of Architectural Importance in and Near Portaferry and Strangford.* Belfast, Ulster Architectural Heritage Society.

Brett C. E. B. 1970. *List of Historic Buildings, Groups of Buildings, Areas of Architectural Importance in the Town of Monaghan.* Belfast, Ulster Architectural Heritage Society.

Brett C. E. B. and McKinstry R. 1971. *Survey and Recommendations for the Joy Street and Hamilton Street District of Belfast.* Belfast, Ulster Architectural Heritage Society.

Brett C. E. B. 1972. *Historic Buildings, Groups of Buildings, Areas of Architectural Importance in the Glens of Antrim.* Belfast, Ulster Architectural Heritage Society.

Brett C. E. B. 1973. *Court Houses and Market Houses of the Province of Ulster.* Belfast, Ulster Architectural Heritage Society.

Brett C. E. B. 1973. *Historic Buildings, Groups of Buildings, Areas of Architectural Importance in the Towns and Villages of East Down.* Belfast, Ulster Architectural Heritage Society.

Brett C. E. B. 1974. *Historic Buildings, Groups of Buildings, Areas of Architectural Importance in the Island of Rathlin.* Belfast, Ulster Architectural Heritage Society.

Brett C. E. B. 1974. *Historic Buildings, Groups of Buildings, Areas of Architectural Importance in the Towns and Villages of Mid Down.* Belfast, Ulster Architectural Heritage Society.

Brett C. E. B. 1975. *Buildings in the Town and Parish of St Peter Port.* Belfast, Ulster Architectural Heritage Society for the National Trust of Guernsey.

Brett C. E. B. 1976. *Buildings of the Island of Alderney.* Belfast, Ulster Architectural Heritage Society for the Alderney Society.

Brett C. E. B. 1976. *Roger Mulholland: Architect, of Belfast, 1740-1818.* Belfast, Ulster Architectural Heritage Society.

Brett C. E. B. 1977. *Buildings in the Town and Parish of St Helier.* Belfast, Ulster Architectural Heritage Society for the National Trust of Jersey.

Brett C. E. B. 1978. *Long Shadows Cast Before: Nine Lives in Ulster, 1625-1977.* Edinburgh, J. Bartholomew.

Brett C. E. B. 1981. *Architectural Schizophrenia.* Belfast, Ulster Architectural Heritage Society.

Brett C. E. B. 1985. *Buildings of Belfast 1700-1914.* 2nd rev ed. Belfast, Friar's Bush Press.

Brett C. E. B. 1986. *Housing a Divided Community.* Dublin, Institute of Public Administration in association with the Institute of Irish Studies, Queen's University of Belfast.

Brett C. E. B. and O'Connell M. 1996. *Buildings of County Antrim.* Belfast, Ulster Architectural Heritage Society and the Ulster Historical Foundation.

Brett C. E. B. 1997. *Five Big Houses of Cushendun and Some Literary Associations.* Belfast, Lagan Press.

Brett C. E. B. and O'Connell M. 1999. *Buildings of County Armagh.* Belfast, Ulster Architectural Heritage Society.

Brett C. E. B. and Merrick A.C.W. 2002. *Buildings of North County Down.* Belfast, Ulster Architectural Heritage Society.

Rechts, Albert (anagrammatic pseudonym). 1986. *Handbook to a Hypothetical City.* Mullingar, Lilliput.

Contributions to edited works

Brett C. E. B. 1967. 'The Edwardian town: Belfast about 1900' in J. C. Beckett and R. E. Glasscock (eds.) *Belfast. The Origin and Growth of an Industrial City*: 120-131. London, BBC.

Brett C. E. B. 1967. 'The Georgian town: Belfast about 1800' in J. C. Beckett and R. E. Glasscock (eds.) *Belfast. The Origin and Growth of an Industrial City*: 67-77. London, BBC.

Brett C. E. B. 1971. 'The architectural heritage' in Michael Longley (ed.) *Causeway. The Arts in Ulster*: 11-27. Belfast, Arts Council of Northern Ireland. Dublin, Gill and Macmillan.

Brett C. E. B. 1985. 'Introduction' in *No Mean City. A Synopsis of Papers Presented to the Conference Organised by the Ulster Architectural Heritage Society at the Ulster Museum, Belfast on Wednesday 3 October 1984*: 1-3. Belfast, Ulster Architectural Heritage Society.

Brett C. E. B. 1989. 'Architect and client: a layman's view' in John Graby (ed.) *150 Years of Architecture in Ireland*: 77. Dublin, Royal Institute of the Architects of Ireland.

Brett C. E. B. 1990. 'Two eighteenth century provincial attorneys: Matthew Brett and Jack Brett' in Daire Hogan and W.N. Osborough (eds.) *Brehons, Serjeants and Attorneys. Studies in the History of the Irish Legal Profession*: 175-179. Blackrock, Irish Academic Press in association with the Irish Legal History Society.

Brett C. E. B. 1992. 'The celestial steam packet' in Agnes Bernelle (ed.) *Decantations. A Tribute to Maurice Craig*: 3-9. Dublin, Lilliput.

Brett C. E. B. 1995. 'The Hall at the Argory' in Gervase Jackson-Stops (ed.) *The National Trust 1895-1995. 100 Great Treasures: 100 Celebrities Select Their Personal Favourites from the Trust's Collections: 18-19.* London, Apollo Magazine Ltd.

Brett C. E. B. 2001. 'Victorian and Edwardian Belfast: preserving the architectural legacy of the inner city' in William J. V. Neill and Hanns-Uve Schwedler (eds.) *Urban Planning and Cultural Inclusion. Lessons from Belfast and Berlin*: 85-99. Basingstoke, Palgrave.

Journal articles

Brett C. E. B. 1964. 'The Legal Aid and Advice Bill (Northern Ireland)'. *Northern Ireland Legal Quarterly*, 15, No. 3: 352-382.

Brett C. E. B. 1970. 'The lessons of devolution in Northern Ireland'. *Political Quarterly*, 41, No. 3: 261-280.

Brett C. E. B. 1971. 'The duty of the architect towards Ulster's architectural heritage'. *RSUA Yearbook and Directory*, 1971/1972: 92-93.

Brett C. E. B. 1974. 'Biographical dictionary of Irish architects: Roger Mulholland'. *Quarterly Bulletin of the Irish Georgian Society*, 17, No. 1/2: 19-21.

Brett C. E. B. 1974. 'Conservation amid destruction'. *Country Life*, 156, No. 4032: 1016-1018.

Brett C. E. B. 1974. 'Ulster's architectural heritage'. *The Architect*, June: 38-42.

Brett C. E. B. 1975. 'Ulster Architectural Heritage Society'. *National Trust Magazine*, No. 22: 16.

Brett C. E. B. 1980. 'Triumph of plush and gilt'. *Country Life*, 168, No. 4344: 1983-1985.

Brett C. E. B. 1982. 'Housing in Northern Ireland'. *Housing Review*, May-June: 75-76.

Brett C. E. B. 1986. 'Belfast: conservation amidst conflict'. *ICOMOS Information*, October-December:15-20.

Brett C. E. B. 1986. 'Sounding board: the future of the common (or garden) gnome'. *Ulster Architect*, May: 25-26

Brett C. E. B. 1990. 'Brett on Belfast: changing Belfast: for better, for worse?' *Ulster Architect*, 7, No. 3: 44-46.

Brett C. E. B. 1990. 'The International Fund for Ireland, 1986-1989'. *Political Quarterly*, 61, No. 4: 431-440.

Brett C. E. B. 1991. 'The design philosophy of the Northern Ireland Housing Executive'. *Ulster Architect*, 7, No. 9: 23-26.

Brett C. E. B. 1991. 'Facadism, and the new Halifax building'. *Ulster Architect*, 7, No. 7: 41-44.

Brett C. E. B. 1991. 'Hearth & home'. *National Trust Magazine*, No. 64: 42-43.

Brett C. E. B. 1992. 'Another view'. *Ulster Architect*, 9, No.11: 52-53.

Brett C. E. B. 1992. 'The environment: the next twenty five years'. *Ulster Architect*, 9, No. 10: 50-51.

Brett C. E. B. 1993. 'Brett on Hong Kong and Macau'. *Ulster Architect*, 11, No. 1: 6-8.

Brett C. E. B. 1993. 'Brett on Sri Lanka'. *Ulster Architect*, 10, No. 10: 10-11.

Brett C. E. B. 1994. 'Brett blows his top'. *Ulster Architect*, 11, No. 2: 10-11.

Brett C. E. B. 1994. 'Brett goes to market'. *Ulster Architect*, 11, No. 3: 4-7.

Brett C. E. B. 1994. 'Brett on castles in Spain'. *Ulster Architect*, 12, No. 1: 4-5.

Brett C. E. B. 1994. 'Brett on John Millar, Architect, of Belfast'. *Ulster Architect*, 11, No. 9: 4-6.

Brett C. E. B. 1994. 'Brett on second thoughts'. *Ulster Architect*, 11, No. 8: 8-9.

Brett C. E. B. 1994. 'Brett on stuffed dummies'. *Ulster Architect*, 11, No. 4: 4-6.

Brett C. E. B. 1994. 'Charles Brett at Galgorm: County Hall revisited'. *Ulster Architect*, 11, No. 6: 12.

Brett C. E. B. 1994. 'Charles Brett on Antrim's new courthouse'. *Ulster Architect*, 11, No. 10: 5-7.

Brett C. E. B. 1994. 'Charles Brett on conservation'. *Ulster Architect*, 11, No. 5: 20-21.

Brett C. E. B. 1994. 'A splendiferous Commission'. *Perspective*, 2, No. 6: 23-27.

Brett C. E. B. 1995. 'Brett goes green'. *Ulster Architect*, 12, No. 2: 4-5.

Brett C. E. B. 1995. 'Brett on Alderney revisited'. *Ulster Architect*, 12, No. 6: 4-5.

Brett C. E. B. 1995. 'Brett on electricity'. *Ulster Architect*, 12, No. 7: 10-11.

Brett C. E. B. 1995. 'Brett on Laganside'. *Ulster Architect*, 12, No. 4: 4-6.

Brett C. E. B. 1995. 'Brett on markets'. *Ulster Architect*, 12, No. 8: 4-5.

Brett C. E. B. 1995. 'Brett on retrospections'. *Ulster Architect*, 12, No.10: 4-5.

Brett C. E. B. 1995. 'Brett on St Brigid's new church, Belfast'. *Ulster Architect*, 12, No. 3: 4-5.

Brett C. E. B. 1995. 'Brett on the Hillsborough Fort controversy'. *Ulster Architect*, 12, No. 5: 8-9.

Brett C. E. B. 1995. 'Brett on the Ordnance Survey Memoirs'. *Ulster Architect*, 12, No. 9: 6-7.

Brett C. E. B. 1995. 'St Brigid's new church, Belfast'. *Architects' Journal*, 12, No. 3: 4-5.

Brett C. E. B. 1996. 'Brett goes to the opera'. *UA International*, 13, No. 6: 4-6.

Brett C. E. B. 1996. 'Brett is back from Bulgaria'. *UA International*, 13, No. 8: 4-5.

Brett C. E. B. 1996. 'Brett on architectural competitions'. *UA International*, 13, No. 5: 4-5.

Brett C. E. B. 1996. 'Brett on music in Venice and on Wellington Park Terrace, Belfast'. *UA International*, 13, No. 3: 4-5.

Brett C. E. B. 1996. 'Brett on the over visiting of country houses'. *UA International*, 13, No. 1: 4-5.

Brett C. E. B. 1996. 'Brett takes a day-trip to London'. *UA International*, 13, No. 9: 6-7.

Brett C. E. B. 1996. 'Brett - up in the air'. *UA International*, 13, No. 2: 4-5.

Brett C. E. B. 1996. 'Brett visits Liverpool'. *UA International*, 13, No. 7: 4-5.

Brett C. E. B. 1996. 'Charles Brett on round towers'. *UA International*, 13, No. 4: 4-5.

Brett C. E. B. 1999. '7 & 9: the end of an affair'. *UA International*, 16, No. 1: 16-17.

Brett C. E. B. 1999. 'Victorian and Edwardian Belfast: preserving the architectural legacy of the inner city'. *Irish Architectural and Decorative Studies*, 2: 8-25.

Brett C. E. B. 2001. 'Letter from Alupka'. *Times Literary Supplement*, No. 5144: 19.

Brett C. E. B. 2002. 'Alupka Palace, Crimea'. *Country Life*, 196, No. 30: 74-79.

Brett C. E. B. 2002. 'Vorontsov and Pushkin'. *Times Literary Supplement*, No. 5154:

Brett C. E. B. 2003. 'Crimea's garden city'. *Country Life*, 197, No. 6: 68-71.

Unpublished documents

Brett C. E. B. 1978. *The Ulsterness of Ulster Architecture.* The Canon Rogers Memorial Lecture delivered at St Joseph's College of Education, Belfast on 24 November 1978.

Brett C. E. B. 1993. *Growth, Greenth and Greed – the Current State of Conservation in Northern Ireland.* A Critical Survey. Seminar paper delivered to the Ulster Architectural Heritage Society.